A People Armed and Free

The Truth About the Second Amendment

By Jack Reynolds, J.D.

This book is a work of non-fiction. The events and situations are true.

© 2003 by Jack Reynolds, J. D. All rights reserved.

No part of this book may be reproduced, stored in a retrieval system, or transmitted by any means, electronic, mechanical, photocopying, recording, or otherwise, without written permission from the author.

ISBN: 1-4107-4547-3(e-book)
ISBN: 1-4107-4546-5(Paperback)
ISBN: 1-4107-4545-7(Dust Jacket)

Library of Congress Control Number: 2003092668

This book is printed on acid free paper.

Printed in the United States of America
Bloomington, IN

1st Books - rev. 05/30/03

A People Armed and Free

Chapter 1
Introduction, or "Why am I writing this book?"

And the debate rages on!

"A well regulated Militia, being necessary to the security of a free State, the right of the people to keep and bear Arms, shall not be infringed."[1]

In May 2002, I was watching the news debate show Hannity & Colmes on the Fox News Network. This happened to be right after the U.S. Attorney General, John Ashcroft, had announced that the government had changed its official position on what the Second Amendment to the Constitution means.[2] Previously, the U.S. government position had been that the amendment only protects the states' right to have a militia; it did not protect any individual right to have firearms. Mr. Ashcroft was changing this, to declare the position of the government to be that there is a right of individuals to have firearms, though the extent of this right is not known, because Mr. Ashcroft says that the government still has the power to regulate this possession, at least to some extent. On the Hannity & Colmes show, they had two guests, one pro-gun rights, and one pro-gun control. They were debating, with the hosts, the legal positions on this issue. Unfortunately, with the short amount of time allotted to each segment of the show, the debate (better described as an argument) went something like this:

Pro-Gun Control Advocate: The 2d Amendment only grants the right to the states to have a militia. This is what the *Miller*[3] case holds.

Pro-Gun Rights Advocate: No it doesn't. The 2d Amendment guarantees an individual right. *Miller* doesn't say that. Look at the wording and history of the 2d Amendment.

Pro-Gun Control Advocate: No it doesn't. It is militia.

Pro-Gun Rights Advocate: No it isn't. It is individual.

Pro-Gun Control Advocate: Militia!

Pro-Gun Rights Advocate: Individual!

Jack Reynolds, J. D.

This degenerated into to an argument that my kids would have been proud of. Needless to say, at the end of it I felt that I had been cheated in that no real information or legal knowledge on the issue had been imparted. How could I possibly decide for myself which side is right? What does the 2d Amendment really mean?

It was at that point that I decided to do something for myself. I am an attorney, licensed in both Texas and Utah, and have been practicing law for about 19 years. I am Board Certified in Personal Injury Trial Law by the Texas Board of Legal Specialization. While I am certainly not a constitutional law professor, I am fairly intelligent (or at least I like to think that I am), and I know how to research a legal issue inside and out. So, I reasoned, if these expert talking heads on television would not give me the full story on the 2d Amendment, I could research it myself, and then make up my own mind.

So, I looked up the *Miller* case on the Internet. After reading it, I realized that this is probably one of the worst written opinions ever to come out of the Supreme Court. Once you read it, you can understand the reason for the argument above as to what it says. It can literally be read to support both sides of the argument! Gee, that did not get me anywhere. So what to do now?

Being on the Internet, I decided to do a search for law review articles to try to find out what the professors say about the case law interpreting the Second Amendment, any history on it, what the text means, etc. I determined to look for articles that were on both sides of the issue, so that I could get the full range of opinions and backup for those opinions, so that hopefully I could make up my own mind. I decided to approach this as if I were a judge and had the two sides presenting briefs and oral arguments to me, supporting their positions. I found several articles that were interesting, but as expected, I found a conflict of opinions. At least these conflicting opinions were backed up by historical facts, legal reasoning, and grammatical construction analysis of the text itself, all appropriately footnoted so that I could evaluate the arguments. But, each side accused the other of distorting historical facts, taking quotes out of context, and so on. So what now?

I decided to start to check out some of the original sources cited in the legal papers, and go to the local law library, where I could get the annotations to the Amendment and look up the cases myself. At that point, I decided that since I was putting so much work now into what had started out as a simple curiosity-fulfilling project, I might as well

A People Armed and Free

write my own paper on the subject, once I had made my mind up as to what the law is. However, the more I dug for the truth, the more complex the issue became. This was not going to be something that could be confined to a paper to be submitted to a law journal or law review. If I write anything, in order to be even close to comprehensive on the issue, presenting all sides in fairness, addressing all arguments, it would have to be a book. Then it occurred to me that such a book could be of value to other people who might have the same questions that I have. Additionally, by publishing my research, analysis and opinions I might influence the public debate on this important topic (who knows, I might even get invited on Hannity & Colmes myself to join in the debate; hopefully doing a better job than the earlier guests), and besides, I might make a little money for my efforts (ah yes, the free market/capitalist motivator; at least I am honest about it).

At this point, it would be a good idea to explain that whatever we as individuals may think about what a statute, or in this case the Constitution, means, it is ultimately the Supreme Court that decides what it means. However in doing so, the Court has a standard way of approaching the issue. It looks at six categories. They are: The text itself, the history of the Amendment, the structure of the government itself, doctrinal sources (primarily the opinions of prior cases dealing with the issue, but also open to secondary sources such as law review articles, legal treatises, legal encyclopedias, etc.), public policy, and ethos of the American culture. While this book treats each of these in a separate chapter, as shown in the diagram below, they are all interrelated:

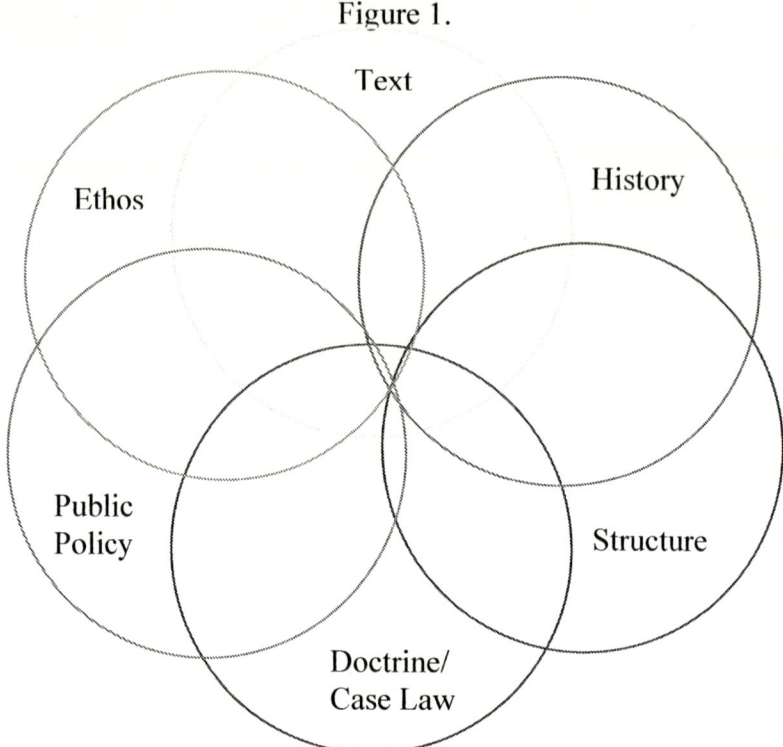

Figure 1.

Six Modalities of Constitutional Argument

Pretty isn't it. Also confusing. But what it shows is that when you start looking at the text of the Amendment, you will invariably wind up looking at the history to see what words meant back in the 1790's when it was passed. You will also look at case law, because often the legal definitions of words and phrases are pronounced in these cases. When looking at the history, you cannot escape the public policy involved at the time, (and therefore even now), nor the overall ethos of the American culture. When looking at case law, you will find historical arguments, textual discussions, and the fact that the cases are spread throughout history means they will show a historical analysis as you move from one case to another. Therefore, there is overlap, even though we will try to look at each item separately.

I should note that as in medicine, engineering, computers, or any other complex profession, this issue, dealing as it does with the law, often uses language that does not seem to have any relation to

English. In fact some of it does not, coming instead from Latin or French. But even the English is often hard to understand. So, I will try to do my best to explain what there is to be said in plain English. Sometimes there is no other way to analyze a point than to quote some difficult portion of a case or some other document, or to use an off-the-wall word or phrase, but when I do, I will try to explain it. If you understand what I say in this book, then I will have succeeded.

Along the same vein, I must warn you that portions of this book are full of quotes from other sources. When we are discussing the historical arguments or case law on this subject, we simply cannot do that without looking at exactly what the people involved in the passage of the Constitution and the Bill of Rights, or the judges who wrote opinions in the cases had to say about the topic. Some of the quotes are long. That is because if I were to delete portions, I might be subject to attacks for taking material out of context. I still find all of this very interesting, but for some, it may be tedious at times. Bear with me. The destination is worth the journey, and you may learn much about what is actually out there in our history and jurisprudence.

Before you proceed in this book, or for that matter any book or article dealing with a political issue, the law or history (which all come into play in this book), you should be aware of something. I am human. As such, as all humans, I have my biases. While I did resolve to approach this topic objectively, that is to say with an open mind as to what the law is, I must admit that when I started out I knew what I thought the law **should** be. Being a civil libertarian, I believe that the law should be interpreted to maximize individual rights, including in the Second Amendment area. However, having lost my share of cases as an attorney, I also knew that sometimes the law is not what I think it should be. Certainly, in the area of economic regulations, my civil libertarian beliefs, regardless of how strong of an argument I can make, are not followed and are not what the law **is**. Therefore, I was willing to accept a result in my research contrary to my beliefs. However, I am not now, nor have I ever been, a member of the National Rifle Association (NRA) or any other advocacy group pertaining to this issue, on either side. Now, as you read, you can decide whether this book is tainted by my personal bias, or is an objective analysis of the facts, arguments, and the law involving the Second Amendment. Whether that should cause you to reject the positions herein, or accept them more strongly, is up to you, but at least you are aware. But also apply this awareness to any other books or commentaries (as I have tried to do herein when discussing the arguments of both sides) before you make up your mind.

Another similar point. Other people upon whose works I have relied to form the arguments on all sides of this issue also have biases. Usually, these biases are easy to see because of the arguments made, but they are not stated, and instead of trying to present the material in an objective manner with both sides of the argument presented and reasoned through, they spin the argument greatly to their side. Of course, this is to be expected. One would hardly expect the Brady Center to present the NRA's position in a favorable light, nor the NRA to express a deep respect for Handgun Control, Inc. What this does point out, however, is that one should be careful whenever reading papers from someone with an agenda. A radio commentator, Neal Boortz, has expressed this best:

> **WARNING!**
> Do not believe anything you hear on my show, or anything you read on the Internet unless it is consistent with what you already know to be true — or you have actually taken the time to verify the information with another source. That's called "doing your homework."[4]

I would recommend that you follow this advice when reading this book, and certainly when you are reading any of the papers put out by organizations that have a vested interest in this issue. It only makes sense. I can tell you that in following this advice I found some misrepresentations on both sides, and some outright lies. I will point these out for you as we go along. While not all of you will agree with my analysis and ultimate conclusions, at least you will see that I have tried to be honest and open to all logical arguments on this issue.

One point that I found in my research is that while most people believe that this is an issue with only two totally opposite positions, either you are for gun control or for gun rights, I found that actually there is a spectrum of positions, running from basically that the Second Amendment might as well not exist, no one has any right to any firearm and all firearms should be confiscated, to the other extreme that the government cannot pass any law pertaining to

A People Armed and Free

firearms at all and everyone has a right to have and carry any weapon they may want to. See the figure below:

Figure 2.

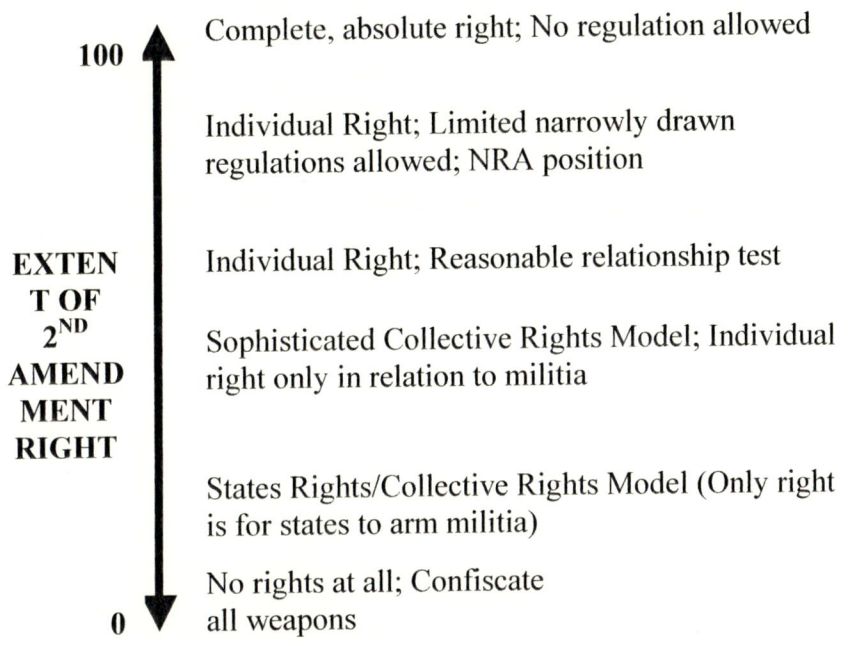

Spectrum of Opinions on Second

While there is some difference in the language used to support their positions, as a practical matter there is actually no difference in the positions of the Sophisticated Collective Rights Model and the States Rights/Collective Rights Model for our purposes. If **either** of these two models or arguments is accepted by the courts, the result is that there is no individual right to have or carry any weapon, and while different people may have different views as to what should be done by the government as to the regulation of gun ownership and use, there is no barrier whatsoever to any regulation or, for that matter, to confiscation.

One last point before we begin. While I am an attorney, and I do give my opinions in this book, this book is not to be taken as legal

Jack Reynolds, J. D.

advice. For any individual case, so much depends on the specific facts of that case that you cannot depend on any book for legal advice. Additionally, once this book is published, there may be new case law published that may change some of the opinions that I give herein. New historical facts may be discovered. Who knows what all could happen? If you get involved in any case where the Second Amendment may apply, hire your own attorney. Do not bring a lawsuit against me if you try to use my opinions and lose. While I have confidence that I am correct in my analysis, I have been wrong in the past, and I am not accepting responsibility for your case without you hiring me as your attorney.

So with all of that said, let's join the debate!

Chapter 2
Whither the Bill of Rights?

But before we actually jump into the debate and analysis, we need to make sure that everyone understands where the concepts of our government come from. Why did the American Revolution occur? Why did we go from the Articles of Confederation to the Constitution? Why did we pass the Bill of Rights? Where did these rights come from? Without knowing the answers to these basic questions, it becomes difficult, if not impossible, to understand either side of the argument on the Second Amendment.

While this will have to take a look at history, structure of government, and the American ethos, it will be done not directly with the Second Amendment in mind, but our history, government, and the Bill of Rights in general. The specifics for the Second Amendment are saved for the appropriate chapters.

Ever since the prophet Samuel anointed Saul as the first king of Israel[5], monarchs, rulers, kings, despots, and governments in general have espoused the political theory or philosophy of "divine rights of Kings". The concept seems to go something like this: In the beginning God held all power and rights to himself. Once He had established governments here on Earth, whether by having his personal representative (known as a prophet) anoint the king, or otherwise, he transferred those powers and rights (though obviously he held some of them back; I have not heard of any kings making new worlds to rule over) to the government. Therefore, the people, or individuals, had no rights, other than what the rulers might give them. An example of this is the Magna Charta, long considered to be the beginning of the freedoms that we all enjoy. What had happened was that a bunch of the barons in England, displeased with the way things were going, forced the king, at the point of the sword, to sign the document, giving up some of the power and/or rights that he had been granted from God, to the barons themselves. The barons were not so radical as to have all of these rights given to the people at large. In fact, while as a practical matter it was the first document in our history giving certain freedoms or rights to certain people, it really did not come from the philosophy that our modern government came from.

While the actual possession of rights by people in general, as opposed to their governments, gradually evolved over the years (or perhaps more appropriately, over the centuries), the philosophy of these rights radically changed in the late 1600's and 1700's. Political philosophers, lawyers and historians, such as Locke, Montesquieu, Hume, and Blackstone had come up with a new theory called the "social-compact theory". While I am greatly paraphrasing and simplifying here, under this theory, God did not give all power to the governmental authorities. Instead, one must look back to the first man and woman. At that time, there was no government. They were given total free agency (although given commandments, they could obey or disobey) to do whatever they thought was right. The individuals therefore held all rights and power themselves. As they had children, these children, once they were grown up and on their own, also had all of the same rights and powers. Once a large number of people began to be living on this planet (or at least within a small area of it), disagreements between some of the people were bound to occur. Therefore, some of these people joined together in communities for protection from others, to resolve their disputes with others, to help each other when needed, and for various other reasons. In so doing, they created governments, whether through tribal councils, chiefs, judges, kings, or whatever. Since these governments were formed by people, the governments were given their powers by the individuals in the community giving up some of their rights and powers to the government. This, not God, was the rightful source of governmental power. This also meant that whatever powers and rights that were not given up by the people to the government were retained by the people, as individuals, to themselves.

Our Founding Fathers were well read and very much aware of the writings of these political commentaries. They relied upon these new theories in their arguments proposing independence from England, and in forming our governments here.[6]

The American Revolution had several root causes. If you read the Declaration of Independence you will see that there was much more than what is generally taught in high school American History courses. But basically, regardless of what the specific complaints were, they all amounted to the accusation that the British government (mostly the king, but also Parliament) had assumed certain powers that had never been given to the government, and denied the American colonists certain rights. Therefore, the Americans were justified in throwing off that government, by force of arms, and constituting a new government.

At the same time it must be remembered that each colony had its own colonial government. These differed from each other to some degree. Some had the governor appointed by the king; some were elected. Some of these colonial governments supported independence; some did not. In any event, once independence was declared, the colonial government became the government of the state, which became a sovereign country in its own right. In other words, we did not have one country, but thirteen countries, joined together much as the United Nations joins many countries together today.

Each of these new states[7], of course, received its powers from the consent of the people governed. But the states preexisted the federal government. Initially, the federal government was formed, not by the people directly, but by the states (again, similar to the United Nations being formed by the various countries involved). As a result, the states could only give to the federal government powers which the states themselves held, and could not grant any power or rights which the people continued to hold. In the process of setting up this federal government (under the Articles of Confederation), the states actually granted very little power, and withheld most of it to themselves. In fact, each state held a veto in Congress over any action the federal government might try to take. This meant that all decisions had to be unanimous. As you might well expect, even if you do not remember from your high school history class, this did not work too well. Most people have a hard time getting their family to agree to what to eat for dinner, much less trying to get thirteen different states with different cultures and interests, to agree on anything.

Even so, we won the Revolutionary War. We continued to try to operate under the Articles of Confederation for a few years, but while some success stories came out of Congress during this time frame, there were many problems. Without going into detail, there were dangers of the new nation falling apart into the original thirteen separate nations (some people even still considered them to all be separate nations). Several attempts were made to amend the Articles of Confederation, but nothing could get unanimous consent from all of the states, which was required under the Articles.

When the Constitutional Convention was convened in Philadelphia in 1787, the delegates put much thought and debate into what the government should look like. What they came up with was truly as revolutionary as the earlier Revolutionary War. Instead of creating the federal/national government from the states, it was to be created directly by the people. The states were still there and had important roles to play, but the federal government came from powers given by the people, not the states. This is stated in the Constitution itself ("We the People ..."). This is also shown by the fact that the Constitution was required to be approved not by the state legislatures, but by special conventions of the people called for that purpose.[8] This resulted in a governmental structure that, in theory, looked something like this:

Figure 3.

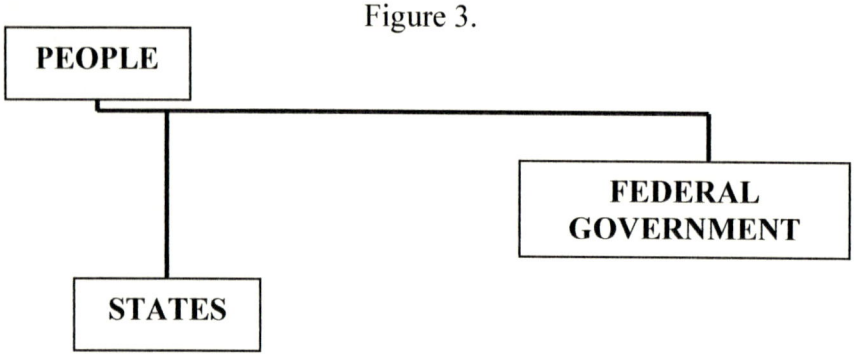

Constitutional Governmental Structure

The people came first and have a superior position to both the states and federal governments. While state governments preexisted the federal government, due to the supremacy clause in the new constitution, the federal government was superior in power to the states.

One of the great debates in both the Constitutional Convention in Philadelphia, and many of the state ratifying conventions, was the extreme amount of power (as seen by the people at that time) given to the federal government, and the protection needed for the people from this power. This all boiled down to a question of whether or not to have a Bill of Rights in the Constitution.

There were two sides to this argument (as in most arguments). Those in favor of the Bill of Rights, and what were called Anti-Federalists in general, asserted that the central government was so strong, that it was bound to begin to usurp powers not granted to it, and to thereby take away rights which the people felt belonged to them as individuals. Therefore, there needed to be some protections of those rights, that is to say a Bill of Rights, prohibiting the government from infringing on those rights held so dear by the American people. On the other side of the argument, the Federalists (most notably James Madison and Alexander Hamilton) argued that under the prevailing social-compact theory, this new central government was one of limited enumerated powers; it could only exercise those powers given to it in the Constitution and no others, and the people retained all rights and powers not given to the central government, or previously given to the states, so the Anti-Federalists fears were unfounded. Additionally, if an attempt were made to list the protected rights in a Bill of Rights, it would invariably leave some rights out. No one could think of all rights that people possess, or that may come up as important in the future. Such an incomplete list, if made, might imply that whatever rights were not included in the list had been given up by the people, or never existed at all, simply because they were not listed. So not only was no Bill of Rights needed, it would be dangerous to the rights of the people to try to make one.[9]

The Federalist argument won out at the convention in Philadelphia, and in relatively short order, five states had ratified the proposed Constitution.[10] Only in Pennsylvania was there any real debate on these points. While ratified by a clear majority in Pennsylvania, the minority there did draft a proposal for amendments to the Constitution, including a Bill of Rights. Then problems began.

Other state conventions began to demand amendments to the Constitution. Not all of these proposed amendments dealt with a Bill of Rights, but a Bill of Rights was always on the minds of the people and always included in the proposed amendments. The problem was, the Constitution was submitted in a "take it or leave it" fashion. Any attempt to amend it now would require a new national convention to consider and adopt the amendments (including a Bill of Rights). With five states already having ratified it (by its own terms, the Constitution only required nine states to ratify, not the unanimous consent required by the Articles of Confederation), the Federalists were over half-way there and did not want to start over. And if they did start over, there was no guarantee that people could agree on the proposed amendments. Therefore, the Federalists continued to push forward with their arguments noted above to get the Constitution ratified. By the end of May, 1788 three more states had ratified the Constitution, but had published recommended amendments that they wanted the new Congress to take up, pass and submit to the states for ratification in its first session.[11]

There was one state that everybody believed they had to have to make the federal government work: Virginia. It was the most populous state at the time, and the most prosperous. It also sat in the middle of the new nation, so if it did not ratify and join the union, it would cut the new country in two. Here some of the strongest debates were held. While he was a Federalist, and opposed to putting a Bill of Rights into the Constitution, Madison realized that in order to get Virginia to ratify he would have to compromise and agree to submit a Bill of Rights once the new government was formed. So he did. While New Hampshire ratified before Virginia, thereby making the Constitution effective, Virginia ratified soon after, followed the next day by New York.[12]

So the new government was formed. When Congress convened in 1788 three states still had not ratified. Even so, Madison, who had lost out on a bid to be a senator from Virginia, and therefore ran for and won a seat in the House of Representatives, drafted and submitted a list of proposed amendments, ten of which became the Bill of Rights.[13] Realize that the Bill of Rights never pretended to grant any rights, but merely guaranteed the protection of certain rights that the people already had before the government was formed. Therefore, they are not really "Constitutional rights", but constitutionally protected rights.

So, that is how we got the government we have, and how the Bill of Rights came to be. With this common starting point, let us now turn to the Second Amendment and the analysis system that the courts use to determine its meaning.

Chapter 3
The Text Itself

Courts quite logically have decided that when trying to interpret a statute or a portion of the Constitution, the first thing they do is look at the words themselves. Sometimes, the provision is clear-cut and the problem can be solved there.[14]

However, the cause of the problem in this case is those darn pesky words. Why couldn't the Founding Fathers be more explicit and clear in what they meant when they drafted the Second Amendment? While I believe that the Founding Fathers had a clear intent in mind when they drafted the Second Amendment (I do not believe that they were trying to confuse people or hide their real purpose or conduct some fraud on the people), the use of two clauses (one dealing with militias, the other with a right of the people), which, at first glance, in today's political environment seem to almost be mutually exclusive, makes it harder to determine just what this original intent was.

It is almost like trying to read the King James Version of the Bible, especially some of the Old Testament prophets such as Daniel or Isaiah. Why couldn't those prophets just write in plain English? Probably because they did not speak English, nor did anyone else on the face of the Earth at the time, but even when translated into English, it is still hard to understand. That is partially because the English used when the King James Version was written differs from our English today. While the English used in the 1780-90's is not as different, it is still somewhat different.

Let's look again at the Second Amendment:
"A well regulated Militia, being necessary to the security of a free State, the right of the people to keep and bear Arms, shall not be infringed." This can be divided into two clauses: 1. *A well regulated Militia, being necessary to the security of a free State* and 2. *the right of the people to keep and bear Arms, shall not be infringed.*

The issue is one of two different interpretations of the same words. The gun control advocates interpret the first clause as controlling over the second. In other words, The Founding Fathers expressed the only purpose for keeping and bearing arms in the first clause, therefore the whole amendment means that the States have a right to have militias, and only the states' militias have the right to keep and bear arms. While this may be jumping ahead of myself, they consider the National Guard to be the militia, therefore, the Second Amendment only gives a right to keep and bear arms to the National Guard.

The gun rights advocates take a different approach. Some ignore the first clause altogether. Those who do not ignore it, read it to mean just **a** purpose stated (not the **only** purpose), and that the second clause controls, giving the right to the people, that is to say, to individuals.

So, what do we do? How do we get started? Who is right as to what the words of the Second Amendment say? I will start from the inside out. I will start with the rights clause, looking at the nouns and defining them. Then I will look at the verbs in that same clause and define them. I will then put that clause together to determine the meaning of the clause. Then I will go to the militia clause and do the same thing, only including the adjectives and adverbs contained therein in the definitions. I will then put the two clauses together to determine the meaning of the Amendment as a whole.

A.   *The "Right"*

The first place to start looking for definitions of words, as I tell my children, is to go look it up in the dictionary. And believe it or not, often times that is exactly what the courts do too. In this case, I happened to pick up the dictionary on my desk and looked up the word "right"[15]. While "right" has many definitions, as an adjective, noun, adverb, and verb, both transitive and intransitive, only two seem to even come close to any possible use in the Second Amendment. They are as a noun, definitions 5 ("Something that is due to a person by law, tradition, or nature"), and 6 ("A just or legal claim or title")[16]. Of the two, I think definition 5 has more application, because while 6 could apply to a "claim" to keep and bear arms, it more likely refers to a "claim" to property (for example: He has a right to the house because he owns it). Notice that in definition 5, a right is something that is due to a **person**, not a government. This is to be contrasted with "power", which the same dictionary defines in several ways applicable here: "1. The ability or capacity to act or perform effectively... 4. The ability or official capacity to exercise control; authority... 6. The might of a nation, political organization, or similar group."[17] I have long been taught that only people have rights; governments can only have powers. People can also have powers (since all of the "powers" that a government has must have come from the people to begin with), and people can give up rights, but governments do not have rights.[18] The Founding Fathers, in fact, did not use the two terms interchangeably. They clearly used the word **"right"** only when referring to something belonging to people as individuals. **"Power"** is usually reserved for use with some governmental entity (such as in Article I, Section 8, clause 1 of the Constitution where the powers of Congress are listed), though in the Tenth Amendment it is used with both the states and the people.[19] It seems to me that this indicates that the "right" is something that is supposed to belong to the people as individuals, not to the states. If it were to belong to the state, it would have been listed as a power. It should be noted that in the same dictionary, under the word "right" there is a list of synonyms: "right, privilege, prerogative, perquisite, franchise, birthright, title."[20] It then states: "These nouns apply to powers and possession and one's established claim to them. Right refers to a just claim, legally, morally, or traditionally."[21] While in listing synonyms the word "power" is used, it is no more a synonym of "right" than is the word "possession" which is also used. The "power" referred to in this quote is something that a person may have a "right" to have. Therefore, the conclusion so far remains the same, the "right" mentioned in the Second Amendment is something that would belong to people as individuals, not to the state.

B.   *"The People"*

Let us start with the dictionary again. Same dictionary, different word. When only the word "people" is used, there is one definition that could be stretched to mean something close to a government: "1. A body of persons living in the same country under one national government; nationality."[22] This would be quite a stretch, but I have seen worse from attorneys in their arguments, and from courts in their rulings. Even so, I do not believe that the stretch of trying to make "people" into "state", even using the above definition, is valid. It still reads to me as a group of individuals. But I need not argue this point. Because, the dictionary has a series of definitions using the phrase "the people", which is what is used in the Second Amendment, which is very clear: "4. **the people.** The mass of ordinary persons; the populace. 5. The citizens of a nation, state, or other political unit;

electorate. 6. Persons subordinate to or loyal to a ruler, superior, or employer."[23] This clearly shows that "the people" is not a governmental unit or entity, but a collection of individuals ("citizens", or "persons"). This again corresponds with the use made in the constitution, and the first ten amendments. The Preamble of the Constitution states:

> We **the People** of the United States, in Order to form a more perfect Union, establish Justice, insure domestic Tranquility, provide for the common defence, promote the general Welfare, and secure the Blessings of Liberty to ourselves and our Posterity, do ordain and establish this Constitution for the United States of America.[24]

As pointed out in Chapter Two, the reason that the phrase "the People" is used here, and not "the States", is that the new national government was to be formed directly by the people, not by the states. The Founding Fathers knew how to use the correct phrase where and when they wanted it. Also, take a look at the other nine Amendments in the Bill of Rights. In the First Amendment, the phrase "the people" is used in reference to the right of individuals to peaceably assemble and to petition the government for a redress of grievances.[25] I have not heard of anyone trying to say that this right actually belongs to the states, or that in this context, "the people" really means "the states". Then, a mere sixteen words into the next Amendment, the same phrase is used, but this time there is an argument over whether it means individuals, or states. Then forty-four words later, in the Fourth Amendment, the same phrase is used again, this time in relation to another right of individuals to "be secure in their persons, houses, papers, and effects, against unreasonable searches and seizures ..."[26] Again, no argument is made that the states are to be secure, but it is universally admitted that this applies to individuals. In the Fifth Amendment[27], a different wording is used: "person", which while not the exact same as "the people", is certainly closer to "the people" than "the states" is. Yet "person" again clearly refers to individuals. Then in the Ninth Amendment it is acknowledged that "the people" retain rights not listed in the rest of the constitution, including the first eight amendments.[28] This again does not apply to the states, but to individual rights. The Tenth Amendment reserves "powers" (not "rights"), not given to the federal government, nor prohibited to the states, to both the states and "the people"[29]. This shows that the Founding Fathers knew how to distinguish between the states and the people, and knew which phrase to use where they wanted it.

This interpretation of what "the people" means, and the ability of the Founding Fathers to use the correct word when they wanted to, is not mine alone. In the Supreme Court case of *United States v. Verdugo-Urquidez*[30] the court stated:

> "[T]he people" seems to have been a term of art employed in select parts of the Constitution. The Preamble declares that the Constitution is ordained and established by "the people of the United States." The Second Amendment protects "the right of the people to keep and bear Arms," and the Ninth and Tenth Amendments provide that certain rights and powers are retained by and reserved to "the people." See also U.S. Const., Amdt. 1 ("Congress shall make no law ... abridging ... the right of the people peaceably to assemble") (emphasis added); Art. I, 2, cl. 1 ("The House of Representatives shall be composed of Members chosen every second Year by the people of the several States") (emphasis added). While this textual exegesis is by no means conclusive, it suggests that "the people" protected by the Fourth Amendment, and by the First and Second Amendments, and to whom rights and powers are reserved in the Ninth and Tenth Amendments, refers to a class of persons who are part of a national community or who have otherwise developed sufficient connection with this country to be considered part of that community.[31]

While this was not a Second Amendment case, but a Fourth Amendment case that had nothing to do with keeping or bearing arms, the language clearly supports the interpretation that I have given of the phrase "the people". Since the Founding Fathers selected the phrase "the people" and not "the states" to use in the Second Amendment, it appears that they meant that "the right of the people" would be something belonging to individuals, not to state governments. To come out with the result asked for by the gun-control advocates, the phrase should have read: "the power of the states". The Founding Fathers knew what they were doing when they used the phrase they used.

C.   *"Arms"*

The gun-control advocates have written articles where they claim that the use of the word "arms" indicates that the intent had to have been to reserve this right to the states' militias, because the only definition of "arms" is as a military weapon.[32] They quote a historian, Gary Wills, as saying "one does not bear arms against a rabbit."[33] (We will get to the word "bear" momentarily.)

> "Indeed, the definition, then and now, of the word 'arms' has a primarily military connotation. The term 'arms' refers to instruments used in war. Accordingly, the Second Amendment was not meant to protect the rights of hunters and sportsmen, as some interpret it now, but was purely a means of protecting a state's right to maintain an armed force."[34]

Now when I first read this, I must confess that I was a little bit puzzled. I knew that "arms" could certainly have a military connotation. However, I always thought that it could have other meanings too, such as in "armed and dangerous". So, again I went to the dictionary, looking under the singular "arm".[35] I did find the meaning proposed by the gun-control advocates (2. A branch of a military force, such as the infantry. 3. **arms**. Warfare.)[36] However, I found the first definition given to be: "A weapon, esp. a firearm."[37] Therefore, "arms" would be more than one weapon, esp. more than one firearm. While definition number 3 applies to "arms" as opposed to "arm" (and therefore, it might be argued, is the correct definition) and the definition given is "warfare", I doubt that the meaning of the Second Amendment is to "keep and bear warfare." I am sorry, but that is one right I do not want, either as an individual or for my state. No, this only makes sense as a multiple of arm, which can have a military connotation, or not. It can apply to any weapon, but mostly to any firearm. Admittedly, the understanding of the term could have been different two hundred years ago, but we will reserve that for the history portion of this book, in Chapter 4.

D. "Keep"

This one is relatively easy. There are three definitions that may apply here: "1. To retain possession of. 2. To have as a supply... 4. To store; put customarily."[38] All three of these could be applied to either an individual right, or a state power. An individual could retain possession of weapons, could have them as a supply, or could store them. So could a state. So while the definition is easy, it does little, by itself, to resolve the question of what the Second Amendment means.

E. "Bear"

Again, the definition found could be applied to either the individual, or the state. "To move while supporting; carry."[39] Certainly an individual can carry a weapon, but then so can the state's militia. What this does do, however, is contradict the argument that "one does not bear arms against a rabbit." Furthermore, there is evidence that the people at the time of the adoption of the Constitution and the Second Amendment understood the term as meaning to carry. The minority report from the Pennsylvania ratification convention proposed an amendment: "That the people have a right to bear arms for the defense of themselves and their own state, or the United States, or for the purpose of killing game; ..."[40] So, I guess that they thought that a person could "bear arms" against animals, presumably including rabbits. Early state constitutional provisions, or their declarations of rights often spoke of the right of the people to bear arms in defense of themselves and the state.[41] The 1828 edition of Webster's American Dictionary of the English Language has a definition of "[t]o wear; to bear as a mark of authority or distinction, as, to bear a sword, a badge, a name; to bear arms in a coat."[42] A bill drafted by Thomas Jefferson and proposed to the Virginia legislature by James Madison in 1785 would have imposed penalties on those who violated hunting laws if they "shall bear a gun out of his [the violator's] inclosed ground, unless whilst performing military duty."[43] Obviously since military duty is exempted from the penalty, a person could bear arms out of his "inclosed" grounds for purposes other than military duty. In a 1998 Supreme Court case,[44] Justice Ginsburg, in a dissent joined by Justices Rehnquist, Scalia, and Souter, asserted that the word carry meant to bear:

> Surely a most familiar meaning is, as the Constitution's Second Amendment ("keep and *bear* Arms")(emphasis added) and Black's Law Dictionary,

at 214, indicate: "wear, bear, or carry ... upon the person or in the clothing or in a pocket, for the purpose ... of being armed and ready for offensive or defensive action in a case of conflict with another person."[45]

Therefore, clearly a person can bear arms in more ways than just in a military manner. To bear arms, combining the two definitions would be to "carry a weapon, especially a firearm." Certainly an individual can carry a weapon against a rabbit, or a deer, or a bear, or anything else. Or he could just carry it, keeping it at the ready for if, and when, it may ever be needed. For example, bearing arms in self-defense.

F. *"Infringed"*

The past tense of infringe. Infringe means "1. To violate or go beyond the limits of (a law, for example). 2.Obs. To defeat; invalidate. –intr. To encroach upon something: *a law that infringed upon the rights of property owners.*"[46] Again, if you assume that the "right" could belong to the state, it could be infringed just as a right belonging to an individual could be. So again, this could apply in either case.

G. *"The right of the people to keep and bear Arms, shall not be infringed"*

Let us now put all of these definitions together to see what this clause means: "The just claim due to a person (citizen/individual) by law, tradition or nature, to possess or carry a weapon, especially a firearm, shall not be violated/invalidated/encroached upon." Pretty simple, huh? If this was the only clause involved, the answer to the question of what the Second Amendment means would be easy. But then, if that was the only clause in the Second Amendment, we probably would not even be having the argument, I would not have written this book, and you would not be reading it. But there is that other clause, which surely has some meaning (I cannot assume that the Founding Fathers threw the militia clause in there for no reason at all, or as a practical joke, just to confuse us two hundred years later). So let's go through the same drill with the militia clause.

H. *"Militia"*

Here things begin to get more complicated. What did the term "militia" mean when the Constitution was adopted and when the Second Amendment was passed? What does it mean now?

A People Armed and Free

The gun control advocates assert that the militia is the National Guard. The problem with this assertion is that the National Guard did not exist when the Second Amendment was passed. So this would require the "militia", whatever it was at the time, to have morphed into the National Guard of today. This is exactly what the gun control advocates claim has happened.

The gun rights advocates dispute this. They claim that the "militia" as originally used meant the people as a whole, being armed for their own defense, and to stop possible tyranny from the government. Since the National Guard consists of a small percentage of the people, it is to be considered more as a "select militia", which is controlled by the very government that the militia is supposed to protect the people from. Therefore, the National Guard cannot be the "militia" intended by the Second Amendment.

So which is right? Or is there some middle ground, or combination, or third definition that is better? Invariably this portion of the argument leads to a discussion of the history of the Revolution, the arguments concerning adoption of the Constitution, even old English history, leading to the intent of the Founding Fathers. While that discussion is important and fruitful, it is premature at this point. These matters will be discussed in detail in Chapter 4. At this point, we need to look more at what the Founding Fathers thought the definition of "militia" was when they used that term in the Second Amendment, and how it should be applied to us today.

Gun control advocates admit that in the 1700's the militia consisted of the entire adult, white, male population from ages 18 to either 45 or 60, depending on the state (or colony). But they claim that because the state government controlled the militia, the meaning of militia refers to the state's army, so to speak, not to the people. When the Constitution was drafted and adopted, it contained provisions that split the authority over the militia.[47] They provided that the federal government could call out the militia for specified purposes ("execute the Laws of the Union, suppress Insurrections and repel Invasions"), and would have the power "[t]o provide for organizing, arming, and disciplining, the Militia, and for governing such Part of them as may be employed in the Service of the United States, reserving to the States respectively, the Appointment of the Officers, and the Authority of training the Militia according to the discipline prescribed by Congress."[48] Another clause authorized the federal government to raise and support armies.[49] However, critical to this was another clause that prohibited the states from maintaining troops without the consent of Congress.[50] I will return to this point shortly.

Coming forward to today, gun control advocates assert that this militia had dwindled from inattention by both the state governments and the federal government. As a result, in the early 1900's Congress changed the militia into the National Guard. The gun control advocates cite two Supreme Court cases for the proposition that the militia became the National Guard, or that today's National Guard is the militia referred to in the Second Amendment. The first case, *Maryland v. United States*,[51] involved an Air National Guard captain from Maryland who had committed negligence while flying a fighter jet, causing a midair collision with a privately owned plane. This captain, when not on duty as a member of the Air National Guard, was, as a civilian, an employee of the Air National Guard. A suit was brought against the federal government under the Federal Tort Claims Act.[52] The Supreme Court held that whether working as a civilian, or as a captain in the Air National Guard, this individual was an employee of the State of Maryland, not of the United States; therefore, there were no grounds to sue the national government. As a part of its lead up to this holding, the Court said: "The National Guard is the modern Militia reserved to the States by Art. I. 8, cl. 15, 16, of the Constitution."[53]

The second case, *Perpich v. Department of Defense*,[54] involved the question of whether or not a governor of a state could prohibit the federal government from sending its National Guard members out of the country for training. The Supreme Court said that the governor could not stop such training. In so doing, the Court seemed to both say that the National Guard is the militia, and that it is not. While there are words indicating that the National Guard is the militia, the Court makes it clear that the National Guard is also a part of the army, under the federal power to raise armies, whenever the federal government wants to federalize the guard. This creates a problem dealing with intent, as will be seen in Chapter 4. For right now, it is enough to say that there is some support and some logic for the gun control advocates position.

Gun rights advocates, however, assert "militia" means "the people" armed. They quote several political figures of the time to this effect. George Mason, a Virginian delegate at the Constitutional

Convention who refused to sign the Constitution due to the federal power that it gave, without a Bill of Rights: "Who are the militia? They consist now of the whole people."[55] The Federal Farmer, an Anti-Federalist writer, referred to a "militia, when properly formed, [as] in fact the people themselves."[56] Tenche Coxe, of Pennsylvania, another commentator of the time: "The militia, who are in fact the effective part of the people at large, ..."[57] and "Who are the militia? Are they not ourselves?"[58]

Our current dictionary defines "militia" in this way:

> 1.a. A citizen army as distinct from a body of professional soldiers. B. The armed citizenry as distinct from the regular army. 2. A military force that is not part of a regular army and is subject to call for service in an emergency. 3. The whole body of physically fit male civilians eligible by law for military service.[59]

Gun rights advocates point out that the militia still exists, apart from the National Guard: "The militia of the United States consists of all able-bodied males at least 17 years of age and ... under 45 years of age who are or who have made declaration of intention to become citizens of the United States and of female citizens who are commissioned officers of the National Guard."[60] A law review article from 1987[61] gave a good summation of all of this:

> [Gun control advocates] argue that the introductory phrase of the Amendment implies that the right to keep and bear arms is restricted to officially organized military units, such as the National Guard. The language of the Constitution, however, actually refutes this claim. In the eighteenth century, the term "militia" was rarely used to refer to organized military units, and indeed, eighteenth century *legal* usage seems never to have adopted that meaning. Rather, the "militia" included all citizens who qualified for military service (i.e., most adult males). This definition continues to be included in the United States Code today. There is thus no apparent reason for supposing that the term "militia" in the Constitution refers solely or even primarily to organized military units. Indeed, article I,

section 8 of the Constitution clearly assumes the existence of the "Militia" in the states, but article I, section 10 *forbids* the states to "keep Troops" without the consent of Congress.

The point of all of this is that there is a reasonable argument to be made on both sides, looking at just the term "militia". I tend to believe the individual rights point of view. When looked at as a whole, it is too incredible to believe that the Founding Fathers meant a special militia that would not exist for over a hundred years. They meant an armed citizenry that would be subject to regulations and receive some minor training. As a retired Lieutenant Colonel from the Marine Corps Reserve, and having worked with Army Reserve and National Guard officers and units, I can tell you that we all consider ourselves as professional soldiers, only not full time. We have a civilian profession, and a military profession, that is to say, two professions. We are not an armed citizenry, as the current dictionary definition requires. You are free to agree or disagree.

This does not take into consideration the intent of the framers (by that I mean the reasons for the Second Amendment and what the purpose of it was), nor the case law that has tried to apply these proposals, nor other factors. Those will be considered later, and may modify your opinion of what "militia" means. In the meantime, a question arises: Does the adjective "well-regulated" affect the acceptance of one definition of militia over the other? Gun control advocates say it does.

I.   *"Well regulated"*

Gun control advocates assert that the addition of the adjective phrase "well regulated" supports their proposed definition of militia, because the unorganized militia of today is totally unregulated. It is just a body of names, or people, with a title put to that body. There is no requirement, as there was in the early days, for them to supply their own weapons. They are not provided weapons. They are not subject to any military laws or regulations. They are not organized into any units, companies, battalions, etc.[62] The gun control advocates quote Noah Webster's Dictionary of 1828:

> "The militia of a country are the able bodied men organized into companies, regiments and brigades,

A People Armed and Free

with officers of all grades, and required by law to attend military exercises on certain days only, but at other times left to pursue their usual occupations." N. Webster, II, <u>An American Dictionary of the English Language</u> (1828).⁶³

Professor Lund admits that at first glance this phrase supports the gun control advocates. However, he then points out that:

> [T]he reference [to a well regulated militia] indicates only that the Framers intended for the militia to be regulated in some way, as for example, by being organized into formal military units *or* by being comprised of individuals already familiar with the principal instruments of military combat.⁶⁴

He then, at footnote 8 appended to the quoted material, adds that "[I]n eighteenth century military usage, 'well regulated' meant 'properly disciplined,' not 'government-controlled.' *See Hardy, Armed Citizens [Citizen Armies: Toward a Jurisprudence of the Second Amendment, 9 Harv. J.L. & Pub. Pol'y 559] at 626 n. 328."*

Today's dictionary has only one definition of "regulate" that could apply here: "To control or direct according to a rule."⁶⁵ This is closer to the Lund and Hardy definition of properly disciplined than to an organized unit under government control. Of course the question could be "How regulated is well regulated?" Marines think that the army, navy, and air force, even on active duty, are not well regulated. And some members of the army's elite units, such as the Rangers, tend to agree, at least as to the other units of the army.

One could think of "well regulated" as being relative, on a scale from least regulated to most regulated, as shown below:

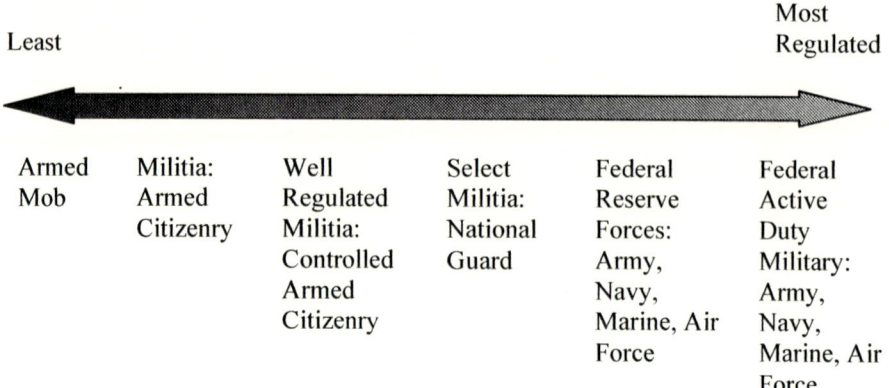

In any event, one would have to assume that once called out, the militia would be subject to the same military rules, laws and regulations that active duty units are subject to. Therefore, at that point, the militia would be well regulated. Furthermore, if allowed to have their own firearms, which they could shoot, whether by target practice or hunting, the individuals who make up the militia could make themselves better trained, or "regulated", which result would be in harmony with the complete text of the Second Amendment.

J.   "State"

Gun control advocates seem to take it for granted that the word "state" when used in the Second Amendment means the states of the United States, and that this then means that the Second Amendment protects the security of the states.[66] Clearly one definition of "state" is "[o]ne of the more or less internally autonomous territorial and political units composing a federation under a sovereign government."[67] However this is not the only definition. Though not used this way as often among most people now as it was in the 1700's, it also means "[a] body politic, esp. one constituting a nation."[68] This is the manner in which the Framers meant to use "state". Notice that the use in the Second Amendment is singular, not plural, as in the Tenth Amendment.[69] Notice that the adjective "free" is used prior to "state". In fact, when Madison first submitted his proposed amendment, it contained the phrase "best security of a free country".[70] It was later changed to "free State". There is no indication that I could find that the reason for this change was to change the meaning to being the security of the individual states. It was probably just a change to the preferred language of the times for indicating a nation. When we get into the intent of the Founding Fathers, it will become clear that one of the main reasons for the Second Amendment was to keep the central government from becoming oppressive or tyrannical towards the people. This means that "free State" meant to have a government where the people were free from oppression and tyranny. Therefore, the "state" that was to have its security and freedom protected is the national government, not the individual states.

K. *"Necessary"*

This word was actually an upgrade from what Madison had proposed in his initial draft of the Amendment. Madison had originally proposed "the best security".[71] The dictionary defines "necessary" as "absolutely essential; indispensable."[72] This is even more important than merely "the best".

L. *" Security"*

"Freedom from risk or danger; …"[73] This is probably not in dispute. Now let us combine the militia clause.

M. *"A well regulated Militia, being necessary to the security of a free State"*

Gun control advocates appear to read this clause as being "An organized part-time military organization being absolutely essential or indispensable to the freedom from risk or danger of the individual states." Did I leave out a word? Oh yeah. "Free." But they leave that word out too, as if it were redundant to the word state. "It is noteworthy that the Pennsylvania language recognizing the people's right to bear arms 'for defense of themselves' did not find its way into the 2nd Amendment, **leaving only the security of the state as the proper object of the right being recognized**."[74] Notice the glaring omission of "free" from this point?

However, putting our definitions together, this clause reads like this: "A properly disciplined or controlled armed citizenry, being absolutely essential or indispensable to the freedom from risk or danger of the national government violating the freedom of its people."

N. *The Whole Second Amendment*

Now let's put the definitions together. First the gun control advocates: "An organized part-time military organization being absolutely essential or indispensable to the freedom from risk or danger of the individual states, the just claim due to a person (citizen/individual) by law, tradition or nature, to possess or carry a weapon, especially a firearm, shall not be violated/invalidated/encroached upon." Does this make any sense? The two clauses seem to at best be disjointed; at worst they actually conflict. One rule of statutory, contract or other document construction is that whenever possible the document/statute/amendment should be read as a whole so as to make sense of all of its parts. In other words, interpretations should not be imposed that would conflict with each other within the document. If possible, all of the parts should harmonize. This only makes sense. Who would purposefully draft a document with intentionally conflicting provisions? Most people would draft a document so that all of its parts go together to make sense with each other and as a whole. And certainly, the wisdom of our Founding Fathers precludes the assumption that they would violate this rule, unless there was a compelling reason to do so. We will see that the Founding Fathers did in fact have a compelling reason to do so with some of the provisions of the Constitution, but not internally to the Second Amendment.

Now let's try the gun rights advocates definitions: "A properly disciplined or controlled armed citizenry, being absolutely essential or indispensable to the freedom from risk or danger of the national government violating the freedom of its people, the just claim due to a person (citizen/individual) by law, tradition or nature, to possess or carry a weapon, especially a firearm, shall not be violated/invalidated/encroached upon." Now, does this make sense? Do these clauses go together and complement each other? I think so.

Now let's assume that I am wrong on the reading of the militia clause. Let's assume that it does not mean an armed citizenry, but a military unit controlled by the states. There is still the problem of grammar.

As noted towards the beginning of this chapter, the sentence that makes up the Second Amendment consists of two clauses. There are two types of clauses: Independent and subordinate (sometimes called dependent).[75] An independent clause is one that could stand alone as a sentence itself if taken out of the sentence being studied. A subordinate clause is one that does not express a complete thought and therefore cannot stand alone.[76] In the Second Amendment, the militia clause is a subordinate clause; by itself it does not make a complete sentence, and does not express a complete thought, therefore it cannot stand alone. The second clause is an independent clause, since it could stand alone as a complete sentence on its own. One law journal points out the importance of this:

> To begin with, the first clause, discussing the well-regulated militia, seems to be the dependent clause. According to this reading, a well-regulated militia depends on the right of the people to keep and bear arms. The language does not support the opposite reading, that the right of the people to keep and bear arms depends on the maintenance or preservation of a well-regulated militia. It should also be noted that the Amendment has two parts: (1) an observation, or perhaps a cautionary note ("A well regulated militia, being necessary to the security of a free State") and (2) a command or legal requirement ("the right of the people to keep and bear Arms, shall not be infringed"). The plain language of the first clause appears to impose no legal requirement or restriction on the federal government. Only the second clause indicates a right that the government cannot infringe.[77]

Not being content with accepting a law journal's opinion on the use of the English language, I called up a friend of mine, Stacy Stair. I used to share office space with him about eleven years ago. He is an attorney, but his undergraduate degree was in English. I had not talked with him for a couple of years. After exchanging a few pleasantries, I came to the point. I told him that I needed not a legal opinion, but an English major's opinion, based on the grammatical structure of the Second Amendment, as to what it means. He could not remember what the Second Amendment was,[78] so I read it to him, complete with punctuation. I did not tell him what my opinion was, nor what my bias was, only that I wanted an honest opinion from him. I did give him a couple of interpretations found in my research: 1. That the right to keep and bear arms belongs to the states and their militias, or can be exercised only through the state militias, and 2. That in order to have a militia for the security of a free state, we must allow the people to keep and bear arms. I then asked him which one of these was correct, or was it some kind of combination of the two, or some third option not listed. His response was: "It is the second one. The second interpretation is grammatically correct." Now Stacy is not an English professor, but he certainly knows more about grammar than I do, and more than the average Joe. Having read so many articles by people on both sides with agendas to push on this issue, I did not trust going to a strange English professor (is that redundant?) that I did not know that I could trust for an opinion. I do trust Stacy to have given me an honest opinion. The fact that he could not remember what was in the Second Amendment indicates that he probably does not have an agenda one way or the other. This merely adds to his credibility.

For more backup, I went to a library and checked out a book on English grammar. Looking up clauses, I found that subordinate clauses can be classified as either noun clauses, adjective clauses or adverb clauses.[79] The militia clause is not a noun clause. It is not used to name a person, place, thing, or idea.[80] What is does do is give a reason why the right to keep and bear arms shall not be infringed. (Whether or not it is **the only reason** will be discussed in later chapters). According to this grammar book, an adverb clause is a subordinate clause that performs one of the "typical adverbial functions of telling *how, when, where,* **why***, to what extent,* or *under what conditions.*"[81] Therefore, it appears that the militia clause must be an adverb clause. As such, it cannot modify the noun "right", but must modify the verb phrase "shall not be infringed." Therefore, the militia clause cannot restrict the "right of the people" to being exercised only in the militia, but merely gives a reason why that right "shall not be infringed."

To show this more graphically, perhaps we should diagram the sentence that is the Second Amendment. What?! Diagram?! Most people have not even thought about doing that since the sixth or seventh grade. But the fact remains that it is a good tool to see just what is being done in a sentence. So dust off the old memory chips in your brain housing group, and here goes:

A People Armed and Free

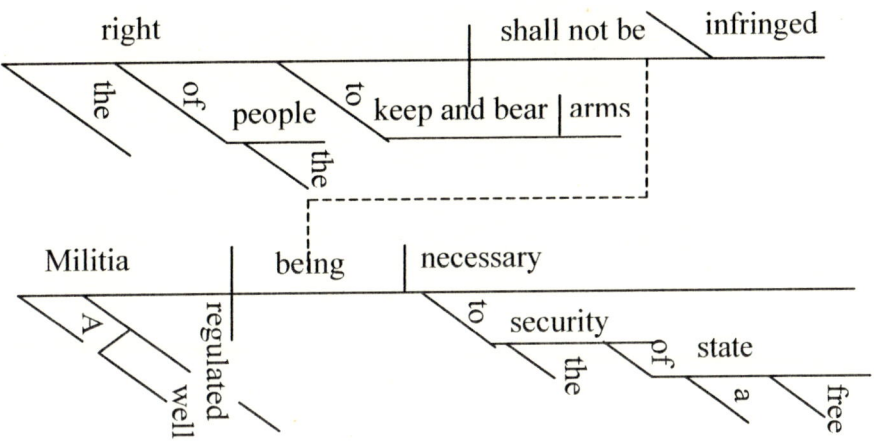

While this looks rather imposing, what it shows is that the dependant clause (the militia clause) modifies the predicate (verb phrase, "shall not be") in the independent clause. The means, as said before, that the militia clause does not restrict (or modify) the "right", which is the subject of the independent clause, but merely states a reason why the right shall not be infringed. The right remains one "of the people", not of "A well regulated Militia", as shown in the diagram above. The exercise in diagramming may be painful, but it is instructive.

Another way to look at this subject is to give it a common sense reading. What the Second Amendment actually says is that, in order to keep the security of a free state, we must have a well regulated militia. In order to have a well regulated militia, we must make sure that the right of the people to keep and bear arms is not infringed. Again, this merely gives a reason to make sure that the right is not infringed, it does not limit that right to being exercised only in connection with a well regulated militia, whether that amounts to the National Guard or something else.

Therefore, under any reasonable way of reading the text of the Second Amendment, whether by going painstakingly through the definitions, or by looking at the grammar, or any other way, it is clear that it does not give a right to states, but to individual people, like you and me, to keep and bear arms. A reason for not infringing this right is stated, but that does not limit the right.

To illustrate this point, I found an interesting concept in my research on the Internet. It was an analogue, or an analogy, to the Second Amendment. I found this at www.guncite.com. Normally this information would be in the endnotes, but I am so impressed by this website, that I want to make my comments here in the body of the book. This is probably the best website dealing with the issues surrounding the Second Amendment. Both sides of the issues are presented. Links are provided to home pages for both gun control advocates and gun rights advocates. Errors or mistakes from both sides are pointed out. While I do not agree with everything the owner of this website says, he/she has done an outstanding job of researching the issues and putting it all together. Unfortunately whoever this is does not name himself or herself. But I highly recommend the website.

Anyway, back to the analogue. The concept is that an amendment that does not exist is drafted along the same lines as the Second Amendment. It reads: "A well-educated electorate being necessary to the preservation of a free society, the right of the people to read and compose books shall not be infringed." The point of this is, if we had such an amendment, it would not mean that only well educated voters have the right to read or write books, nor that the right to read books of one's own choosing can be restricted to only those subjects which lead to a well-educated electorate. It should not be construed to deny one's pre-existing right to read books if there are not enough well educated people to be found. Remember, rights are not granted by the Constitution; they preexisted the Constitution and remained with the people when the Constitution was formed. The Bill of Rights merely guarantees that the government will not infringe these pre-existing rights. The purpose of the provision in this analogue is that while not everyone may end up being well educated, enough people will become well educated to preserve a free society. While this is the purpose stated, it is only one reason given for not abridging the right to read and write; there may be others.

Now before you say that this is a ridiculous example that could never exist, in fact a similar analogue has existed in real life. The 1842 Rhode Island Constitution had a free press clause which stated: "The liberty of the press being essential to the security of freedom in a

A People Armed and Free

state, any person may publish his sentiments of any subject, being responsible for the abuse of that liberty ..."[82] Now, I ask you, would anyone try to argue that because of the first clause, the right to publish belongs only to those who own or run newspapers or other such items? Or would anyone argue that in order to publish opinions one would have to do so in connection with some organization connected with the press (newspapers, magazines, radio, television, etc.)? No! Of course not! The right clearly belongs to everybody as individuals and can be exercised by individuals acting alone. Nor could the subject matter be restricted to only those subjects involving security of freedom, but would include all subjects.

One last argument from the gun control advocates. They say that the Framers knew how to draft an amendment that clearly gave rights to individuals, as they did in the other portions of the Bill of Rights. They did not do that in this case; in this case they added the clause about the militia and security of a free state, therefore the Framers must have intended something different, and that difference is that the right belongs to the states.[83] There is some truth and logic to this argument, in that the Framers surely did know how to write their amendments to grant what they wanted to. But, the same argument could be made the other way. If what the Framers wanted to do was to reserve something to the states, why didn't they just say so? Why didn't they draft the Second Amendment to read: "The power of the states to keep and arm their militias shall not be infringed." Or why did they not draft a different amendment saying, "Congress shall have no power to prohibit state-organized and directed militias."[84] In fact, another proposed amendment drafted by a senator would have done virtually that, but it was rejected by the Senate, and therefore never submitted to the states for ratification[85] The body of this rejected amendment read as follows:

> That each state, respectively, shall have the power to provide for organizing, arming, and disciplining, its own militia, whensoever Congress shall omit or neglect to provide for the same; that the militia shall not be subject to martial law, except when in actual service, in time of war, invasion, or rebellion; and when not in the actual service of the United States, shall be subject only to such fines, penalties, and

punishments, as shall be directed or inflicted by the laws of its own state.[86]

Notice the use of the word "power" in relation to what is reserved or given to the state government, instead of the word "right". And if the purpose of what became the Second Amendment was to protect the states' militias, then why did this senator, who already had Madison's proposed amendment before him, also draft this one? He was not trying to replace Madison's amendment, but to add this new one. If they both do the same thing, why try to pass both?

We are now passing from the text into the intent of the Framers or Founding Fathers, as shown by the history surrounding the Second Amendment, so it is time for a new chapter.

Chapter 4
The History of Gun Rights and the Second Amendment

Do you enjoy history? I do. In fact, my wife complains that if I am not watching the Fox News Channel, I am watching the History Channel. The problem that most people have with history courses is that the teachers treat it as an exercise in memorization of dates and events. While some events and dates are important to memorize (July 4, 1776, or November 10, 1775[87]), to treat all of history in this manner is boring. What really makes history interesting is learning the why and how of what happened. Learning what was really behind these events, and how the story all played out in the end.

I am also interested in politics. That is probably why I watch the Fox News Channel. Politics and history are interrelated. Much of history is about politics. Even war, as Clauswitz said, is politics through another means.[88] Yet, history also drives politics. Much of our thoughts and beliefs, our biases, if you will, are formed by our history. What has happened in the past, and how our ancestors or we have dealt with it, helps to form our points of view, be they liberal, conservative, libertarian, or something else.

This is the concept behind the courts' use of history in determining what a constitutional provision means, or what the effect of it is. Not only does the text itself show what was intended, but the history surrounding the particular provision may also show what the intent was. What were the historical facts leading up to the provision being enacted? What were the problems that the Founding Fathers saw that caused them to enact the provision? How did the Framers of the provision envision it working? What were some of the comments made at the time in question concerning these problems and the provision itself? How did the people and the governments seem to view the provision from shortly after its passage up to the present? All of this is designed to discover the **intent** of the Framers. Once that intent is known, then we should know what the provision means and how to apply it today.

Jack Reynolds, J. D.

Much of the history of the Second Amendment is undisputed. However, both sides accuse each other of ignoring certain facts and taking other facts out of context. Even those facts that both sides agree on may be interpreted differently. I will try to present all of the facts used by both sides, including the additional context when the other side has accused someone of taking something out of context. Unfortunately, this makes some of the quotes rather long, so please bear with me on this. If I have omitted any particular facts (such as quotes from some commentators), it is only because they were redundant or not really relevant, or perhaps because they are agreed to by both sides. I will present both points of view as to the interpretation of these facts as we go along. In the end, with everybody having all of their cards laid face up on the table, hopefully you can determine for yourself what the truth is and what the real intent of the Framers was. You may agree or disagree with my analysis, but at least you will have all of the pertinent facts available.

Before we get into the actual historical facts, it would be good to review the basic positions of the advocates in this matter, so that you can spot potential evidence for or against them as we go along. The gun control advocates contend that the intent of the Framers was to protect the states' militia from the potential encroachment of the federal government. The concern was that since the new Constitution gave the federal government the power to have a standing army, this standing army could be used by the federal government to attack the states and possibly even do away with the state governments, which were considered to be the best protection of the freedom of the people. By doing this, the federal government could then oppress the people themselves. The states had militias at the time which could be used to defend against such an usurpation of power by the federal government, but the new Constitution gave the federal government certain powers over the militia, and if not protected by a new amendment, the federal government could reduce the effectiveness of the militia or even do away with it, and the states would not have anything with which to resist an attack by the standing army of the central government. Therefore, the reasoning goes, the Second Amendment was passed to make sure that the states could keep their militias. And, this was the **only** reason for the Second Amendment, therefore, there is no other right given to anyone by the Second Amendment. "[I]t is precisely [the militia clause] language that

A People Armed and Free

expresses the **purpose, and limit,** of the right to keep and bear arms."[89] In regards to what evidence there is available on the other side in this argument, the gun control advocates have said: "There is no evidence that the Framers discussed, much less intended, that the amendment provide a guarantee to individuals of a right to be armed for purposes unrelated to militia service."[90]

Before I go into the gun rights advocates position, let me address a point of observation here. I have learned from 19 years of practicing law that it is generally dangerous to use absolutes such as always, never, all, none, etc. It invites the opposing party to come up with one example that violates your absolute statement, and once that has been done, you lose your credibility. And the other side can usually find such an example. What you will see me doing in this book is qualifying my absolutes, such as "I could not find any such example." Note I did not say such an example does not exist, only that I could not find one. That way, if the other side finds one, at least I retain my credibility.

The gun rights advocates, not surprisingly view history differently. They start with the proposition that people, or at least citizens, have a number of God given rights, including the right to keep and bear arms. These rights all pre-existed the Constitution. Therefore, the Second Amendment did not grant anything, it merely guaranteed that the federal government would not infringe that right. Under this argument, the pre-existing right to keep and bear arms was there for any number of valid reasons. One of these reasons was to allow the states to have their militias. But that was not the only reason. Other reasons included self-defense, hunting, sport (including target shooting contests), and the protection of the people, as opposed to the states, from the possible tyranny and oppression of a strong central government (called by some "the insurrectionist theory"). Therefore, absent an express waiver of this right of the people to keep and bear arms for purposes other than maintaining a militia, the Second Amendment could not restrict that right. They claim that there is evidence in the historical context that such other reasons for this right existed, that the Founding Fathers and Framers knew of these other reasons, and embraced them. Therefore, the intent of the Framers of the Second Amendment had to be to state one major purpose of protecting the right to keep and bear arms, but not the only reason, and then guarantee the protection of that right. Therefore, the right to keep and bear arms belongs to individuals, not to the states or militias, and can be exercised without any relation to a militia.

Which position is right? Which position does the historical record support? Let's find out!

A.   Old English History

The American history of individuals keeping and bearing weapons actually begins in England with the "Assize of Arms", a decree (assize) issued by King Henry II in 1181, which required every free man to keep arms suited to his station in life, in order to aid in the defense of the kingdom.[91] Note that this was prior to the Magna Charta, which was signed on June 15, 1215, by King John, and therefore it really does not grant any right, but places a requirement on the people. However things do have a way of evolving. In 1285 the Statute of Winchester was passed, which specified the military obligations of English freemen, basically setting up the first militia system, requiring that every freeman have his own arms, train periodically, and bring his own weapons if called upon to defend the country.[92] However, these requirements were not just for providing military service, but to also provide local police services, such as pursuing criminals and guarding the villages.[93]

A little bit of religious history gets involved now. After King Henry VIII broke away from the Catholic Church, the English monarchy went back and forth between Protestants and Catholics. The Kings often tried to reduce the power of the militia (in fact, King James I repealed the Statute of Winchester in 1603) and build up standing armies. However, the English people saw the standing army as a "sign of tyranny, a tool used by an absolutist ruler."[94] In the 1640's Oliver Cromwell, a Protestant, took over as a military dictator, with a standing army even larger than the King's. The Catholics returned in 1660 with Charles II, and the army was disbanded. However, Charles II, and his successor, James II, began to disarm many of their Protestant subjects.[95] James II increased the standing army again, to 30,000, asked Parliament to abandon the militia in favor of the standing army (saying that the militia was too inefficient to rely upon), and replaced Protestant officers and soldiers with Catholics.[96] From 1686-88 the army grew to 53,000.[97] All of this (along with other dastardly deeds by the king) led to the Glorious Revolution, during which King James II fled England.[98] In the aftermath of this revolution, Parliament passed the English Bill of

Rights in 1689.[99] Among other things, this Bill of Rights addressed the individual right to bear arms:

> Whereas the late King James II did endeavor to subvert and extirpate the Protestant religion and the laws and liberties of this kingdom by ... raising and keeping a standing army within this kingdom without the consent of Parliament and quartering soldiers contrary to law, by causing several good subjects being Protestants to be disarmed at the same time when papists were both armed and employed contrary to law ... and ... [therefore] for the vindicating and asserting [our] ancient rights and liberties ... [we] declare ... that the raising or keeping a standing army within the kingdom in time of peace, unless it be with consent of Parliament, is against the law; that the subjects which are Protestants may have arms for their defense suitable to their conditions and as allowed by law.[100]

Several things should be noted from the above passage (which gun control advocates claim is usually cited out of context by gun rights advocates; therefore, I have quoted the whole passage from the gun control point of view). First, the gun control advocates are heavy on the emphasis of the restriction of the standing army. This, they say, implies that the real problem behind the passage of the Second Amendment was fear of a standing army and the desire to strengthen the militia.[101] However, nothing in this passage even mentions the militia. And there is no restriction on the use of the arms, although as we will see shortly, some of the "laws" did restrict their use. Second, The right to have arms is not universal (it applied only to Protestants), nor absolute (that is to say, it could be restricted, "as allowed by law"). It is limited to Protestants, and only goes so far as allowed by law. This, gun control advocates argue, shows that there never was a real individual right to bear arms.[102] They seem to think that unless the right granted is absolute and universal, there is no right. However, as will be documented with quotes and citations later, our Founding Fathers recognized that the English Bill of Rights was deficient in these respects and that the American right to bear arms was universal to all people (or at least to all freemen), and while maybe not absolute, it could not be restricted merely on the whim of the legislative body. In other words, the American right was always considered to be better and stronger than the English right; the English Bill of Rights was merely a starting point for recognizing the pre-existing right. Finally, note that a major concern was that the King had disarmed many of the Protestants. Therefore, the Founding Fathers had reason to fear the power of the central government to disarm its people.

In 1765, the famous English jurist William Blackstone wrote his *Commentaries on the Laws of England*. This was the key treatise on what the law was at the time. In this Commentary, Blackstone listed the three principal absolute rights of Englishmen as personal security, personal liberty and private property. He then listed five auxiliary rights, which were designed to protect the three principle rights (since merely naming the rights would not protect them, the people had to have some method of protecting them). The first four of these auxiliary rights were: 1. Parliament; 2. Limitation of the King's prerogative; 3. Right to apply to the courts for redress of injuries; and 4. The right to petition the king or either house of Parliament for the redress of grievances. The fifth auxiliary right addressed the right to have arms:

> [T]he last auxiliary right of the subject ... is that of having arms for their defence, suitable to their condition and degree, and such as are allowed by law. Which is also declared by the same statute ... and is indeed a public allowance, under due restrictions, of the natural right of resistance and self-preservation, when the sanctions of society and laws are found insufficient to restrain the violence of oppression.

****

> ... [T]o vindicate [the three primary rights], when actually violated or attacked, the subjects are entitled, ... lastly, to the right of having and using arms for self-preservation and defence.[103]

A People Armed and Free

Several notes about this commentary. The right belongs to the subject, that is to say, to individuals, not to some subordinate governmental entity such as a county or city or township, or colonies (England did not have states). There is also no mention of a militia. Therefore, whatever right there was would not support a reading of the Second Amendment as belonging to the states or militia, but it would belong to individuals. Next, the purpose of the right extends to a "natural right" of resistance and self-preservation. This is a right that must have pre-existed even the English Bill of Rights, since it is a natural right, and it includes self-preservation, or self-defense. Therefore, there is here an indication of purposes other than military, to allow people to have guns.

As stated above, the English right was not absolute. It expressly says that it only goes so far as allowed by law. Blackstone recognized this in his *Commentaries*, and even added that the allowance was under due restrictions. In fact, the English Parliament did pass rather restrictive gun control laws at the time. The Game Act of 1671[104] limited possession of firearms to English noblemen ostensibly to reduce over hunting of the forests (the earliest environmentalists?). The Militia Act of 1662 empowered British officials "to search for and seize all arms in the custody or possession of any person or persons whom the said lieutenants or any two or more of their deputies shall judge dangerous to the peace of the kingdom."[105] This appeared to be for crime prevention, as many of our present day gun control laws and proposed laws appear to be. Gun control advocates assert that this shows that the right to bear arms, from the earliest days, was subject to severe regulation, and was therefore no right at all; meaning that guns can be heavily regulated today. However, Blackstone recognized that "prevention of popular insurrections and resistance to the government, by disarming the bulk of the people is a reason oftener meant than avowed."[106] So gun rights advocates assert that what this really means is that our Founding Fathers knew of the dangers of such regulations being used to disarm the populace, and therefore, given the stronger right to bear arms that Americans claimed, enacted the Second Amendment for the very purpose of prohibiting such regulations and gun confiscation. How our Founding Fathers looked at this is the subject of the next few sections.

B. The Colonial Period

As the English subjects came to America, they brought with them their ideas and philosophies as to their natural rights, and the protections due them as English citizens. In fact, in order to induce people to go to America, the English government pledged that the immigrants and their children would continue to possess "all the rights of natural subjects, as if born and abiding in England."[107] It appears reasonable to say that these English citizens also brought with them a distrust of standing armies as discussed above.[108]

The laws of the colonies required all free males to provide and maintain their own firearms. For example, In Virginia, a 1631 law required "all men that are fitting to beare armes, shall bring their pieces to church ... for drill and target practice."[109] And a 1640 statue required "all masters of families" to provide themselves and "all those of their families which shall be capable of arms ... with arms both offensive and defensive."[110] In Connecticut, the law required "every listed souldier and other house-holder (except troopers)" to be "always provided with, and have in continual readiness, a well-fixed firelock ... one pound of good powder" and "four pounds of bullets."[111] South Carolina required its inhabitants to have arms and ammunition.[112] Rhode Island likewise required men to have arms and ammunition.[113] Some colonies even required its people to carry firearms when traveling. Maryland required all householders to own guns and those capable of bearing arms to bring their guns to church and carry them when traveling a considerable distance from home.[114] Massachusetts required men to provide themselves with ammunition and travelers were "not to go unarmed." In fact, all persons traveling over a mile from home "except in places wheare other houses are neare together" were to be armed.[115] Massachusetts also had a statute which encouraged all of its inhabitants to own arms that were useful both to their own defense and the colony's defense, and therefore required that only certain kinds of muskets would be acceptable for militia duty.[116] While certainly the maintenance of the militia was one reason behind all of these laws, the requirements to carry firearms when traveling and the encouragement to own arms for the inhabitants' own defense does not sound like they have anything to do with the militia. They sound like self-defense was the motivating factor. Indeed, "[t]hese laws served the twofold purpose of providing individual self-defense while giving England a reserve force available

A People Armed and Free

in time of war."[117] This is not surprising, since no organized police force existed until the middle of the 19th century. Some gun control advocates have even admitted:

> [F]rontier life and the need for self-sufficiency created a climate in which almost everyone had guns, whether to hunt food or to fight off bandits and Indians. The populace was already well trained in the use of weapons and generally had their own, making the militia much cheaper and more effective.[118]

This points out that in addition to the militia and self-defense, hunting was a valid reason to own a firearm. All of this together shows that, contrary to the gun control advocates position that the limitations on the English Bill of Rights right to bear arms applied in the colonies, the American right had become much more universal, and much more extensive, including rights for self-defense and hunting as well as forming the militia.

At this point it would be appropriate to address a side issue. A book has been published which its author (Michael A. Bellesiles, a history professor) claims to have been extensively researched, which puts forth the conclusion that guns were not prevalent in early America, in fact they were rare. The thesis is that the gun culture or ethos did not begin to develop until around the time of the Civil War.[119] While the last quote shows some acknowledgement of the extensive use of guns in colonial America, many gun control advocates have jumped on this bandwagon, citing this as proof that the reasons cited above for people having a right to have firearms could not have existed. The problem with this argument is that numerous other historians, including some who initially supported this work, have tried to replicate Bellesiles's research, and they have found that either the facts claimed for the books conclusions do not exist, or even worse, they actually support the opposite conclusion and that Bellesiles simply lied. This is a strong word, but I did not initiate this conclusion.

> I can say with great confidence that he isn't *honestly* mistaken; he is intentionally deceiving his readers. Let me be very clear on this. I am not saying that Bellesiles

missed books and papers that showed that early America had lots of guns and lots of hunters. Bellesiles' own sources, the ones that he listed in his footnotes, demonstrate that in some cases, he read materials that directly contradict his claims. In other cases, Bellesiles makes claims about guns and hunting in early America, but when I checked the sources that he lists, there is nothing there. Often, the sources he lists, even the particular pages that he lists, contain evidence that contradicts his claims. Most blatant of all, Bellesiles quotes parts of sentences from some sources and makes false statements about what was in the rest of the sentence.[120]

While it is not the purpose of this book to go into great detail refuting Bellesiles, let me give you a few examples of the problems found with his work.

He quotes a letter from George Washington for the proposition that all of the militia were poorly armed. In fact, the letter says that **a few** of the militia were poorly armed.[121] He cites a Massachusetts census of arms, alleging that it included all arms in the colony, and found that there were only 21,549 guns in the colony of some 250,00 people. But the census does not indicate the categories of firearms counted. It appears that only military arms and publicly owned arms were counted. Additionally, a committee report, contained in the same book relied upon by Bellesiles for this census information, indicates that only a few of the inhabitants are destitute of firearms.[122] Bellesiles claims to have reviewed numerous travel journals and books that allegedly show that hunting was not often conducted and that guns were sparse. Yet a reading of those books show tens to hundreds of pages in each where hunting is described and the use of firearms is described as being commonplace.[123] He supposedly researched probate records during the target time period and found that only 48% of them mention firearms, of which 33% were old and useless. Now, being an attorney, I question the validity of using probate records to determine the percentage of households owning anything. Too many estates are not probated. Of those that are, many will leave items of personal property, such as firearms, out of the inventory of the estate. Even so, people who have checked the records that Bellesiles bases his claim on have found that they actually show that 62% of them show firearms, of which only 9% were old.[124]

And my personal favorite, my being an attorney, Bellesiles claims that no gun ever belonged unqualifiedly to an individual and that all guns were to be made into property of the state. When I read this I almost fell over. This totally contradicts everything I knew from both history and my legal training, about the sanctity of private property rights in early America. When his cites were checked, the best that could be said for them was that some of them allowed weapons to be *"impressed"*.[125] Now, this means that the government could take them for public use, but the owners were to be paid for them. Even today, the Fifth Amendment, which prohibits the taking of private property without due process or just compensation, allows private property to be taken by the government for public use if the government pays for it. People sometimes have their houses taken so that the government can build a new road, or expand an existing one. Does this mean that all houses are now to be considered not as individually owned, but as property of the state? Hardly! All of this reminds me of the admonition I gave you from Neal Boortz in the first chapter. If something does not sound right, do not believe it until you have checked it out. Many people have done just that to the claims made by Bellesiles and found them to be false. What I have presented is but a small part of those findings. If you are interested, I would encourage you to check out the sources cited in my endnotes, and the additional sources cited in those documents, for yourself, to see just how pervasive this attempt to foist a fraud on the American people is. Clearly Bellesiles is wrong, and his thesis is wrong. There were a large number of guns in early America and they were used for numerous purposes.

In any event, it is also clear that until the time of the French and Indian War (1760's) there was no standing army in English America. As a result of this war, the king and Parliament imposed taxes on the American colonists to help pay for this army (all without representation). As the colonists began to object to these taxes, the king sent more troops to enforce his taxes. This caused additional problems, with quartering the soldiers in people's homes, abuses of citizens, the assumption of governmental powers by the military, and the like. As problems began to grow, a patriot, "A.B.C." (probably Samuel Adams) wrote: "It is reported that the Governor has said, that he has Three Things in Command from the Ministry, more grievous to the People, than any Thing hitherto made known. It is conjectured 1st, that the Inhabitants of the Province are to be disarmed..."[126] In February 1769, a report was made that, as of October 1768, the inhabitants had been ordered to bring in their arms.[127] Samuel Adams wrote an article in which he cited the Blackstone *Commentaries* discussed above, as to the right to bear arms being the fifth auxiliary right used to protect the three primary rights, and used it to justify the people now keeping their arms in preparation for self-preservation against the violence of oppression. He further accused the same persons that wanted to take away their guns as also wanting to prevent the people from petitioning their king.[128] Nothing was said about the arms being kept as a part of a militia.

Things gradually escalated. In 1770 the Boston Massacre occurred. In 1774 England put an embargo on shipments of arms to America. In September of that year, some of the pro-British rulers in Boston proposed the disarming of the people, but the measure was voted down. There may have been concern about what would happen if they tried to do this:

> It is said, it was proposed in the Divan last Wednesday, that the inhabitants of this Town should be disarmed, and that some of the newfangled Counsellors consented thereto, but happily a majority was against.—The report of this extraordinary measure having been put in Execution by the Soldiery was propagated through the Country, with some other exaggerated stories, and, by what we are told, if these Reports had not been contradicted, we should by this date have had 40 or 50,000 men from the Country (some of whom were on the march) appear'd for our relief.[129]

Even though this was not passed, the British began trying to disarm the colonists any way. They began seizing arms and ammunition, and entrapping individuals for trying to buy guns.[130] On April 19, 1775, the "shot heard round the world" was fired at Lexington Green. Three days later General Gage told the Selectmen of Boston that "there was a large body of men in arms" hostilely

A People Armed and Free

assembled. The next day a town committee met with Gage, who promised that if the people would turn in their weapons, the people could leave the town and that the arms would be returned to them at a suitable time. The people proceeded to turn in 1778 muskets, 634 pistols, 973 bayonets and 38 blunderbusses. General Gage then set a guard over the weapons and refused to allow the people to leave town. On June 12, 1775, General Gage proclaimed martial law and offered a pardon to everyone who would turn in his arms, except John Hancock and Samuel Adams.[131] Needless to say, few took him up on this offer. It is important to realize that these attempts to disarm the citizens of Boston were directed against people who were not even involved in the hostilities at Lexington and Concord.

This message was not lost on the other colonies. On June 24, 1775, a report was published in Virginia, and on July 20, 1775, in Maryland, that the British were gong to require all of the colonists to turn in their weapons, and that anyone who did not would be deemed a rebel.[132] All of this caused the Continental Congress to adopt the Declaration of Causes of Taking Up Arms on July 6, 1775, which specifically addressed the taking of the people's arms from them.

Of course on July 4, 1776, independence was declared. A portion of the Declaration of Independence is important to the "insurrectionist theory" of the right to bear arms:

> That whenever any Form of Government becomes destructive of these ends, it is the **Right of the People** to alter or to abolish it, and to institute new Government, laying its foundation on such principles and organizing its powers in such form, as to them shall seem most likely to effect their Safety and Happiness. Prudence, indeed, will dictate that Governments long established should not be changed for light and transient causes; and accordingly all experience hath shewn, that mankind are more disposed to suffer, while evils are sufferable, than to right themselves by abolishing the forms to which they are accustomed. But when a long train of abuses and usurpations, pursuing invariably the same Object evinces a design to reduce them under absolute Despotism, **it is their right, it is their duty, to throw**

off such Government, and to provide new Guards for their future security.

(Emphasis added). Surely this notes a natural right, belonging to people, not states or colonial governments, which pre-existed the forming of the Constitution, to fight against an oppressive government.

Then in 1777, William Knox, the Under Secretary of State in the British Colonial Office made a proposal that the government create a ruling aristocracy loyal to the crown in America, the Church of England be established throughout the colonies, and that the government be given an unlimited power to tax. To further this, his proposal contained the following:

> The Militia Laws should be repealed and none suffered to be re-enacted, & the Arms of all the People should be taken away, & every piece of Ordnance removed into the King's Stores, nor should any Foundry or manufactory of Arms, Gunpowder, or Warlike Stores, be ever suffered in America, nor should any Gunpowder, Lead, Arms or Ordnance be imported into it without License; they will have but little need of such things for the future, as the King's Troops, Ships & Forts will be sufficient to protect them from any danger.[133]

In 1778, while occupying Philadelphia, General Howe of the British army, attempted to disarm the populace there.[134]

All of this points out several important facts. In addition to the other reasons the Americans had for wanting to keep their right to bear arms, they wanted it as individuals, in addition to the militia, so that they could resist the oppression and tyranny of the government. The government was not trying to disarm only those who actually were trying to fight against it, but to disarm all citizens. My theory on this is that it is easier to disarm law abiding citizens, and the collection of a large number of weapons gives the government a false sense of security, so the government went after the guns that were easiest to get (though admittedly they also went after the stores elsewhere, such as at Concord). The clear reason for the taking of the people's arms was to be to allow the government to be oppressive. And finally, the attempt to take away the people's arms was one of the reasons the Americans were fighting the British.

It must be noted here, in all fairness, that one of the big reasons for the Revolutionary War was the maintenance of a standing army in the colonies. The problem was expressly listed in the Declaration of Independence: "He has kept among us, in times of peace, Standing Armies without the consent of our legislatures." This appears to indicate that since the English Bill of Rights precluded the maintenance of a standing army without the consent of Parliament, neither should a standing army be maintained in a colony without its legislature's consent.

At the start of the war, the king controlled the colonial/state governments. Therefore, the colonies held conventions in order to establish new state governments. Now to me this indicates another problem with the gun control advocates position. It clearly was not the colonial/state governments that led the rebellion, nor their militias. It was independent and free thinking people, such as Samuel Adams and John Hancock, and a separately organized militia, formed of the people, that started this whole thing off. Of course once the new state governments were formed, it could be said that the new state governments and their militias were involved in the revolution, but not at the beginning of the resistance to tyranny. Therefore, it seems incredible to me to argue that the purpose of the Second Amendment was to give the right to keep and bear arms to the state governments and their militias in order to protect them against a strong central government and standing army, when that was not who initially used this right to resist the tyranny from England.

In forming the new state constitutions, four states put in provisions protecting the right to bear arms. Those states, the dates, and the pertinent provisions are as follows:

1776 *North Carolina:* **That the people have a right to bear arms, for the defence of the State;** and, as standing armies, in time of peace, are dangerous to liberty, they ought not to be kept up; and that the military should be kept under strict subordination to, and governed by, the civil power.

1776 *Pennsylvania:* **That the people have a right to bear arms for the defence of themselves and the state;** and as standing armies in the time of peace are dangerous to liberty, they ought not to be kept up; and that the military should be kept under strict subordination, to, and governed by, the civil power.

1777 *Vermont:* **That the people have a right to bear arms for the defence of themselves and the State** — and as standing armies in time of peace are dangerous to liberty, they ought not to be kept up; and that the military should be kept under strict subordination to and governed by the civil power.

1780 *Massachusetts:* **The people have a right to keep and to bear arms for the common defence.** And as, in time of peace, armies are dangerous to liberty, they ought not to be maintained without the consent of the legislature; and the military power shall always be held in an exact subordination to the civil authority, and be governed by it.

Note that in three of these, the right extends to self-defense, as well as defense of the state. North Carolina has only defense of the state listed, but it is not known if this was supposed to limit the right to bear arms. Also, in each of these there is a reference to not having standing armies in time of peace, and the subordination of the military to civil authority. The other nine states did not put a right to bear arms in their constitutions, but did mention the avoidance of standing armies, militias, and/or civil authority.[135]

Of course, we won the Revolutionary War. And, as shown in chapter 2, there became a time when a new constitution was needed. We will now turn to the proceedings of the constitutional convention, and the state ratification conventions, to see what the attitudes were toward the people keeping firearms.

C.   *The Constitutional Convention and Ratification*

The Articles of Confederation did not contain a Bill of Rights, nor anything resembling one.[136] This was because the central government was so limited in its powers that there was no need to list any such rights; the central government could not infringe on the rights of the people if it had to.

At the Constitutional Convention very little was said about any Bill of Rights. Most of the time and effort was spent on the weighty matters that had caused the convention to be called; the need for a stronger central government, the method of checks and balances to prevent the central government from abusing this additional power, within these checks and balances, was one branch being given too much power in relation to the other branches, etc. Part of the problem to be resolved dealt with experiences seen from the state governments themselves. James Madison had noticed majorities tended to impose on the rights of minorities and individuals. Thus, the central government was to be set up to prevent possible oppression by majorities. Madison even proposed that the federal government have an absolute veto over the laws of each state, in order to protect the private rights of individuals from "vicious" state legislation.[137] This also caused Madison to distrust the utility of a Bill of Rights. He saw them as "parchment barriers." "Not only had they failed to restrain the state assemblies, they had done nothing to brake the factious passions swirling among the people at large."[138] Even so, some rights were placed in the Constitution. Article I, section 9, clause 2 guarantees the right to a writ of habeas corpus. Clause 3 prohibits bills of attainder and ex post facto laws. Article III, section 2, clause 3 guarantees trial by jury in criminal cases. Article IV, section 2, clause 1 provides that the citizens of each state shall be entitled to all privileges and immunities of citizens in the several states. So some few rights were discussed and adopted. But "[n]one of these provisions invoked the natural rights and first principles that Americans expected a declaration of rights to contain."[139]

An actual Bill of Rights was not proposed until September 12, 1787, five days prior to the Convention adjourning.[140] At that time George Mason moved to appoint a committee to draft a bill of rights to be a preface to the Constitution. The motion was voted down unanimously.[141] Nothing was said about what this bill of rights should contain. It must be noted that there does not seem to have been any discussion of the right to keep and bear arms at the Constitutional Convention,[142] however the same can be said for other rights later put into the Bill of Rights.

There was some discussion of standing armies and the militia, and a lot of talk about whether or not the central government was too strong. The federalists (those supporting a strong central government, and later favoring the ratification of the proposed Constitution) wanted both a standing army and national control of the militia. Anti-federalists (those favoring a weak central government and stronger state governments, and later opposed to the ratification of the Constitution) opposed both of these measures. While both sides distrusted standing armies, the infallible logic was that the nation could not be forced to wait until it was attacked to begin to raise an army. Therefore, the compromise was to allow the creation of a standing army, but to limit its funding to no more than two years at a time.[143]

On the question of the militias, the Federalists argued that if the nation could rely on the militia, this would reduce the need for a standing army. Even so, the Anti-Federalists saw a danger in this as taking away the states' ability to defend themselves from outside forces (such as Indians, Spaniards, Frenchmen, and the British), from internal insurrections (such as Shays Rebellion) and from the central government and its standing army. They were even concerned that if the federal government had total control over the militia, it could march the militia from one state to another to oppress that second state. They were also concerned that if Congress had the sole power to arm and train the militia, it could neglect the militia and leave it useless to the states. The Federalists responded that since the militia was the people, and the American people are armed, they could successfully resist any standing army attempting to oppress them, and would not allow themselves to be used against their own people, nor their brethren in other states.[144] Again, the result of this conflict of opinions was a compromise. Article I, section 8, clause 15 allowed Congress to call out the militia for limited purposes ("to execute the Laws of the Union, suppress Insurrections and repel Invasions"), and clause 16 gave Congress the power "[t]o provide for organizing, arming, and disciplining, the Militia, and for governing such Part of them as may be employed in the Service of the United States" but reserved to the states "the Appointment of the Officers, and the Authority of training the Militia according to the discipline prescribed by Congress;" This, obviously guaranteed the states the authority to have state militias.[145] Therefore, it seems strange to argue that the Second Amendment was needed to guarantee the states a right to have militias that could keep and bear arms. Since the existence of the state militia was guaranteed in the body of the Constitution, clearly they could be armed by somebody (for what good is a militia without arms), so it would be redundant to make that guarantee again in the Second Amendment.

At the same time, article I, section 10, clause 3 prohibited states from keeping troops without permission of Congress. Clearly, the militia that the states had the right to have was not to be considered as

A People Armed and Free

troops, nor could troops be considered as militia. Therefore, if the National Guard of today is considered to be a state army (since Congress has given its permission for the National Guard to exist) it cannot be the militia.

These compromises settled most of the concerns of the opposing camps. However, it still was not settled as to who had the power to arm the militia. Article I, section 8, clause 16 gave this power to Congress, but was that power only in Congress, or could the states also arm the militia? This question was to be raised again many times during the ratification debates, and is used by the gun control advocates to argue that the Second Amendment really means that the states have the power to arm the militias. I take a different view. Madison and other federalists continually asserted that the power to arm the militia was a shared power. While the Congress could arm the militia, so could the states. And since the practice up to that time was to rely primarily on the citizens to arm themselves and then use these armed citizens as the militia (states had provided some arms to those who could not afford to arm themselves or for other reasons did not have appropriate arms), the citizens could continue to arm themselves, thereby providing arms for the militia. Therefore, there was no danger that the state militias would ever be disarmed through neglect by the federal government. And the Second Amendment guaranteed that this would always be the case, by providing that "the right of the people to keep and bear arms shall not be infringed" so that the state militias would be guaranteed to have arms, even if the national government and state governments both neglected the militia.

As support for this view, I offer some of the statements from the convention itself. When the committee that drafted the militia clause reported it back to the convention as a whole, the following discussion took place:

> MR. [Rufus] KING [of Massachusetts], by way of explanation, said that by *organizing,* the committee meant, proportioning the officers and men—by *arming,* specifying the kind, size, and caliber of arms—and by *disciplining,* prescribing the manual exercise, evolutions, &c.

****

> MR. [James] MADISON [of Virginia] observed, the *"arming,"* as explained did not extend to furnishng arms; nor the term *"disciplining,"* to penalties, and courts martial for enforceing them.
> MR. KING added to his former explanation, that *arming* meant not only to provide for uniformity of arms, but included the authority to regulate the modes of furnishing, either **by the militia themselves,** the state governments, or the national treasury; that *laws* for disciplining must involve penalties, and everything necessary for enforcing penalties.[146]

This clearly shows that the state government and the militia are not the same entity, since the arms could be provided by the militias themselves or by the state government. It also shows that the Congress could, under the militia clause, decide who furnished the arms to the militia. This Congress did, with state ratification, by enacting the Second Amendment ensuring that the right of the people to keep and bear arms shall not be infringed; that is to say, the arms could always be furnished by the militia (people) themselves, even if the state and national governments failed to do so. Another exchange took place between James Madison and Luther Martin where Madison complained about the states neglecting the militias, and Martin responded that if the states were neglecting them, they would be less attended to by the general government than by the state governments. Therefore, it is seen that there was concern about neglect of the militias by both the federal governments and the state governments.

We are now ready to look at the process of ratifying the Constitution. Before we do, a couple of things should be explained. First, there are basically two categories of historical documents that we will be looking at: Published commentaries and letters from both Federalists (most notably the Federalist Papers, mostly written by James Madison and Alexander Hamilton) and Anti-Federalists, and the records of the state ratifying conventions. Second, we should understand what we are looking for. As noted earlier, gun control advocates argue that the only reason for the Second Amendment is to guarantee the states the right (power) to have and arm their militias. Gun rights advocates argue there were other reasons. The problem

A People Armed and Free

that gun control advocates have, as I see it, is that for them to prevail, virtually all of the historical evidence has to express their purpose. Regardless of how many statements indicate a desire to make sure that the states maintain control over their militias and can arm them without Congress's approval, if we find any evidence for other reasons to pass the Second Amendment, it begins to shoot holes in the states rights theory. And the more evidence we find for other reasons for a right to keep and bear arms, the further the states rights theory sinks beneath the waves of historical commentary.

Let us start off with a quote from the ultimate Anti-Federalist, Thomas Jefferson:

> God forbid we should ever be twenty years without such a rebellion ... And what country can preserve its liberties, if its rulers are not warned from time to time, that this people preserve the spirit of resistance? Let them take arms... The tree of liberty must be refreshed from time to time, with the blood of patriots and tyrants.[147]

How about a few more, such as Luther Martin (a delegate to the Constitutional Convention, mentioned above): "By the principles of the American revolution arbitrary power may, and ought to be, resisted even by arms, if necessary."[148] Another writer in the *Pennsylvania Gazette,* April 23, 1788 criticized "the loyalists ..., who objected to associating, arming and fighting, in defense of our liberties, because these measures were not constitutional. A free people should always be ... with every possible power to promote their own happiness."[149] This all sounds like the "insurrectionist theory" of the Second Amendment. Then there was James Madison himself, the man who later drafted what became the Second Amendment, addressing the danger of a standing army being used to oppress the people:

> Let a regular army, fully equal to the resources of the country, be formed; and let it be entirely at the devotion of the federal government; still it would not be going too far to say, that the State governments, **with the people on their side,** would be able to repel

the danger. The highest number to which, according to the best computation, a standing army can be carried in any country, does not exceed one hundredth part of the whole number of souls; or one twenty-fifth part of the number able to bear arms. This proportion would not yield, in the United States, an army of more than twenty-five or thirty thousand men. To these would be opposed a militia amounting to near half a million of **citizens with arms** in their hands, officered by men chosen from among themselves, **fighting for their common liberties, and united and conducted by governments** possessing their affections and confidence. It may well be doubted, whether a militia thus circumstanced could ever be conquered by such a proportion of regular troops. Those who are best acquainted with the last successful resistance of this country against the British arms, will be most inclined to deny the possibility of it. **Besides the advantage of being armed, which the Americans possess over the people of almost every other nation, the existence of subordinate governments, to which the people are attached,** and by which the militia officers are appointed, forms a barrier against the enterprises of ambition, more insurmountable than any which a simple government of any form can admit of. Notwithstanding the military establishments in the several kingdoms of Europe, which are carried as far as the public resources will bear, **the governments are afraid to trust the people with arms. And it is not certain, that with this aid alone they would not be able to shake off their yokes. But were the people to possess the additional advantages of local governments chosen by themselves,** who could collect the national will and direct the national force, and of officers appointed out of the militia, by these governments, and attached both to them and to the militia, it may be affirmed with the greatest assurance, that the throne of every tyranny in Europe would be speedily overturned in spite of the legions which

A People Armed and Free

surround it. Let us not insult the free and gallant citizens of America with the suspicion, that they would be less able to defend the rights of which they would be in actual possession, than the debased subjects of arbitrary power would be to rescue theirs from the hands of their oppressors. Let us rather no longer insult them with the supposition that they can ever reduce themselves to the necessity of making the experiment, by a blind and tame submission to the long train of insidious measures which must precede and produce it.[150]

The reason that I have quoted such a long passage here is that the gun control advocates often accuse gun rights advocates of taking portions of this out of context, and the gun control advocates then try to argue that what Madison is really talking about is the importance of state governments and their militias to resist possible oppression from a standing army. However, from the whole text, noting the bolded portions, several things can be seen. First, Madison distinguishes between the state governments and the people. The state governments could not resist tyranny alone; they would have the people on their sides. It is not the armed states, but the militia of citizens with arms, united and conducted by the state governments, again distinguishing between the two. Second, it is not the state governments that hold the advantage of being armed, but the American people. There are two separate and distinct advantages listed: The fact that the people are armed, and the existence of state governments. Again distinguishing between the two, the people have the **additional** advantage of having subordinate governments to help in this resistance. If we were really only talking about the state governments with their militia, how would this be an additional advantage? Finally he compares the American people being armed with the European people who were not armed, implying that it would be much better for the European's if they were. The European countries did not have subordinate governments, which as Madison said would make it harder for them to resist tyranny even if they did have arms, but they might be able to throw off the yokes of oppression if they were armed. He is clearly talking about arming the people, not subordinate (state) governments, and the purpose is for the people to resist oppression by a standing army belonging to a strong central government. The "insurrectionist theory" asserted by the drafter of the Constitution and the Second Amendment himself!

An Anti-Federalist, Richard Henry Lee, writing as the Federal Farmer, addressed the concern that the federal government might use the militia itself to oppress the people:

> It is true, **the yeomanry of the country** possess the lands, the weight of property, **possess arms**, and are too strong a body of men to be openly offended—and, therefore, it is urged, they will take care of themselves, that men who shall govern will not dare pay any disrespect to their opinions. It is easily perceived, that if they have not their proper negative upon passing laws in congress, or on the passage of laws relative to taxes and armies, **they may** in twenty or thirty years **be** by means imperceptible to them, **totally deprived of that boasted weight and strength**: This may be done in a great measure by congress; if disposed to do it, **by modelling the militia**. Should one fifth or one eighth part of the men capable of bearing arms, **be made a select militia**, as has been proposed, and those the young and ardent part of the community, possessed of but little or no property, and all the others put upon a plan that will render them of no importance, **the former will answer all the purposes of an army, while the latter will be defenseless**.... I see no provision made for calling out the *posse comitatus* for executing the laws of the union, but provision is made for congress to call forth the militia for the execution of them—and the militia in general, or any select part of it, may be called out under military officers, instead of the sheriff to enforce an execution of federal laws, in the first instance, and thereby introduce an entire military execution of the laws.[151]

Here it is again clearly seen that the fear was that the people ("yeomanry") would be disarmed; that the militia would be "modeled" into a "select militia" of only a small percentage of the people, mostly young and ardent, and that thereby the government

A People Armed and Free

could use this select militia to enforce federal laws, thereby oppressing the people. Notice that nothing is said about protecting the states, or that having the power over the militia in the states would protect the people. In fact, if all the Second Amendment does is give the states power to have and arm a militia, it does nothing to address this fear. Furthermore, by the gun control advocates' own theory, that today's National Guard is the militia of yesteryear, the fear expressed above is exactly what has come to pass. Only a small percentage of the people are in the National Guard, mostly the young and ardent. The federal government can federalize the National Guard and use it to enforce federal law. As examples, witness the use of the National Guard to enforce desegregation in Arkansas in the 1950's (where the governor initially used the National Guard to stop the desegregation, and President Eisenhower federalized the National Guard to forcibly desegregate the high school), and the same use in Alabama in the 1960's involving Governor Wallace and the attempt to exclude blacks from the university there, with the exact same actions and results. Now whether or not you believe that this use of the National Guard was justified or right (I personally believe in desegregation, that the governors were wrong in trying to stop it, and that the presidents were right in using the National Guard to enforce the law), the point remains that this use of the National Guard, and the institution itself, is exactly what the Federal Farmer feared. And even if you like the use made in the desegregation disputes, you may not like it the next time it is used in a like manner over some other issue. No, what the Anti-Federalists were calling for was not state control of something that could later be made into a select militia, but for the right of all people to keep and bear arms, so that no form of a standing army, whether a full blown army or a select militia, or a National Guard, could oppress the people.

As noted in Chapter 2, the first five states to ratify the Constitution did so rather uneventfully. It was in Pennsylvania that the first fireworks began to be set off. During the debate, one of the delegates, John Smilie, made the following argument: "Congress may give us a select militia which will, in fact, be a standing army—or Congress, afraid of a general militia, may say there shall be no militia at all. When a select militia is formed; the people in general may be disarmed."[152] Sounds a little like the Federal Farmer quoted above. And in fact, Congress has given us a select militia, the National

Guard, which is called "in fact, a standing army". A Federalist, James Wilson, responded: "In its principles, it [the Constitution] is surely democratical; for, however wide and various the firearms of power may appear, they may all be traced to one source, the people."[153]

Despite the arguments of the Anti-Federalists[154] the majority of the Pennsylvania Convention—46 to 23— voted to ratify the Constitution on December 12, 1787. However, on December 18, 1787, the Anti-Federalist delegates published the "Dissent of the Minority of the Convention", which demanded amendments to the Constitution, including a declaration of rights. This contained 14 principles, among which were included:

    7.   That the people have a right to bear arms for the defense of themselves and their own state, or the United States, or for the purpose of killing game; and no law shall be passed for disarming the people or any of them, unless for crimes committed, or real danger of public injury from individuals; and as standing armies in the time of peace are dangerous to liberty, they ought not to be kept up; and that the military shall be kept under strict subordination to and be governed by the civil powers.[155]

    11.   That the power of organizing, arming, and disciplining the militia (the manner of disciplining the militia to be prescribed by Congress) remain with the individual states, and that Congress shall not have authority to call or march any of the militia out of their own state, without the consent of such state, and for such length of time only as such state shall agree.

    Clearly the minority saw two different issues, one being the right of the people to bear arms, the other being the power of the states in organizing, arming and disciplining the militia, since they wanted two separate amendments addressing these separate issues. If the right to bear arms only belonged to the states, why have two different amendments; one would do. Additionally, other reasons for the right were added, for defense of themselves, as well as their own state and the United States, and for hunting. It seems that they were well aware of the British attempt to disarm the people under the guise of game laws. It did allow for criminals or those posing a real danger to the public to be disarmed. Finally, it mentions bearing arms for hunting (or killing game). So much for the concept that one does not bear arms against rabbits.

While Pennsylvania had already ratified the Constitution, another group gathered at Harrisburg and on September 3, 1788, repeated the demand for amendments. In their demands, instead of wanting specific rights listed, they asked that "every reserve of the rights of individuals, made by the several constitutions of the states in the Union, to the citizens and inhabitants of each state respectively, shall remain inviolate, except so far as they are expressly and manifestly yielded or narrowed by the national Constitution."[156] This would have protected an individual right to bear arms. To make it even more clear that this applied to individual rights, this convention also proposed, in a separate article, that "each state, respectively, shall have power to provide for organizing, arming, and disciplining the militia thereof, whensoever Congress shall omit or neglect to provide for the same."[157] Do you begin to see a pattern here? Doesn't it seem that the people involved in forming our country at this time saw a distinction between the right of the people to bear arms and the power of the states over the militia?

The Federalists responded to these calls for amendments. Among the responses pertaining to the issue of private ownership of firearms, and the militia, is Alexander Hamilton's Federalist No. 29.[158] Now this paper actually cuts both ways to some degree, but in the end it still supports private ownership. Gun rights advocates have often quoted his language in this paper (somewhat out of context) to support the people bearing arms in order to not have a standing army, but Hamilton actually calls for a select militia to do this job. Let's take a look at what Hamilton has to say:

> The project of disciplining all the militia of the United States is as futile as it would be injurious, if it were capable of being carried into execution... Little more can reasonably be aimed at, **with respect to the people at large, than to have them properly armed and equipped**; and in order to see that this be not neglected, it will be necessary to assemble them once or twice in the course of a year... The attention of the government ought particularly to be directed to the

> formation of a select corps of moderate extent, upon such principles as will really fit them for service in case of need. By thus circumscribing the plan, it will be possible to have an excellent body of well-trained militia, ready to take the field whenever the defense of the State shall require it. This will not only lessen the call for military establishments, but if circumstances should at any time oblige the government to form an army of any magnitude that army can never be formidable to the liberties of the people while there is a large body of citizens, little, if at all, inferior to them in discipline and the use of arms, who stand ready to defend their own rights and those of their fellow-citizens. This appears to me the only substitute that can be devised for a standing army, and the best possible security against it, if it should exist.

(Emphasis added). While it is clear that Hamilton is calling for a select militia here, and this must have sent shock waves through the Anti-Federalist community, he still insists on having the people at large armed. Again, this shows a distinction between the militia controlled by the state governments and the people.

James Madison sent a copy of his Federalist 46 (quoted at length above; see text at note 150) to his friend, and fellow Federalist commentator, Tench Coxe (who later became Assistant Secretary of the Treasury, under Alexander Hamilton), for his comments. Coxe approved of Madison's comments and wrote his own article with the following:

> The power of the sword, say the minority of Pennsylvania, is in the hands of Congress. My friends and countrymen, it is not so, for THE POWERS OF THE SWORD ARE IN THE HANDS OF THE YEOMANRY OF AMERICA FROM SIXTEEN TO SIXTY. The militia of these free commonwealths, entitled and accustomed to their arms, when compared with any possible army, must be tremendous and irresistible. **Who are the militia? Are they not ourselves?** Is it feared, then, that we shall turn our arms each man against his own bosom. Congress have

> no power to disarm the militia. Their swords, and every other terrible implement of the soldier, **are the birth-right of an American.... [T]he unlimited power of the sword is not in the hands of either the federal or state governments, but, where I trust in God it will ever remain, in the hands of the people.**[159]

This clearly states that the right to keep and bear arms belongs not to the federal, **nor the state governments**, but to **the people**. And the militia is not referred to as being part and parcel with the state governments, but as being "ourselves", in other words, the people.

At the Massachusetts Ratifying Convention, William Symmes warned that at some point the new federal government "shall be too firmly fixed in the saddle to be overthrown by any thing but a general insurrection."[160] This, again sounds like asserting the "insurrectionist theory". But the Federalist, Theodore Sedwick, attempted to put the fears of a standing army to rest, asking "if raised, whether they could subdue a nation of freemen, who know how to prize liberty, and who have arms in their hands?"[161] Again note that this comment pertains to people, not states, having arms and prizing liberty. And again, this seems to support the "insurrectionist theory" of the people having arms for the purpose of resisting the federal government.

Samuel Adams, the firebrand who probably did as much to start the Revolutionary War as anyone, proposed the following amendments to the Constitution at the Massachusetts Convention:

> And that the said Constitution be never construed to authorize Congress to infringe the just liberty of the press, or the rights of conscience; or to prevent the people of the United States, who are peaceable citizens, from keeping their own arms; or to raise standing armies, unless when necessary for the defence of the United States, or of some one or more of them; or to prevent the people from petitioning, in a peaceable and orderly manner, the federal legislature, for a redress of grievances; or to subject the people to unreasonable searches and seizures of their persons, papers or possessions.[162]

While this proposed amendment was rejected by the Massachusetts Convention, note that in addition to the language similar to the Second Amendment, it contains language very similar to the First and Fourth Amendments to the Constitution. Only the portion about not raising standing armies was not eventually adopted by the federal government. Additionally, in this proposal there is absolutely no mention whatsoever of militias or state governments. The right clearly belongs to the people. This was clearly Samuel Adams's attitude toward this issue. This becomes more important when we look at the ratification of the Second Amendment.

In New Hampshire, the Convention approved the Constitution 57 to 47, but recommended twelve amendments. Two of them are relevant here:

> X. That no standing army shall be kept up in time of peace, unless with the consent of three fourths of the members of each branch of Congress; nor shall soldiers in a time of peace, be quartered upon private houses without the consent of the owners.

****

> XII. Congress shall never disarm any citizen, unless such as are or have been in actual rebellion.[163]

Notice again how the treatment of the problem of the standing army is separate and apart from that of the right to have arms. Additionally, notice that the right to have arms goes to the citizens (in other words, the people), not the militia or states. Gun control advocates assert that the provision for disarming those who have been in actual rebellion proves the fallacy of the insurrectionist theory. While I will address this in more detail in Chapter 7 on public policy, at this point just let me say that in my mind we can both have a right to rebel when the government goes too far in oppression, and the government can have the power to suppress insurrections and disarm those involved in them, when the government is not being oppressive. It is really a matter of degree in the amount of governmental oppression, and a question of who wins the rebellion.

A People Armed and Free

Some additional commentaries were published prior to the Virginia Convention. Alexander White, a Federalist who would later serve at the Virginia Convention, wrote a response to the Pennsylvania Minority Report:

> There are other things so clearly out of the power of Congress, that the bare recital of them is sufficient, I mean the "rights of conscience, or religious liberty—**the rights of bearing arms for defence, or for killing game**—the liberty of fowling, hunting and fishing ...." These things seem to have been inserted among their objections, merely to induce the ignorant to believe that Congress would have a power over such objects and to infer from their being refused a place in the Constitution, their intention to exercise that power to the oppression of the people.[164]

Again, the federalists recognized an inherent right that pre-existed the constitution and could not be taken away by the federal government, for the people to bear arms for defense and hunting.[165]

In May 1788, Richard Henry Lee issued another *Letter from the Federal Farmer*. In it, he again addressed the concern over a select militia:

> A militia, when properly formed, are in fact the people themselves, and render regular troops in a great measure unnecessary.... [T]he constitution ought to secure a genuine [militia] and guard against a select militia, ...

****

> But, say gentlemen, the general militia are for the most part employed at home in their private concerns, cannot well be called out, or be depended upon; that we must have a select militia; that is, as I understand it, particular corps or bodies of young men, and of men who have but little to do at home, particularly armed and disciplined in some measure, at the public expense, and always ready to take the field. These

67

corps, not much unlike regular troops, will ever produce an inattention to the general militia; and the consequence has ever been, and always must be, that the substantial men, having families and property, will generally be without arms, without knowing the use of them, and defenceless; whereas, **to preserve liberty, it is essential that the whole body of the people always possess arms, and be taught alike, especially when young, how to use them;** nor does it follow from this, that all promiscuously must go into actual service on every occasion. The mind that aims at a select militia, must be influenced by a truly anti-republican principle; and when we see many men disposed to practice upon it, whenever they can prevail, no wonder true republicans are for carefully guarding against it.[166]

This appears to be worded to respond to Hamilton's Federalist No. 29. It clearly indicates that the people must possess arms, and that a select militia should not be developed, because it is the same as a standing army, and by having a select militia, the people could be disarmed. That seems in fact to be the gun control advocates position in regard to the National Guard and the current power of the governments, both state and national, in regard to gun control (see Chapter 7 on Public Policy).

Another writer, "Aristocrats",[167] published a satire asserting the good the power of the central government could be used for as a way to show its potential abuses, pointing out that the active, or select, militia, could:

> [Q]uell insurrections that may arise in any parts of the empire on account of pretensions to support liberty, redress grievances, and the like... The second class or inactive militia, comprehends all the rest of the peasants; viz., the farmers, mechanics, labourers, &c. which good policy will prompt government to disarm. It would be dangerous to trust such a rabble as this with arms in their hands.[168]

A People Armed and Free

Obviously, with tongue-in-cheek, "Aristocrats" is talking about the people having arms and being dangerous to the government, not the states having arms.

Yet another writer, "M.T. Cicero" wrote to the "Citizens of America":

> Whenever, therefore, the profession of arms becomes a distinct order in the state ... the end [or goal] of the social compact is defeated ...
>
> No free government was ever founded, or ever preserved its liberty, without uniting the characters of the citizen and soldier in those destined for the defence of the state .... Such are a well regulated militia, composed of the freeholders, citizen and husbandman, **who take up arms** to preserve their property, **as individuals**, and their rights as freemen.[169]

Again, while the militia is mentioned, it is to be composed of citizens who take up arms as **individuals**, not as a state.

The gun control advocates point to much of the debate at the Virginia Ratifying Convention for the proposition that the real concern on everybody's minds was the ability of the states to arm their own militias. The reasoning goes that the Anti-Federalists were afraid that since Congress was given the power to arm the militia, this power was taken away from the states. The Federalists countered that the power was concurrent, that is to say, both the Congress and the states could arm the militia. So if everybody was concerned about the governments arming the militia, the right to obtain arms, and therefore keep and bear them, must have been in the governments, not the individuals. While I will grant them the fact that a lot of the debate had to do with whether or not the states could arm the militia — in fact there was such a debate in every state where there was any pertinent debate at all — the conclusion drawn by the gun control advocates is a stretch. The mere fact that this was a concern does not preclude other concerns, and as we will see shortly, the Virginia convention also addressed the right of the people to have arms.

At the Virginia Convention, Patrick Henry ("Give me Liberty or Give me Death!"), in response to an argument that any abuse of power could be remedied by calling another constitutional convention, argued that the power to resist oppression is based upon the right to possess arms:

> Guard with jealous attention the public liberty. Suspect every one who approaches that jewel. Unfortunately, nothing will preserve it but downright force. Whenever you give up that force, you are ruined... O sir, we should have fine times, indeed, if, to punish tyrants, it were only sufficient to assemble the people! Your arms, wherewith you could defend yourselves, are gone .... Did you ever read of any revolution in a nation ... inflicted by those who had no power at all?"[170]

Sounds like the insurrectionist theory raising its ugly head again, to me. Another delegate, Francis Corbin, opposing the need for a bill of rights, asked: "Who are the militia? Are we not the militia? Shall we fight against ourselves?"[171] George Mason, who had written the Virginia Declaration of Rights, and wrote the Virginia proposals for amendments to the Constitution, warned of the dangers of a gradual disarmament:

> Forty years ago, when the resolution of enslaving America was formed in Great Britain, the British Parliament was advised by an artful man [Sir William Keith], who was governor of Pennsylvania, to disarm the people; that it was the best and most effectual way to enslave them; but that they should not do it openly, but weaken them, and let them sink gradually, by totally misusing and neglecting the militia. [Here Mr. Mason quoted sundry passages to this effect.] This was a most iniquitous project. Why should we not provide against the danger of having our militia, our real and natural strength, destroyed? The general government ought, at the same time, to have some such power. But we need not give them power to abolish our militia. If they neglect to arm them, and prescribe proper discipline, they will be of no use .... I wish that, in case

A People Armed and Free

the general government should neglect to arm and discipline the militia, there should be an express declaration that the state governments might arm and discipline them.[172]

While this clearly talks about the state governments being able to arm the militia, it also provides a warning to us today, concerning all of our rights, against allowing them to be gradually eroded until they exist no more.

As a key to understanding what this discussion of the state's power to arm the militia was about, we turn again to Patrick Henry. In saying that if the power was concurrent, then the people from their taxes would have to pay for two sets of arms for the militia, he pointed out:

> **The great object is, that every man be armed**. But can the people afford to pay for double sets of arms, &c.? **Every one who is able may have a gun**. But we have learned, by experience, that, necessary as it is to have arms, and though our Assembly has, by a succession of laws for many years, endeavored to have the militia completely armed, it is still far from being the case. When this power is given up to Congress without limitation or bounds, how will your militia be armed? You trust to chance; for sure I am that nation which shall trust its liberties in other hands cannot long exist.[173]

Here, Patrick Henry has pointed out that those who are able can provide themselves with arms. The real question is which government has the power to provide arms to the rest of the people. Therefore, all people have a right, independent of the state government providing them, to have arms. And notice the distrust shown in the last sentence, which again supports the "insurrectionist theory". I would expect nothing less from Patrick Henry.

The proposed amendment from Virginia combined the right of the people with language concerning a well-regulated militia and avoiding standing armies:

> 17th. That the people have a right to keep and bear arms; that a well-regulated militia, composed of the body of the people, trained to arms, is the proper, natural, and safe defence of a free state; that standing armies, in time of peace, are dangerous to liberty, and therefore ought to be avoided, as far as the circumstances and protection of the community will admit; and that, in all cases, the military should be under strict subordination to, and governed by, the civil power.[174]

Gun control advocates argue that this combination of provisions show that this is not to be an individual right, but a right of the state government to maintain its militia. This argument might be more persuasive if it were not for two things. First, this was from a section of proposed amendments entitled as a bill of rights. The entire bill of rights proposed by the Virginia Convention, of which the above quoted provision was a part, asserted "the essential and unalienable rights of the people."[175] Therefore, in both the provision itself, and the general preamble to the bill of rights, it is the "rights of the people" that is being protected, not the states. Second, the Virginia convention also proposed a separate amendment, in a separate section not involved with the bill of rights, but proposing other amendments dealing with substantive changes to the Constitution, which dealt directly with the power of the states to maintain their militias: "11th. That each state respectively shall have the power to provide for organizing, arming, and disciplining its own militia, whensoever Congress shall omit or neglect to provide for the same."[176] The gun control advocates have ignored both of these facts. How many times does it have to be said? This provision of two separate amendments shows that the people involved must have two objects in mind; the one was to guarantee a right to the people, the other was to secure the power of the states. The gun control advocates have ignored this repeatedly.

In New York, prior to their convention, the author of "Common Sense", an Anti-Federalist paper, wrote "that the chief power will be in the Congress, and that what is to be left of our government is plain, because **a citizen may be deprived of the privilege of keeping arms for his own defence**, he may have his property taken without a trial by jury ...."[177] Notice here that the fear expressed is the loss of the privileges by the citizens, not the state governments. Also notice that the privilege, or right, extended to self-defense.

On July 26, 1788, New York ratified the Constitution 30 to 27. The Convention predicated its ratification, however, on the following propositions:

> That the powers of government may be reassumed by the people whensoever it shall become necessary to their happiness ...
> That the people have a right to keep and bear arms; that a well regulated militia, including the body of the people *capable of bearing arms*, is the proper, natural, and safe defence of a free state.[178]

They also provided in a separate portion of their proposals, additional amendments to the body of the Constitution affecting the states' powers over the militia and the keeping of a standing army during peace:

> That the militia of any state shall not be compelled to serve without the limits of the state, for a longer term than six weeks, without the consent of the legislature thereof.[179]
> That no standing army or regular troops shall be raised, or kept up, in time of peace, without the consent of two thirds of the senators and representatives present in each house.[180]

Again, separate proposed amendments, with separate purposes. And, again an indication that the people have a right to rebel to reform the government, that is to say, the "insurrectionist theory".

The North Carolina Convention refused to ratify the Constitution.[181] Their convention demanded the same Declaration of Rights as proposed by Virginia, and like Virginia and the other states, proposed a separate amendment dealing with the powers of the states:

> That each state respectively shall have the power to provide for organizing, arming, and disciplining its

own militia, whensoever Congress shall omit or neglect to provide for the same; that the militia shall not be subject to martial law, except when in actual service in time of war, invasion, or rebellion; and when not in the actual service of the United States, shall be subject only to such fines, penalties, and punishments, as shall be directed or inflicted by the laws of its own state.[182]

Again redundant if the language in the Declaration of Rights is to protect the states powers over the militias as asserted by the gun control advocates.

Rhode Island did not ratify the Constitution until May 29, 1790, by a vote of 34 to 32, and even then it incorporated a bill of rights into its ratification and proposed 21 amendments to the Constitution. Like the other states just discussed, Rhode Island's right to bear arms amendment listed that right as belonging to the people, then in philosophical language mentioned the well-regulated militia, not keeping standing armies during peace, the military should be subject to civil power, and no soldier should be quartered in any private house. Then in the amendment section, again like the other states, they proposed a specific prohibition on keeping a standing army in time of peace.[183]

I think that we have shown clearly that while there was significant concern and debate about the states losing their power over the militia, and the need for the states to have some protection of their power to maintain and arm their militias, there was also a lot of debate and concern over whether or not the federal government could disarm the people, and the need to protect the people's right to keep and bear arm, not only to defend the states from the federal government, but for self defense, hunting, and ultimately for the people to be able to rise up, not necessarily under the state governments, but possibly the state governments could assist in organizing and directing their efforts, in defense of their liberties if the federal government began to usurp powers and began to oppress the people under a tyrannical rule.

With the ratification process completed, we now turn to the drafting, passage and ratification of the Second Amendment. And some real surprises, that most people do not even have a clue of, and the gun control advocates certainly will never tell you about, are in store for you.

D.   *The Drafting, Passage and Ratification of the Second Amendment*

Gun control advocates have asserted: "There is no evidence that the Framers discussed, much less intended, that the amendments provide a guarantee to individuals of a right to be armed for purposes unrelated to militia service."[184] This statement is a lie. I would be kinder and gentler, but the article that this statement is pulled from is so well researched in so many obscure areas of history, and there is so much evidence available contrary to the statement, that I simply cannot believe that the authors had missed the evidence, overlooked it, or were simply mistaken. This has to be a conscious effort to deceive. And this point, the effort to deceive, is what for me cost the gun control advocates all of their credibility. While I can accept someone putting a different interpretation on the facts, or coming up with a different argument from the facts, I cannot accept a knowing attempt to say that the facts do not exist, when in fact they do. It is bad enough that they refuse to discuss the facts during the ratification of the Constitution that show the desire to have an individual right to keep and bear arms for reasons other than militia service, since that undermines their position, but when they say that such facts do not exist, whether pertaining to the ratification of the Constitution or the passage and ratification of the Second Amendment itself, this is simply too much.

So what facts are there that do show such an intent and discussion of an individual right to be armed for other purposes? Let us start with James Madison, who would soon draft the Second Amendment. James Madison, after losing out on his bid to be appointed as a Senator from Virginia,[185] ran for the House of Representatives. While during the ratification process he had been against a bill of rights, during his campaign he changed his mind and expressed his support for it: "That the change of circumstances produced by the secure establishment of the plan proposed, leaves me free to espouse such amendments as will, in the most satisfactory manner, guard essential rights, and will render certain vexatious abuses of power impossible ..."[186] This shows that the intent of the coming bill of rights was to be to "guard essential rights". In a letter to Edmund Pendleton, dated October 20, 1788, Madison referred to the coming proposal for amendments as "those further guards for private rights ..."[187] In preparing for a speech to deliver to Congress introducing the bill of rights, Madison made a first draft which contained the following:

> The following appears to be the most important objects of such an instrument. It should more especially comprise a doctrine in favor of the equality **of human rights**; of the liberty of conscience in matters of religious faith, of speech and of the press; of the trial by jury of the vicinage in civil and criminal cases; of the benefit of the writ of habeas corpus; **of the right to keep and bear arms** .... If these rights are well defined, and secured against encroachment, it is impossible that government should ever degenerate into tyranny.[188]

Again, this shows that the right to keep and bear arms would be a human right, not governmental. That was not the speech he delivered, but in his notes for the speech that he did deliver, he made the following entries: "They [the proposed amendments] relate first to private rights –fallacy on both sides espec[iall]y as the English Decl[aratio]n of Rights –1. mere act of parl[iamen]t. 2. no freedom of press—Conscience ... attainders—arms to protest[an]ts." What does this mean? The rights that would be proposed, such as freedom of the press and the right to keep and bear arms, would be "private rights". The problem ("fallacy") with the English Declaration of Rights was two fold: First, it was a mere act of Parliament, which could also be changed by a mere act of Parliament. Ours would be in a Constitution that would require a super majority in Congress and approval of three-fourths of the states to change. Second, the English Declaration omitted certain rights, and others, such as the right to have arms, was restricted. This would not be the case in America. We would have a general right to keep and bear arms. In the speech itself, Madison indicated that he wanted to prove that those who had accused the Federalists of trying to set up a government for the purpose of instituting an aristocracy or despotism were wrong. Even so, he did not want to open the door for a reconsideration of the whole structure of government. Then he said:

A People Armed and Free

> But I do wish to see a door opened to consider, so far as to incorporate those provisions **for the security of rights**, against which I believe no serious objection has been made by any class of our constituents: such as would be likely to meet with the concurrence of two-thirds of both Houses, and with the approbation of three-fourths of the State Legislatures.[189]

Madison then proposed his bill of rights. Most people do not know that initially, the rights were not to be appended at the end of the Constitution, as they are now. The initial proposal was to place the particular provisions into the body of the Constitution where they would most appropriately belong. For example, Madison proposed changing the preamble to the Constitution to include "all power is originally vested in, and consequently derived from the people;" "government is instituted ... for the benefit of the people;" and "the people have an indubitable, unalienable, and indefeasible right to reform or change their government..."[190] Then Madison proposed that certain personal rights, such as freedom of religion, non-establishment of religion, freedom of conscience, freedom of speech, freedom of the press, peaceable assembly, and others, be placed in Article I, section 9, which restricts the powers of Congress, between clauses 3 and 4 (right after the guarantee of the writ of habeas corpus in clause 2 and the prohibition of bills of attainder and ex post facto laws in clause 3—all personal rights—and the prohibition of capitation or other direct taxes in clause 4).[191] Other portions were proposed to be placed elsewhere in the Constitution, such as a proposed amendment to guarantee the right to jury trial in civil cases was proposed to be put in Article III, which concerns the judiciary, and which is where the guarantee of jury trials in criminal trials is found.[192] Guess where the proposal for the right to keep and bear arms was to be put? Right with the rest of the personal rights! Now Article I, section 8, clause 16 already has a reservation to the states of certain powers pertaining to the militia (the Appointment of the Officers, and the Authority of training the Militia). It would have made sense, the way Madison was doing this, if the real purpose of what became the Second Amendment was to reserve to the states the power to maintain and arm their militias, to have put it in or right after clause 16.

77

The text of the amendment, as initially proposed by Madison was as follows: "The right of the people to keep and bear arms shall not be infringed; a well armed, and well regulated militia being the best security of a free country: but no person religiously scrupulous of bearing arms shall be compelled to render military service in person."[193] Of note is the fact that while Madison made proposals for many rights, and some procedural protections, he did not draft any proposal that clearly stated any reservation of power over the militia in the states.

Other people, inside and outside of Congress understood this proposed amendment to belong to the people. Representative Fisher Ames of Massachusetts wrote: "Mr. Madison has introduced his long expected amendments… It contains a bill of rights … the right of the people to bear arms."[194] Ames wrote another letter where he said that "[t]he rights of conscience, **of bearing arms**, of changing the government, are declared to be **inherent in the people**."[195] Does this sound like the Framers thought the right would go to the states? Doesn't this sound like there is some evidence that the Framers thought that the right to be armed was an individual right? But wait, there's more! Senator William Grayson of Virginia wrote to Patrick Henry: "Last Monday a string of amendments were presented to the lower House; **these altogether respected personal liberty…**"[196] Joseph Jones wrote to Madison that the amendments are "calculated to secure **the personal rights of the people**…"[197] William L. Smith wrote to Edward Rutledge that the amendments "will effectually secure **private rights**…"[198] Ten days after the amendments were proposed, the Philadelphia Gazette published an article by Tench Coxe entitled "Remarks on the First Part of the Amendments to the Federal Constitution. In this article, which was a complete study of the entire Bill of Rights, Coxe stated:

> As civil rulers, not having their duty to the people duly before them, may attempt to tyrannize, and as the military forces which must be occasionally raised to defend our country, might pervert their power to the injury of their fellow-citizens, **the people** are confirmed by the next article in their right to keep and bear their **private arms**.[199]

A People Armed and Free

Notice that nothing is said about state governments or state militias. The right is for the people to resist tyranny, and they are to use their **private** arms, presumably kept at home, not governmentally supplied arms kept in a National Guard armory. Also note, that this would also satisfy the Federal Farmer since this would work against both a standing army and a select militia. All of this sounds to me like the intent was to guarantee individuals the right to bear arms, not to give the states the power to have a militia.

Coxe then sent a copy of this article to Madison. Madison responded positively to the article, approving of what Coxe had said, saying himself: "It will however be greatly favored by explanatory strictures of a healing tendency, and is therefore already indebted to the co-operation of your pen."[200] Therefore, Madison agreed that his proposal that became the Second Amendment protected private arms, which has nothing to do with states or militias, other than the people could use these private arms when serving in the militia.

A former member of the Massachusetts Ratification Convention who had voted against the Constitution, Samuel Nasson, wrote the following to Representative George Thatcher, a Federalist from the same state:

> I find that Amendments are once again on the Carpet. I hope that such may take place as will be for the Best Interest of the whole. A Bill of Rights well secured that we the people may know how far we may Proceed in Every Department. Then there will be no Dispute Between the people and rulers in that may be secured **the right to keep arms for Common and Extraordinary Occasions such as to secure ourselves against the wild Beast and also to amuse us by fowling and for our Defence against a Common Enemy**.[201]

He then continued to discuss the importance of people learning how to use their firearms so that everybody could always be prepared to defend the country and discourage a standing army and potential abuse by the government. Note that in the highlighted portion, the additional purposes of common, that is to say ordinary (self-defense, hunting, sport) and extraordinary occasions (defense of freedoms), to secure ourselves against wild beasts, for fowling, and for defense against common enemies. Obviously, reasons other than militia service were discussed.

Richard Henry Lee, in a letter of May 28, 1789 to Patrick Henry said: "I think, from what I hear and see, that many of our amendments will not succeed, but my hopes are strong that such as may effectually secure **civil liberty** will not be refused."[202] Again this indicates that an individual right, not a state government power was intended.

Madison's proposals were submitted to a select committee to consider them. This committee included Roger Sherman of Connecticut. While, as noted above, Madison did not draft any proposal for a reservation of power over the militia in the states, Roger Sherman did. While Sherman's draft of amendments did not include many of the rights that Madison had proposed, he did include the following:

> The militia shall be under the government of the laws of the respective states, when not in the actual service of the United States but such rules as may be prescribed by Congress for their uniform organization and discipline shall be observed in officering and training them; but military service shall not be required of persons religiously scrupulous of bearing arms.[203]

This proposal clearly reserves to the states powers over the militias, and does nothing to guarantee any right to the people. The problem (for gun control advocates) is, the committee rejected this proposal. They accepted Madison's proposal, modifying it slightly to read: "A well regulated militia, composed of the body of the people, being the best security of a free state, the right of the people to keep and bear arms shall not be infringed; but no person religiously scrupulous shall be compelled to bear arms."[204] So, the Congress rejected a proposed amendment that would have done exactly what the gun control advocates say the Second Amendment does, but approved a proposed amendment that all of the contemporaries indicate preserved an individual right to bear arms for not only militia service, but for self-defense, hunting, fowling, sport, and for the people to resist tyranny. Yet the gun control advocates attempt to turn this history on its head by requiring the exactly opposite result of what the Congress did. Shades of George Orwell's 1984 double speak!

Newspaper commentaries continued during this time. An article in the Boston Independent Chronicle of Aug. 20, 1789, compared the amendments as reported by the House committee, with those proposed by Samuel Adams at the Massachusetts Ratification Convention:

> It may well be remembered, that the following "amendments" to the new constitution of these United States, were introduced to the convention of this commonwealth by ... SAMUEL ADAMS ... [E]very one of the intended alterations but one [i.e., proscription of standing armies] have been already reported by the committee of the House of Representatives, and most probably will be adopted by the federal legislature. In justice therefore for that long tried Republican, and his numerous friends, you gentlemen, are requested to republish his intended alterations, in the same paper, that exhibits to the public, the amendments which the committee have adopted, in order that they may be compared together....
> "And that the said constitution be never construed to authorize congress ... to prevent the people of the United States, who are peaceable citizens, from keeping their own arms ...."[205]

This shows that the thought at this time was that the proposed Second Amendment was the same in effect as that proposed by Samuel Adams, which did not mention militias and could not possibly be construed to do anything but secure the right of the people to have their own firearms. It is acknowledged in the article that the one item that Samuel Adams proposed that was not passed was the prohibition of a standing army. The newspapers of the time did not even think about the Second Amendment possibly being argued to mean that the states were granted some power over the militias.

With the proposed amendments now before the entire House of Representatives, they proceeded to debate them. In a letter dated

August 9, 1789, from Representative William L. Smith of South Carolina to his colleague Edward Rutledge, Smith pointed out that "[t]he Committee on Amendments have reported some, which are thought inoffensive to the Federalists & may do some good on the other side... There appears to be a disposition in our house to agree to some, which will more effectually secure **private rights, without affecting the structure of the Government**."[206] In other words, the goal was to secure private rights, and not change the structure of the government, internally, or as between the states and the federal government. So in the case of the Second Amendment, this would guarantee the individual's right to keep and bear arms, but would not affect the relationship between the state and federal government as to the militias.

On August 18, 1789, Pennsylvania Congressman Frederick A. Muhlenberg wrote to Benjamin Rush, concerning the Bill of Rights, "... I hope it will be satisfactory to our State, and as it takes in the principal Amendments which our Minority had so much at Heart, I hope it may restore Harmony & unanimity amongst our fellow Citizens..."[207] Remember that the amendment proposed by the Pennsylvania Minority Report specifically allowed for the keeping of arms by people for self-defense and hunting, not dealing with militias. While they also requested an amendment dealing with militias, that proposal was defeated in the House Committee, so it could not be what Muhlenberg was referring to.

There was little recorded debate concerning the Second Amendment. There appears to have been nothing recorded concerning the extent of the right to keep and bear arms, nor any objection to it. Some have accused the official House reporter, Thomas Lloyd as being incompetent and drunk.[208] Even so, gun control advocates often cite what was recorded as evidence that the purpose of the Second Amendment related only to the militia and the states. What they are referring to is a discussion centering on the objection of Representative Elbridge Gerry to the exemption of those who are religiously scrupulous from rendering military service. His point was that with that clause in there, the government could determine who was religiously scrupulous, and prevent them from bearing arms. Gerry argued that the government should not be allowed to do this. The gun control advocates argue that if this interpretation of this clause is correct, then the amendment as proposed would not have protected anyone's rights to have arms, since the government could prevent them from bearing arms once it determined that they were religiously scrupulous. Therefore, the Amendment had to only relate to the maintenance of a militia, since the government could determine who could serve in the militia. However, this ignores the portion of the amendment concerning keeping arms. The religiously scrupulous could not be forced to bear arms, in the military context, but they still had the right to keep arms. In fact, Gerry's remarks show that the Amendment as worded at that time did not restrict federal power over the militia, since it did not expressly grant the federal government any power to prevent people from bearing arms, but merely said that certain people could not be **forced** to bear arms. So that restriction of power had to come, if it existed at all, from the body of the Constitution, the militia clauses found in article I, section 8, clauses 15 and 16. Therefore, according to Gerry, the proposed amendment would not do what the gun control advocates say it does; it would not protect the states powers over the militia.

In any event, the House of Representatives passed the proposed amendment on August 24, 1789, after amending it by including the words "in person" at the end of the clause: "but no person religiously scrupulous shall be compelled to bear arms in person."[209]

After the House passed this version of the amendment, one article in a newspaper criticized it, not for not ensuring the people a right to keep and bear arms, but for it not ensuring the states more power over their militias:

> It is remarkable that this article only makes the observation, 'that a well regulated militia, composed of the body of the people, is the best security of a free state;' it does not ordain, or constitutionally provide for, the establishment of such a one. The absolute command vested by other sections in Congress over the militia, are not in the least abridged by this amendment. The militia may still be subjected to martial law ... may still be marched from state to state and made the unwilling instruments of crushing the last efforts of expiring liberty.[210]

Jack Reynolds, J. D.

This clearly states that the proposed amendment does not do what the gun control advocates say it does. It does not constitutionally ordain the establishment of a militia. The absolute command over the militia, given to Congress in article I section 8, clauses 15 and 16, is not reduced or restricted at all. So, if it does not do anything to protect the states' control of the militia, as asserted by the gun control advocates, it must protect the individual's right to keep and bear arms as asserted by the gun rights advocates.

The author of this article was "Centinel", who was actually Samuel Bryan, the author of the Pennsylvania Dissent of the Minority, which you may remember called for, in addition to an amendment protecting the militias, an amendment protecting the individual's right to bear arms for self defense, for hunting, and for defense of the state and country. Now it is significant that "Centinel" did not object to the proposed amendment on the grounds that it did not protect personal rights, only that it did not protect militias. In the military, when calling in indirect fire (air strikes, mortars or artillery), we have a rule called "silence is consent". If you call in fire on a target or on certain grid coordinates, and other people listening in on the radio for this call for fire do not object, by getting on the radio and saying "wait a minute, there are friendly troops there", then this silence is considered to be consent to fire at the target and it is assumed that there are no friendly forces in the impact area. Likewise, in the law, when we look at the history of a provision such as this, the fact that no objection was made indicates that it was consented to. One would assume that the people who were so vocal in their objections to the Constitution would be willing to object if the proposed amendment did not do what they wanted it to do. Certainly "Centinel" showed that he was willing to object since militias were not protected. His silence on the issue of an individual's rights to bear arms speaks as loudly as if he had actually said that it does protect those rights. We will see other examples of the "silence is consent" rule in a moment.

With the passage by the House, all of the proposed amendments went to the Senate, which was not as friendly to them as was the House. While the Senate met in secret on these items, so we do not have a record of what was said in the debates, we do have a record of what they did in regards to each of the amendments. The Senate made numerous changes to several of the proposed amendments. Of course, what we are concerned with is what they did in relation to the one that became the Second Amendment.

The Senate considered and rejected a motion to add the following clauses to the amendment:

> That standing armies, in time of peace, being dangerous to liberty, should be avoided, as far as the circumstances and protection of the community will admit; and that in all cases the military should be under strict subordination to, and governed by, the civil power; that no standing army or regular troops shall be raised in time of peace, without the consent of two-thirds of the members present in both Houses; and that no soldier shall be enlisted for any longer term than the continuance of the war.[211]

The vote was six in favor, nine against. Those in favor included the Anti-Federalists such as William Henry Lee and William Grayson. The Senate did approve motions to drop the phrase "composed of the body of the people" which had been right after the word "militia", and deleted the clause "but no one religiously scrupulous of bearing arms, shall be compelled to render military service in person."

On September 8, 1789, the Senate considered renewed proposals to require a two-thirds majority of Congress to have a standing army and limits on the terms of enlistment, which again failed.[212] They then took up a new proposal to reserve power to the states to maintain militias, in accordance with the proposals from several of the state ratifying conventions:

> That each state, respectively, shall have the power to provide for organizing, arming, and disciplining its own militia, whensoever Congress shall omit or neglect to provide for the same; that the militia shall not be subject to martial law, except when in actual service, in time of war, invasion, or rebellion; and when not in the actual service of the United States, shall be subject only to such fines, penalties, and

punishments, as shall be directed or inflicted by the laws of its own state.[213]

This proposal shows some interesting points when compared with the Second Amendment. First, it specifically mentions the states as the beneficiaries of the proposal, not the people. Second, it says that the thing being guaranteed is a "power", not a "right". Remember our discussion in Chapter 3 about the difference between powers and rights, and that governments can only have powers; only people have rights? The above proposal also clearly gives the states control over their militias, as opposed to the Second Amendment, which has to be spun out of control to get to that point. Well, guess what? You will not find the above proposal anywhere in today's Constitution, because, just like the House of Representatives, the Senate rejected such a reservation of powers to the states. Now it must be said that gun control advocates try to say that the probable reason for this rejection is that it would have been redundant of the Second Amendment. However, this simply does not wash. Several state ratifying conventions, as has been shown above, did not think the two were redundant, since they proposed both, usually with the proposal most closely related to the Second Amendment being included in a section dealing with personal rights, and the proposal most closely linked to the above proposal being in a separate section, not involving personal rights. Some significant number of the members of Congress did not think they were redundant, since such measures were brought up both in the House and Senate and received some votes. No, it is much more likely that the reason that the proposals were defeated in both the House and Senate is that the majority of the members of Congress simply did not want to reserve such power to the states, but did want to guarantee an individual right to keep and bear arms.

On September 9, the Senate rejected another proposal that might have restricted this individual right. The proposal was to add the words "for the common defense" right after the words "bear arms" (to read "the right to keep and bear arms for the common defense"). While the preamble to the Second Amendment, as a philosophical declaratory statement giving a reason for guaranteeing the right of the people to keep and bear arms, does not restrict that right, the addition of the words in the manner proposed here might have restricted that right to just for the common defense. However, that's right, you

A People Armed and Free

guessed it, the Senate rejected this proposal too.[214] Again, the Senate simply did not want to restrict the right to keep and bear arms to any specific purpose; it is a natural pre-existing right, and it is up to the law-abiding citizens to determine to what purpose they will apply that right.

The Senate finally changed a small part of the preamble to the Second Amendment. Instead of "the best security", the militia was now declared to be "necessary" to a free state.[215] This change appeared to be in response to some comments made in the House debates that the words "the best security" implied that there may be other acceptable methods of securing a free state, and the number two method might be a standing army. By using the word "necessary" it made it clear that guaranteeing that the people could keep and bear arms so that a militia would always exist, would always have to be done in order to secure our free state.

The Senate then passed the final version of what became the Second Amendment: "A well regulated militia being necessary to the security of a free State, the right of the people to keep and bear arms shall not be infringed." Since this amendment, and others, had been changed by the Senate, a conference committee met to resolve the differences. The House accepted the Senate version of this amendment. On September 25, 1789, the Senate agreed to the House Resolution approving the final version of the Bill of Rights, sending it to the states for ratification. Attached to the amendments was a preamble which stated: "The conventions of a number of the states having, at the time of their adopting the constitution, expressed a desire, in order to prevent misconstruction or abuse of its powers, that further declaratory and restrictive clauses should be added ...."[216] The point here is that the Second Amendment indeed does have a declaratory clause (the militia clause) which does not limit or produce any governmental power, nor limit or produce any personal right, but merely states a reason for the right itself, and a restrictive clause (the right of the people to keep and bear arms, which does guarantee this right). The Congress recognized the difference between declaratory clauses and restrictive clauses. Again, evidence that our grammatical analysis in Chapter 3 is correct.

It was now up to the states to ratify the proposed amendments, or not. In fact, the first two amendments proposed were not ratified at that time.[217] What is now the First Amendment was actually passed by Congress as the Third Amendment, and the subject of this book, the Second Amendment, was initially to be the Fourth.

During this time, political positions fell into three camps: 1. The Amendments were good as presented; 2. Additional guarantees were needed, so more amendments were needed; and 3. There were still people who said that there was no need for any Bill of Rights. While there were commentaries between these camps about the adequacy of the various amendments, and some of this commentary included objections that no guarantee of state power over the militia was included, and that there was no restriction on a standing army, I have not seen any commentary that complained that the amendments did not protect individuals' rights to have firearms, for self-defense, hunting, or any other purpose, or just in general. Let's take a look at some of these comments.

> The right of the people to keep and bear arms has been recognized by the General Government; but the best security of that right after all is, the military spirit, that taste for martial exercises, which has always distinguished the free citizens of these States; From various parts of the Continent the most pleasing accounts are published of reviews and parades in large and small assemblies of the militia .... Such men form the best barrier to the Liberties of America.[218]

"The whole of that Bill [of Rights] is a declaration of the right of the people at large or considered as individuals… [I]t establishes some rights of the individual as unalienable and which consequently, no majority has a right to deprive them of."[219] President Washington told the House of Representatives that "a free people ought not only to be armed, but disciplined…"[220] Patrick Henry was said to be "pleased with some of the proposed amendments; but still asks for the great desideratum, the destruction of direct taxes."[221] Richard Henry Lee said that the Bill of Rights was "short of some essentials, as Election interference & Standing Army & C…"[222] Theodorick Bland wrote Patrick Henry that "I have founded my hopes to the single object of securing (*in terrorem*) the great and essential rights of freemen from the encroachments of Power—so far as to authorize resistance when they should be either openly attacked or insidiously undermined."[223] This again sounds like the "insurrectionist theory" to me. Thomas Jefferson was dissatisfied with the Bill of Rights, but did not object to the arms-bearing provision in the Second Amendment.[224] Samuel Adams was curiously quiet on the issue. But remember that his proposed amendments, while putting forth an individual right to keep and bear arms, did not say anything about a militia. Therefore, his silence is perfectly in keeping with the Second Amendment being an individual right. He simply had nothing to complain about, with the protection of the state militia being left out. I have already quoted Centinel's objection that the amendments did not do anything to guarantee states' power over their militias. The Massachusetts General Court rejected the Bill of Rights and published a large Report of the Committee of the General Court on Further Amendments explaining why. It did not object that there was no individual right to keep and bear arms, but it did propose an amendment which would have recognized a state power to veto Congressional action establishing a "system for forming the militia" or making an "establishment of troops in a time of peace."[225] With all of these complaints that these people were willing to make about the amendments, and as vociferous as they had been at the state ratifying conventions and in public commentaries prior to the ratification of the Constitution in calling for an amendment to guarantee an individual's right to bear arms, and as strongly as they obviously held their beliefs that people should have the right to bear arms, it would be amazing indeed if they had believed that the Second Amendment did not protect the right of the people as individuals to keep and bear arms for whatever reason and did not say anything about it. Again, the "silence is consent" rule shows that all of these people, all very influential in the forming of our country, believed that the Second Amendment did in fact protect an individual right of the people to keep and bear arms, and did not reserve any power to the states over the militias.

 E. *Post Amendment Ratification History*

 I have read some objections about continuing the historic analysis beyond the ratification of the Second Amendment. The position seems to be that if what we want is to discover the intent of the Framers; that must be done before the amendment is ratified. Once ratified, the intent has been accomplished and is now over, so nothing that happens after that shows intent. However, the Framers did not just magically disappear once the amendment was ratified. They did not all suddenly die. They continued to be influential in politics, in office, and in commentaries. The way they treated issues related to the Second Amendment surely provides some evidence of their interpretation of it, and therefore, their intent in passing it. They surely conveyed their thoughts, attitudes and feelings about the issues involved, people owning firearms and states controlling militias, to their friends and colleagues, their children, their political successors. These people probably carried the same thoughts, attitudes, feelings and beliefs concerning the Second Amendment for some years. Therefore, their actions and commentaries, as they relate to the Second Amendment, also remain important as to what the Amendment was originally supposed to do. Of course, the farther away that we get from the ratification of the Second Amendment in time, the less certain it is that these understandings remain the same as the Framers'.

The first action that occurred that has any relation to the Second Amendment was the passage by Congress of the Federal Militia Act of 1792. While not directly involving the Second Amendment, it does have a relationship to some of the arguments presented about what it means. The Militia Act, at the federal level, required every "free able bodied white male citizen" aged 18 through 45 to "provide himself with a good musket or firelock," bayonet and ammunition. Horsemen were to provide themselves with a pair of pistols, ammunition and a sabre. It was originally introduced in the House of Representatives on December 14, 1790.[226] Some gun rights advocates cite this provision as being further evidence that the word "militia" meant all of the people. We have already addressed this in Chapter 2, and found that there is actually some logic and support on both sides of this point of the argument. However, I have another interpretation of the meaning of the Militia Act that I have not seen addressed by either side up to this time.

Now remember that the gun control advocates say that the purpose of the Second Amendment was to guarantee the power/right of the state governments to maintain and arm the militia. Do you see a conflict here? Doesn't it strike you as a little strange, if the gun control advocates' position is correct, that the same people who had worked so hard for a constitutional guarantee of the states' power to arm the militia would all of a sudden, within the next year, introduce a bill, then pass it, that would virtually pull the rug out from under this

A People Armed and Free

state power by having the federal government order all of the people to provide their own arms, totally skipping the states? This does not make any sense to me. If Congress had done something to encourage the states to exercise this newly guaranteed power and arm their militias, the argument might make sense. Instead, the Congress ordered individuals to arm themselves, leaving the states out of it. If the gun control advocates are right, it seems to me that the Militia Act would have violated the Second Amendment. Of course the gun control advocates might argue that this was just another allowed method of arming the militia and therefore did not conflict with the states' power. If it were the states ordering the people to arm themselves I would agree. But for the federal government to usurp the power supposedly just given to the states, by Congress determining how all of the state militias in the country would be armed, is a conflict with any supposed grant of the power to the states to arm the militia. The gun control advocates could say that the Second Amendment merely made it clear that the power to arm the militia is a joint power, existing both in the state and federal government, so that this act would merely be the federal government exercising its portion of that power. But this does not wash either, for two reasons. First, if that was all the Amendment did, then why all the fuss? The power to arm was supposed to be concurrent to begin with. Second, if making the power concurrent is what the Amendment does, it does not satisfy the concerns expressed that once the federal government arms the militia, it could then take those arms away, leaving the militia unarmed and useless to the states. This could occur even if the states had the concurrent power. What do you think would happen today if the federal government all of a sudden took away all of the arms from the National Guard. The states would be disarmed! Until they could raise enough money in additional taxes (a lot of money; a lot of taxes) and procure the additional arms from manufacturers who would have to make them in massive quantities, the states would be without arms. During this time, the states would be defenseless against the standing army. Therefore, a concurrent, or joint, power to arm the militia does nothing to address the concerns that the gun control advocates say led to the Second Amendment.

A review of the debates in the Congress concerning this act confirms my position. One of the issues involved was whether or not the **federal** government should provide arms to those individuals too poor to provide them for themselves. Comments were made about the burden having to provide their own weapons would put on individuals. Congressman Josiah Parker of Virginia moved to amend the act to have the **federal** government pay for the arms for those who were too poor to comply with the law's requirement of arming themselves. Several objections were voiced to this motion. Some objections related to the desire of the people to arm themselves. Some argued that there were too few people who were that poor, so the Congress should not be concerned with it. Another argument was that if the United States offered to provide arms, then it could also disarm those that it had provided arms to. The motion was defeated.[227] Then Representative Thomas Fitzsimmons of Pennsylvania moved to strike the words "provide himself" and to substitute "shall be provided" with arms. James Madison (remember him) objected that this "would leave it optional with the States, or individuals, whether the militia shall be armed or not." This proposed amendment was also defeated.[228]

All of this is incongruous with a guarantee of state power to maintain and arm the militia. The federal government is establishing the militia itself, and some of the Representatives are arguing that the federal government should arm some of the militia members. None of the objections to these proposals said "we can't do that; we just gave this power to the states." If Congress did not think that the Second Amendment gave power to maintain and arm the militia to the states, then what could the Amendment do? The only other choice is that it guarantees the pre-existing right to keep and bear arms for individuals.

In 1799, this country almost exploded. There was a great dispute between the two camps headed by John Adams (then President) and Thomas Jefferson. The Sedition Acts had been passed. Tench Coxe had aligned himself with Thomas Jefferson and a Philadelphia newspaper supporting him. Some soldiers in the Federalists (Adams) faction had attacked the newspaper, destroying some property and assaulting its editor. In response, Tench Coxe wrote the following:

> But as men intent upon hostility have associated themselves in military corps, it becomes your duty to associate likewise-**Arm and organize yourselves immediately** ....

A People Armed and Free

> Do you wish to preserve your rights? **Arm yourselves**-Do you desire to secure your dwellings? **Arm yourselves**-Do you wish your wives and daughters protected? **Arm yourselves**-Do you wish to be defended against assassins or the Bully Rocks of faction? **Arm yourselves**-Do you desire to assemble in security to consult for your own good or the good of your country? **Arm yourselves.-To arms, to arms**, and you may then sit down contented, each man under his own vine and his own fig-tree and have no one to make him afraid....
>
> If you are desirous to counteract a design pregnant with misery and ruin, **then arm yourselves**; for in a firm, imposing and dignified attitude, will consist your own security and that of your families-**To arms, then to arms**.[229]

This appears to be an exhortation to be prepared to exercise the insurrectionist theory. And it is not a call for a state militia to come to the rescue, but for individuals to arm themselves.

Now let us turn to some early legal commentary on the Second Amendment. First is that of St. George Tucker. Never heard of him? That's O.K. Neither had I, nor I suspect have most people, prior to my research for this book. He was a colonel in the Virginia militia during the Revolutionary War, a law professor at William and Mary, and a justice on the Virginia Supreme Court from 1804 to 1811. In 1803 he published an annotated five-volume edition of Blackstone's Commentaries on the Laws of England. In this publication, he comments on the Second Amendment:

> 8.A well regulated militia being necessary to the security of a free state, the right of the people to keep and bear arms, shall not be infringed. Amendments to C.U.S. Art. 4.
>
> **This may be considered as the true palladium of liberty .... The right of self defence is the first law of nature**: in most governments it has been the study of rulers to confine this right within the narrowest limits

> possible. Wherever standing armies are kept up, and the right of the people to keep and bear arms is, under any colour or pretext whatsoever, prohibited, liberty, if not already annihilated, is on the brink of destruction. **In England, the people have been disarmed, generally, under the specious pretext of preserving the game: a never failing lure to bring over the landed aristocracy to support any measure, under that mask, though calculated for very different purposes**. True it is, their bill of rights seems at first view to counteract this policy: but the right of bearing arms is confined to protestants, and the words suitable to their condition and degree, have been interpreted to authorize the prohibition of keeping a gun or other engine for the destruction of game, to any farmer, or inferior tradesman, or other person not qualified to kill game. So that not one man in five hundred can keep a gun in his house without being subject to a penalty.
>
> The congress of the United States possesses no power to regulate, or interfere with the domestic concerns, or police of any state: it belongs not to them to establish any rules respecting the rights of property; **nor will the constitution permit any prohibition of arms to the people;**..."
>
> If, for example, **a law be passed by congress**, prohibiting the free exercise of religion, according to the dictates, or persuasions of a man's own conscience or **abridging** the freedom of speech, or of the press; **or the right of the people** to assemble peaceably, **or to keep and bear arms**; it would, in any of these cases, be the province of the judiciary to pronounce whether any such act were constitutional, or not; and if not, to acquit the accused from any penalty which might be annexed to the breach of such unconstitutional act.[230]

While this is a rather long quote, it is important. In 1803, one of the great legal scholars of this country was saying that the Second Amendment guaranteed the right of the people to keep and bear arms for, among other reasons, self-defense, prevention of the need for

A People Armed and Free

standing armies, and for opposing oppression. The Constitution does not allow any prohibition of arms to the people, and if Congress tries to abridge this right, it would be up to the courts to set things right. Also notice the distinction made between the English Bill of Rights and the American. Our right was always meant to be broader than the British. While this was about 14 years after the ratification of the Second Amendment, you should remember that at this time Thomas Jefferson, who wrote the Declaration of Independence, was President, and others of the Founding Fathers were still around, so it gives a very contemporary look into what the amendment meant to the Framers.

In 1814, Tench Coxe, now working for the federal government procuring arms for the country, made a report to President Madison concerning the arms industry in America. In it he pointed out that cannon, the largest military weapons of the time, were made "for sale to associations of citizens, and to individual purchasers, for use at home, or for exportation."[231]

What about the state governments? How did they treat this whole issue of the Second Amendment and the right of the people to keep and bear arms during the early history of our country? While state court opinions are certainly not binding authority on the federal courts as to the interpretation of the United States Constitution, they are interesting from the historic perspective of what people thought about the issues at the time. In 1822, in the case of *Bliss v. Commonwealth*,[232] the Kentucky Supreme Court held that a law that made it illegal to carry certain concealed weapons was unconstitutional. While the real issue was the application of the state constitution, not the Second Amendment, the logic used applies to our discussion. The point was asserted by the government in trying to uphold the statute, that the law was not prohibiting the right to carry arms, but merely regulating the manner of exercising that right; that while people were prohibited from wearing concealed weapons, they could nevertheless bear arms in any other admissible form. The Kentucky Supreme Court refuted this by pointing out that the law did diminish the liberty. In addition, the court used what I consider to be irrefutable logic in pointing out that if the argument of the government was correct, then the government could have allowed people to carry concealed weapons, but then made it illegal to carry weapons openly, and that too would have been constitutional. But if both laws would be constitutional on their own, then the legislature could prohibit the carrying of all weapons, not matter how it is done, which would destroy the right to bear arms. The court acknowledged that some people might say that the government could restrict one, but not both at the same time. In response to this proposal the court said:

> [T]he absurd consequence would thence follow, of making the same act of the legislature, either consistent with the constitution, or not so, according as it may precede or follow some other enactment of a different import... But it should not be forgotten, that it is not only a part of the right that is secured by the constitution; it is the right entire and complete, as it existed at the adoption of the constitution; and if any portion of that right be impaired, immaterial how small the part may be, and immaterial the order of time at which it be done, it is equally forbidden by the constitution.[233]

Now let us turn to William Rawle, another person that I suspect that most of you have never heard of. He was President Washington's first choice as the nation's first attorney general, but he declined the appointment. He was later appointed by President Washington as a United States Attorney for Pennsylvania. In 1829 he wrote A View of the Constitution of the United States of America. Back at that time, lawyers did not have the case reporter system that we have now. They depended on treatises such as Blackstone's and St George Tucker's books to let them know what the law was. Rawle's book was, at the time, considered to be the primary resource on constitutional law. Another long quote is in the offering—remember only attorneys can draft a fifty-page document and call it a brief—but let us see what he has to say about the Second Amendment:

> In the second article, it is declared, that a ***well regulated militia is necessary to a free state***; a proposition from which few will dissent. Although in actual war, in the services of regular troops are confessedly more valuable; yet while peace prevails, and in the commencement of a war before a regular force can be raised, the militia form the palladium of

the country. They are ready to repel invasion, to suppress insurrection, and preserve the good order and peace of government. That they should be well regulated, is judiciously added. A disorderly militia is disgraceful to itself, and dangerous not to the enemy, but to its own country. The duty of the state government is, to adopt such regulation as will tend to make good soldiers with the least interruptions of the ordinary and useful occupations of civil life. In this all the Union has a strong and visible interest.

The corollary, from the first position, is that the right of the people to keep and bear arms shall not be infringed.

The prohibition is general. No clause in the Constitution could by any rule of construction be conceived to give to congress a power to disarm the people. Such a flagitious attempt could only be made under some general pretence by a state legislature. But if in any blind pursuit of inordinate power, either should attempt it, this amendment may be appealed to as a restraint on both.

In most of the countries of Europe, this right does not seem to be denied, although it is allowed more or less sparingly, according to circumstances. In England, a country which boasts so much of its freedom, the right was secured to protestant subjects only, on the revolution of 1688; and is cautiously described to be that of bearing arms for their defence,'suitable to their conditions, and as allowed by law.' An arbitrary code for the preservation of game in that country has long disgraced them. A very small proportion of the people being permitted to kill it, though for their own subsistence; a gun or other instrument, used for that purpose by an unqualified person, may be seized and forfeited. Blackstone, in whom we regret that we cannot always trace expanded principles of rational liberty, observes however, on this subject, that the prevention of popular insurrections and resistance to government by disarming the people, is oftener meant than avowed, by the makers of forest and game laws.[234]

Notice that while he says that the maintenance of a well regulated militia is important, the **right** belongs to the people, and is a general right, that is to say for any purpose, one that the Congress could not infringe by trying to disarm the people. Then notice that he too distinguishes the English situation from ours, indicating that our right is broader, and that the English actually try to disarm the people to prevent insurrections.

Next is Justice Joseph Story, who was appointed to the United States Supreme Court in 1811 by President James Madison (yes, the same one we have been discussing, who drafted the Constitution and the Bill of Rights). In 1833 Justice Story wrote Commentaries on the Constitution of the United States. Here are his comments on the Second Amendment:

> "§ 1000. The next amendment is: "A well regulated militia being necessary to the security of a free state, the right of the people to keep and bear arms shall not be infringed.
> § 1001. The importance of this article will scarcely be doubted by any persons, who have duly reflected upon the subject. The militia is the natural defence of a free country against sudden foreign invasions, domestic insurrections, **and domestic usurpations of power by rulers**. It is against sound policy for a free people to keep up large military establishments and standing armies in time of peace, both from the enormous expenses, with which they are attended, and the facile means, which they afford to ambitious and unprincipled rulers, to subvert the government, or trample upon the rights of the people. **The right of the citizens to keep, and bear arms has justly been considered, as the palladium of the liberties of a republic; since it offers a strong moral check against the usurpation and arbitrary power of rulers; and will generally, even if these are**

successful in the first instance, enable the people to resist, and triumph over them. And yet, though this truth would seem so clear, and the importance of a well regulated militia would seem so undeniable, it cannot be disguised, that among the American people there is a growing indifference to any system of militia discipline, and a strong disposition, from a sense of its burthens, to be rid of all regulations. How it is practicable **to keep the people duly armed** without some organization, it is difficult to see. There is certainly no small danger, that indifference may lead to disgust, and disgust to contempt; and thus gradually undermine all the protection intended by this clause of our national bill of rights.[235]

While gun control advocates claim that the discussion of the militia and the need to have some organization to keep the people armed shows that the purpose of the Second Amendment was to allow the states to arm the militias, Story did not say that. He said that the purpose was to allow the people to be armed, and that this would be difficult without the organizations of state militias. This does not mean that only the state can arm the people, only that they can help; the bottom line is, the people have the right to keep and bear arms. And, he included as a purpose, to defend against domestic usurpations of power, the insurrectionist theory.

Let us now travel outside the United States to the Mexican state of Texas for our next example of actions taken with regard to the right to keep and bear arms. Being from Texas, I am rather partial to Texas history myself. In any event, Stephen F. Austin had brought colonists from the United States into Mexico to settle in Texas. Being formerly American citizens, they brought with them their understandings of the rights that people have, or should have. Even so, they gave up their right to religious freedom, agreeing to convert to the Catholic Church as a condition to their being admitted to settle there. To make a long story short, problems developed with the Mexican government. The state government, controlled by the Mexican army, had given a small cannon to the people of the town of Gonzales for protection from the Indians in 1831. In 1835, the military commander of Texas, Domingo de Ugartechea, ordered the colonists to return the cannon. When they refused, he sent 100 soldiers under Francisco de Castaneda to retrieve it. The colonists refused to give it back, raising a flag with a depiction of the cannon on it, with the words "COME AND TAKE IT" written underneath. They fought the Mexican army in a small skirmish and drove them off, keeping their cannon. This has caused historians to proclaim the Battle of Gonzales as the "Lexington of the Texas Revolution."[236] The people clearly were defending their right to keep and bear arms, even larger arms than rifles, against what they considered to be a despotic central government. And it was not the state government that was using a well-regulated militia to resist this despotic central government, because the state government was under control of the Mexicans and was actually trying to take the cannon away. No, it was the people. While certainly this is not controlling authority on the construction of the United States Constitution, this shows the general attitude of the people, coming from the United States, during this period of time.

The Texans, in 1836, published a Declaration of Independence similar to the United States, listing the despotic acts of the central government.[237] Included in this Declaration was the following complaint: "It [the Mexican Government] has demanded us to deliver up our arms, which are essential to our defense – the rightful property of freemen – and formidable only to tyrannical governments." When they drafted the Constitution for the Republic of Texas, again in 1836, they included the following right to bear arms: "**Every citizen shall have the right to bear arms in defence of himself and the republic. The military shall at all times and in all cases be subordinate to the civil power.**"[238] Again, at least the Texans, who took many provisions of their new Constitution from that of the United States, considered the right to bear arms to extend to self-defense.

O.K., let's return to the United States, this time in the area of Ohio, Missouri and Illinois. During the 1830's and 1840's the members of the Church of Jesus Christ of Later Day Saints (the Mormons) were being persecuted. They had been run out of Kirtland, Ohio. They had tried to settle in western Missouri, but conflicts with others not of their faith resulted in the governor using the militia to arrest some of their leaders, kill some of the members, and chase the rest out of the state. The governor even issued what was called the "Extermination Order", ordering that all Mormons either leave the state or be killed. The Mormons formed their own militia (before

A People Armed and Free

leaving Ohio) and had marched it to Missouri to help their members who had settled there. They wound up not using this militia, and returned to Ohio. After being kicked out of Missouri by the state militia, they settled in Nauvoo, Illinois. The governor of Illinois promised them protection. Even so, the Mormons formed their own militia again, which did not answer to the state, but to their church leaders. It was called the Nauvoo Legion, and at that time was the third largest military organization in the United States. Despite this, with problems again developing with nearby people not of their faith, the governor ordered the leaders of the Mormons arrested, ostensibly under the protection of the Illinois militia. However, despite the governor's promises of protection, two of those leaders, Joseph Smith and his brother, Hiram Smith, were killed by those militia members who were supposed to be protecting them. Now what does all of this have to do with the Second Amendment? According to the gun control advocates, the Second Amendment granted power to the states. But it is clearly seen here that the members of the Mormon religion armed themselves and formed their own militias, separate and apart from the states involved. None of this was contested as being illegal or violating the power of the state. The problems were religious, not the people arming themselves. It further shows the need for people to be able to arm themselves to protect themselves not only from possible oppression from the national government, but also from possible oppression from the state governments, which in each case was involved in the persecution of the Mormons, using the very militia which was supposed to protect the people from oppression. It should be noted that Joseph Smith went to Washington D.C. to ask for federal help to protect their religious rights, but because the Bill of Rights, including the freedom of religion, applied at that time only to restrict the federal government, not the states, the federal government could not do anything; it was a state internal matter.

Now let us go back to some state court opinions on this issue. In 1842, the Supreme Court of Arkansas held, opposite to that of Kentucky, that a law prohibiting the carrying of concealed weapons was constitutional. The case of *State v. Buzzard*[239] is really interesting because the logic set forth by both the majority and the dissent sounds almost like today's public policy debate. While these arguments are saved for the chapter on public policy, suffice it to say that the majority found that the sole reason for having the right in the

Constitution was to allow the states to provide for their militias, and does not protect any right of individuals to have arms. The dissent, of course, disagreed. The point is, this is the first statement that I have found in the historical analysis that can be said to truly support the position that the militia was the sole reason for the Second Amendment and that there was no right of an individual to keep and bear arms. This was about 50 years after the passage of the Second Amendment, but still it is about 75 to 90 years before the first such historical event that most gun rights advocates will acknowledge as having taken place. I do not know if this is an intentional misrepresentation or lie or their part, or merely an unknowing misstatement of fact, since this is a rather old, obscure case. Even gun control advocates do not mention it often, so one would hardly expect the gun rights advocates to know about it. Still it is there.

Four years later, in the case of *Nunn v. State*,[240] the Georgia Supreme Court split the difference between Kentucky and Arkansas. They ultimately held that a law which prohibited the carrying of concealed weapons was constitutional, but to the extent it prohibited the carrying of weapons openly it was unconstitutional, against the Second Amendment (even though the United States Supreme Court had already held that the Bill of Rights did not apply to restrict the state governments). What is really interesting here is the historical analysis and logic set forth by the Georgia court:

> [T]hese instruments [state constitutions] confer no *new rights* on the people which did not belong to them before. When, I would ask, did any legislative body in the Union have the right to deny to its citizens the privilege of keeping and bearing arms in defence of themselves and their country?
> If this right, "inestimable to freemen," has been guaranteed to British subjects since the abdication and flight of the last of the Stuarts and the ascension of the Prince of Orange, did it not belong to our colonial ancestors in the western hemisphere? Has it been a part of the *English* Constitution ever since the bill of rights and act of settlement? And been forfeited here by the substitution and adoption of our own Constitution? No notion can be more fallacious than this! On the

A People Armed and Free

contrary this is one of the fundamental principles, upon which rests the great fabric of civil liberty, reared by the fathers of the Revolution and of the country. And the Constitution of the United States, in declaring that the right of the people to keep and bear arms, should not be infringed, only reiterated a truth announced a century before, in the act of 1689, "to extend and secure the rights and liberties of English subjects"...

*****

The language of the *second* amendment is broad enough to embrace both Federal and State governments—nor is there anything in its terms which restricts its meaning. The preamble which was prefixed to these amendments shows, that they originated in the fear that the powers of the general government were not sufficiently limited. Several of the States, in their act of ratification, recommended that further restrictive clauses should be added. And in the first session of the first Congress, *ten* of *these* amendments having been agreed to by that body, and afterwards sanctioned by three-fourths of the States, became a part of the Constitution. But admitting all this, does it follow that because the people refused to delegate to the general government the power to take from them the right to keep and bear arms, that they designed to rest it in the State governments? **Is this a right reserved to the *States* or to *themselves*? Is it not an unalienable right, which lies at the bottom of every free government?** We do not believe that, because the people withheld this arbitrary power of disfranchisement from Congress, they ever intended to confer it on the local legislatures. **This right is too dear to be confided to a republican legislature.**

... In solemnly affirming that a well-regulated militia is necessary to the *security* of a *free State,* and that, in order to train properly that militia, **the unlimited right of the *people* to keep and bear arms shall not be**

> **impaired,** are not the sovereign people of the State committed by this pledge to preserve this right inviolate?
>
> *****
>
> Nor is the *right* involved in this discussion less comprehensive or valuable: "The right of the people to bear arms shall not be infringed." The right of the **whole people**, old and young, men, women and boys, and **not militia only**, to keep and bear *arms* **of every description**, and **not** *such* **merely as are used by the** *militia*, shall not be *infringed*, curtailed or broken in upon, in the smallest degree; and all this for the important end to be attained: the rearing up and qualifying a well-regulated militia, so vitally necessary to the security of a free State. Our opinion is, that any law, State or Federal, is repugnant to the Constitution, and void, which contravenes this *right*... And Lexington, Concord, Camden, River Raisin, Sandusky and the laurel crowned field of New Orleans, plead eloquently for this interpretation![241]

Do you see that this court clearly determined that the right belongs to all individuals, for any purpose, and extends to all weapons, not only those pertaining to militia service?

Anyone for a little Civil War History (or War Between the States, if you are from the South)?[242] The southern states thought that the federal government had failed to live up to the provisions of the Constitution and the social compact upon which the Constitution was based. Each of the states' articles of succession listed grievances, including a failure of both the northern states and the federal government itself to follow the constitution (such as in article IV, section 2, clause 3, which required runaway slaves to be returned to their masters; claiming that the northern states and the federal government were not following or enforcing this, among others). Therefore, the southern states broke away. In the Constitution of the Confederate States of America, they basically copied the Constitution of the United States, with some notable changes. Since they wanted to keep the rights from the Bill of Rights, but were starting with a new

Constitution, so that it would not make sense to list them as amendments, they had to put these rights somewhere else. Where did they put them? The first eight amendments went into article I, section 9, at the end, similar to where Madison had wanted to put most of his proposed amendments dealing with personal rights.[243] The Ninth and Tenth Amendments went into Article VI, which also contains the supremacy clause, so they were apparently designed to limit the supremacy of the central government. But the others, including what had been the Second Amendment, were clearly put where the restrictions on the powers of Congress are listed. The Second Amendment was not put in a place indicating that it was a grant of power to the states. Again, the Constitution of the Confederate States of America is by no means binding authority on the United States, but this placement does indicate the thoughts of those people involved as to what the Second Amendment meant.

The Civil War itself was basically an execution of the "insurrectionist theory" of the Second Amendment. The Southerners were attempting to exercise the right (or power) to replace what they thought was an abusive government with a correct one. Actually, the soldiers on both sides thought they were fighting for a continuation of the ideals expressed in the Declaration of Independence, the Constitution, and the Bill of Rights.[244] You can agree or disagree with this position of the Southern soldiers, but the point is that is what they thought, so they were using the insurrectionist theory. As will be discussed later in Chapter 7 on public policy, the problem with this theory, and the problem that the Southerners had, was that if you are going to try to execute the theory, you had better make sure you win. They did not.

With the ending of the war and the freeing of the slaves, all former slaves should have incurred the same rights as the whites. However, many states passed laws that restricted the rights of blacks. As a result, Congress passed the Civil Rights Act of 1866. Part of the reason for this Act was that blacks were being denied the right to have firearms.[245] This statute guaranteed that blacks would have the same rights as whites, including the right to keep and bear arms.[246] This is significant because at the time each state that was restricting blacks from having firearms probably also excluded them from being in the militia. Therefore, this Act's application of the right to keep and bear arms had nothing to do with the militia, but had everything to do with an individual right.

Not satisfied with a mere statute, the Radical Republicans of the Reconstruction era passed the 14th Amendment. The pertinent part is section 1:

> No state shall make or enforce any law which shall abridge the privileges or immunities of citizens of the United States; nor shall any state deprive any person of life, liberty, or property, without due process of law; nor deny to any person within its jurisdiction the equal protection of the laws.

While admittedly the early Supreme Court cases refused to read this as making any of the Bill of Rights applicable to the states to restrict their powers[247]—these cases have been overruled in numerous more recent cases which have used the 14th Amendment to apply many of the provisions of the Bill of Rights to the States—and no federal court has yet held that it does apply the Second Amendment to the states, there is a large amount of evidence presented by Justice Black in a dissenting opinion joined by Justice Douglas (both noted liberals on the Supreme Court), in *Adamson v. California*,[248] that the Representatives and Senators who were involved in drafting and passing the 14th Amendment intended it to apply the whole Bill of Rights to restrict the powers of the states. More will be discussed about this in detail in Chapter 9 concerning the application of the Second Amendment to the states. For our present purposes, it is enough to note that if the 14th Amendment was intended to apply all of the Bill of Rights (including the Second Amendment) to restrict the states, even if it was merely argued by a substantial number of the members of Congress that this was to be the result, then the conclusion is inescapable that the Second Amendment cannot be a grant of power to the states, but must be a guarantee of an individual right. For what does the 14th Amendment say? "No state shall make or enforce any law which shall abridge the privileges or immunities of citizens of the United States; ..." This would mean that the states could not make any law that would abridge the right, whatever it is, stated in the Second Amendment. It does not make sense to talk about not allowing a state to make a law abridging its own power to

A People Armed and Free

maintain and arm a militia. It only makes sense to talk about prohibiting a state from making any law that would abridge an individual right to keep and bear arms. While obviously this position is stronger if the courts hold that the purpose of the 14th Amendment is in fact to apply the Bill of Rights to the state governments, even if that is not so held, as the courts to this date continue to piecemeal apply the rights from the Bill of Rights, one at a time as they come up, to the states, the point that it was argued to so apply in the Congress that passed it still indicates that they, at least, considered the Second Amendment to guarantee an individual right, not a state power. Again, this seems to have been the nearly unanimous interpretation (except for a portion of the Arkansas Supreme Court) of the Second Amendment up to this point of history.

The gun control advocates have said that the individual right of insurrection theory, especially if applied to the individual state governments, is preposterous because the Founding Fathers had in mind ensuring the existence of the militia. How could individuals be allowed to use their right to keep and bear arms against the very militia mentioned in the Second Amendment? Yet, as an example, in 1870, in North Carolina, the governor called out the militia, under a Colonel Kirk, to supposedly suppress an insurrection in Alamance County.[249] This was in the midst of an election for governor, and the militia was said to have:

> occupied the courthouse at Graham and at Yanceyville in Caswell County. They terrorized the section, robbing, and plundering without hindrance. It became their custom to undress and bathe in full sight of the town, and women did not appear on the streets for fear of insult.
> Eighty-two men were arrested, confined, and treated with great brutality and cruelty.[250]

Even so, apparently, the local citizens did utilize their private firearms to resist this tyranny, for in a later case, the North Carolina Supreme Court referred to this event as a reason to support the right of individuals to keep and bear arms:

> In our own State, in 1870, when Kirk's militia was turned loose and the writ of habeas corpus was suspended, it would have been fatal if our people had been deprived of the right to bear arms, and had been unable to oppose an effective front to the usurpation.[251]

Therefore, it can be seen that the people have historically used their private arms to protect themselves from the very states that the gun control advocates say the Second Amendment was made for. This is totally incongruous with the gun control position on what the Second Amendment means. If the people can use their arms against the state governments, then the Second Amendment should be interpreted to guarantee individual rights, not state powers.

One more commentary before we leave the 19th century. Thomas Cooley was a justice on the Michigan Supreme Court, and was recognized as the leading constitutional commentator of the late 1800's. In 1898 he wrote Principles of Constitutional Law. He wrote the following about the Second Amendment:

> Section IV.—The Right to Keep and Bear Arms
> The Constitution. — By the Second Amendment to the Constitution it is declared that "a well regulated militia being necessary to the security of a free State, the right of the people to keep and bear arms shall not be infringed.
> The amendment, like most other provisions in the Constitution, has a history. It was adopted with some modification and enlargement from the English Bill of Rights of 1688, where it stood as a protest against arbitrary action of the overturned dynasty in disarming the people, and as a pledge of the new rulers that this tyrannical action should cease. **The right declared was meant to be a strong moral check against the usurpation and arbitrary power of rulers, and as a necessary and efficient means of regaining rights when temporarily overturned by usurpation.**
> **The Right is General. — It may be supposed from the phraseology of this provision that the right to keep and bear arms was only guaranteed to the**

A People Armed and Free

militia; but this would be an interpretation not warranted by the intent. The militia, as has been elsewhere explained, consists of those persons who, under the law, are liable to the performance of military duty, and are officered and enrolled for service when called upon. But the law may make provision for the enrollment of all who are fit to perform military duty, or of a small number only, or it may wholly omit to make any provision at all; **and if the right were limited to those enrolled, the purpose of this guaranty might be defeated** altogether by the action or neglect to act of the government it was meant to hold in check. **The meaning of the provision, undoubtedly is, that the people, from whom the militia must be taken, shall have the right to keep and bear arms, and they need no permission or regulation of law for the purpose, but this enables the government to have a well regulated militia**; for to bear arms implies something more than the mere keeping; it implies the learning to handle and use them in a way that makes those who keep them ready for their efficient use; in other words, it implies the right to meet for voluntary discipline in arms, observing in doing so the laws of public order."

"Standing Army. — A further purpose of this amendment is, to preclude any necessity or reasonable excuse for keeping up a standing army. A standing army is condemned by the traditions and sentiments of the people, as being as dangerous to the liberties of the people as the general preparation of the people for the defence of their institutions with arms is preservative of them."

"What Arms may be kept. — The arms intended by the Constitution are such as are suitable for the general defence of the community against invasion or oppression, and the secret carrying of those suited merely to deadly individual encounters may be prohibited.[252]

No one could have ever been clearer about what the Second Amendment means. Cooley addressed the potential argument that the Second Amendment is limited to use in a militia context and expressly says that such an interpretation would be wrong. It is a right of the people, and this right enables the government to have a well-regulated militia. Now admittedly Colley is writing some hundred years after the ratification of the Second Amendment, but he is a lot closer in time than we are today, and than the courts that have addressed this issue were. He was also writing before the National Guard was formed.

Despite allegations from the gun control advocates and others of failures in the militia system, the militia had served the country well up through the Civil War. Did you ever hear of the Battle of New Orleans? Most of General Andrew Jackson's forces there were militia. In the Civil War itself, the first forces deployed on both sides were mobilized militia units. Why do you think that both sides organized their regiments under state designations? Even later, in the Spanish American War, the militia was used. Teddy Roosevelt's Rough Riders were not a part of a standing army, but were recruited by him from citizens who were accustomed to riding and handling firearms as civilians.

Even so, in 1901 President Theodore Roosevelt stated that "[o]ur militia law is obsolete and worthless."[253] Congress that year repealed the Militia Act of 1792.[254] In 1903 Congress passed the Dick Act that began the National Guard. It established an "organized militia", entitled the National Guard, and the rest of the able bodied males from age 18 through 45 were called the "reserve militia". The table of organization of the National Guard corresponded to the Regular Army, and federal funds and Regular Army instructors were used to train the National Guard. This was all done under the authority given to Congress under the militia clauses, article I, section 8, clauses 15 and 16 of the Constitution. While gun control advocates try to say that this was merely a gradual transformation of the militia, and that the National Guard is the militia of old, guaranteed to the states by the Second Amendment, it clearly is not. From instruction that I have received at the Naval War College, I have learned that the concept of the National Guard, while feared and opposed during the ratification of the Constitution and the passage and ratification of the Second Amendment, was actually brought into viability by the successful

German experience with its highly trained reserve forces in European wars during the later half of the 19th century. Reading the rest of President Roosevelt's message to Congress confirms that the political concern was that in modern warfare, we simply could not afford the luxury of having to train civilians to military standards once called up. We had to have a select militia in the modern world to protect us from outside aggression. Much like the standing army that we have had since the end of World War II, which would have been revolting to the Founding Fathers, yet it has been necessary. So the National Guard was necessary when it was brought into being. But it was not, and is not, the militia intended by the Founding Fathers and the Framers of the Second Amendment.

Initially, Congress intended that the National Guard would only be used on "the soil of the United States or of its Territories."[255] However, in 1908 Congress amended the act to expressly provide for its use "either within or without the territory of the United States."[256] During General Pershing's incursions into Mexico, chasing Poncho Villa, the army wanted to utilize the National Guard in that campaign. However, then Attorney General Wickersham expressed the opinion that the militia clauses of the Constitution prohibited the use of the National Guard outside of the United States, despite the statute.[257] As a result of this, in 1916, as the war in Europe became more threatening, Congress decided to federalize the National Guard.[258] The statute doing this further provided "[T]hat the Army of the United States shall consist of the Regular Army, the Volunteer Army, the Officers' Reserve Corps, the Enlisted Reserve Corps, the National Guard while in the service of the United States, and such other land forces as are now or may hereafter be authorized by law."[259] The statute also provided that all members of the National Guard had to take a dual oath, to support the nation and obey the President, as well as supporting their states and obeying their governors, and provided for additional federal funding and control of the Guard.

In 1933 Congress again amended the statutes pertaining to the National Guard. This time they set up two overlapping but distinct organizations: The National Guard of the various States and the National Guard of the United States. Everyone who enlisted in a State National Guard unit simultaneously enlisted in the National Guard of the United States, and thereby became a member of the Enlisted Reserve Corps of the Army. They could be called to active duty whenever Congress declared a national emergency and authorized the use of troops in excess of those in the Regular Army.[260]

In 1952, Congress again amended these provisions, this time removing the national emergency requirement, broadly authorizing orders to active duty or active duty for training, but providing that such orders could not be issued without gubernatorial consent.[261] This gubernatorial consent requirement was then basically repealed in 1986 by another amendment that provided: "The consent of a Governor described in subsections (b) and (d) may not be withheld (in whole or in part) with regard to active duty outside the United States, its territories, and its possessions, because of any objection to the location, purpose, type, or schedule of such active duty."[262] It should be noted that in 1986 "the Army National Guard provide[d] 46 percent of the combat units and 28 percent of the support forces of the Total Army."[263]

So what is the National Guard? Is it the militia of old? Certainly some of the language used in the statutes of being an organized militia and some of the cases have treated it as being the militia. However, it clearly is a part of the standing army, the select militia, which the Founding Fathers, except for Alexander Hamilton, feared. Calling it the original militia is a little bit like calling today's Democratic Party the party of Thomas Jefferson. While it is true that Thomas Jefferson founded the political party that has evolved into today's Democratic Party, with the Democratic Party's insistence on centralized government, high taxes, regulation of personal matters of individuals, regulations of property rights, and the like, I doubt that Thomas Jefferson would want to claim it.

The same can be said for today's National Guard. While it can be called a descendant of the original militia, it should not be construed to be the militia named in the Second Amendment, because this kind of militia is exactly what the Founding Fathers and the Framers of the Second Amendment were trying to avoid by guaranteeing the right of the people to keep and bear arms.

Now let's step back for just a moment. While the ultimate authority to pronounce what the Constitution and Bill of Rights actually mean rests with the United States Supreme Court, the Congress, as a co-equal branch of government often gives its opinions, which are given due respect and deference by the Court in its opinions. In the last century, after the decision in *Miller*, there are

A People Armed and Free

two occasions that I am aware of when the Congress has expounded on the Second Amendment.

The first was in 1941, as the United States was preparing for entry into World War II. Congress authorized the President to requisition property from the private sector, with payment of fair compensation. However, they prohibited any attempt:

> (1) to authorize the requisitioning or require the registration of any firearms possessed by any individual for his personal protection or sport (and the possession of which is not prohibited or the registration of which is not required by existing law), (or) (2) to impair or infringe in any manner the right of any individual to keep and bear arms ...[264]

Additionally, with the passage of that law, one of the House Committees made the following report:

> In view of the fact that certain totalitarian and dictatorial nations are now engaged in the willful and wholesale destruction of personal rights and liberties, our committee deem it appropriate for the Congress to expressly state that the proposed legislation shall not be construed to impair or infringe the constitutional right of the people to bear arms... There is no disposition on the part of this Government to depart from the concepts and principles of personal rights and liberties expressed in our Constitution.[265]

The second instance was in 1986, when the Congress passed the Firearms Owners' Protection Act. The introductory clause that gives the reason for its enactment says: "The Congress finds that — (1) the rights of citizens — (A) to keep and bear arms under the second amendment to the United States Constitution ... require additional legislation to correct existing firearms statutes and enforcement policies."[266] In another committee report, the Senate Subcommittee on the Constitution, Senate Judiciary Committee, said:

> The conclusion is thus inescapable that the history, concept, and wording of the second amendment to the Constitution of the United States, as well as its interpretation by every major commentator and court in the first half-century after its ratification, indicates that what is protected is an individual right of a private citizen to own and carry firearms in a peaceful manner.[267]

So it sounds like Congress, even with the knowledge of *Miller* and many of the courts of appeals cases cited by gun control advocates, has expressed its opinion that the Second Amendment protects individual rights, not a power of the states.

One more legal commentary needs to be addressed here before we move from the historic analysis. It is a quote from former Chief Justice Warren Burger in 1991: "[The Second Amendment] has been the subject of one of the greatest pieces of fraud, I repeat the word 'fraud,' on the American public by special interest groups that I have ever seen in my lifetime."[268] Gun control advocates often quote this statement in their literature. The reason is that Chief Justice Warren is accusing the gun rights advocates of committing the fraud. Now this position is hard to take. If you have only read this far in this book (believe me, there is more to come), you can choose to disagree with my interpretation of the facts that exist, but you can hardly call my position fraudulent. In fact, I have already expressed my belief that it is the gun control advocates that are committing the fraud by claiming that there is no evidence of any discussion of an individual right involving any purpose other than militia service.

In all fairness to the Chief Justice, judges, even Supreme Court Judges, are no smarter on any given issue than are other attorneys. No one can know what all of the law is, what all of the history is on every statute and constitutional provision. Judges generally do not have any special expertise on a particular provision of the law except for the law that applies to the cases that have been before them. When an issue first comes before a judge, the attorneys on both sides present their briefs on the issue, explaining their positions on the issue and what they believe the law is. They may do the same with oral arguments, where the judge may ask questions. The judge, depending on what level of court he or she is at, may then have a law clerk do

A People Armed and Free

some independent legal research, or may do it himself/herself. In any event, this process is designed to educate the judge and, by giving the judge all sides of the issue, allow the judge to apply wisdom to determine which side is correct, to determine what the law is. At that point, the judge then gains an extra expertise in the law on that particular point, and not before. I cannot tell you how many times I have been before a judge on some small, esoteric issue that he has never seen before, and realized that the judge knows nothing about this issue. So I would have to educate him. Now applying this to the former Chief Justice (and I am not saying that he knows nothing about the issue), he did not have any Second Amendment cases come before him, as far as I know. I do not know of any scholarly articles (which would indicate that he had done some independent research on the topic) that he wrote on the subject. If all he did was to read some gun control advocates articles, he may have been convinced that their position was correct and the gun rights advocates were committing a fraud on the American people without having the entire picture, without knowing any better. This is the very reason that courts, at least in the federal system, and in many of the state systems as well, do not give advisory opinions. They require a real case and controversy to be before them, with real contending parties, and real facts, so that they may have the benefit of hearing all sides of an issue before deciding it. Incidentally, this is an important point in the one case on the Second Amendment that has been decided by the Supreme Court, which will be discussed in Chapter 6. In any event, giving Chief Justice Burger the benefit of the doubt, I can only believe that if he had had the benefit of an exhaustive research of both sides of the Second Amendment controversy, while he might not have agreed with me on what the final ruling and outcome of that controversy should be, he at least would not have accused the gun rights advocates of committing a fraud. He would at least have concluded that the whole matter is an honest disagreement on what the law is, as are most cases that are brought before the courts. Of course, I could be wrong on this, but if I am, then I can only say that the former Chief Justice himself would have been involved in helping the gun control advocates commit a fraud on the American people in attempting to take away their right to keep and bear arms.

Jack Reynolds, J. D.

Chapter 5
The Structure of the Government and the Constitution

After the long chapter on history, with all of its quotes, you will probably be glad to know that this chapter will be rather short. What we are talking about when we say "structural analysis" is how the particular structures of the government as set up by the Constitution, including the checks and balances set up by having the three branches of the government, the separate existence of the federal government, the state government and the people as sources of power and rights, and how the Second Amendment relates to other provisions of the Constitution and the Bill of Rights.

Most of this has already been discussed in earlier chapters. Remember I told you that there is an overlap of each of the six approaches to determining what a constitutional provision means. Even so, let me expound just a little bit about the structure of our governments and the Constitution.

Remember the points made in Chapter 2 about the source of all power being the people? Remember that the concept was that the people originally had all power and rights that could possibly be conceived of, and that in making the social compact that we call a government they conveyed some of those powers to the government and thereby restricted some of their rights? The result of this is that the people retained all rights not given up by giving powers to the government. And these rights pre-existed the establishment of the Constitution. Now this means that before the Constitution was formed, all people had the right to keep and bear arms. Whether or not they had given up any measure of this right to their state governments depended on the social compact made in forming the state governments, not on the Constitution. As far as the federal government was concerned, the people had that right before the Constitution was enacted.

Now look at the Constitution. Nowhere in it does it give the federal government the power to regulate or restrict the ownership, possession or carrying of firearms. This was the whole point of the

Federalist arguments that no Bill of Rights was needed. There was, however, a grant of authority and power over the militias to the federal government. Now, therefore, if it has been held that the Second Amendment did not grant or create any right, which you will see in the next chapter it has been so held by the U.S. Supreme Court, then it must be applying an individual right interpretation to the Amendment. If on the other hand it is held that the Second Amendment does grant something, it would only apply to the granting of some of the power over the militias, given to the federal government by the people, to the states. I have not seen any holding that the Second Amendment grants anything; it merely protects what already existed.

It is, after all, called the "Bill of Rights". It is not the Bill of Powers. As discussed before, rights only belong to people, not governments. It would be strange if when we call it the Bill of Rights, we really mean to exclude the second one, because it really grants a power to the states. Only the Tenth Amendment mentions powers, and in that context it distinguishes between the states and the people. Both the Ninth and Tenth Amendment show that "the people" are an important part of the government construct, and that they do retain all of their rights and powers not given to the federal government. In fact, it has been said that the collective rights' or states' rights idea that the Second Amendment can only be viewed in terms of the state vs. federal power construct "ignores the implication that might be drawn from the Second, Ninth, and Tenth Amendments: the citizenry itself can be viewed as an important third component of republican governance as far as it stands ready to defend republican liberty against the depredations of the other two structures, however futile that might appear as a practical matter."[269] One can even argue that if the Second Amendment is not designed to protect an individual's right to keep and bear arms, the Ninth Amendment, by expressly recognizing that there are additional rights that people have which are not listed in the first eight amendments, and by the indisputable fact that there is a large body of evidence that many of our founders saw a right of individuals to keep and bear arms for many different purposes both before the Constitution was ratified and after, then this must be one of those additional rights, and the federal government would have no power to infringe that right. And, in fact, a form of that argument

Jack Reynolds, J. D.

was made by one federal court of appeals judge in a case, as will be seen in the next chapter.

While this structural analysis and chapter have been rather short, its impact is clear: There is an individual right to keep and bear arms. So now let's see what the courts have to say about all of this.

Chapter 6
Case Law

Gun control advocates are fond of complaining about the gun rights advocates attempts to assert an individual right to keep and bear arms as being guaranteed by the Second Amendment, especially in lobbying members of Congress or state legislators. They say that it is one of the most well settled principles in constitutional law that there is no individual right. And, if you look only at federal lower court opinions, they have a point. Up until the *Emerson* case was decided in December 2001,[270] each court of appeals that had addressed the issue, except for one that did not explicitly rule on the issue, but treated it like an individual right, had found not an individual right guarantee in the Second Amendment, but a state power over the militia. And all of these lower courts have upheld government regulations of firearms. But, fortunately, if you are a gun rights advocates, while the lower courts certainly impact the situation in the areas where they have jurisdiction, they do not declare for the nation what the Constitution means. Only the U.S. Supreme Court can do that.

And what has the Supreme Court done in the area of the Second Amendment. Well, as I pointed out in Chapter 1, I began my research by looking at the only Supreme Court opinion that attempts to deal directly with what the Second Amendment means, and found that it can be read to support both sides. So they really have not directly ruled on the issue. The reason that this is important is that while the courts do look at such things as the text, history and public policy involving the particular part of the Constitution in issue, a very important part of their analysis will always be what previous court opinions have had to say on the issue involved, especially the Supreme Court.

But before we continue this discussion of Supreme Court cases, there are some basic matters that I need to make sure that you understand, so that you can understand the rest. It is kind of like needing to learn algebra before you try to do calculus, although I hope that this will not be as hard as either of those.

Jack Reynolds, J. D.

First you need to understand how the federal judiciary is organized. While there are certainly other types of federal courts (such as military courts and bankruptcy courts), we will only look at three types of courts: The U.S. Supreme Court, Courts of Appeals, and District Courts. Let's look at the lower courts first.

The federal district courts are where the lawsuits or criminal cases start. This is where the actual trial occurs, with or without a jury. Each state has at least one federal district court. Depending on the population and size of the state, it may have multiple districts. For example, Texas has a Northern District, Southern District, Eastern District, and Western District. Each district may have more than one judge. Each judge has his own court, with his own staff of clerks and legal interns. Each judge will try his own cases. If the case is a criminal one, the party bringing the case is the United States of America, and is represented by the local U.S. Attorney's office. The defendant is the person charged with the crime. In civil cases, any person or legal entity (such as a corporation) can bring a suit against another person, legal entity or government. The person who brings the suit is called the plaintiff; the one that the suit is brought against is called the defendant.

As the case proceeds in the district court, certain issues may come up that require a decision by the judge. Sometimes this happens before the case even gets to trial, sometimes during the trial, sometimes after the trial is over. When the judge makes a ruling on the issue, usually after having reviewed briefs from all sides and possibly hearing oral argument from the parties (this means their attorneys), and probably after having the court's own legal interns research the issue, the judge will usually write an opinion on the issue and his decision. Sometimes this opinion will be published for all of the world to see. The place that all of these opinions are published is in the West Reporter system called the Federal Supplement (we are actually now up to the Federal Supplement 2d). These opinions are supposed to be binding, as to the issues addressed, on all other judges within the same district, but many times I have seen judges go their own way despite what other judges in their own district may have held. As a practical matter, these decisions do not have much binding authority, and certainly no binding authority on the courts of appeals or Supreme Court, but may have persuasive authority because of how well they are written and reasoned through. I will explain binding and persuasive authority in a moment.

Once a case has reached a final judgment at the district court level, and in some instances before a final judgment is reached, the losing party on any given issue has a right to appeal the results of the case, or the individual rulings or decisions of the district court judge on any particular issue, to the appropriate U.S. Circuit Court of Appeals. There are twelve circuit courts of appeals (eleven numbered circuits, and the D.C. circuit). Each circuit covers multiple states and is responsible for all appeals coming from the district courts in those states. For example, the 5th Circuit covers all federal district courts in Texas, Louisiana, and Mississippi. Each Circuit has many judges sitting on the Court of Appeals, the number differing between the circuits and from time to time within a circuit as judges retire and are appointed. The number may be as low as ten, or as high as forty. For any case coming before a court of appeals, usually a panel of three judges is appointed to hear the case.

If a party from a district court case appeals to the court of appeals, without going into great detail about the procedures for this appeal, briefs from both sides are filed, oral arguments usually heard, and again the court's own legal interns (attorneys hired by the court) will research the issues involved on the appeal. No evidence, testimony or otherwise, is taken at the court of appeals. That is all done at the district court level. The Court does, however, have a copy of the transcript of the testimony and proceedings that occurred at the district court, and all of the other exhibits introduced into evidence there, such as documents, guns, tape recordings, etc. The court of appeals does not retry the case, but merely reviews the record, in light of the issues asserted on appeal, applies the law, and makes its ruling or decision on the issues. The court will publish its opinion in writing, which will be published for all of the world to see in the Federal Reporter, Federal Reporter 2d, or now, the Federal Reporter 3d. Sometimes, a case may be reheard by the whole circuit court of appeals, that is to say not by a three judge panel, but by all of the circuit judges together. This is called an *en banc* review.

The opinions of the court of appeals panel, even though there are other panels hearing other cases, are supposed to be binding on all other panels of that circuit, as to those issues involved in the opinion, and on all district courts and judges within that circuit's jurisdiction. I have, on occasion, seen different panels of the same circuit reach opposite rulings on the same issue, though in different cases. This does not occur as often as at the district court level. In any event, the court of appeals' opinions have no binding authority on the other circuits, nor on the Supreme Court, though again, depending on how well written and reasoned the opinion is, it may have persuasive authority on these other courts.

Unlike the right to appeal to the court of appeal, there is (in most cases) no right to appeal to the Supreme Court. The party that losses at the court of appeals can request the Supreme Court to hear his case (usually done by a request for a *writ of certiorari*; an order from the Supreme Court to the court of appeals to send the case up to it for review), but the Supreme Court can either agree to hear the case or refuse. It has the power to choose which cases it hears. With the thousands of cases where such requests are made each year, the Supreme Court cannot possibly hear all of the cases. So it picks and chooses which cases to hear, based on a number of factors, including how important the issues involved are to the country as a whole, whether or not there is a disagreement between the circuits' opinions on the issues, and, so say the cynics, on whether or not the judges think that they have a majority of the court on their side to reach the end result that they want. If it refuses to hear a case, usually this does not mean that the Supreme Court took any particular position on the issues involved. It usually is treated as if there was no attempt to appeal to the Supreme Court at all, as far as being any authority on other courts hearing other similar cases.

In any event, once the Supreme Court accepts a case, briefs are filed again, the record (transcript of the testimony and proceedings, and all exhibits) is reviewed, oral argument is usually heard, the legal interns do their thing again, and the judges make their decisions. The majority decision is binding on the Supreme Court itself in later cases involving the same issues (this is called the doctrine of *stare decisis*), and is binding on all of the lower courts, courts of appeals and district courts, throughout the country. I used the plural when referring to the decisions here because there are nine judges on the Supreme Court.[271] Usually they all sit on and hear each case, though occasionally one or more may be absent from any given case. Have you ever tried to get nine people to try to agree on anything? It is hard. Therefore, it is common for the judges to come out with multiple opinions of what

A People Armed and Free

the law is and what the decision should be. It is to the explanation of the various types of opinions that might come out of the Supreme Court that we now turn.

There are basically four types of opinions that we may run into: Majority Opinions, Plurality opinions, Concurring Opinions, and Dissenting Opinions. We will use the Supreme Court as the example here because, other than *en banc* hearings, the court of appeals, operating as it does, in three judge panels usually only runs into two of these types of opinions.

Majority opinions are just that. If we use the nine-judge court as the base number, then if you have five or more judges joining in everything that is said in the opinion, it is a majority opinion. Only a majority opinion is actually binding authority. All of the other types of opinions are merely persuasive authority.

A plurality opinion occurs when you get a majority agreeing on the result in a case, but you cannot get a majority to agree on why. For example, you might get four judges to say that the result should be X, because of A, B, and C, and another judge to agree that the result should be X, but the reason is D, E, and F. The four-judge opinion would be a plurality opinion. While not exactly binding authority, it is usually followed because it was the opinion with the most judges agreeing, and which was on the winning side. Therefore, while not binding, it is stronger authority than the next two types.

The next type of opinion is the concurring opinion. This is an opinion by one or more judges, which agrees with the result, but expresses different reasons. For example, the one judge opinion in the paragraph above would be a concurring opinion. Or, even if there is a majority opinion, another judge may agree that the same party should win, but express different reasons, saying that he might reach a different holding, but still let the same party win, or just express a different logic as to how he got to the same result. Concurring opinions are not binding authority, but they can be persuasive authority, and are certainly better authority than the next type of opinion, the dissenting opinion.

Out of nine judges it is not unusual to get at least some of them that disagree with the majority as to the result, as to what the law is or should be, what the holding is, and what the logic or reasoning is that should be used in the case involved. When a judge, or multiple judges, disagrees with the result in the case, he usually writes a dissenting opinion setting forth the reasons he disagrees, and how he would resolve the case if he could just persuade the majority to go along with him. Obviously this type of opinion cannot have any binding authority, because his opinion lost. But, on any given issue, if the logic and reasoning used in the opinion is very good, it may have some persuasive authority on an issue not directly involved with the holding of the majority opinion. Even on the exact issue involved in the holding of the majority opinion, occasionally the Supreme Court in a later case may adopt a dissenting opinion if the Supreme Court decides to overrule the holding of the prior case where the dissenting opinion lost out. These are the reasons that the judges whose positions lost out go to the trouble to write their dissenting opinions. While the weakest authority of all of the types of opinions, it cannot be ignored. After all, it was written by a Supreme Court justice, and if the facts in a future case are just a little bit different than the original case, maybe the dissenting opinion may prevail.

Just like there are different types of opinions, with different levels of authority, not everything that is said within an opinion is of equal value. There are four parts of an opinion that you need to understand. They are the issues involved, the holding, the reasoning, and dicta.

The issue involved is the ultimate question that the case turns on. It is usually drawn as narrowly as possible, to avoid a broad discussion that someone might later try to apply to a situation where it should not be applied. For example, in a given case, the issue might be does a criminal defendant have the right to an attorney to represent him at trial. If the criminal defendant in this particular case has plenty of money, the question of whether or not the government has to appoint an attorney, and pay him, for a poor defendant is not part of the issue. That question would be saved for a later case where the defendant might be poor and therefore the question might be an issue then. If the question about providing an attorney for a poor defendant was addressed in an opinion in the first case, without a party that really has a stake in that question, it might not get properly briefed and the court could use reasoning and reach a holding that would simply prove to be wrong when a truly interested party was to bring such a case with fully developed facts on that issue.

The holding is likewise narrowly drawn, to apply just to the issue presented. In the above example, the appropriate holding would be that a criminal defendant does have the right to an attorney at trial, not that a criminal defendant does have the right to an attorney at trial and if he does not have the money to obtain one, the government will appoint one, and pay him, for the defendant. While the last part of this bad holding might be true, and might become a holding in a case presenting the appropriate facts to bring up the appointment of an attorney as an issue, it would not be appropriate in the first case. Only holdings are actually binding authority, that is to say, what the court itself and all of the lower courts under it are required to follow and apply in future cases.

With that said, it must be realized that very seldom are any two cases exactly the same. The closer the facts in a subsequent case are to the original case, the stronger the binding authority of the original case is. As you begin to get more differences between the cases, the more likely it is that someone can convince the court that the new case is different enough from the original case that a different result should be had. For example, let us say that the holding in a prior case was to the effect that a poor defendant is entitled to have the government appoint and pay an attorney for him. Now let us say that a subsequent case shows that the defendant himself is poor, but he has rich relatives. Maybe this changes the situation enough to change the result; maybe it does not. Then let us say that in yet another case the defendant himself is not rich, but he has somewhat more assets than the defendant in the prior case. The court will be presented with the question on where to draw the line. So the holding is binding, but if the new case can be distinguished enough from the case with the holding, a different holding on the new facts may result.

Which leads us to the logic or reasoning of the case. While not exactly binding, it is very strong authority as to how to handle the various differences that might come up. The logic used might tell a future court if a new case is really different enough to merit a different result and holding, or if it really falls within the same class of cases and should be ruled on the same. The reasoning shows how the court went from the facts presented, applied the law, and reached its result and holding. Therefore, this reasoning should be applied to any set of similar facts. For example, let us go back to our first example of the criminal defendant with enough money to get his own attorney. Now let us assume that this case came up after the case of the poor person. Perhaps the court might say that since it has been held in a previous case that a poor criminal defendant has the right to have the government appoint and pay an attorney for him, then surely a rich person has the right to hire his own attorney and have that attorney represent him at trial. The holding would still be only that he has a right to an attorney at trial, but the matter of the government appointing and paying for an attorney for a poor defendant would be a part of the reasoning of the case. Therefore, while not a holding itself, as reasoning it could be forcefully applied to future cases involving poor defendants.

Dicta, technically, has no authority whatsoever. Dicta is basically a gratuitous statement of the court. For example, let us say that the issue involved is one of whether or not a particular statement of a defendant is protected under the free speech clause of the First Amendment. Then let us assume that in addressing this issue the court makes a statement that because people have a right to have an attorney at trial, and even to have one appointed and paid for by the government if they cannot afford one themselves, the person involved could have consulted an attorney before he made the statement in question. The statement that people have the right to an attorney at trial might be reasoning or dicta, depending on the particular facts of the case and how critical this statement was to reaching the holding of the case, but the statement about poor defendants is probably just dicta, because it is thrown in more for dramatic effect, and is not likely to be crucial to the holding. The line between logic and dicta is not always clear. While, as said, dicta technically has no authority, it is usually better than not having any statements from court opinions in your favor at all. At least a court said something in your favor. A good attorney can usually take dicta and, using his own logic, show why it should be applied as reasoning in his particular case to reach the result he wants. It then becomes a question of how persuasive the attorney's logic is as to whether or not the court will decide to apply that dicta as reasoning or even a holding in the new case.

Now if all of this seems a bit much to try to understand all at once, do not feel bad. Lawyers often do not understand all of this. And as we go through the cases in this chapter, applying these concepts, you will begin to see how they work and will understand them better. So let's take a look at what the courts have to say about the Second Amendment, starting with the U.S. Supreme Court.

A. U.S. Supreme Court Cases

Since I have told you that there is only one Supreme Court case that has addressed the issue of what the Second Amendment means, you might think that this section is really going to be short. No such luck. Remember I said that there are other cases where the Supreme Court has at least talked about the Second Amendment. There are actually over 30 of them. While some of these statements are dicta, some are used in the reasoning or logic of the case, even though the Second Amendment is not directly the issue involved in the case. I will go in chronological order, since statements in later cases may relay on the statements in the earlier cases. So let's get started.

1. *Houston v. Moore*[272]

This first case was decided in 1820. Actually, a normal legal research would not find this case because the reference to the Second Amendment is botched up. A typographical error called it the Fifth Amendment, but the text clearly is talking about the Second Amendment.[273] The case involved a Pennsylvania man, Mr. Houston, who failed to report for federal militia duty during the War of 1812. This was in violation of both a federal statute and a state statute, which was identical to the federal one. Mr. Houston was tried and convicted before a Pennsylvania court martial for violating the state statute. During the trial, his attorney argued that due to the federal statute, and the powers given to the federal government by the militia clauses of the Constitution, the Pennsylvania court lacked jurisdiction or authority to hear the case; only the federal government could prosecute him. On appeal to the U.S. Supreme Court, the same argument was made.[274] The attorneys for the State of Pennsylvania replied that the federal power over the militia was concurrent with the states (have you heard this before?). They then relied on the Tenth Amendment, the reservation of powers to the states, to argue that the states retained this power over the militia. They did not invoke the Second Amendment.

Now this seems a little strange. While the case does not involve arming the militia (unless you consider getting the members to report for duty has something to do with arming the militia, which while a stretch, is an arguable point), it certainly involves the ability of the states to maintain a militia, for without the power to enforce a requirement to report for duty, how can a state maintain its militia? Everybody could just decide to not show up, and there goes your militia. So, if the Second Amendment grants the states the power to maintain and arm their militias, why didn't the attorneys argue that the Second Amendment was the basis of Pennsylvania's power to prosecute Mr. Houston, instead of, or at least in addition to, the Tenth Amendment? Maybe they were incompetent, but I doubt it. The more likely reason is that they had no reason to even think that the Second Amendment applied to this situation, because it does not grant the states any power; it guarantees an individual right.

The majority opinion agreed with the state's attorneys and held that Pennsylvania did have the power to prosecute Mr. Houston. Like the attorneys, the court did not rely on, or even allude to the Second Amendment. A concurring opinion came to the same result, again without even discussing the Second Amendment. So where is the Second Amendment in this case?

In a dissenting opinion, written by Justice Story, whom we have discussed in Chapter 4. Justice Story would have held that the state could not prosecute because the power to do so was solely in the federal government. He was willing to accept the concept of concurrent powers, to be used by the states when the federal government was not exercising its powers. "But when once Congress has carried this power into effect, its laws for the organization, arming, and discipline of the militia, are the supreme law of the land; and all interfering State regulations must necessarily be suspended in their operations."[275] He then proposed a hypothetical:

> If, therefore, the present case turned upon the question, whether a State might organize, arm, and discipline its own militia in the absence of, or subordinate to, the regulations of Congress, I am certainly not prepared to deny the legitimacy of such an exercise of authority. It does not seem repugnant in its nature to the grant of a like paramount authority to Congress; and if not, then it is retained by the States. The fifth [sic] amendment to the constitution, declaring that "a well regulated militia being necessary to the security of a free State, the right of the people to keep and bear arms shall not be infringed," may not perhaps, be thought to have any important bearing on this point. If it have, it confirms

A People Armed and Free

and illustrates, rather than impugns the reasoning already suggested.[276]

He then goes on to say that once the militia has been employed in the service of the United States, the states can have absolutely no power over the militia. All of the power is in the federal government.[277] Therefore, Justice Story said, Pennsylvania should not have been able to prosecute Mr. Houston.

Now what does all of this mean? Justice Story is saying that if Congress does not exercise the power given to it, the states may exercise concurrent powers. He does not believe that the Second Amendment applies, but if it does, it supports his position. Now that can be read two ways, either it supports his position that if Congress does not act the states can, or it supports his position that Congress is not limited in the exercise of its powers, but the states are, because the Second Amendment does nothing to help the states, being designed to only grant individual rights to keep and bear arms. It is not clear which "reasoning already suggested" Story is referring to. In any event, once Congress acts in any area of the militia, the states cannot act in that same area. If that is the case, under the states' rights model, of what use is the Second Amendment? It is not doing what they claim for it. It does not guarantee any power to the states, because by merely acting in the area of militias the federal government denies the power to act to the states. It does not restrict the power of Congress to act. The only restrictions that Justice Story mentions are those contained in the body of the Constitution. Under Justice Story's reasoning, the Second Amendment might as well be non-existent if it only applied to a states' right to maintain and arm its militia. And since we cannot assume that the Framers intended to pass an amendment that would have absolutely no effect, therefore, it must apply to guarantee an individual's right to keep and bear arms, since this is the only other purpose proposed.

2. *Scott v. Sandford*[278]

The next case is the infamous Dred Scott case. I can almost hear the gasps now. "You're not really going to rely on **that** case, are you?" Well, yes. Even though I may not like the end result of the case supporting slavery, it still provides a useful tool to find out what the early Supreme Court thought about the Second Amendment. The issues that were involved there were whether or not a free black could be a U.S. citizen, and the extent of the power of the Congress to restrict slavery in the territories.

On the first issue the majority opinion held that a free black man could not be a U.S. citizen. The reasoning was that many states, both north and south, restricted the activities of blacks, even those who were free. If they were to be considered U.S. citizens, these special laws would be unconstitutional, or the free blacks would at least be exempt from them.

> It would give to persons of the Negro race, who were recognized as citizens in any one State of the Union, the right to enter every other State whenever they pleased, singly or in companies, without pass or passport, and without obstruction, to sojourn there as long as they pleased, to go where they pleased at every hour of the day or night without molestation, unless they committed some violation of law for which a white man would be punished; and it would give them the full liberty of speech in public and in private upon all subjects upon which its own citizens might speak; to hold public meetings upon political affairs, **and to keep and carry arms wherever they went.**[279]

I think that most of us today would agree that blacks, as citizens, would, and do indeed, have all of the rights listed in this quote. What is significant for our purposes, however, is that the right to keep and carry arms (keep and bear) is listed as a right that would go to a black individual, not a state or militia. In fact, blacks, even free ones, at that time, were not even allowed to be a part of the federal militia (which was limited to free **white** males), and certainly not most state militias, so this could not involve the militia at all. It could only be applied here as an individual right.

On the second issue of the territories, the Supreme Court reasoned that since Congress could not restrict individuals' rights such as freedom of religion, freedom of speech, **and the right to keep and bear arms**, in a territory, it also could not restrict the property rights of slave owners by not allowing slavery in any of the territories. This again treats the right to keep and bear arms as purely an individual right, because of the way it reads, listing all of these rights together as individual rights, because of the logic used (it would make no sense to include the Second Amendment provision to allude to the protection of individuals' property rights if it were only a grant of power to the states), and because we are now talking about territories, not states, and certainly the power of the federal government as opposed to the territorial government is much broader than when compared to that of state governments. On both issues, the Second Amendment is used in the reasoning as an individual right.

3. *Ex Parte Milligan*[280]

This case involved the civil war conviction of civilians, with a death sentence, by a military court-martial. This would normally be considered a violation of the Fifth Amendment's requirement of trial only after indictment by a grand jury, and the Sixth Amendment right to trial by jury. However, the U.S. Attorney General argued that there are exceptions to all of the rights listed in the Bill of Rights, and that during war, there are, or at least should be, an exception to the Fifth and Sixth Amendments' requirements, so as to allow trial of civilians by courts-martial. As an example of the exceptions to the other rights in the Bill of Rights, the Attorney General included the following:

> It cannot properly be so argued, any more than it could be that it was intended by the second article (declaring that "the right of the people to keep and bear arms shall not be infringed") to hinder the President from disarming insurrectionists, rebels, and traitors in arms while he was carrying on war against them."[281]

This argument does not make any sense if the Second Amendment only grants a power to the states over their militias. Such a grant would be absolutely no impediment to the disarming of "insurrectionists, rebels, and traitors" (want to bet on who he was referring to, being right after the Civil War?), as the gun control advocates argue today that the Second Amendment is absolutely no impediment to the disarming of law abiding citizens. The argument only makes sense if the Second Amendment is considered as an individual right to begin with. Also, it is claimed to be a right that there needs to be an exception to, to allow the government to disarm these individuals.

The Supreme Court did not address the Second Amendment in its opinion, so we do not know if the Court agreed with the interpretation placed on the Second Amendment by the Attorney General or not. Therefore, this case, while showing an individual right argument being made, really abstains from the issue.

4. *United States v. Cruikshank*[282]

In this case, which arose toward the end of the reconstruction era, some members of the KKK had been depriving blacks in Louisiana of their rights. The specific rights involved were the rights to peaceable assembly and the right to bear arms for a lawful purpose. Prior to this, Congress had passed the Enforcement Act of 1870, which made it a criminal act for any two or more persons to act or conspire together to deprive anyone of any right or privilege granted or secured to him by the constitution or laws of the United States. Therefore, these KKK members were charged with a criminal indictment. The issue was whether or not this statute was constitutional, to where these people could be charged with any federal crime.

The Supreme Court, in another majority opinion, said that no, the statute was not constitutional and therefore, there could be no federal crime committed. The reason was that these rights were not granted by the Constitution. They pre-existed the Constitution as natural rights of men. Therefore, while the First and Second Amendments, which were the ones involved, restricted the powers of Congress to deprive people of these rights, the federal government could not prevent individuals from depriving others of these rights. It was up to the state governments to provide that protection from other individuals. Let's look at the words used:

> The first and ninth counts state the intent of the defendants to have been to hinder and prevent the citizens named in the free exercise and enjoyment of their "lawful right and privilege to peaceably assemble together with each other and with other citizens of the United States for a peaceful and lawful purpose." The right of the people peaceably to assemble for lawful purposes existed long before the adoption of the Constitution of the United States. In fact, it is, and always has been, one of the attributes of citizenship under a free government. It "derives its source" ...

A People Armed and Free

"from those laws whose authority is acknowledged by civilized man throughout the world." It is found wherever civilization exists. It was not, therefore, a right granted to the people by the Constitution. The government of the United States when established found it in existence, with the obligation on the part of the States to afford it protection.

* * * *

The particular amendment now under consideration [First Amendment] assumes the existence of the right of the people to assemble for lawful purposes, and protects it against encroachment by Congress. The right was not created by the amendment; neither was its continuance guaranteed, except as against congressional interference. For their protection in its enjoyment, therefore, the people must look to the States. The power for that purpose was originally placed there, and it has never been surrendered to the United States.

* * * *

The second and tenth counts are equally defective. The right there specified is that of "bearing arms for a lawful purpose." This is not a right granted by the Constitution. Neither is it in any manner dependent upon that instrument for its existence. The second amendment declares that it shall not be infringed; but this, as has been seen, means no more than that it shall not be infringed by Congress. This is one of the amendments that has no other effect than to restrict the powers of the national government, leaving the people to look for their protection against any violation by their fellow-citizens of the rights it recognizes, to what is called, ... the "powers which relate to merely municipal legislation, or what was, perhaps, more properly called internal police," "not surrendered or restrained" by the Constitution of the United States.[283]

Notice how the description of the issues involving the First and Second Amendment are framed identically, as are the holdings. The Court treats both amendments the same. If the Second Amendment did something different, such as protecting the powers of the state government over its militia, you would expect it to be treated differently from the First Amendment by the Court. Also note that the opinion indicates that the people must look to the state government for the protection of their Second Amendment rights. This would make no sense at all if the Court thought that the Second Amendment only protected the state's power over its militia.

One additional note here. I have seen some gun control advocates quote the one sentence above: "This is not a right granted by the Constitution." They do this by itself, totally out of context, and then argue that this means that the Constitution does not grant or recognize any right of people to keep and bear arms. This sounds persuasive to those who do not understand the concept of pre-existing rights as we have discussed them. But you should be clear on this. The Constitution and the Bill of Rights do not grant **any** rights. They merely confirm their existence and restrict the powers of the federal government to infringe on those rights. This does not mean that the rights do not exist, as implied by this usage and argument by the gun control advocates.

Finally, some gun control advocates have cited this case for the proposition that the 14th Amendment does not apply the Second Amendment to restrict the powers of the state governments. While some of the reasoning used in *Cruikshank* can be applied to that argument, such was not, nor could it have been, a holding of the case. The issue involved was other individuals violating the rights of the people, not the state governments violating the rights. Without the state governments being involved in the restriction of the rights, the question of using the 14th Amendment to apply any of the Bill of Rights to restrict the powers of the states simply could not have been in issue. But that is OK, since it has been in other cases.

5. *Presser v. Illinois*[284]

Presser is an interesting case of class conflict. It arose in the late 19th century when labor strife was rising. In response to the labor

A People Armed and Free

problems, many state governments had violently suppressed attempts by workingmen to exercise their economic and collective bargaining rights. Due to this violent response by the state governments, some of the workers created self-defense organizations. In response to that, some state governments, including Illinois, enacted laws against armed public parades. In defiance of this law, a German working-class self-defense organization held a parade in which one of its leaders carried an unloaded rifle. This was Herman Presser. In this case Presser argued that the law violated the Second Amendment, violated the militia clauses of the Constitution, and violated the Militia Act of 1792.

The Supreme Court, in a unanimous opinion (that's the strongest authority you can get), ruled that the statutes did not violate the militia clauses, nor the Militia Act. On the Second Amendment it said the following:

> We think it clear that the sections [of the Illinois statute that Presser was accused of violating] under consideration, which only forbid bodies of men to associate together as military organizations, or to drill or parade with arms in cities and towns unless authorized by law, do not infringe the right of the people to keep and bear arms. But a conclusive answer to the contention that this amendment prohibits the legislation in question lies in the fact that the amendment is a limitation only upon the power of Congress and the National government, and not upon that of the States.[285]

Now, if the Second Amendment was actually only a guarantee of power to the states, why didn't the Court just say so, instead of throwing in the gratuitous statement that it did not think that the statutes involved infringed upon the right of the people (for the reason that the statute really did not prohibit much)? Of course what ever it said on this point was, or would have been dicta, because the real holding was that the Second Amendment does not limit the power of the states. But even here it is interesting to note the reasoning used. The Court did not say that the Second Amendment could not restrict the power of the states because it is in actuality a grant of power to the state, or a protection of the states' power over their militias, as might be appropriate and expected if the gun control advocates' interpretation of the Second Amendment is correct. No, instead the Court used the same logic as in *Cruikshank*, even quoting the portion that I quoted above.

The Court went on to address whether or not the 14th Amendment, specifically its first section, would make the Second Amendment applicable to the states. While a full discussion of the Court's reasoning on this point is reserved until Chapter 10 on the application of the Second Amendment to the States, and the 14th Amendment, at this point it is adequate to say that the Court treated it as an individual right, but not as a privilege or immunity of a citizen of the United States (which did not include even freedom of speech, religion or assembly (except when assembling to petition the federal government), but included only things such as the right to travel between the states, the right to vote in federal elections, the right to petition the federal government, in other words, rights pertaining directly to federal citizenship), therefore the 14th Amendment would not make the Second Amendment apply to the states. This treatment of the issue makes no sense at all if the gun control advocates' position is correct. If the Second Amendment merely guarantees some state power over militia, how could the 14th Amendment's prohibition of a state making or enforcing any law abridging the privileges or immunities of citizens of the United States ever be thought to have anything to do with causing the Second Amendment to be applied to the states? And if that is the case, why in the world did the Supreme Court go through three whole pages of the discussion showing why the Second Amendment was not a privilege or immunity of citizens of the United States when it could have dismissed the issue in one sentence using the gun control advocates position? The reason is clear. The Supreme Court had to have considered the Second Amendment to protect individual rights, but the 14th Amendment merely did not apply to those rights to restrict the states.

6. *Logan v. United States*[286]

This discussion will be relatively short. The Second Amendment was not involved in this case. This case, like *Cruikshank*, involved the Enforcement Act of 1870. In *Logan*, however, the situation was that a mob had kidnapped a handful of prisoners, who had been held in custody by federal law enforcement officials. There is no indication that their rights to bear arms had been infringed. The issue was whether the prisoners, by their kidnapping, and been deprived of any of their federal rights. What the Court did, which brings the case to our attention, is repeat the analysis from *Cruikshank*, including the favorable comparison of the First and Second Amendments to each other, and the treatment of the Second Amendment as an individual right. Since it is basically a repeat of the logic in *Cruikshank* (which shows that the Supreme Court still accepted the interpretation of the Second Amendment given therein), and is purely dicta, we will move on to the next case.

7. *Miller v. Texas*[287]

Franklin P. Miller was a white man in love with a black woman. This was not socially acceptable in late 19th century Texas. After learning that Miller might be carrying a handgun without a license, a group of Dallas police officers, after some heavy drinking, broke into Miller's store with guns drawn. While it was disputed who fired first, and whether or not Miller realized that his attackers were police officers, suffice it to say a gunfight ensued. Miller, being sober, got the better of the deal, killing one of the police officers, but being outnumbered, he was captured. He was charged with murder of the police officer and convicted.

Once his case had gotten to the U.S. Supreme Court, Miller was alleging violations of his Second, Fourth, Fifth and 14th Amendment rights. As to the Second Amendment, Miller claimed that it made the Texas statute against concealed carrying of a weapon unconstitutional. In another unanimous opinion, the Supreme Court held that "it is well settled that the restrictions of these amendments operate only upon the federal power, and have no reference whatever to proceedings in state courts."[288] The concept that the Bill of Rights, including the Second Amendment, by themselves did not operate directly against state governments was hardly new. As to the 14th Amendment claim, the Court first held that Miller had waived this claim because he had not asserted it at the trial court level, saying: "If the Fourteenth Amendment limited the power of the States as to such rights, as pertaining to the citizens of the United States, we think it was fatal to this claim that it was not set up in the trial court."[289] The Court then went on to cite several cases for the proposition that "nor did the law of the state, to which reference was made, abridge the privileges or immunities of citizens of the United States as such privileges and immunities are defined in the Slaughterhouse Cases, ..."[290] The logic here is the same as in the last three cases.

Now at least one gun rights advocate has argued that the holding on the waiver of the 14th Amendment right by not asserting it at the trial court might mean that the Court would have been willing to possibly find such a right as to extending the Second Amendment to the states.[291] I disagree. Usually, if a court can get rid of a case, or an issue in a case, by some procedural method, such as the failure to assert a right at the right place and time in a lower court, without dealing with the substantive issues of what the right entails or whether or not it is to be extended to the states, the court will do so. That is what the Supreme Court did here. By doing so, it made the rest of the statements about the 14th Amendment not applying the Bill of Rights to the states dicta. However, my best guess, given the state of the law at the time, and given that dicta, is that the Supreme Court still would not have extended the Bill of Rights to apply to restrict the state governments. In any event, the mere fact that the Court was still discussing the issue in this manner indicates that the Court still looked at the Second Amendment as an individual right, just like the rest of the Bill of Rights, not as a state power.

8. *Brown v. Walker*[292]

Brown involved a witness before a grand jury regarding an Interstate Commerce Commission investigation. The witness had invoked the Fifth Amendment protection against self-incrimination and refused to testify. However, the majority of the Supreme Court ruled that he had to testify because a provision of the federal statute involved protected the witness from any criminal prosecution growing out of the testimony. In a dissenting opinion, Justice Stephen Field argued that the infamy and disgrace that might result from the testimony was enough reason to allow the Fifth Amendment protection; it did not require the danger of criminal prosecution. As part of his argument, Justice Field said the following:

> **The abuses and perversions of sound principles which would creep into the law by yielding to arguments like these-to what is supposed to be necessary for the public good**-cannot be better stated than it was by the late Justice Bradley... Said the learned justice:

"Illegitimate and unconstitutional practices get their first footing in that way, namely, by silent approaches and slight deviations from legal modes of procedure. This can only be obviated by adhering to the rule that constitutional provisions for the security of person and property should be liberally construed. A close and literal construction deprives them of half their efficacy, and leads to gradual depreciation of the right, as if it consisted more in sound than substance. It is the duty of courts to be watchful for the constitutional rights of the citizens, and against any stealthy encroachments thereon. Their motto should be, 'Obsta principiis."
As said by counsel for the appellant:
'The freedom of thought, of speech, and of the press; **the right to bear arms**; exemption from military dictation; security of the person and of the home; the right to speedy and public trial by jury; protection against oppressive bail and cruel punishment,-are, together with exemption from self-crimination, the essential and inseparable features of English liberty. Each one of these features had been involved in the struggle above referred to in England within the century and a half immediately preceding the adoption of the constitution, and the contests were fresh in the memories and traditions of the people at that time."[293]

Of course, this is all dicta in a dissenting opinion, hardly the strongest authority. Even so, he makes some interesting points. First, we should be wary of the gradual erosion of our rights for what is supposed to be the public good. Does that sound like the gun control advocates' arguments that even if the Second Amendment does protect some individual right, that it is now out of date and due to high crime rates with guns, for the public good we should restrict them? Second, Justice Field equates the right to keep and bear arms to other individual rights, as being essential and inseparable features of English liberty. In other words, it would have to be an individual right, because it came from English liberties, since the English had no states, and since it would then precede the Constitution, and even the Declaration of Independence, it could not belong to the states.

Jack Reynolds, J. D.

Again, this is just dicta in a dissenting opinion, but I have not found even that much authority up to this point for the gun control advocates' position.

9. *Robertson v. Baldwin*[294]

In this case, the Congress had passed a law that called for the arrest and impression of all merchant seamen who had deserted their ships. Some seamen caught and detained under this statute asserted the 13th Amendment (prohibition of involuntary servitude or slavery), claiming that the statute involved was unconstitutional and that they could not be forced back into service aboard the ships. The Supreme Court, in another majority opinion, held that even though the 13th Amendment was absolute on its face (which is to say that just by reading it you might think that involuntary servitude was never allowed), it would have to be subject to various exceptions. To support this concept of exceptions to what otherwise would read as absolute rights, the Supreme Court noted that other rights, specifically those rights protected in the Bill of Rights, though absolute on their face, also have exceptions:

> The law is perfectly well settled that the first 10 amendments to the constitution, commonly known as the 'Bill of Rights,' were not intended to lay down any novel principles of government, but simply to embody certain guaranties and **immunities which we had inherited from our English ancestors, and which had, from time immemorial, been subject to certain well-recognized exceptions**, arising from the necessities of the case. In incorporating these principles into the fundamental law, there was no intention of disregarding the exceptions, which continued to be recognized as if they had been formally expressed. Thus, the freedom of speech and of the press (article 1) does not permit the publication of libels, blasphemous or indecent articles, or other publications injurious to public morals or private reputation; **the right of the people to keep and bear arms (article 2) is not infringed by laws prohibiting the carrying of concealed weapons**; the provision that no person shall be twice put in jeopardy (article 5)

A People Armed and Free

does not prevent a second trial, if upon the first trial the jury failed to agree, or if the verdict was set aside upon the defendant's ... ; nor does the provision of the same article that no one shall be a witness against himself impair his obligation to testify, if a prosecution against him be barred by the lapse of time, a pardon, or by statutory enactment... Nor does the provision that an accused person shall be confronted with the witnesses against him prevent the admission of dying declarations, or the depositions of witnesses who have died since the former trial.[295]

    A couple of points here. First, the Court again calls the Second Amendment right as something inherited from our English ancestors. We did not inherit state powers from our English ancestors. Second, the Second Amendment is again treated the same as all of the other individual rights mentioned in the quote, and is listed as a right of the people. None of the other items listed is a power (nor even any possible right, if such a thing could exist) of any government. Finally, the fact that there is an exception to the Second Amendment right is interesting on two counts. Since there were no such federal laws at the time, the Court had to be talking about state laws that amounted to the exception. While many states did prohibit the carrying of concealed weapons at the time, these statutes did not prohibit state militias from carrying concealed weapons. So, first, it makes no sense to talk about a state passing laws that would be exceptions to its own powers over its militia. Second, since the exception to the right (that is to say, the prohibition of carrying concealed weapons) did not apply to the militia, but only to individual citizens, in order to be an exception, the right also had to go to individual citizens. All of the above quoted passage can be considered reasoning of the Court, and therefore, is stronger than dicta.

    Finally, this disproves some statements that I have seen from gun control advocates, that since the right to keep and bear arms was never absolute, even going all the way back to the English Bill of Rights, there never was any right at all. Rights can, and do, exist, even though there are limits on those rights.

    Incidentally, in case you are interested, the seamen had to go back to work on the ships.

10. Maxwell v. Dow[296]

The issue here was whether or not the 14th Amendment could be used to apply the Sixth Amendment right to a jury trial to the state government. In holding that it could not be used to do that, the Supreme Court cited *Presser* as holding that "the Second Amendment to the Constitution, in regard to the right of the people to bear arms, is a limitation only on the power of the Congress and the National Government, and not of the States."[297] Once more, this is used as reasoning by the Court, that if the Second Amendment cannot be applied to the states, neither can the others. Again, this indicates that the Second Amendment is a right of the people, and again it does not make sense to even talk about it possibly limiting the states if it protects a state's power/right to have, maintain and/or arm its militia.

11. Trono v. United States[298]

After the Spanish-American War, the United States assumed control over the Philippines. In 1902, Congress passed a law that imposed most, but not all, of the Bill of Rights, on the Territorial Government of the Philippines. *Trono* was a criminal case where the defendant claimed that his rights had been violated. The Supreme Court, in explaining the statute imposing these rights on the Philippines, stated:

> This language is to be found in connection with other language in the same act, providing for the rights of a person accused of crime in the Philippine Islands. The whole language is substantially taken from the Bill of Rights set forth in the amendments to the Constitution of the United States, **omitting** the provisions in regard to the right of trial by jury and **the right of the people to bear arms**, and containing the prohibition of the 13th Amendment, and also prohibiting the passage of bills of attainder and ex post facto laws.[299]

Notice again how it is listed as a right of the people. Notice also how it is listed with nothing but individual rights. Gun control advocates might try to argue that the reason that the Second Amendment was omitted from the statute was that it protects state powers, not individual rights, which would be perfectly logical. Except, the Tenth Amendment, which also protects state powers, also was not included in the statute imposing things (rights or powers) on the Philippines (which in itself is also logical), but the Tenth Amendment is not listed by the Court in its opinion as having been omitted from the statute. If, other than the Second Amendment, the Supreme Court does list those rights that were omitted from the statute, but does not list those state powers that were omitted from the statute, then why would it be that the Court included the Second Amendment in its list? Could it be that the Court believed that the Second Amendment is a right of the people as it said, and not a power of the states? I think so. Incidentally, if you are keeping track, this would probably be considered dicta, in a majority opinion.

12. *Twining v. New Jersey*[300]

This is another case dealing with whether or not a portion of the Bill of Rights (in this case the Fifth Amendment's protection against self-incrimination) will be applied to the states through the 14th Amendment. This case was overruled in *Malloy v. Hogan*,[301] which we will discuss later. The Supreme Court again cited *Presser* for the concept that the 14th Amendment could not be used to apply the Second Amendment to the states. Again, it only makes sense to even discuss the concept this way if the Second Amendment is an individual right and not a state power. So, as of 1908, the Supreme Court still treats the Second Amendment as an individual right, in yet another majority opinion, in its reasoning (therefore not dicta), though it has not had the occasion to directly address the issue of whether or not it is an individual right. Still, no opinions that I have found up to that date have even alluded to any possibility of it being a state power. In case you are keeping score, so far it is 11 opinions (9 majority, 2 dissenting) for individual right, 0 for state power, 1 abstention.

13. *Stearns v. Wood*[302]

After what became World War I had broken out in Europe, the United States War Department sent "Circular 8" to the National Guards of the various states, putting restrictions on promotions above the rank of Lieutenant Colonel. The plaintiff in this case, Major Stearns, claimed that this denied him a possible promotion. However, since, being a major, he was not even eligible to be promoted above Lieutenant Colonel at the time, the Supreme Court summarily dismissed the case as lacking standing and genuine controversy, refusing to give an advisory opinion. So where does the Second Amendment come in? For the first time that I can find, in a U.S.

Jack Reynolds, J. D.

Supreme Court case, the prospect of the Second Amendment protecting state power over the militia was raised in the plaintiff's brief as a reason that the federal government could not limit promotions. While this indicates that as of 1915 someone had come up with this theory, since it was not even addressed, one way or the other, by the Supreme Court, this case has absolutely no precedential value for either side. Score this one as an abstention.

14. United States v. Schwimmer[303]

This case involved a female pacifist who tried to become a citizen of the United States. In a majority opinion, the Supreme Court held that active pacifism was inconsistent with good citizenship; therefore, Ms. Schwimmer could be denied citizenship. As part of its reasoning, the Court cited various provisions of the Constitution pertaining to the national defense:

> That it is the duty of citizens by force of arms to defend our government against all enemies whenever necessity arises is a fundamental principle of the Constitution. The common defense was one of the purposes for which the people ordained and established the Constitution. It empowers Congress to provide for such defense, to declare war, to raise and support armies, to maintain a navy, to make rules for the government and regulation of the land and naval forces, to provide for organizing, arming, and disciplining the militia, and for calling it forth to execute the laws of the Union, suppress insurrections and repel invasions; it declares that, a well-regulated militia being necessary to the security of a free state, the right of the people to keep and bear arms shall not be infringed. We need not refer to the numerous statutes that contemplate defense of the United States, its Constitution and laws, by armed citizens. This court, ... speaking through Chief Justice White, said that 'the very conception of a just government and its duty to the citizen includes the reciprocal obligation of the citizen to render military service in case of need...[304]

A People Armed and Free

While this language used certainly does mention the Second Amendment in the same context as other powers, it does so in relation to national powers, not state powers, it also mentions armed citizens, not armed states, and its purpose is to show the duty that citizens have to defend the national government (therefore, a person not willing to do this could be denied citizenship). Therefore, this passage could be read as being consistent with either the states powers claimed by the gun control advocates, or the individual rights claimed by the gun rights advocates. I really do not think that the Court was expressing any opinion, one way or the other, but merely showing that in order to obtain citizenship, a person has to be willing to be an armed citizen to support and defend this country. Count this one as another abstention.

15. *Hamilton v. Regents*[305]

This case can be read to support the states' power theory, but it is still a little shaky. It involved a couple of college students in California who wanted to be excused from ROTC due to a claim of being conscientious objectors. The training program was set up as part of the state's militia program. A unanimous court held that the state had the power to regulate its own program and make its own decisions about whether or not students had to train in the program if they were going to attend the particular university. In so doing, the Supreme Court used the following reasoning:

> So long as its action is within retained powers and not inconsistent with any exertion of the authority of the national government and transgresses no right safeguarded to the citizen by the Federal Constitution, the state is the sole judge of the means to be employed and the amount of training to be exacted for the effective accomplishment of these ends. Second Amendment; Houston v. Moore, 5 Wheat. 1, 16, 17; Dunne v. People (1879) 94 Ill. 120, 129, 34 Am.Rep. 213; 1 Kent's Commentaries, 265, 389. Cf. Presser v. Illinois, 116 U.S. 252, 6 S.Ct. 580.[306]

Certainly the citing of the Second Amendment in the above is used in the context of state powers over the militia, but no explanation is given of it. Sometimes, in order to make the Court's position clearer, it helps to look at the other sources cited in the opinion and relied upon. In this case, each of the other sources cited upheld state powers over the militia without relying on the Second Amendment, except *Dunne v. People*, a state court case addressing state power over the militia. It also explained how a state's constitutional duty to operate a militia depended on the right of the citizens to keep and bear arms:

> "A well regulated militia being necessary to the security of a free State," the States, by an amendment to the constitution, have imposed a restriction that Congress shall not infringe the right of the "people to keep and bear arms." The chief executive officer of the State is given power by the constitution to call out the militia "to execute the laws, suppress insurrection and repel invasion." This would be a mere barren grant of power unless the State had power to organize its own militia for its own purposes. Unorganized, the militia would be of no practical aid to the executive in maintaining order and in protecting life and property within the limits of the State. These are duties that devolve on the State, and unless these rights are secured to the citizen, of what worth is the State government?[307]

This state court language has both some indication that the Second Amendment involves the states powers, and involves an individual right of citizens to keep and bear arms. I suppose that it is not inconceivable that the two could exist together in the same amendment. In any event, due to the purpose that the Second Amendment appears to be cited for in the United States Supreme Court Opinion, even though it certainly does not hold that the Amendment protects states' powers over the militias (realize that none of the earlier cases discussed held that it was an individual right either; they merely implied it in their reasoning or dicta), it does imply that the amendment does protect the states powers. Therefore, I score this case on the gun control advocates side, making the score now 11 opinions (9 majority, 2 dissenting) for individual right, 1 (majority) for state power, 3 abstentions.

16. United States v. Miller[308]

This is the case that has caused all of the problems. If it had clearly held one way or the other on what the Second Amendment does, I would probably not be writing this book. But ...

I have heard it often said that bad cases make bad law. This turned out to be a bad case, and as you will see, it is bad law, not because I do not agree with its holding or logic, but because it is impossible to determine just what its holding and reasoning is in relation to the theories espoused today. This is the only case in which the United States Supreme Court has tried to directly address what the Second Amendment means.

What makes this a bad case? Its facts. Congress had passed a law requiring the registration and taxing of certain firearms, specifically machine guns and sawed-off shotguns.[309] This was the first attempt, that I have seen, by the federal government to regulate, in any way, firearms. The two defendants in the case were moon shiners in the Oklahoma/Arkansas area. They were arrested and charged with a violation of this statute, in that they had a double barrel 12-gauge shotgun with a barrel less than 18 inches. In response to the charge, the defendants' attorney asserted the Second Amendment. The district court where the case would have been tried agreed that the statute violated the Second Amendment and quashed the indictment.

Now, if you were a moon shiner and had just been released by the trial court quashing the indictment what would you do? Would you stick around to see how things might come out when the government appeals? Or would you leave the area? Well, the defendants left. Therefore, when the U.S. Attorney's office appealed the case directly to the U.S. Supreme Court (one of the few instances where this is allowed), nobody showed up to argue on behalf of the defendants. No briefs were filed on their behalf, no oral arguments, nothing! In other words, the Supreme Court had only one position on the case presented to it. Now, if I go into a court without the opposing side there to resist me, I can usually convince the court to do anything I want it to.[310] This makes *Miller* a bad case. Anytime the court does not have both sides presented, it does not bode well for what the court is likely to do.

So what did the Court in *Miller* do? What is all of the fuss about? Why can't a smart attorney like me figure out what the Supreme Court says the Second Amendment means? For the answer, let's first look at the holding of the Court, remembering that the issue is whether or not the restrictions on the possession of shotgun with a barrel of less than eighteen inches violate the Second Amendment:

> In the absence of any evidence tending to show that possession or use of a 'shotgun having a barrel of less than eighteen inches in length' at this time has some reasonable relationship to the preservation or efficiency of a well regulated militia, we cannot say that the Second Amendment guarantees the right to keep and bear such an instrument. Certainly it is not within judicial notice that this weapon is any part of the ordinary military equipment or that its use could contribute to the common defense. Aymette v. State of Tennessee, 2 Humph., Tenn., 154, 158.[311]

The Supreme Court remanded the case back to the district court for further proceedings, presumably to receive evidence on the question of whether or not the shotgun in question had some reasonable relationship to the preservation or efficiency of a well-regulated militia. The refusal to take judicial notice (which means that the Court is accepting some proposition, such as the earth is round, as fact, without having to hear evidence on it) and the statement that there was no evidence in front of the court at that time on this issue, merely means that the trial court had not heard evidence, and needed to. Had the Court decided that it was impossible for the shotgun to have such a relationship, it would have reversed and rendered the case (that is, found for the government as a matter of law) on this issue. It did not. Remand means that the district court gets to try the case, that is, hear evidence on the issue.

Now what does this holding mean? That is a good question. The only thing actually held is that the possession or use of the weapon in question must have some reasonable relationship to the preservation or efficiency of a well-regulated militia, what ever that means. As a retired lieutenant colonel in the Marine Corps Reserve, I can tell you that a sawed-off shotgun can, and does, have a relationship to military forces. In fact, almost any modern firearm can be shown to have a relationship to military forces. In fact, the argument has been made that the above holding means that virtually all firearms should be unregulated. Certainly, machine guns, bazookas, artillery, mortars, tanks, fighter and bomber aircraft, etc., would all have a reasonable relationship to a well regulated militia. Gun control advocates say that that is ridiculous, that no one could want their next-door neighbor to have the right to have a M-1 tank. Lower courts have agreed with the gun control advocates, but the only logic used is that they do not think it is a good idea; there is nothing in *Miller* that produces that result.

Such positions, without more than just the individuals' opinions that it would not be a good idea to allow people to have such high powered weapons, is about like some conservatives saying that it is ridiculous for the First Amendment Freedom of Speech and Press provisions to be interpreted to protect the publication of pornography, because the Founding Fathers never would have intended such a result, and in their opinions it simply is not a good idea to allow that freedom to go that far. In fact, there is probably more evidence that if the Founding Fathers had ever thought about the publication of pornographic pictures, videos, and other materials, they probably would have been more inclined to ban them, than there is that they would have been inclined to allow the government to ban machine guns, antitank weapons, and other heavy weapons. But since they could never have even thought about either issue because the technology did not exist on either point, it is probably speculative to try to say one way or the other. I may not like pornography being spread around, but I will defend the constitutional right of people to publish it. Let's see the gun control advocates make a similar magnanimous statement about the Second Amendment and guns. I doubt it!

What about the reasoning used in *Miller*? Maybe it can help us to understand what the holding means. Good luck! Here is some of it:

> The Constitution as originally adopted granted to the Congress power- 'To provide for calling forth the Militia to execute the Laws of the Union, suppress Insurrections and repel Invasions; To provide for organizing, arming, and disciplining, the Militia, and for governing such Part of them as may be employed in the Service of the United States, reserving to the States respectively, the Appointment of the Officers, and the Authority of training the Militia according to

> the discipline prescribed by Congress.' U.S.C.A.Const. art. 1, 8. With obvious purpose to assure the continuation and render possible the effectiveness of such forces the declaration and guarantee of the Second Amendment were made. It must be interpreted and applied with that end in view.
>
> The Militia which the States were expected to maintain and train is set in contrast with Troops which they were forbidden to keep without the consent of Congress. The sentiment of the time strongly disfavored standing armies; the common view was that adequate defense of country and laws could be secured through the Militia- civilians primarily, soldiers on occasion.
>
> The signification attributed to the term Militia appears from the debates in the Convention, the history and legislation of Colonies and States, and the writings of approved commentators. These show plainly enough that the Militia comprised all males physically capable of acting in concert for the common defense. 'A body of citizens enrolled for military discipline.' And further, that ordinarily when called for service these men were expected to appear bearing arms supplied by themselves and of the kind in common use at the time.[312]

This passage clearly points to the need for some relationship to the militia, as stated in the holding, but then goes on to describe the militia as "civilians primarily, soldiers on occasion" and as "[a] body of citizens enrolled for military discipline." The court then goes on, in unquoted portions of the opinion, to give some history of the militia, how the colonies and early states declared all free, white, able-bodied males to be members of the militia, and the Militia Act of 1792, all of which we have already discussed (though the Court's discussion of the history involved was nowhere near as comprehensive as ours). It should be noted that in the history cited in *Miller*, no reference was made to any "select militia" or the National Guard.

So now let's use the same method we used in the last case of looking at the law relied on by the Court for its holding to see what it says. The case is *Amyette v. State*[313] an 1840 case from Tennessee that involved a defendant who had been convicted of carrying a concealed Bowie knife. He claimed that under the Tennessee constitutional provision ("the citizens of this State have a right to keep and bear arms for their common defense; but the legislature shall have power, by law, to regulate the wearing of arms with a view to prevent crime") he had a constitutional right to carry the knife. In holding otherwise the Tennessee Supreme Court said:

> [E]very free white man may keep and bear arms. But to keep and bear arms for what? ... The object, then, for which the right of keeping and bearing arms is secured is the defence of the public. The free white men may keep arms to protect the public liberty, to keep in awe those who are in power, and to maintain the supremacy of the laws and the constitution... As the object for which the right to keep and bear arms is secured is of a general and public nature, to be exercised by the people in a body, for their common defence, so the arms the right to keep which is secured are such as are usually employed in civilized warfare, and that constitute the ordinary military equipment. If the citizens have these arms in their hands, they are prepared in the best possible manner to repel any encroachments upon their rights by those in authority. They need not, for such a purpose, the use of those weapons which are usually employed in private broils, and which are efficient only in the hands of the robber and the assassin... The right to keep and bear them is not, therefore, secured by the constitution.[314]

This clearly has both elements in it, that is, a requirement that the weapons have something to do with military service, and the right apparently belongs to the people, not the state, as they are to be available to be used against the government (those in authority) if need be. Sounds like the "insurrectionist theory" again. In any event, it is also clear how this relates to the *Miller* holding when one remembers the problems that were occurring at the time regarding gangsters and prohibition. Sawed-off shotguns were used by criminals in their trade, and the Supreme Court was questioning their utility in a military context in an effort to allow their restriction in order to fight crime. But, this still does not clearly get to the question of whether the Supreme Court in *Miller* was holding that the Second Amendment guarantees an individual right, or grants a state power.

If we go to the brief of the government in *Miller*, two reasons for upholding the statute involved are given:

> *First,* it contends that the right secured by the Second Amendment is "only one which exists where the arms are borne in the militia or some other military organization provided for by law and intended for the protection of the state." ...
>
> The *second* ... "While some courts have said that the right to bear arms includes the right of the individual to have them for the protection of his person and property as well as the right of the people to bear them collectively (*People v. Brown,* 253 Mich. 537; *State v. Duke,* 42 Tex. 455), the cases are unanimous in holding that the term "arms" as used in constitutional provisions refers only to those weapons which are ordinarily used for military or public defense purposes and does not relate to those weapons which are commonly used by criminals.[315]

The government's brief then went on to quote the passage from *Aymette*. The first reason given is the position of the gun control advocates today, that the Second Amendment only protects the keeping and bearing of arms in the militia, or in other words, a state's power to maintain and arm its militia. The second reason supports an individual right, but limits the types of weapons that may be kept and borne. The Supreme Court appears to have adopted the second reason, although the opinion itself can be read either way.

Now, while this will be addressed in more detail in the discussion of the lower court cases as they come up, let's look at some of the arguments that have proceeded from *Miller*:

Gun Rights Advocates: Since weapons only have to have some relationship to the militia, and virtually all weapons can pass that test, no regulations are allowed.

A People Armed and Free

Gun Control Advocates: No, that would be ridiculous, besides, in order for the possession or use of a weapon to have a reasonable relationship to the militia, not only must the weapon have a relationship, but so must the individual involved.

Gun Rights Advocates: OK, so we have here a person that falls in the definition, by state law and federal law, of belonging to the Militia (albeit, the unorganized militia). And he wants to have a M-16 or AK-47, which clearly have reasonable relationships to the military, so the federal prohibition against these "assault weapons" violates the Second Amendment.

Gun Control Advocates: No, because of the phrase "well-regulated", the unorganized militia does not count.

Gun Rights Advocates: OK, we now have a member of the National Guard who wants to have the same weapons, and another member of the National Guard who has designed and built his own prototype machine gun that he wants to sell to the government. Both situations involve organized militia members, and weapons reasonably related to military purposes, and the fact that they can use these weapons on their own time, at their own costs, for target practice, improves the efficiency of the militia, and the possible invention of a new and better machine gun by the one National Guard member could improve the efficiency of the militia, so these individuals have the right to keep and bear these firearms.

Gun Control Advocates: No, what Miller means is that not only do the weapons have to have a reasonable relationship to the militia, and the individuals have to be members of the National Guard, but the weapons have to belong to the National Guard, so there is no right of an individual to have any firearm, period.

Now I defy any of you to find any support for these arguments on either side in *Miller*, whether to portions discussed in this book or anywhere else in the whole opinion; read it for your self. They just are not addressed. Or maybe the problem is that while there is nothing direct in *Miller* that can support these arguments, you can take what is said in *Miller* and argue its implications in support of both positions. Either way, we are still left wondering just what *Miller* **does** mean. Does it support only a state power over the militia? Or, does it support an individual citizen's right to keep and bear arms as long as some reasonable relationship to the preservation and efficiency of the militia (whatever that means) can be shown? Or is it some combination of the two? Or is it something that I have not thought of? We just do not know.

Since I can sit here, with whatever biases I may have, and present logical arguments on both sides of the issue from *Miller,* I score it a tie. It is not an abstention, since it did address the issue, but we just cannot tell what the result is.

Incidentally, just in case you are interested, one of the defendants was killed before the case made it back to the district court, the other defendant struck a plea bargain, so we do not have any subsequent history to help us resolve the meaning of these issues.

17. *Adamson v. California*[316]

This is a very interesting case, in that the opinion that we are concerned with is a dissenting opinion which since has been adopted, at least in part, by the Supreme Court in numerous other cases. This shows what I had pointed out earlier in this chapter, that while dissenting opinions are not binding authority, if they are well written and well reasoned, they may turn out later to be good law.

Adamson was a criminal defendant, charged with a state law crime and tried in a state court in California. It was a jury trial. He opted to exercise his right against self-incrimination and not testify. California law allowed the judge to comment to the jury on the fact that the defendant did not testify, instructing them that they could draw adverse inferences from the defendant's failure to testify. Now if this had been a federal case, in federal court, under the cases interpreting the Fifth Amendment, this comment/instruction would have clearly been improper. But the issue involved here was, could this Fifth Amendment restriction be applied to a state judge, in a state court, involving a state law, with a state criminal defendant?

Remember that all of the cases that we have looked at so far (and we have not looked at all of them, only the ones that mentioned the Second Amendment in some way) have held that the Bill of Rights did not apply directly to the states, and that the first section of the 14th Amendment did not cause the Bill of Rights to be applied to the states. It only applied the privileges and immunities of national citizenship, narrowly defined, to the states. Well, the majority opinion of the Court in *Adamson* continued this holding in regards to the Fifth Amendment.

In a lengthy dissent, Justice Black, joined by Justice Douglas, two of the most liberal judges to ever sit on the Supreme Court, asserted

A People Armed and Free

that the history of the 14th Amendment was such that it was, in fact, supposed to make all of the first eight amendments to the Constitution apply to the states. We will go into this history in much more detail in Chapter 9, but at this point it is adequate to again point out that the language of Justice Black's dissent, as well as the history he relies on, equates the Second Amendment with the other individual rights contained in the Bill of Rights, and the mere talk of applying the whole Bill of Rights, including the Second Amendment, against state governments, means that the amendment would have to protect individual rights; otherwise it could not be used to restrict a state government against its own power.

Chalk this one up as an individual rights case. This makes the running score now 12 opinions (9 majority, 3 dissenting) for individual right, 1 (majority) for state power, 1 tie, 3 abstentions.

18. Johnson v. Eisentrager[317]

This is another very interesting case, but for a different reason. It is just a very interesting mental exercise in applying the words in the Bill of Rights.

After Germany had surrendered in World War II, some of the German soldiers in China continued to help the Japanese army prior to its surrender. They were captured by the American army and tried by military court-martial in China as war criminals. The Germans appealed asserting a Fifth Amendment right to not be tried by court-martial, pointing out that the Fifth Amendment is not by its language limited to American citizens, but applies to all "person[s]". The applicable portion of the Fifth Amendment reads as follows: "No person shall be held to answer for a capital, or otherwise infamous crime, unless on a presentment or indictment of a Grand Jury, except in cases arising in the land or naval forces, or in the Militia, when in actual service in time of War or public danger; ..." Since courts-martial are not held under an indictment of a grand jury, and only the land and naval forces, and the militia when in actual service in time of war or public danger, are exempted from this protection, the reasoning proposed was that, as persons, the Germans could not be tried by court-martial, but had to be indicted by a grand jury and tried in a civilian court. The court of appeals bought off on this argument and reversed the court-martial conviction. The Supreme Court did not agree.

Jack Reynolds, J. D.

Justice Jackson, who had been a judge at the Nuremberg war crimes trials, wrote the majority opinion for the Supreme Court. In it, he pointed out that none of the other rights contained in the Bill of Rights were limited to citizens, and therefore if this argument to apply the Fifth Amendment to enemy soldiers was correct, then the other rights would also have to be applied to enemy soldiers, with some pretty ridiculous results:

> If the Fifth Amendment confers its rights on all the world except Americans engaged in defending it, the same must be true of the companion civil-rights Amendments, for none of them is limited by its express terms, territorially or as to persons. **Such a construction would mean that during military occupation irreconcilable enemy elements, guerrilla fighters, and "werewolves" could require the American Judiciary to assure them freedoms** of speech, press, and assembly as in the First Amendment, **right to bear arms as in the Second**, security against "unreasonable" searches and seizures as in the Fourth, as well as rights to jury trial as in the Fifth and Sixth Amendments.[318]

Notice that the Court lists the Second Amendment right with other individual rights. Also, enemy prisoners could hardly have any claim to any right stemming from a guarantee of power to the states to maintain and arm their militias. They have absolutely no relationship to any of our states. Therefore, even if a member of their own country's militia, the Second Amendment, under the states' power theory, simply could not apply to them. Additionally, if we are looking at guerrilla fighters and "were-wolves", these simply are not members of any militia, but are small groups or individuals functioning in enemy territory beyond the reach of any friendly government. Therefore, that reference could have nothing to do with anyone's militia. This reference to the Second Amendment only makes sense if it is a protection of an individual right.

In case you could not tell, the Supreme Court said that the Germans were not entitled to the protection of the Fifth Amendment.

19. Knapp v. Schweitzer[319]

This is another case where the issue is a question of the applicability of the Fifth Amendment to the states. The majority again refused to apply it to the states, and in so doing reeled off a list of the other rights that had been held to not apply to the states. Included in this list of rights was the Second Amendment, citing *Cruikshank*. Again, this discussion lists the Second Amendment with other individual rights and it does not make sense to talk about applying the Second Amendment to the states unless it is an individual right. So, score another case for the individual right interpretation.

20. Poe v. Ullman[320]

This involved the right of privacy, a right not expressly found in the Constitution or any of its amendments. The issue was whether or not married persons had a right to use contraceptives. The majority said no. However two judges dissented with separate opinions that are of interest to us here.

First, Justice Douglas wrote, concerning the 14th Amendment: "The first eight Amendments to the Constitution have been made applicable to the States only in part. My view has been that when the Fourteenth Amendment was adopted, its Due Process Clause incorporated all of those Amendments."[321] Again this implies an individual right interpretation of the Second Amendment, but it must be noted that if Justice Douglas intended such an interpretation, he abandoned it in a later case.

Second, Justice Harlan also wrote that the 14th Amendment would guarantee the right of privacy, and that the 14th Amendment is not limited to those found in the Bill of Rights, specifically including the Second Amendment as an individual right:

> This **"liberty"** is not a series of isolated points pricked out in terms of the taking of property; the freedom of speech, press, and religion; **the right to keep and bear arms**; the freedom from unreasonable searches and seizures; and so on. It is a rational continuum which, broadly speaking, includes a freedom from all substantial arbitrary impositions and purposeless restraints, see Allgeyer v. Louisiana, 165 U.S. 578 ; Holden v. Hardy, 169 U.S. 366 ; Booth v. Illinois, 184 U.S. 425 ; Nebbia v. New York, 291 U.S. 502 ; Skinner v. Oklahoma, 316 U.S. 535, 544 (concurring

opinion); Schware v. Board of Bar Examiners, 353 U.S. 232 , and which also recognizes, what a reasonable and sensitive judgment must, that certain interests require particularly careful scrutiny of the state needs asserted to justify their abridgment. Cf. Skinner v. Oklahoma, supra; Bolling v. Sharpe, supra.[322]

Of course, this comes out to be the same interpretation as many prior 14th Amendment cases. It lists the Second Amendment as an individual right, and that is the only way to consider it if one is going to talk about applying it, through the 14th Amendment, to the states. But there is another interesting point here. Did you notice that in this quote I left in cites to other cases, while most of the time when I put a quote in I have taken such cites out (to make it easier for you to read)? Supreme Court Judges have quoted this text in later cases. But their quotes are not complete. They leave out two of the cases cited: Allgeyer v. Louisiana, 165 U.S. 578 , and Nebbia v. New York, 291 U.S. 502 . These cases supported the use of the 14th Amendment to protect economic rights. Economic rights, while important to our Founding Fathers, have not been in vogue for the last 70 years. Therefore, this shows that these later justices knew how to delete material from this quote that they did not want to be seen as endorsing, and were willing to do so. However, as you will see, they did not delete the reference to the Second Amendment as being a point of liberty like freedom of speech, etc. This adds strength to the individual rights arguments, since the repetition of quotes is seen to not be just a mindless copy of statements for some other purpose, but a reasoned decision as to what to leave in and what to take out.

What is our score now? I have 15 opinions (11 majority, 4 dissenting) for individual right, 1 (majority) for state power, 1 tie, and 3 abstentions.

21. Konigsberg v. State Bar of California[323]

The State Bar of California had refused to grant a law license to a man who refused to answer questions about his beliefs regarding communism. He complained that this violated his First Amendment rights to freedom of speech and freedom of association. The majority opinion, written by Justice Harlan, upheld the denial of the law

A People Armed and Free

license, saying that the First Amendment rights are not absolute, and comparing it to the Second Amendment:

> That view [of an absolute right of freedom of speech], which of course cannot be reconciled with the law relating to libel, slander, misrepresentation, obscenity, perjury, false advertising, solicitation of crime, complicity by encouragement, conspiracy, and the like, is said to be compelled by the fact that the commands of the First Amendment are stated in unqualified terms: "Congress shall make no law ... abridging the freedom of speech, or of the press; or the right of the people peaceably to assemble ..." But as Mr. Justice Holmes once said: "[T]he provisions of the Constitution are not mathematical formulas having their essence in their form; they are organic living institutions transplanted from English soil. Their significance is vital not formal; it is to be gathered not simply by taking the words and a dictionary, but by considering their origin and the line of their growth." ... In this connection also compare the equally unqualified command of the Second Amendment: "the right of the people to keep and bear arms shall not be infringed." And see United States v. Miller, 307 U.S. 174.[324]

This use of the Second Amendment to show that it is not absolute, and that therefore the First Amendment is not absolute, only makes sense if it involves an individual right. If the Second Amendment only grants a power to the states over the militia, how can the *Miller* case be read to show that the First Amendment does not protect an absolute right? There just is no relationship to the argument presented in the *Konigsberg* case using the states' power model. Therefore, chalk up another majority opinion using the Second Amendment in its reasoning as implying that it is an individual right.

Another interesting sidelight to this case is that Justice Black dissented, saying that in his opinion the First Amendment is an absolute protection. He had expressed this opinion the year before in the First Annual James Madison Lecture at the New York University

School of Law, where he said that all of the rights guaranteed in the Bill of Rights are absolute.[325] While Justice Black did not mention the Second Amendment in his dissenting opinion, he did in his lecture. Here is what he said:

> Amendment Two provides that: "A well regulated Militia being necessary to the security of a free State, the right of the people to keep and bear Arms, shall not be infringed." Although the Supreme Court has held this Amendment to include only arms necessary to a well-regulated militia, as so construed, its prohibition is absolute.[326]

Now this could be interpreted in two different ways. The power of the states to maintain and arm their militias is absolute, or the right of individuals to keep and bear arms, as long as they are arms that are necessary to a well-regulated militia, is absolute. So which is it? Well, his earlier dissenting opinion in *Adamson*, already discussed, indicates that he thought that the Second Amendment guarantees an individual right. Additionally, we have already seen case law that shows that the states' power over their militias is not absolute, so that would be an unlikely logic for the justice to follow. While none of this is in his opinion anyway, and therefore does not really count in our search for how the Supreme Court has treated the Second Amendment, I think it makes more sense to read his lecture as saying that the Second Amendment is an absolute guarantee of an individual right, as long as the weapon involved has "a reasonable relationship to the preservation or efficiency of a well-regulated militia" (the actual words used in *Miller*).

22. Malloy v. Hogan[327]

Malloy was another case where the issue was whether or not the 14th Amendment could be used to extend the Fifth Amendment protection against self-incrimination to the states. Only this time, the result was different. *Malloy* expressly overruled (which means that the Supreme Court said "our decision in those earlier cases were wrong and their holdings, at least on these issues, are no longer good law") *Twining* and *Adamson*, previously discussed herein, and ruled that the Fifth Amendment does apply to the states, through the 14th Amendment. In doing so, the Court went through the history of applying the individual rights of the Bill of Rights to the states through the 14th Amendment, including the fact that the Second Amendment was not applied. Again, it discusses the Second Amendment in context with other individual rights, and the discussion makes sense only if the Second Amendment is considered as an individual right. The words used by Justice Brennan, who wrote the opinion, are interesting:

> The extent to which the Fourteenth Amendment prevents state invasion of rights enumerated in the first eight Amendments has been considered in numerous cases in this Court since the Amendment's adoption in 1868. Although many Justices have deemed the Amendment to incorporate all eight of the Amendments, 2 the view which has thus far prevailed dates from the decision in 1897 in Chicago, B. & Q. R. Co. v. Chicago, 166 U.S. 226, which held that the Due Process Clause requires the States to pay just compensation for private property taken for public use...
>
> The Court has not hesitated to re-examine past decisions according the Fourteenth Amendment a less central role in the preservation of basic liberties than that which was contemplated by its Framers when they added the Amendment to our constitutional scheme.
>
> * * * *
>
> We hold today that the Fifth Amendment's exception from compulsory self-incrimination is also protected by the Fourteenth Amendment against abridgment by the States. Decisions of the Court since Twining and Adamson have departed from the contrary view expressed in those cases.
>
> [Footnote 2] Ten Justices have supported this view... Decisions that particular guarantees were not safeguarded against state action by the Privileges and Immunities Clause or other provision of the Fourteenth Amendment are: United States v. Cruikshank, 92 U.S.

<u>542, 551</u> [which dealt with the Second Amendment];³²⁸

So, apparently ten justices have, as of the time of *Malloy*, supported the view that all of the first eight amendments to the Constitution should be made to apply to the states, although they did not all sit on the Supreme Court at once. If they are right, then the Second Amendment has to be an individual right, for only then could it be applied to restrict states' powers over their citizens. This case, along with many of the cases that it cites, indicate that the Supreme Court is willing, in the right case, to revisit the issue as to whether or not a particular right should be applied to the states. This gives gun rights advocates hope that eventually the Second Amendment will be applied to the states through the 14th Amendment. Score another majority opinion for individual rights.

23. Duncan v. Louisiana³²⁹

This is another case about applying a portion of the Bill of Rights to the states, this time the Sixth Amendment right to a jury trial. By this point in time, the Supreme Court was much more receptive to this concept than it had been in the late 1800's. The Court ruled that it would be applied to the states through the 14th Amendment. This continues to strengthen gun advocates hopes that the Second Amendment will also be applied to the states, as one after another of the other rights in the Bill of Rights are so applied.

But that is not the point of this case. Our point comes from the concurring opinion of Justice Black (he is finally on the winning side in applying the Bill of Rights to the states). In his concurring opinion, he addresses the dissent's position that the Bill of Rights should not apply to the states, and restates some of his arguments from his long dissent in *Adamson*. He also points out some of the rights that have already been applied to the states:

> [O]ur Court has since the Adamson case held most of the specific Bill of Rights' protections applicable to the States to the same extent they are applicable to the Federal Government. Among these are the right to trial by jury decided today, the right against compelled self-incrimination, the right to counsel, the right to compulsory process for witnesses, the right to confront

witnesses, the right to a speedy and public trial, and the right to be free from unreasonable searches and seizures.[330]

Justice Black then sees fit to quote at length Senator Howard, who had introduced the 14th Amendment in the Senate:

> Such is the character of the privileges and immunities spoken of in the second section of the fourth article of the Constitution [the Senator had just read from the old opinion of Corfield v. Coryell, 6 Fed. Cas. 546 (No. 3,230) (E. D. Pa. 1825)]. **To these privileges and immunities**, whatever they may be - for they are not and cannot be fully defined in their entire extent and precise nature - to these **should be added the personal rights guarantied and secured by the first eight amendments of the Constitution; such as** the freedom of speech and of the press; the right of the people peaceably to assemble and petition the Government for a redress of grievances, a right appertaining [391 U.S. 145, 167] to each and all the people; **the right to keep and to bear arms**; ... Now, sir, **here is a mass of privileges, immunities, and rights**, some of them secured by the second section of the fourth article of the Constitution, which I have recited, **some by the first eight amendments** of the Constitution; and it is a fact well worthy of attention that the course of decision of our courts and the present settled doctrine is, that all these immunities, privileges, rights, thus guarantied by the Constitution or recognized by it, **are secured to the citizens solely as a citizen of the United States** and as a party in their courts. They do not operate in the slightest degree as a restraint or prohibition upon State legislation...
> "... **The great object of the first section of this amendment is, therefore, to restrain the power of the States and compel them at all times to respect these great fundamental guarantees.**" Cong. Globe, 39th Cong., 1st Sess., 2765-2766 (1866).[331]

If this quoted material was from a majority opinion in a case where the issue was the application of the Second Amendment to the states, I would end this book here – if I had ever started it – because you cannot find any more explicit statement than that of Senator Howard in explaining the effect of the 14th Amendment, that the Second Amendment is a privilege, immunity and right belonging to citizens, not to states, and it should be applied to restrict the states' ability to infringe this right. Score one concurring opinion for individual right. And I could not ask for a stronger statement or better reasoning to this effect.

So, where are we now? I have 18 opinions (13 majority, 1 concurring, 4 dissenting) for individual right, 1 (majority) for state power, 1 tie, and 3 abstentions.

24. *Burton v. Sills*[332]

This is basically a non-case. The Supreme Court refused to hear it. However, it can be argued to have some meaning.

New Jersey had passed a new gun licensing law. It did not ban any guns, but did require licensing to screen out people with serious criminal convictions and other problems. The plaintiffs claimed, in the state supreme court, that the law violated the Second Amendment. The New Jersey Supreme Court rejected this argument, saying that the Second Amendment is not an individual right. The plaintiffs filed an appeal (not a request for a writ of certiorari) to the United States Supreme Court. The Supreme Court rejected the appeal saying: "The motion to dismiss is granted and the appeal is dismissed for want of a substantial federal question."

While a refusal to grant a writ of certiorari does not mean approval of anything that has occurred below in a case, the dismissal of an appeal does have some meaning:

> Summary affirmances and dismissals for want of a substantial federal question without doubt reject the specific challenges presented in the statement of jurisdiction and do leave undisturbed the judgment appealed from. They do prevent lower courts from coming to opposite conclusions on the precise issues presented and necessarily decided by those actions... Summary actions, however, ... should not be

understood as breaking new ground but as applying principles established by prior decisions to the particular facts involved.[333]

Therefore, a lower court would be precluded from holding that the particular New Jersey statute in question violated the Second Amendment, but not necessarily that the reasoning in the case was correct. It does not amount to an approval of the holding in the state court that the Second Amendment is not an individual right. It could be that the Supreme Court decided not to hear the appeal because it was not ready to apply the Second Amendment to the states. There are any number of other reasons that the Supreme Court decided not to hear the case. Perhaps the Supreme Court decided that the particular statute did not infringe on the right enough to cause it to violate the Second Amendment. No one knows. Since we can only guess at what the Court had in mind, and the Court did not say anything at all to guide us, I count this as another abstention.

25. *Laird v. Tatum*[334]

This was a case involving the military spying on civilians in this country. While the majority held that the case could not be brought because the plaintiffs (the civilians being spied on) could not show any damages, past or future, Justice Douglas, joined by Chief Justice Warren, vigorously dissented.

While meant to show that the militia had no power to spy on civilians, the following quote from the dissent is interesting for another reason:

> The start of the problem is the constitutional distinction between the "militia" and the Armed Forces. By Art. I, 8, of the Constitution the militia is specifically confined to precise duties: "to execute the Laws of the Union, suppress Insurrections and repel Invasions."
> This obviously means that the "militia" cannot be sent overseas to fight wars. It is purely a domestic arm of the governors of the several States, save as it may be called under Art. I, 8, of the Constitution into the federal service.[335]

Jack Reynolds, J. D.

Does anybody besides me remember the National Guard being sent overseas to fight wars? If this Supreme Court Justice's reading of the Constitution is correct, then unless there has been another amendment authorizing the sending of the militia overseas to fight wars, which there has not been, the National Guard, since it has been sent overseas to fight wars, cannot be the militia spoken of in the Constitution. A mere statute could not override the Constitution. And any argument that what happened was that the federal government nationalized the National Guard and then sent it overseas (therefore it could still be the militia until nationalized) is disingenuous. That would allow legal sophistry to make an end run around a Constitutional prohibition.

Then Justice Douglas quoted a law review article written by then Chief Justice Warren about the Bill of Rights safeguarding the people from possible military dominance:

> As Chief Justice Warren has observed, the safeguards in the main body of the Constitution did not satisfy the people on their fear and concern of military dominance:

> "They were reluctant to ratify the Constitution without further assurances, and thus we find in the Bill of Rights Amendments 2 and 3, specifically authorizing a decentralized militia, guaranteeing the right of the people to keep and bear arms, and prohibiting the quartering of troops in any house in time of peace without the consent of the owner. Other Amendments guarantee the right of the people to assemble, to be secure in their homes against unreasonable searches and seizures, and in criminal cases to be accorded a speedy and public trial by an impartial jury after indictment in the district and state wherein the crime was committed. The only exceptions made to these civilian trial procedures are for cases arising in the land and naval forces. Although there is undoubtedly room for argument based on the frequently conflicting sources of history, it is not unreasonable to believe that

our Founders' determination to guarantee the preeminence of civil over military power was an important element that prompted adoption of the Constitutional Amendments we call the Bill of Rights." 336

This is another listing of the Second Amendment provision with a host of other individual rights. In the next case we will see that Justice Douglas does not necessarily believe that it is an individual right, or if it is, it should be "watered-down". Even so, this case, due to its exposing the National Guard as not being the militia, and its coextensive treatment of the Second Amendment as an individual right, should be scored in the individual right category.

26. *Adams v. Williams*[337]

The question in this case involved the Fourth Amendment's protection of the people's right to be free of unreasonable searches and seizures. In this particular case, a police officer, acting on a tip, stopped a motorist for questioning, and then grabbed a revolver hidden in the driver's waistband. The majority upheld the police officer's actions as a reasonable action to protect his safety under the case of *Terry v. Ohio*.[338] Justice Douglas, joined by then Chief Justice Marshall, filed a vigorous dissent, claiming that the search did violate the defendant's Fourth Amendment rights. In doing so, in a statement that is pure dicta, because it is not even reasoning of why the Fourth Amendment applies or was violated, but is merely stating an opinion of the Second Amendment totally unrelated to the issue in the case, Justice Douglas decried the Second Amendment as allowing people to carry guns:

> The police problem is an acute one not because of the Fourth Amendment, but because of the ease with which anyone can acquire a pistol. A powerful lobby dins into the ears of our citizenry that these gun purchases are constitutional rights protected by the Second Amendment, which reads, "A well regulated Militia, being necessary to the security of a free State, the right of the people to keep and bear Arms, shall not be infringed."

There is under our decisions no reason why stiff state laws governing the purchase and possession of pistols may not be enacted. There is no reason why pistols may not be barred from anyone with a police record. There is no reason why a State may not require a purchaser of a pistol to pass a psychiatric test. There is no reason why all pistols should not be barred to everyone except the police.

* * * *

Critics say that proposals like this water down the Second Amendment. Our decisions belie that argument, for the Second Amendment, as noted, was designed to keep alive the militia. But if watering-down is the mood of the day, I would prefer to water down the Second rather than the Fourth Amendment. I share with Judge Friendly a concern that the easy extension of Terry v. Ohio, 392 U.S. 1 , to "possessory offenses" is a serious intrusion on Fourth Amendment safeguards. "If it is to be extended to the latter at all, this should be only where observation by the officer himself or well authenticated information shows 'that criminal activity may be afoot.'" 436 F.2d, at 39, quoting Terry v. Ohio, supra, at 30.[339]

Now some might try to say that there is still room for an individual right here, only "watered-down". I disagree. While that language is there, the earlier language stating that there is no reason that pistols could not be barred from everyone except the police is just too strong for me to accept it even as a watered-down individual right. Even so, there are a few things to note about this opinion, beyond the fact that it is pure dicta.

First, there is no background analysis to support this statement. He merely takes some words from *Miller* out of context. There is no historical analysis, as in Justice Black's dissents and concurring opinion.

Second, I have a real hard time with the logic. Now remember that I am basically a libertarian. As such, I feel strongly that **all** individual rights, including the right against unreasonable searches and seizures, should be strongly protected. I certainly do not want to personally be subjected to any unreasonable searches, and I do not think that the police should be able to just stop people at will, for no reason at all, and search them. However, Justice Douglas's opinion would lead to the ludicrous result of criminals being allowed to carry guns, because once a stop is made, under probable cause, the police still would not be able to search the individual's person, while law-abiding citizens would be prohibited from having pistols, and because they are law-abiding, would probably comply with that law. So, Justice Douglas would deny law-abiding citizens a constitutional right, while protecting criminals' ability to exercise the same right. Amazing logic.

Finally, it should be noted that, unlike Justice Black's dissent concerning the history and application of the 14th Amendment, or that of Justice Harlan, Justice Douglas's dissenting language concerning the Second Amendment has never been quoted in another opinion. Again, to become well received and possibly become the law at a later time, the dissenting opinion has to be well written and well reasoned. Justice Douglas's opinion is neither.

Given all of that, it is still an opinion in favor of the gun control advocates, so I will count it as in favor of the states' power position. The score is now 19 opinions (13 majority, 1 concurring, 5 dissenting) for individual right, 2 (1 majority, 1 dissenting) for state power, 1 tie, and 4 abstentions.

27. Roe v. Wade[340]

That's right. The abortion case. What in the world could abortion have to do with the Second Amendment?

Well, according to the Supreme Court, whether you agree or not, the issue of abortion involves a Constitutional right, applied to the states through the 14th Amendment. Justice Stewart, in a concurring opinion quoted the language from Justice Harlan's dissent in *Poe v. Ullman*,[341] which calls the right to keep and bear arms a "liberty". As predicted earlier, Justice Stewart left out the cites to the economic rights cases, but left in the reference to the Second Amendment. Since this is a quote of language that we have already considered, I will not go into more detail, but just say that this too indicates an individual right.

28. Moore v. East Cleveland[342]

Jack Reynolds, J. D.

This case involved a zoning law that prohibited extended families from living together. In holding that the law was unconstitutional, Justice Powell, writing a plurality opinion, again quoted Justice Harlan's dissent in *Poe v. Ullman*. In a dissent, Justice White also quoted the same language, which referred to the Second Amendment. So this case counts as two opinions for an individual right; 1 plurality and 1 dissenting. Again, the justices left out the cites to the economic rights cases, but left in the reference to the Second Amendment.

It should be noted, in all fairness, that either Justice Powell did not realize what he was saying in his opinion, or he later changed his mind after he retired from the bench. In 1988 he gave a speech to the American Bar Association where he said that the Second Amendment should not be construed to guarantee a right to own handguns,[343] and in 1993 he suggested in a television interview that the Constitution should not be read as guaranteeing a right to own a sporting gun.[344] But, David Kopel has pointed out that Justice Powell's comments in this television interview show that he was not sure of what case held that the Second Amendment involved the militia, and was not sure what it said (saying: "This court decided a case that I haven't seen decided, I am not a hundred percent sure, …). He also was completely wrong on his history when he asserted that "hand guns certainly were not even dreamed of in the sense that they now exist at the time the second amendment was adopted."[345] Not that movies are always accurate historically (in fact, **NEVER** trust Hollywood), but anyone who has seen the movie Patriot knows that handguns existed during the Revolutionary War, well before the Second Amendment. In truth, as we have seen, some of the early militia statutes, prior to the Second Amendment, required horsemen to provide themselves with pistols. Justice Powell was simply wrong on this point.

The score now: 22 opinions (13 majority, 1 plurality, 2 concurring, 6 dissenting) for individual right, 2 (1 majority, 1 dissenting) for state power, 1 tie, and 4 abstentions.

29. *Lewis v. United States*[346]

Gun control advocates often cite this case in support of their position, but it is beyond me as to why. The case does not hold that the Second Amendment only protects states' powers over militias; it merely upholds a law prohibiting the possession of a firearm by a convicted felon. And guess what. Even the NRA would agree with that! While the Second Amendment is mentioned in a footnote, it is not in issue in the case.

In 1961 Lewis had been convicted of a felony in Florida, based on his guilty plea. However, he was not represented by an attorney in that case. Now this may have been in violation of a later Supreme Court case, *Gideon v. Wainwright*,[347] which the Supreme Court ruled had a retroactive effect to overturn all prior convictions where the right to an attorney had been improperly denied. Even so, Lewis never sought any legal action to overturn his conviction, or receive a pardon.

In 1968, Congress passed a law that prohibited certain categories of people, including convicted felons, from possessing firearms. In 1977, Lewis was arrested and charged with receiving and possessing a firearm, as a convicted felon. The question before the Supreme Court was, since his earlier conviction may have been invalid, should the statute be applied to him? The Supreme Court reasoned that the Congress had the power to extend the prohibition of firearms, not only to those who had totally valid convictions, but also to those who had been convicted, whose convictions might possibly be subject to being overturned, but which were not overturned. The Congress could conceive of these people as also being dangerous, and therefore a category of people who should be prohibited from having firearms. While conceivably it could have been brought up as an issue in this case, the Second Amendment was not brought up as an issue. The whole point was should Lewis have been provided counsel in the earlier case, and should the statute be applied to him.

In trying to find an intention of Congress to apply the statute to those such as Lewis, the Court quoted Senator Long, who introduced the bill in the Senate:

> So, under Title VII, every citizen could possess a gun until the commission of his first felony. Upon his conviction, however, Title VII would deny every assassin, murderer, thief and burglar of the right to possess a firearm in the future except where he has been pardoned by the President or a State Governor and had been expressedly authorized by his pardon to possess a firearm.[348]

Now, this sounds like Senator Long is calling the possession of firearms a right, albeit a right that can be taken away if a person commits a felony. And the fact that the Supreme Court quoted this passage would indicate that it recognizes the possession of firearms as a right.

The Court went on to say that "[t]he firearm regulatory scheme at issue here is consonant with the concept of equal protection embodied in the Due Process Clause of the Fifth Amendment if there is 'some rational basis for the statutory distinctions made ... or ... they have some relevance to the purpose for which the classification is made.'"[349] Now this compares the firearm regulation to a right guaranteed in the Fifth Amendment, indicating that the possession of a firearm would be a right. Additionally, the "rational basis" test referred to, as will be seen in more detail in Chapter 10 on the extent of the Second Amendment protection, is usually reserved for certain economic rights, which are rights, though not as preferred as some others, such as freedom of speech.

This interpretation is further supported by additional language from the case:

> Congress could rationally conclude that any felony conviction, even an allegedly invalid one, is a sufficient basis on which to prohibit the possession of a firearm... This Court has recognized repeatedly that a legislature constitutionally may prohibit a convicted felon from engaging in activities far more fundamental than the possession of a fire arm. See Richardson v. Ramirez, 418 U.S. 24 (1974)(disenfranchisement); De Veau v. Braisted, 363 U.S. 144 (1960)(proscription against holding office in a waterfront labor organization); Hawker v. New York, 170 U.S. 189(1898)(prohibition against the practice of medicine).

* * * *

Congress' judgment that a convicted felon, even one whose conviction was allegedly uncounseled, is among the class of person who should be disabled from dealing in or possessing firearms because of potential dangerousness is rational.³⁵⁰

The use of the word "rational" is, again, part of the "rational basis" test. Additionally, the Court has compared the possession of firearms to more "fundamental" rights, implying that the possession of firearms may be a right, though not as fundamental as voting, etc.

Finally, footnote 8 to the opinion, the portion most quoted by gun control advocates, states the following:

> These legislative restrictions on the use of firearms are neither based upon constitutionally suspect criteria, nor do they trench upon any constitutionally protected liberties. See United States v. Miller, 307 U.S. 174, 178 (1939)(the Second Amendment guarantees no right to keep and bear a firearm that does not have "some reasonable relationship to the preservation or efficiency of a well regulated militia"); United States v. Three Winchester 30-30 Caliber Lever Action Carbines, 504 F.2d 1288, 1290, n.5 (CA7 1974); United States v. Johnson, 497 F.2d 548 (CA4 1974); Cody v. United States, 460 F.2d 34 (CA8), cert. Denied, 409 U.S. 1010 (1972)(the latter three cases holding, respectively, that 1202 (a)(1), 922 (g) and 922 (a)(6) do not violate the Second Amendment).³⁵¹

This does not say that no conceivable restrictions would trench upon any constitutionally protected liberties, only that the ones at issue do not. In other words, the Second Amendment is not absolute, convicted felons can be prohibited from possessing firearms without running afoul of the Second Amendment. The mere fact that the statement is phrased the way it is indicates to me that there is some right, but this statute does not infringe on it. If there was no right, or if the Second Amendment only guaranteed state power over the militia, why did the Court discuss trenching on liberties? Why not just say, there is no right, so the Second Amendment does not apply?

What about the cases relied on in this quote? Do they seem to hold for an individual right or a state power? We already know what *Miller* says, and that it could be read either way. The *Three Winchester* case merely says that a convicted felon can be barred from possessing firearms. *Johnson* does assert a "collective right" theory of the Second Amendment, so that would be in favor of a states' power argument. This does not mean that the Supreme Court was necessarily approving of that assertion, however. It could have just been relying on the holding that a convicted felon could be barred from possessing a firearm. *Cody* merely says that the statute in play does not violate the Second Amendment, citing *Miller* as its authority:

> Since United States v. Miller, ... it has been settled that the Second Amendment is not an absolute bar to congressional regulation of the use or possession of firearms. The Second Amendment's guarantee extends only to use or possession which "has some reasonable relationship to the preservation or efficiency of a well regulated militia." ... We find no evidence that the prohibition of 922(a)(6) obstructs the maintenance of a well regulated militia.[352]

This goes no farther than *Miller* in declaring whether the Second Amendment is an individual right (albeit restricted to weapons reasonably related to the preservation or efficiency of a well regulated militia), or a state power over the militia.

So of the cases cited by the Supreme Court in *Lewis*, only one of them supports a state power position, and it is not clear that the Supreme Court is approving of that position. While there is plenty in this case that can be read as supporting a lesser individual right under the Second Amendment, that can be regulated under the "rational basis" test, just like *Miller*, which it relies on, *Lewis* can be read the other way. Therefore, I count this case as another tie. It is also worth noting that while two of the justices joining in this majority opinion are still on the Supreme Court today (Justice Stevens and Chief Justice Rehnquist), both have written opinions in subsequent cases which, as we will see, imply the existence of an individual right.

30. *United States v. Verdugo-Urquidez*[353]

This case involved American drug agents' warrantless search of a Mexican's home in Mexico. If this had been done in the United States, it clearly would have been in violation of the Fourth Amendment. However, since it was done to a Mexican citizen in

A People Armed and Free

Mexico, the question was, does the Fourth Amendment apply? The Court said no.

In his majority opinion, Chief Justice Rehnquist wrote about a narrow definition of the phrase "the people":

The Fourth Amendment provides:

"The right of the people to be secure in their persons, houses, papers, and effects, against unreasonable searches and seizures, shall not be violated, and no Warrants shall issue, but upon probable cause, supported by Oath or affirmation, and particularly describing the place to be searched, and the persons or things to be seized."

That text, by contrast with the Fifth and Sixth Amendments, extends its reach only to "the people." Contrary to the suggestion of amici curiae that the Framers used this phrase "simply to avoid [an] awkward rhetorical redundancy," Brief for American Civil Liberties Union et al. as Amici Curiae 12, n. 4, **"the people" seems to have been a term of art employed in select parts of the Constitution.** The Preamble declares that the Constitution is ordained and established by "the people of the United States." **The Second Amendment protects "the right of the people to keep and bear Arms,"** and the Ninth and Tenth Amendments provide that certain rights and powers are retained by and reserved to "the people." See also U.S. Const., Amdt. 1 ("Congress shall make no law ... abridging ... the right of the people peaceably to assemble") (emphasis added); Art. I, 2, cl. 1 ("The House of Representatives shall be composed of Members chosen every second Year by the people of the several States") (emphasis added). While this textual exegesis is by no means conclusive, it suggests that **"the people" protected by** the Fourth Amendment, and by the First and **Second Amendments**, and to whom rights and powers are reserved in the Ninth and Tenth Amendments, **refers to a class of persons who are part of a national**

> community or who have otherwise developed sufficient connection with this country to be considered part of that community.[354]

This clearly conceives of the Second Amendment, along with the other portions of the Bill of Rights, as expounding rights belonging to the people, not as expressing a reservation of a power to the states. "The people", in each of these amendments means the people, not the states.

Justice Brennan filed a dissent in which he accepted the concept that "the people" means the people, at least as it relates to the Fourth Amendment, only he would broaden the definition of "the people" to include those that become involved in our legal justice system, which these defendants had. While he never mentions the Second Amendment, so it is not clear that he would also accept this definition of the people in that case, he does not dispute the application made by the majority to the other amendments, so his opinion is not inconsistent with the implication derived from the majority opinion.

Finally, a rather interesting side note. The Court of Appeals below had ruled that the Fourth Amendment did apply. The dissenting opinion at the Court of Appeals had made a point similar to that of the majority of the Supreme Court quoted above. When the government filed its brief with the Supreme Court, it quoted the Court of Appeals dissent, but used ellipses[355] in place of that dissent's reference to the Second Amendment.[356] Therefore, if the Supreme Court had wanted to discount the possibility that the Second Amendment should have the same definition of "the people" applied to it as is applied to the other amendments, it had a good opportunity to do so. But it did not. It seems to have purposefully reinserted the reference to the Second Amendment, which indicates that the majority of the Supreme Court at the time did consider "the people" to mean the people. So, score another majority opinion for an individual right.

31. Planned Parenthood of Southeastern Pennsylvania v. Casey[357]

This case, as the name implies, involves abortion restrictions. Justice Sandra Day O'Connor wrote an opinion, which once again quoted Justice Harlan's language from *Poe v. Ullman*[358]. As predicted earlier, Justice O'Connor left out the cites to the economic rights cases, but left in the reference to the Second Amendment. While the opinions in this case were fractured, with different judges agreeing with different parts of each other's opinions, so that it takes some work to figure out just what is a majority opinion on any given point, the portion of Justice O'Connor's' opinion that quoted the Harlan language, was joined in by four other judges, so on the point of law that this quote was intended for, it was the majority opinion. Score another majority opinion for an individual right.

32. Albright v. Oliver[359]

Albright involved a case of alleged malicious prosecution. The issue was whether or not this alleged false prosecution violated the individual's rights under the 14th Amendment. The majority said it did not, asserting that the claim would be better presented as a violation of the Fourth Amendment. In any event, Justice Stevens dissented, and was joined by Justice Blackman, and quoted the same language from Justice Harlan about the 14th Amendment in *Poe v. Ullman*, again implying that the Second Amendment involves a liberty. And again, Justice Stevens left out the cites to the economic rights cases, but left in the reference to the Second Amendment. Score another dissenting opinion for an individual right.

33. Printz v. United States[360]

This case involves the Brady Act, which itself involves the Second Amendment, but this case did not, at least not according to the majority. A portion of the Brady Act required local law enforcement officers to do the background check on prospective purchasers of firearms. Since this is a federal law, the question was raised: Can the federal government require local officials to do its work for it? The majority said no, and declared that portion of the Brady Act unconstitutional under the Tenth Amendment (which reserves powers to the states and people).

Justice Thomas joined in this majority opinion (which did not mention the Second Amendment), but also wrote a separate concurring opinion (which did). In this concurring opinion, Justice Thomas brought up two additional reasons for declaring the Brady Act (at least the provisions in issue) unconstitutional. He first asserted that it applied to purely intrastate sales of firearms, which the Congress does not have power to regulate under the interstate commerce clause.[361] The second reason given was that it **might** (he did not say that it did) violate the Second Amendment:

> Even if we construe Congress' authority to regulate interstate commerce to encompass those intrastate transactions that "substantially affect" interstate commerce, I question whether Congress can regulate the particular transactions at issue here. **The Constitution, in addition to delegating certain enumerated powers to Congress, places whole areas outside the reach of Congress' regulatory authority.** The First Amendment, for example, is fittingly celebrated for preventing Congress from "prohibiting the free exercise" of religion or "abridging the freedom of speech." **The Second Amendment similarly appears to contain an express limitation on the government's authority. That Amendment provides: "[a] well regulated Militia, being necessary to the security of a free State, the right of the people to keep and bear arms, shall not be infringed."** This Court has not had recent occasion to consider the nature of the substantive right safeguarded by the Second Amendment. 1 If, however, the Second Amendment is read to confer a personal right to "keep and bear arms," a colorable argument exists that the Federal Government's regulatory scheme, at least as it pertains to the purely intrastate sale or possession of firearms, runs afoul of that Amendment's protections. 2 As the parties did not raise this argument, however, we need not consider it here. Perhaps, at some future date, this Court will have the opportunity to determine whether Justice Story was correct when he wrote that the right to bear arms "has justly been considered, as the palladium of the liberties of a republic." 3 J. Story, Commentaries §1890, p. 746 (1833).[362]

Then, in the two footnotes shown in the quote, Justice Thomas went on to say:

> 1. Our most recent treatment of the Second Amendment occurred in *United States v. Miller*, 307 U.S. 174 (1939), in which we reversed the District

> Court's invalidation of the National Firearms Act, enacted in 1934. In Miller, we determined that the Second Amendment did not guarantee a citizen's right to possess a sawed off shotgun because that weapon had not been shown to be "ordinary military equipment" that could "contribute to the common defense." Id. at 178. The Court did not, however, attempt to define, or otherwise construe, the substantive right protected by the Second Amendment.
>
> 2. Marshalling an impressive array of historical evidence, a growing body of scholarly commentary indicates that the "right to keep and bear arms" is, as the Amendment's text suggests, a personal right... Other scholars, however, argue that the Second Amendment does not secure a personal right to keep or to bear arms... Although somewhat overlooked in our jurisprudence, the Amendment has certainly engendered considerable academic, as well as public, debate.[363]

Justice Thomas clearly agrees with my interpretation of *Miller*, that it simply does not say what the Second Amendment entails. He is also clearly leaning toward the individual right interpretation, while not saying that that is what he would hold. Incidentally, it would be considered inappropriate for him to say how he would hold without the issue being before him. Finally, he is almost inviting the right case (not one like *Miller*, where one side was a no show) to be brought before the Court so they can make a ruling on this issue. When such a case is heard by the Supreme Court, if Justice Thomas is still on the bench, my money will be on him voting for an individual right. Score another concurring opinion for individual right.

34. Muscarello v. United States[364]

A federal law requires a mandatory five year sentence for anyone who "carries a firearm" while committing a drug trafficking crime. The question in this case involves the definition of "carries". Does it include, say, having a firearm in the trunk of your car while you are sitting in the car and committing the crime? In a 5-4 decision, the majority of the Supreme Court said it does.

Jack Reynolds, J. D.

In a rather unusual combination of judges in dissent (Chief Justice Rehnquist and Justice Scalia from the conservative side, and Justice Ginsburg, who wrote the opinion, and Justice Souter from the liberal side), it was pointed out that there is more than one definition of carry:

> On definitions, "carry" in legal formulations could mean, inter alia [among other things], transport, possess, have in stock, prolong (carry over), be infectious, or wear or bear on one's person... Surely a most familiar meaning is, as the Constitution's Second Amendment ("keep and bear Arms") ... and Black's Law Dictionary, at 214, indicate: "wear, bear, or carry ... upon the person or in the clothing or in a pocket, for the purpose ... of being armed and ready for offensive or defensive action in a case of conflict with another person."[365]

This shows that carry can mean bear, as used in the Second Amendment, therefore, bear, as used in the Second Amendment, can mean carry, which can be done by an individual. Therefore, the gun control advocates' argument that "bear" can only mean use by a militia, is clearly wrong. While this opinion does not say that the word bear has to apply to an individual, clearly it says that it can apply to an individual. Therefore, I count this dissenting opinion in the individual right category.

35. *Spencer v. Kemna*[366]

Spencer had been in prison, but was released on parole. While out on parole, he was again arrested and charged with, but not convicted of, rape. This mere charge was sufficient to cause his parole to be revoked. He appealed this revocation of his parole, but before it could be resolved, the time on his original sentence ran out and he was released from prison as having served his time. The Supreme Court at that point held that the case was moot, that is to say, that it was already over, there was nothing the Supreme Court could do at that point.

Justice Stevens dissented, arguing that the implied finding, from the revocation of his parole, that he had committed a rape, could have consequences besides prison: "An official determination that a person has committed a crime may cause two different kinds of injury. It may result in tangible harms such as imprisonment, **loss of the right** to vote or **to bear arms**, and the risk of greater punishment if another crime is committed."[367] Now common sense will tell you that an individual can only lose a right if he had it to begin with. In order to lose a right to bear arms, Spencer would have had to have the right to bear arms. And since we are talking about an individual, totally out of the context of a state militia, this must be indicating an individual right. Now he could be talking about a state's constitution giving an individual the right to bear arms, but given that this is a judge on the United States Supreme Court, it is more likely that he is talking about the Second Amendment. Even if talking about states' constitutions, the gun control advocates try to argue that those do not guarantee individual rights either, so we are still talking about an individual right existing at some level. Score another dissenting opinion for individual right.

This is the last case to have been decided by the U.S. Supreme Court that mentions the Second Amendment. The final score? 28 opinions (15 majority, 1 plurality, 3 concurring, 9 dissenting) for individual right, 2 (1 majority, 1 dissenting) for state power, 2 ties, and 4 abstentions. Now while it is fun to keep score as we have done, this really does not mean much in and of itself (although it is kind of one sided, isn't it?); the real test is how strong the comments are in favor of the particular position, and how well reasoned the opinions are. Remember that none of these cases, except *Miller,* which was a tie, had the meaning of the Second Amendment as an issue. Some cases are stronger and better reasoned than others. Some amount to little more than passing comments. But, in my humble opinion, the better-reasoned language, and the stronger assertions, lie with the individual right position. Bottom line is, we do not have a ruling on this issue from the only Court that can give a definitive ruling. But it looks like the Supreme Court should/will rule that the Second Amendment guarantees an individual right.

But if the Supreme Court has not ruled on this issue, what have the lower courts done, and what have they based their opinions on?

B.   *Lower Courts' (Courts of Appeals and District Courts) Opinions*

We should note that all of the lower court cases to be discussed arose after *Miller.* There are a couple of reasons for this. First, the federal government had no laws restricting the possession of firearms prior to the 1934 act involved in *Miller*. Since lower federal courts usually do not get involved in state law cases, the contests involving state laws restricting gun ownership/possession went through the state court system. Therefore, the cases just did not come up in lower federal courts before then. Second, even if there are any lower federal court opinions out there before *Miller*, we really need to concentrate on those after, because the lower courts are required to apply the law as it is decided by the Supreme Court. Therefore, any lower court decision before *Miller* could be said to have been overruled or changed by *Miller*.

In case you are tired after the litany of Supreme Court cases, take heart. We will only look at 26 lower court cases, and the analysis of most of them will be much shorter. First, while important for any real analysis the lower court opinions may have, and while certainly important to the individuals involved in them, and if courts of appeals decisions they may be binding authority in that circuit, none of them can determine the law for the nation as a whole. Second, as you will see, most of them have little to no analysis at all, and the analysis that has been done has mostly already been addressed earlier in this book. So let's see what the lower courts have to say.

1. *United States v. Tot*[368]

A portion of the Federal Firearms act made it illegal for any person who had been convicted of a crime of violence (defined as murder, manslaughter, rape, mayhem, kidnapping, burglary, housebreaking; assault with intent to kill, commit rape, or rob; assault with a dangerous weapon, or assault with intent to commit any offense punishable by imprisonment for more than one year) to receive any firearm. The defendant in this case had admittedly been convicted of a crime of violence as defined, and was arrested at home (on a warrant charging theft of cigarettes from an interstate shipment) in possession of a Colt .32 caliber pistol, which of course, was in violation of the statute.

The defendant asserted that the statute violated his rights under the Second Amendment. The court disagreed, but went a lot further than it needed to in order to reach its result. Purporting to base its reasoning on the history of the Second Amendment, but not going into any detail at all, just citing a few sources, the court said the following:

> It is abundantly clear both from the discussions of this amendment contemporaneous with its proposal and adoption and those of learned writers since that this amendment, unlike those providing for protection of free speech and freedom of religion, was not adopted with individual rights in mind, but as a protection for the States in the maintenance of their militia organizations against possible encroachments by the federal power.[369]

This clearly supports the states' power position. But there is no analysis of how the court got there, just a bald statement that history shows that this was the purpose. One wonders if the court reviewed all of the history, or just selected portions of it.

The court went on to cite *Miller* as authority for holding that the weapon in this case could be barred. Then it held that the Second Amendment does not protect an absolute right:

> Weapon bearing was never treated as anything like an absolute right by the common law. It was regulated by statute as to time and place as far back as the Statute of Northampton in 1328 and on many occasions since. The decisions under the State Constitutions show the upholding of regulations prohibiting the carrying of concealed weapons, prohibiting persons from going armed in certain public places and other restrictions, in the nature of police regulations, but which do not go so far as substantially to interfere with the public interest protected by the constitutional mandates. The Federal statute here involved is one of that general type... [The classification made by the statute] is entirely reasonable and does not infringe upon the preservation of the well regulated militia protected by the Second Amendment.[370]

Most gun rights advocates could agree with most of that paragraph (though not the assertion that the Second Amendment protects the militia). Most gun rights advocates do not believe that the right protected is an absolute right, and are very comfortable with the concept of barring convicted violent felons from possessing guns. They just disagree with the gun control advocates as to how far the government can go in regulating the possession of guns. Of course, the quoted paragraph totally ignores the fact that in the United States we always considered our right to have guns to be broader and stronger than the English did. One might argue that by talking about the Second Amendment not being an absolute right implies that it must be some kind of right. But when read as a whole, this opinion cannot be read to imply this. It is clearly in the states' power camp, and however wrong I may believe its holding and logic is, it is the law in the Third Circuit, which covers Pennsylvania, Delaware, New Jersey, and the Virgin Islands. If you live in those states, you have no individual right to own or possess a firearm, according to your federal court of appeals. Wouldn't the people who drafted the Pennsylvania Minority report be surprised that this is the result in their state?

2. *Cases v. United States*[371]

This case (no kidding, *Cases* is the name of the case) came from Puerto Rico. The same statute was at issue here. The defendant here had been convicted in 1922 of aggravated assault and battery. In 1941, he acquired ten rounds of ammunition and a .38 caliber Colt, and went to a club and shot a person. To show that judges are not without a sense of humor, let's read the court's description of the event:

> [E]quipped with a .38 caliber Colt type revolver of Spanish make which, when some one turned out the lights, he used, apparently not wholly without effect, upon another patron of the place who in some way seems to have incurred his displeasure.
> * * * *
>
> He not only brought the arm and ammunition with him to the club but he also pursued the victim of his spleen through a window and around the grounds before bringing him to earth with a well directed shot.[372]

This guy was probably guilty of more than just illegally possessing a firearm.

The court's logic in upholding the statute is interesting. First, it seems to acknowledge that the Second Amendment does protect an individual right: "The Federal Firearms Act undoubtedly curtails to some extent **the right of individuals** to keep and bear arms but it does not follow from this as a necessary consequence that it is bad under the Second Amendment."[373] The court goes on to say that the right to keep and bear arms was not conferred on the people by the Second Amendment. This, we know, is true; it was a pre-existing right that the Second Amendment only guarantees. The court then goes into a discussion of *Miller*, which was probably not necessary to the case, but which is interesting given the different interpretations of *Miller*:

> Apparently, then, under the Second Amendment, the federal government can limit the keeping and bearing of arms by a single individual as well as by a group of individuals, but **it cannot prohibit the possession or use of any weapon which has any reasonable relationship to the preservation or efficiency of a well regulated militia**. However, we do not feel that the Supreme Court in this case was attempting to formulate a general rule applicable to all cases. The rule which it laid down was adequate to dispose of the case before it and that we think was as far as the Supreme Court intended to go. At any rate the rule of the Miller case, if intended to be comprehensive and complete would seem to be already outdated, in spite of the fact that it was formulated only three and a half years ago, because of the well known fact that in the so called 'Commando Units' some sort of military use seems to have been found for almost any modern lethal weapon. In view of this, if the rule of the Miller case is general and complete, the result would follow that, under present day conditions, the federal government would be empowered only to regulate the possession or use of weapons such as a flintlock musket or a matchlock harquebus. But to hold that the Second Amendment limits the federal government to regulations concerning only weapons which can be

classed as antiques or curiosities,— almost any other might bear some reasonable relationship to the preservation or efficiency of a well regulated militia unit of the present day,— is in effect to hold that the limitation of the Second Amendment is absolute. Another objection to the rule of the Miller case as a full and general statement is **that according to it Congress would be prevented by the Second Amendment from regulating the possession or use by private persons not present or prospective members of any military unit, of distinctly military arms, such as machine guns, trench mortars, anti-tank or anti-aircraft guns,** even though under the circumstances surrounding such possession or use it would be inconceivable that a private person could have any legitimate reason for having such a weapon. **It seems to us unlikely that the framers of the Amendment intended any such result.** Considering the many variable factors bearing upon the question **it seems to us impossible to formulate any general test by which to determine the limits imposed by the Second Amendment but that each case under it, like cases under the due process clause, must be decided on its own facts and the line between what is and what is not a valid federal restriction pricked out by decided cases falling on one side or the other of the line.**[374]

The court clearly recognized the points put forth by gun rights advocates, that under *Miller* virtually any modern weapon could be protected by the Second Amendment, because any such weapon could have a military use. It would also protect heavier weapons. Then the court basically says that it does not think that this is what the Framers intended, without any cite to authority to support this. Then the court says that it has no general rule to follow, but that each case must be decided on its own merits, on a case-by-case basis, which will result in a rule eventually being formulated. All of this is only consistent with an individual right in the First Circuit (consisting of Maine, Massachusetts, New Hampshire, Rhode Island and Puerto Rico), at least at the time of this opinion. There is one other opinion from the First Circuit that we will look at later.

3. *United States v. Gross*[375]

This is a district court case from Indiana, decided in 1970. The defendant was engaged in the business of selling firearms, but was not licensed as required in a 1968 federal statute. In addressing the defendant's assertion that the statute violated the Second Amendment, the court cited *Miller*, then said: "In the present case, the defendant has not shown that the licensing of dealers in firearms in any way destroys, or impairs the efficiency of, a well regulated militia."[376] Like *Miller*, which the court relies on, this statement does not indicate whether the Second Amendment protects an individual right or the states' power over the militia. But it does approve a regulation of firearms that some gun rights advocates believe does violate individual rights.

4. *United States v. Synnes*[377]

This is another case of a convicted felon possessing a gun. Here the first argument addressed was whether or not the gun in question had to actually be shown to have been involved in interstate commerce, and if not, was the statute therefore an unconstitutional attempt of Congress to extend its power under the interstate commerce clause of the Constitution. While not directly impacting the Second Amendment, since Justice Thomas of the Supreme Court brought this issue up in his concurring opinion in *Printz v. United States*[378], and since some of you might think that the federal government could not regulate purely intrastate (that is wholly within one state; no connection with any other state) possession of guns, or that the statute by mentioning interstate commerce would not even apply to the intrastate possession of guns, I thought I would include some of the court's analysis on this point. The bottom line is, the federal government can, and did, regulate wholly intrastate possession of guns:

> The Commerce Clause of the Constitution, Art. I, ' 8, cl. 3, combined with the Necessary and Proper Clause, Art. I, ' 8, cl. 18, gives to Congress the power to regulate both interstate commerce and any intrastate activity which '* * * exerts a substantial economic effect on interstate commerce * * *.'

> * * * *
>
> In determining whether the legislation in question is within the limits set out above, we examine: (1) whether Congress had a rational basis for finding that receipt or possession of a firearm by a convicted felon affects commerce, and (2) if it had such a basis, whether the means it selected to protect commerce are reasonable and appropriate.
>
> * * * *
>
> Having found a rational nexus between the regulated activity and interstate commerce, we cannot say that the proscriptions of ' 1202(a)(1) are unreasonable or inappropriate means for eliminating the evil perceived by Congress. Again, our viewpoint must be relative rather than absolute; the exercise of congressional power need not coincide with what we believe to be the optimum choice of available alternatives. It need only be reasonable and appropriate…
> It must be conceded that Congress' regulatory power under the Commerce Clause has been construed liberally, and expanded to meet the needs of our increasingly complex society.[379]

This shows that the interpretation of the interstate commerce clause is broad enough to allow the federal government to regulate wholly intrastate possession of firearms. Going on in this vein, the court then quotes Senator Long, who introduced the bill in the Senate: "It has been said that Congress lacks the power to outlaw mere possession of weapons… Without question, the Federal Government does have power to control possession of weapons where such possession could become a threat to interstate commerce…"[380] Then the court goes on to apply the test to this statute:

> It is clear that the basic concepts of equal protection apply to the federal government through the Due

> Process Clause of the Fifth Amendment. The safeguards of the equal protection doctrine vary in degree depending on the nature of the right being affected by the legislation. In our view, legislation restricting the possession of firearms ' ... will not be set aside if any state of facts reasonably may be conceived to justify it.' ...
> In so doing, **we decide only that the right to bear arms is not the type of fundamental right to which the 'compelling state interest' standard attaches.**
> Judged by these standards, we think that the attacks on the classifications of 'felons' and 'firearms' fall short. While meritorious arguments can be advanced justifying narrower classifications, we view these as policy considerations which do not alter the fact that the classifications chosen have a rational basis.[381]

This shows again that the interstate commerce clause can be used to regulate intrastate possession of firearms. And, while I agree with Justice Thomas's position as a matter of historic intent of our Founding Fathers, I must agree with the court of appeals that their statement is a better representation of what the law is on this point, even from the Supreme Court level, than Justice Thomas's. If Justice Thomas wants to change that law, then he will need to get the right case before the Supreme Court, and convince at least four other justices to agree with him.

As to the applicability of the statute itself to intrastate possession, the court said:

> Section 1202(a)(1) is also attacked on the basis that it creates a presumption that the particular possession is in or has an effect on interstate commerce, and that this presumption is unconstitutional...
> The fallacy in this argument is that it assumes that a connection between possession and interstate commerce is an element of a ' 1202(a)(1) offense. In the cases relied upon by the defendants, the presumption attacked provided the fact finder with a necessary element of the offense and could, at least

> theoretically, be overcome by the defendant. For example, in Tot v. United States, ... the defendant was charged with violating a statute which prohibited certain felons from receiving a firearm which had been transported in interstate commerce. The statutory presumption found wanting stated that possession of a firearm was prima facie evidence that the defendant had received the firearm after it had been transported in interstate commerce.
>
> However, under ' 1202(a)(1), as we have interpreted it, the fact that the possession was in or affecting commerce is not an element of the offense to be proven. It follows that the rationale of Tot and Leary is inapplicable.
>
> We have already upheld the congressional finding that, in general, possession of a firearm by felons affects interstate commerce. This being so, Congress may prohibit the particular intrastate possession '... even though in that instance the effect on interstate commerce is minimal or non-existent.'[382]

In other words, since a connection can be made between almost anything and interstate commerce, it does not have to be shown that the particular firearm involved was at some point itself in interstate commerce.

Moving on to the Second Amendment issue (again, the defendant claimed that the statute violated the Second Amendment), the court of appeals said:

The leading pronouncement of the Supreme Court in this area states:

> 'In the absence of any evidence tending to show that possession or use of ... (the weapon) at this time has some reasonable relationship to the preservation or efficiency of a well regulated militia, we cannot say that the Second Amendment guarantees the right to keep and bear such an instrument.'
> United States v. Miller, 307 U.S. 174, 178, 59 S.Ct. 816, 818, 83 L.Ed. 1206 (1939).

> ... We think it is also applicable here. Although ' 1202(a) is the broadest federal gun legislation to date, we see no conflict between it and the Second Amendment since there is no showing that prohibiting possession of firearms by felons obstructs the maintenance of a 'well regulated militia.'[383]

So, the Eighth Circuit, in this opinion, did not say whether or not the Second Amendment applies to an individual right or a state power, although it did say that it did not protect a fundamental right. One could argue that this means that if it is not a fundamental right, then some other right is implied, but it would also be just as reasonable to say that what the court was saying is that "we do not know what it is, but we know that it is not a fundamental right." There are other cases from the Eighth Circuit, so we will see how its case law plays out. Incidentally, the Eighth Circuit covers North Dakota, South Dakota, Minnesota, Nebraska, Iowa, Missouri, and Arkansas.

5. *Stevens v. United States*[384]

This is another case involving a convicted felon charged with the possession of a firearm. In addressing the constitutional issues, this is what the court said:

> We turn now to the consideration of whether Congress has the power to prohibit the possession of a firearm by a convicted felon. Since the Second Amendment right 'to keep and bear Arms' **applies only to the right of the State to maintain a militia and not to the individual's right to bear arms, there can be no serious claim to any express constitutional right of an individual to possess a firearm**. United States v. Miller, 307 U.S. 174, 178, 59 S.Ct. 816, 83 L.Ed. 1206. Stevens asserts, however, that Congress is without constitutional power to deny him this privilege. We hold that Congress has this authority under the commerce clause.[385]

Do you see the problem with interpreting *Miller*? The same language that gun rights advocates claim support a right to keep any military type weapon is probably the language that this court is using to say that there is no individual right. I happen to disagree with this court's interpretation of Miller, but I can see how they get their interpretation.

6. *United States v. Johnson*[386]

This case looks a lot like *Miller*. The defendant was charged with possessing a sawed-off shotgun that had not been registered to him. On the Second Amendment issue, the court merely quoted *Miller*, and affirmed the conviction. So no indication here of what the Fifth Circuit thinks about what the Second Amendment protects. However, we will see later that the Fifth Circuit strongly holds that an individual right exists. The Fifth Circuit covers Texas, Louisiana and Mississippi.

7. *United States v. Decker.*[387]

The federal law dealing with firearms dealers not only require them to be licensed, but require them to keep a mountain of paper work, that is records, concerning their firearms business, under the possibility of criminal prosecution if it is not done. The defendant here was convicted of failure to make appropriate entries and to properly maintain the records required. Addressing the defendant's claim that these record keeping requirements violate the Second Amendment, the court quoted *Miller*, then said:

> In our view, the record keeping requirements at issue here bear an even more tenuous relationship to the Second Amendment than did the statute involved in Miller. Thus, in light of the defendant's failure to present any evidence indicating a conflict between the requirements of " 922(m) and 923(g) and the maintenance of a well regulated militia, we decline to hold that the statute violates the Second Amendment.[388]

The court then affirmed the conviction. Again, no indication of which way the Eighth Circuit is going to go, individual right or state power.

8. *United States v. Kraase*[389]

In a very short opinion, the case presented was that of Mr. Kraase, who was charged with selling a firearm to an out of state person, without being properly licensed. On the claim that the statute violates the Second Amendment the court said:

> In my opinion, there is no merit in the contention that the defendant's second amendment rights are violated by the statute in question... Second amendment protection to Mr. Kraase might arise if proof were offered at the trial demonstrating that his possession of the weapon in question had a reasonable relationship to the maintenance of the "well-regulated Militia."[390]

The fact that a Second Amendment protection might arise if the weapon had a reasonable relationship to the militia indicates that there might be an individual right. It is not clear what it would take to show a reasonable relationship. Would it merely be a showing that this type of weapon is used in a military setting? Or would it require a showing that this specific weapon is used by the defendant in the National Guard? Or would it be something in between? We do not know.

9. *Cody v. United States*[391]

The federal law requires each buyer of a firearm to fill out and sign a statement that he meets the requirements of the law to be eligible to own a firearm, including a statement that he has not been convicted of a crime punishable by imprisonment for a term exceeding one year. Lying on this form is itself a crime. Well, Cody signed the form, saying that he had not been convicted, but in fact he had, back in 1964, for a felony punishable by up to five years imprisonment. There were two questions: Did this form requirement exceed the power of the interstate commerce clause? And did this requirement violate the Second Amendment?

First, the interstate commerce clause. "[T]he section regulates transactions with licensed dealers, whose general involvement with interstate commerce is ample to justify federal regulation of even intrastate sales."[392] See what I mean about the interstate commerce clause? It may not be right, but it is the law.

As to the Second Amendment issue:

> We find no merit in the contention that ' 922(a) (6) violates appellant's Second Amendment right to bear arms. Since United States v. Miller, 307 U.S. 174, 59 S.Ct. 816, 83 L.Ed. 1206 (1939), it has been settled that the Second Amendment is not an absolute bar to

congressional regulation of the use or possession of firearms. The Second Amendment's guarantee extends only to use or possession which "has some reasonable relationship to the preservation or efficiency of a well regulated militia." Id. at 178, 59 S.Ct. at 818... We find no evidence that the prohibition of ' 922(a) (6) obstructs the maintenance of a well regulated militia.[393]

This still is not clear where the Eighth Circuit stands on the issue of individual right vs. state power. One could argue that since this case does not involve a particular weapon, but an individual lying on a form, then this case is extending *Miller*, to a point where there now has to be some connection, not only of the weapon, but of the individual and/or the statute with the militia. But it still is not clear.

10. United States v. Day[394]

Under federal law, not only are convicted felons prohibited from possessing firearms, but if you are dishonorably discharged from the military, the same law also prohibits you from possessing a firearm. Mr. Day had been dishonorably discharged from the army in 1945. He was convicted in 1972 of possessing firearms.

Again, the court first looks at the interstate commerce issue:

> In Perez v. United States, 402 U.S. 146, 91 S.Ct. 1357, 28 L.Ed.2d 686 (1971), the Supreme Court analyzed anew the scope of Congressional power to regulate purely intrastate activities under the Commerce Clause. As the Court stated:
> "The Commerce Clause reaches, in the main, three categories of problems. First, the use of channels of interstate or foreign commerce which Congress deems are being misused, ... Second, protection of the instrumentalities of interstate commerce, ... Third, those activities affecting commerce." 402 U.S. at 150, 91 S.Ct. at 1359.
> The Perez Court reaffirmed, under the third category of Congressional power, that Congress can constitutionally regulate a class of activities if that class has an effect on interstate commerce.

> "Where the class of activities is regulated and that class is within the reach of federal power, the courts have no power 'to excise, as trivial, individual instances' of the class." The Supreme Court, it should be noted, repeatedly has upheld Congressional regulation of purely intrastate activity. As the Supreme Court wrote in the Heart of Atlanta case, supra: "If it is interstate commerce that feels the pinch, it does not matter how local the operation which applies the squeeze." 379 U.S. at 258, 85 S.Ct. at 358[395]

Does this leave any question that the federal government has the power to regulate intrastate possession of firearms? It only leaves the question of whether or not the Second Amendment recognizes a pre-existing right and prohibits the federal government from exercising that power in the area of arms.

As to the Second Amendment, here is all the court said: "As to the alleged right to bear arms, Day's claim is meritless. There is no absolute constitutional right of an individual to possess a firearm. United States v. Miller..."[396] Again, most gun rights advocates do not dispute this point. They do assert that there is some strong right though.

On the test to be applied to see if due process is violated, the court stated the following:

> In Katzenbach v. McClung, 379 U.S. 294, 303-304, 85 S.Ct. 377, 383, 13 L.Ed.2d 290 (1964), the Supreme Court set out the applicable standard under which the Congressional classification here presented must be tested:
> "[W]here we find that the legislators, in light of the facts and testimony before them, have a rational basis for finding a chosen regulatory scheme necessary to the protection of commerce, our investigation is at an end."[397]

Then to show that there is a rational basis, the court quoted Senator Long:

> "[T]his is a matter of saying that if he cannot be trusted to carry arms for Uncle Sam, he cannot be trusted to carry arms on the streets. This kind of person is part of the criminal element in many instances, the kind of person who does not know how to behave properly, and is a hazard to others when he possesses firearms."
> We hold that the finding by Congress that possession of guns by those dishonorably discharged from the armed services is hazardous was rational. We decline to overturn it.[398]

So again there is no indication from this court whether or not an individual right exists, only that there is no absolute right, and whatever the Second Amendment does, it is subject to the regulatory power of the interstate commerce clause, using the rational basis test.

11. United States v. Johnson[399]

Another convict in possession of a firearm. Most of this case dealt with whether or not Mr. Johnson's prior conviction, for forgery, was a felony or misdemeanor. When it got to the Second Amendment, here is what the court said:

> Johnson's argument that section 922(g) is an unconstitutional violation of his Second Amendment right to keep and bear arms is not new. See, e.g., United States v. Miller, 307 U.S. 174, 59 S.Ct. 816, 83 L.Ed. 1206 (1939). The courts have consistently held that **the Second Amendment only confers a collective right** of keeping and bearing arms which must bear a 'reasonable relationship to the preservation or efficiency of a well regulated militia.' 307 U.S. at 178, 59 S.Ct. at 818. Johnson presents no evidence that section 922(g) in any way affects the maintenance of a well regulated militia.[400]

Miller did not hold that the Second Amendment only confers a collective right, but it did hold that the arms had to have a reasonable relationship to the militia. In any event, this court's holding favors the state power interpretation, and no individual right. The Fourth Circuit includes Maryland, North Carolina, South Carolina, Virginia, and

A People Armed and Free

West Virginia. Now, wouldn't the Federal Farmer and Patrick Henry be surprised?

12. United States v. Swinton[401]

This is another case involving an unlicensed dealer in firearms. The problem in this case was the wording of the statute, which prohibited "any person, other than a licensed dealer, to engage in the business or dealing in firearms." Now, what does it mean to "engage in the business of dealing in firearms"? If you or I sell one of our guns to a friend or relative, would that be sufficient? The answer is no, but what if we have an extensive collection and we sell and buy them like trading cards or art pieces? Well, that may depend on where we get our livelihood. Is it from the selling and trading of the firearms, or is it from some other occupation and the firearms stuff is just a hobby? Do you see the potential problem with trying to define this?

The only issue in this case was whether or not the defendant was engaged in the business of dealing in firearms. The Second Amendment was never raised as an issue in the case. Yet, totally gratuitously, without even relating it to any logic pertaining to the case, the court said the following: "These holdings, when considered within the broad intent of the Act, highlight the established principle that there is no absolute constitutional right of an individual to possess a firearm."[402] While this is undoubtedly a true statement, because even the NRA does not believe that the right is absolute, it still does not say whether there is an individual right at all, or if the Second Amendment protects a state power. The concern that gun rights advocates have, and the probable reason that the gun control advocates like this case, is that since there was absolutely no need to even mention this point (again, it is not related to the case at all), it may show a rather contemptuous nature of the court toward the Second Amendment. There are other Tenth Circuit cases that we will look at.

13. United States v. Warin[403]

This is a very strong gun control case, which holds explicitly that there is no individual right to possess a firearm; that the Second Amendment applies only to a "collective right", that is to say, the states' powers over their militias.

Let's look first at the facts. Mr. Warin was convicted of possessing a 9 mm prototype submachine gun that was not registered as required by federal law. The following facts were then basically stipulated by both sides to be true:

> **that submachine guns are used by the armed forces of the United States, and that submachine guns contribute to the efficient operation of the armed forces of the United States in their function of defending the country** .... (T)hat the weapon involved in this case is a submachine gun .... (T)hat 9-millimeter submachine guns have been used by at least one Special Forces Unit of the Army in the Vietnam, ... although they are not in general use. 9-millimeter submachine guns have been used by the military forces of the United States on at least one occasion during the Vietnam war .... (T)hat submachine guns are part of the military equipment of the United States military— ... and that firearms of this general type, that is, submachine guns, do bear some relationship, some reasonable relationship, to the preservation or efficiency of the military forces.
>
> The district court found that **the defendant**, as an adult male resident and citizen of Ohio, **is a member of the 'sedentary militia' of the State**. It was not contended that Warin was a member of the active militia. The court also found that **the defendant was an engineer and designer of firearms** whose employer develops weapons for the government and—... that **the defendant had made the weapon in question**, which is indeed a firearm as described in the Act. It is also clear from the evidence **that the weapon was of a type which is standard for military use**, and fires the ammunition which is in common military use for the weapons used by individual soldiers in combat. **The defendant testified that he had designed and built the weapon for the purpose of testing and refining it so that it could be offered to the Government as an improvement on the military weapons presently in use**. The weapon was not registered to him as required by law.[404]

So, we have a case where the defendant is admitted to be a member of the militia, the weapon is admitted to be a military type, and in fact it was designed and was being tested for possible purchase and use by the United States military. If this does not have a reasonable relationship to the preservation and efficiency of a well-regulated militia, what does?

The defendant argued that under *Miller*, and quoting it, the above facts bring him under the protection of the Second Amendment. The court, in holding otherwise, said the following:

> Warin argues that the necessary implication of the quoted language is that a member of the 'sedentary militia' may possess any weapon having military capability and that application of 26 U.S.C. s 5861(d) to such a person violates the Second Amendment. We disagree. In *Miller* the Supreme Court did not reach the question of the extent to which a weapon which is 'part of the ordinary military equipment' or whose 'use could contribute to the common defense' may be regulated. In holding that the absence of evidence placing the weapon involved in the charges against Miller in one of these categories precluded the trial court from quashing the indictment on Second Amendment grounds, the Court did not hold the converse—that the Second Amendment is an absolute prohibition against all regulation of the manufacture, transfer and possession of any instrument capable of being used in military action.

* * * *

Agreeing as we do with the conclusion in *Cases v. United States*, supra, that the Supreme Court did not lay down a general rule in *Miller*, we consider the present case on its own facts and in light of applicable authoritative decisions. **It is clear that the Second Amendment guarantees a collective rather than an individual right.** In Stevens v. United States, 440 F.2d

144, 149 (6th Cir. 1971), this court held, in a case challenging the constitutionality of 18 U.S.C.App. s 1202(a)(1):

"Since the Second Amendment right 'to keep and bear Arms' applies only to the right of the State to maintain a militia and not to the individual's right to bear arms, there can be no serious claim to any express constitutional right of an individual to possess a firearm."[405]

While I strongly disagree with the conclusion stated in this case, and while it has absolutely no analysis of the history, language or other Supreme Court case law usage of the Second Amendment, still its pronouncement is clear as a bell: There is no individual right to keep and bear arms in the Sixth Circuit, which covers the states of Michigan, Ohio, Kentucky and Tennessee.

14. United States v. Oakes[406]

Oakes was convicted of possessing an unregistered machine gun. He claimed protection under the Second Amendment, claiming that he was a member of the state militia and, under state law, a member of the "Posse Comitatus", a militia type organization registered with the state. In upholding the conviction, the court said:

> The second constitutional argument that appellant advances is that the prosecution here violated his right to bear arms guaranteed by the second amendment. Defendant presents a long historical analysis of the amendment's background and purpose from which he concludes that every citizen has the absolute right to keep arms. This broad conclusion has long been rejected. *United States v. Miller*, 307 U.S. 174, 59 S.Ct. 816, 83 L.Ed. 1206...
> The purpose of the second amendment as stated by the Supreme Court in *United States v. Miller*, supra at 178, 59 S.Ct. 816, was to preserve the effectiveness and assure the continuation of the state militia. The Court stated that the amendment must be interpreted and applied with that purpose in view. Id. To apply the amendment so as to guarantee appellant's right to keep

an unregistered firearm which has not been shown to have any connection to the militia, merely because he is technically a member of the Kansas militia, would be unjustifiable in terms of either logic or policy. This lack of justification is even more apparent when applied to appellant's membership in "Posse Comitatus," an apparently nongovernmental organization. We conclude, therefore, that this prosecution did not violate the second amendment.

In an expansion on his argument that the right of an individual to bear arms is fundamental, appellant argues that the right is protected by the ninth amendment. This issue was never raised in the district court and, therefore, absent exceptional circumstances or manifest injustice, will not be considered on appeal... We find no such circumstances or injustice here.[407]

A couple of points are important here. First, even when presented with a supposedly extensive history on the Second Amendment, this court was unwilling to hold that an individual right exists (although it could be said that it did not say that an individual right did not exist, only that no **absolute** right exists). It did seem to lean toward an interpretation that the Second Amendment only applies to a state power. Then, with that interpretation, it rejected the membership in a militia as being sufficient to come within the protection of the Second Amendment, whatever it is. The Tenth Circuit consists of the states of Colorado, Kansas, New Mexico, Oklahoma, Utah, and Wyoming.

Do you begin to see that for some of these courts, no matter what the facts are, they simply are going to rule that nobody has any right at all to any firearms? We will discuss later whether under that theory the states have any real power or not.

15. *United States v. Kozerski*[408]

Another convicted felon in possession of a firearm, but this one has a twist: The defendant is a police officer! Do you see the problems that this one causes? A police officer who is not allowed, by law, to possess a firearm may be a problem. Of, course, having a convicted felon as a police officer may be an even worse problem, but that is a whole additional issue that we will not address.

Jack Reynolds, J. D.

The defendant asserted the Second Amendment claiming that he, as a rural police officer, was similar to the militia described in the Amendment, pointing out that as a police officer he was required to purchase and have available his own firearm. In denying this point, the court said:

> It is well established that the Second Amendment is not a grant of a right but a limitation upon the power of Congress and the national government, *United States v. Miller*, 307 U.S. 174, 59 S.Ct. 816, 83 L.Ed. 1206 (1939); *State v. Sanne*, 116 N.H. 583, 364 A.2d 630 (1976), and it is further held that **the right guaranteed by the Second Amendment is a collective right to bear arms rather than an individual right, and has application only to the right of the state to maintain a militia and not to the individual's right to bear arms.** *United States v. Warin*, 530 F.2d 103 (6th Cir.), cert. denied, 426 U.S. 948, 96 S.Ct. 3168, 49 L.Ed.2d 1185 (1976). See also Annot. 37 A.L.R.Fed. 696. The Court finds and rules that the defendant's argument that somehow the Second Amendment bars the instant prosecution is totally without legal merit.[409]

Now, the first sentence is true. The Second Amendment did not **grant** a right, but **guaranteed** that right by limiting the power of Congress and the national government. But the holding that the right is a collective right is strange. This is a district court case from New Hampshire, which is in the First Circuit. But instead of citing its own circuit's opinion in *Cases v. United States*[410], which implied that the Second Amendment protects an individual right, the trial judge chose to rely on another circuit's case which held that it is only a collective right. This was also done without any further analysis of the Amendment, than to cite this case. So, what is the law to be applied in New Hampshire? It is in doubt.

16. *Thompson v. Dereta*[411]

This was a constitutional tort case. A tort is usually some wrongful damage or injury to someone, such as a claim for injuries from a car accident, products liability, libel, slander, medical malpractice, and the like. In this case, it was alleged that the plaintiff's constitutional right to keep and bear arms had been wrongfully denied by the defendants wrongfully refusing to grant him an exemption to the prohibition of possessing a firearm. Such exemptions can be allowed under the federal law that restricts such possession. In holding that the plaintiff's assertion did not amount to a legal claim, the trial court said that "[t]here can be little dispute with the proposition that 'there is no absolute constitutional right of an individual to possess a firearm.' ... The court is unaware of a single case which has upheld a right to bear arms under the Second Amendment to the Constitution, outside of the context of a militia."[412] Of course, neither has there been any case that has upheld the right to bear arms in a militia context.

17. *Quilici v. Village of Morton Grove*[413]

This is another strong gun control case, with a different twist. There is a dissent, but it relies not on the Second Amendment, but the Ninth Amendment.

The Village of Morton Grove, in Illinois, passed an ordinance making it illegal for anyone to possess, within the village, a handgun (mostly pistols), with a few exceptions for policemen, members of the armed services in the performance of their duties, and the like. The question was did this violate the right of individuals to keep and bear arms?

The court first looked at the state constitution, which provided that "[s]ubject only to the police power, the right of the individual citizen to keep and bear arms shall not be infringed." Now this is clearly stated as an individual right of citizens. Even so, the court held that since this ordinance was pursuant to the police power, it did not violate the stated right. Now think about this. All such regulations are made pursuant to the police power of the government, therefore, any such ordinance would be allowed and there would be no right protected, therefore, the state constitutional provision is meaningless. Nothing stops those wanting to take away people's guns.

The court next considers the United States Constitution, Second Amendment. First it cites *Presser v. Illinois*[414] for the holding that the Second Amendment does not apply to the states. While the plaintiffs admitted that this was the holding of *Presser*, based on the numerous changes to the constitutional law where many of the rights in the Bill of Rights have now been applied to the states (where they were not at the time of *Presser*), the plaintiffs asked the court to reconsider this issue. The court declined to do so, saying that only the Supreme Court can do that. Of course, this never stops the courts of appeals from doing this when they want to, but it is a correct statement of the rules that they are supposed to operate under.

Then, in dicta, since the court had already held that the Second Amendment could not apply in this case, the court goes on to espouse its belief on what the extent of the Second Amendment is. "Construing this language according to its plain meaning, it seems clear that the right to bear arms is **inextricably connected** to the preservation of a militia."[415] A rather short-hand rendition of what we did in Chapter 3, with the totally opposite result, indicating that the only reason for keeping and bearing arms is the preservation of a militia. "Under the controlling authority of *Miller* we conclude that the right to keep and bear handguns **is not guaranteed** by the second amendment."[416] Again a different interpretation of *Miller*, than what I would give it, but obviously others give it this same interpretation as well. Then in a footnote, referring to the plaintiffs' contention that handguns are military weapons:

> Appellants devote a portion of their briefs to historical analysis of the development of English common law and the debate surrounding the adoption of the second and fourteenth amendments. This analysis has no relevance on the resolution of the controversy before us. Accordingly, we decline to comment on it, other than to note that **we do not consider individually owned handguns to be military weapons.**[417]

Now, this statement, I have to take great exception with. First, the historical analysis should have some relevance. Beyond that, when I joined the U.S. Marine Corps, in 1975, as a lieutenant my T/O (Table of Organization) weapon was the same as **all** officers and SNCO's, a .45 semiautomatic pistol. When I retired, it was a 9-mm. Semiautomatic pistol. These are clearly handguns, and clearly are military weapons. While I can accept different interpretations of *Miller*, and the unjustified continuing application of an outdated case from the late 1800's as to the use of the 14th Amendment, this statement by the majority on the court tells me that they are either stupid, or they will do anything to justify the prohibition of guns, or both.

Finally, the majority holds that since the Supreme Court has never said anything on whether the Ninth Amendment can be applied to protect a pre-existing individual right to keep and bear arms, this court would not rule on it, saying that the plaintiffs' arguments have no legal significance. Now, one of the purposes of the lower courts is to rule on issues before they get up to the Supreme Court. There is always a first case on every issue. Under this logic, no court of appeals could ever rule on any right until the Supreme Court had ruled on it. I do not believe that that is the way the system is supposed to work.

The dissent says that the ordinance is not allowed, mostly based on state law reasons. However, Justice Coffey also invokes the Ninth Amendment, which the majority rejects. "It has been said that the greatest threat to our liberty is from well-meaning, and almost imperceptible governmental encroachments upon our personal freedom. Today's decision sanctions an intrusion on our basic rights as citizens which would no doubt be alarming and odious to our founding fathers."[418]

> I find today's decision particularly disturbing as it sanctions governmental action which I feel impermissibly interferes with basic human freedoms. I cannot let this opportunity pass without expressing my concern with the erosion of these rights.
>
> The majority cavalierly dismisses the argument that the right to possess commonly owned arms for self-defense and the protection of loved ones is a fundamental right protected by the Constitution. Justice Cardozo in Palko v. Connecticut, 302 U.S. 319, 325, 58 S.Ct. 149, 151, 82 L.Ed. 288 (1937), defined fundamental rights as those rights "implicit in the concept of ordered liberty." Surely nothing could be more fundamental to the "concept of ordered liberty" than the basic right of an individual, within the confines of the criminal law, to protect his home and family from unlawful and dangerous intrusions.

* * * *

In today's decision this court has refused to take cognizance of the natural right of an individual, within the confines of the criminal law, to protect his home and family from unlawful and dangerous intrusions. It is my opinion that Morton Grove Ordinance No. 81-11 impermissibly interferes with the rights of Illinois citizens to guard their personal security, subject to the limits of the criminal law, and that it is the duty of this court to so declare.

The court today has also refused to recognize the tremendous impact of Morton Grove Ordinance No. 81-11 on personal privacy rights. There is no doubt that the right to one's privacy is afforded constitutional protection. The United States Supreme Court has repeatedly recognized a right to privacy implicit in the federal constitution ...

The Morton Grove Ordinance, by prohibiting the possession of a handgun within the confines of the home, violates both the fundamental right to privacy and the fundamental right to defend the home against unlawful intrusion within the parameters of the criminal law. There is no area of human activity more protected by the right to privacy than the right to be free from unnecessary government intrusion in the confines of the home.

The unique importance of the home from time immemorial has been amply demonstrated in our constitutional jurisprudence. Among the enumerated rights in the Bill of Rights are the Third Amendment's prohibition of quartering of troops in a private house in peace-time and the right of citizens to be "secure in their ... houses ... against unreasonable searches and seizures ..." guaranteed by the Fourth Amendment. As early as 1886, the United States Supreme Court recognized that the Fifth Amendment protects against all governmental invasions "of the sanctity of a man's home and the privacies of life." Boyd v. United States, 116 U.S. 616, 630, 6 S.Ct. 524, 532, 29 L.Ed. 746

A People Armed and Free

(1886). The First Amendment had been held to encompass the right to "privacy and freedom of association in the home." Moreno v. United States Dep't of Agriculture, 345 F.Supp. 310, 314 (D.D.C.1972), aff'd, 413 U.S. 528, 93 S.Ct. 2821, 37 L.Ed.2d 782 (1973).

In Stanley v. Georgia, 394 U.S. 557, 89 S.Ct. 1243, 22 L.Ed.2d 542 (1969), the Supreme Court overturned a state conviction for possession of obscene material, holding "that the First and Fourteenth Amendments prohibit making the private possession of obscene material a crime." The Supreme Court had previously held that obscenity is not protected by the First Amendment, but in Stanley the Court made a distinction between commercial distribution of obscene matter and the private possession of such materials in the home and held the Georgia statute unconstitutional because it prohibited the possession of such materials in the home. The Court recited:

"For also fundamental is the right to be free, except in very limited circumstances, from unwanted governmental intrusions into one's privacy." Id. at 564, 89 S.Ct. at 1247.

The Court has made it clear that its Stanley decision was not based on the idea that obscene matter is itself protected under the right of privacy. Rather, the focus in Stanley was on the fact that the activity prohibited by the Georgia statute occurred in the privacy of the home. In United States v. Reidel, 402 U.S. 351, 356, 91 S.Ct. 1410, 1412, 28 L.Ed.2d 813 (1971), the Court rejected the argument that commercial distribution of pornography is constitutionally protected and held that the "focus" of Stanley was "on freedom of mind and thought and on the privacy of one's home." Subsequently, the Court in United States v. Orito, 413 U.S. 139, 142, 93 S.Ct. 2674, 2677, 37 L.Ed.2d 513 (1973) stated "the Constitution extends special safeguards to the privacy of the home" and there exists a "myriad" of activities which may be prohibited in public but which may be lawfully conducted within the privacy and confines of the home.

Most importantly, the Supreme Court in Paris Adult Theatre I v. Slaton, 413 U.S. 49, 66, 93 S.Ct. 2628, 2639, 37 L.Ed.2d 446 (1973), held that Stanley was decided "on the narrow basis of the 'privacy of the home' which was hardly more than a reaffirmation that 'a man's home is his castle.'" (emphasis added).

Privacy in the home is a fundamental right under both the federal and Illinois Constitutions. This does not mean, of course, that a person may do anything at anytime as long as the activity takes place within a person's home. Instead, the right to privacy is limited in two important respects. First, the Supreme Court strictly limited its Stanley holding to possession for purely private, noncommercial use in the home. Second, as noted in Stanley, the right to privacy must yield when it seriously interferes with the public welfare. The government bears a heavy burden when attempting to justify an expansion, as in gun control, of the "limited circumstances" in which intrusion into the privacy of a home is permitted.

Morton Grove has not met that heavy burden. Without question, the state may, should and has placed reasonable restrictions on the possession of handguns outside one's home to protect the public welfare. However, Morton Grove's prohibition of handgun possession within the confines of a person's own home has not been shown to be necessary to protect the public welfare and thus violates the fundamental right to privacy.

The right to privacy is one of the most cherished rights an American citizen has; the right to privacy sets America apart from totalitarian states in which the interests of the state prevail over individual rights. A fundamental part of our concept of ordered liberty is the right to protect one's home and family against dangerous intrusions subject to the criminal law. Morton Grove, acting like the omniscient and paternalistic "Big Brother" in George Orwell's novel, "1984", cannot, in the name of public welfare, dictate to its residents that they may not possess a handgun in the privacy of their home. To so prohibit the possession of handguns in the privacy of the home prevents a person from protecting his home and family, endangers law-abiding citizens and renders meaningless the Supreme Court's teaching that "a man's home is his castle."[419]

This is probably our longest quote. However, if you made it through it, you can see how well reasoned it is. Isn't it a shame that people have a constitutional right to have pornography in their home, but not to keep a weapon with which they can defend themselves? While I do not believe in having pornography for myself, I agree that individuals should have the right to have that material for themselves, in the privacy of their homes. My point is that a person's liberty should also extend to being able to have the implements necessary to defend himself and his family in his home. Some people, and judges (like the majority in this case) only want to acknowledge the rights that they like.

In any event, forget about any individual right in the Seventh Circuit, covering Illinois, Indiana, and Wisconsin.

18. *United States v. Nelson*[420]

This case involved the possession of a switchblade knife, which had been made illegal by a federal statute. The court applied the reasonable basis test to uphold the power of Congress to pass the statute. In regards to the Second Amendment (which applies to arms, not just guns), the court says that the concept of a fundamental right to keep and bear arms has not been the law for at least 100 years. It then quotes *Cruikshank:* "The right there specified is that of 'bearing arms for a lawful purpose.' This is not a right granted by the Constitution."[421] Remember, I told you that some people use this statement to try to make people think that there is no right at all. Of course, the Constitution did not grant this right; it could not grant it since it already existed! But when read out of context like that, it sure sounds to most people like the court is saying that the Supreme Court has long held that there simply is no right to keep and bear arms, period. But, of course, that is not the case.

The court then went on to notice that "[l]ater cases have analyzed the second amendment purely in terms of protecting state militias, rather than individual rights."[422] Again, no analysis of its own, merely relying on prior cases, which also had little to no analysis, to carry forward a mistaken interpretation of the Second Amendment and *Miller*. Anyway, the Eighth Circuit seems to be supporting the state power argument.

19. *Fresno Rifle and Pistol Club, Inc. v. Van De Kamp*[423]

Here the State of California had passed a law restricting the possession of "assault weapons". More will be discussed about this in Chapter 10 on the extent of the Second Amendment protections. Anyway, the plaintiffs in this case wanted to have this state law declared unconstitutional.

While we will address this case more in Chapter 9 on the application of the Second Amendment to the states, at this point it is sufficient to note that the court did not truly address the individual right vs. state power argument (although it assumed, for the sake of argument, that the Supreme Court case of *Verdugo-Urquidez* could be read to support the proposition that the use of "the people" guarantees an individual right). What it did do was to refuse to apply the Second Amendment to the states, following *Quilici* just discussed above.

20. *United States v. Hale*[424]

The defendant was convicted for possession of a machine gun and other unregistered firearms. He tried to argue, under *Miller*, that since these machine guns were military weapons, they could not be regulated by the federal government. Remember we indicated that this was a reasonable reading of *Miller*, and even one court of appeals has recognized this as a plausible reading of *Miller*. In rejecting this argument, the court said the following:

> Hale wants to find in Miller the rule that individual possession of true military weapons is protected under the Second Amendment. When the Second Amendment was ratified in 1791, the state militias functioned as both the principal units of military organization and as an implicit check on federal power. See generally Keith A. Ehrman & Dennis A. Henigan, The Second Amendment in the Twentieth Century: Have You Seen Your Militia Lately?, 15 U.Dayton

L.Rev. 5 (1989). These militias were comprised of ordinary citizens who typically were required to provide their own equipment and arms. The Second Amendment prevented federal laws that would infringe upon the possession of arms by individuals and thus render the state militias impotent. Over the next 200 years, state militias first faded out of existence and then later reemerged as more organized, semi-professional military units. The state provided the arms and the equipment of the militia members, and these were stored centrally in armories. With the passage of the Dick Act in 1903, the state militias were organized into the national guard structure, which remains in place today. Id.

* * * *

Considering this history, **we cannot conclude that the Second Amendment protects the individual possession of military weapons**. In Miller, the Court simply recognized this historical residue. **The rule emerging from Miller is that, absent a showing that the possession of a certain weapon has "some reasonable relationship to the preservation or efficiency of a well- regulated militia," the Second Amendment does not guarantee the right to possess the weapon.** Miller, 307 U.S. at 178, 59 S.Ct. at 818. Miller simply "did not hold ... that the Second Amendment is an absolute prohibition against all regulation of the manufacture, transfer and possession of any instrument capable of being used in military action."

* * * *

[I]t is not sufficient to prove that the weapon in question was susceptible to military use. Indeed, as recognized in Cases, most any lethal weapon has a potential military use. Id. Rather, **the claimant of**

Second Amendment protection must prove that his or her possession of the weapon was reasonably related to a well regulated militia. See id. at 923. Where such a claimant presented no evidence either that he was a member of a military organization or that his use of the weapon was "in preparation for a military career", the Second Amendment did not protect the possession of the weapon.

Since the Miller decision, no federal court has found any individual's possession of a military weapon to be "reasonably related to a well regulated militia." **"Technical" membership in a state militia (e.g., membership in an "unorganized" state militia) or membership in a non- governmental military organization is not sufficient** to satisfy the "reasonable relationship" test. Oakes, 564 F.2d at 387. Membership in a hypothetical or "sedentary" militia is likewise insufficient. See Warin, 530 F.2d 103.

* * * *

Citing dicta from United States v. Verdugo-Urquidez, 494 U.S. 259, 265, 110 S.Ct. 1056, 1060, 108 L.Ed.2d 222 (1990), Hale argues that the Second Amendment protections apply to individuals and not to states or collective entities like militias. This argument is inapplicable to this case. The purpose of the Second Amendment is to restrain the federal government from regulating the possession of arms where such regulation would interfere with the preservation or efficiency of the militia. See Miller, 307 U.S. at 178, 59 S.Ct. at 818; United States v. Oakes, 564 F.2d 384 (10th Cir.1977), cert. denied, 435 U.S. 926, 98 S.Ct. 1493, 55 L.Ed.2d 521 (1978); Cody, 460 F.2d 34. Whether the "right to bear arms" for militia purposes is "individual" or "collective" in nature is irrelevant where, as here, the individual's possession of arms is not related to the preservation or efficiency of a militia.[425]

A People Armed and Free

So now, according to the Eighth Circuit, not only does the weapon have to have a reasonable relationship to the militia, but the individual has to show that he is using it in relation to the militia. And the state or federal unorganized militia is not good enough. This leaves only the National Guard. And guess what? Since nobody is allowed to use their private firearms in the National Guard, *presto*—there is no right to keep and bear arms.

There is a concurring opinion in this case. While the concurring justice agrees that the prohibition of the possession of a machine gun does not violate the Second Amendment, without any further analysis, the justice says:

> I disagree, however, that Cases v. United States, 131 F.2d 916 (1st Cir.1942); United States v. Warin, 530 F.2d 103 (6th Cir.1976); United States v. Oakes, 564 F.2d 384 (10th Cir.1977) and United States v. Nelson, 859 F.2d 1318 (8th Cir.1988) properly interpret the Constitution or the Supreme Court's holding in United States v. Miller, 307 U.S. 174, 59 S.Ct. 816, 83 L.Ed. 1206 (1939) insofar as they say that Congress has the power to prohibit an individual from possessing any type of firearm, even when kept for lawful purposes.[426]

It is not clear just what the justice would hold as to the protection afforded by the Second Amendment, but at least we know that he would not reject it entirely. Despite this, however, the law in the Eighth Circuit is that there is no individual right.

21. *United States v. Friel*[427]

The First Circuit in 1993 again followed *Miller* without expounding on it, in holding that the statute barring convicted felons from possessing firearms does not violate the Second Amendment. The defendant, Mr. Friel, had been convicted of a felony, and was found in possession of a firearm. The court said that "the Second Amendment ... applies only to firearms having a 'reasonable relationship to the preservation or efficiency of a well regulated militia...'"[428] The court also cited *Lewis v. United States* as holding that the "legislative restrictions on the ability of a felon to possess a firearm do not 'trench upon any constitutionally protected liberties.'"[429] So, while this case was probably decided correctly, we still do not know for sure where the First Circuit will fall on the individual right v. state power issue, though in an earlier case it appeared to indicate that an individual right does exist.

22. *Hickman v. Block*[430]

In this case from California, the plaintiff had applied for a concealed carry permit for a gun. In California, the issuance of such permits is discretionary with the governmental official, not mandatory (if the prerequisites to obtain the permit are met) as in most states. Upon being denied the permit, while he met all of the criteria, the plaintiff filed suit. In upholding the denial of the permit, the 9th Circuit said: "We follow our sister circuits in holding that the Second Amendment is a right held by the states, and does not protect the possession of a weapon by a private citizen."[431] The plaintiff therefore lacked standing to bring his suit. Clearly, the 9th Circuit does not recognize an individual right. The 9th Circuit includes California, Oregon, Washington, Arizona, Montana, Idaho, Nevada, Alaska, and Hawaii.

23. *United States v. Haney*[432]

The defendant in this case was rather unusual. He walked into a police station, found a police officer, and told him that he owned two fully automatic guns, which were illegal. He told the officer they were not licensed. Either he was gutsy, really believed that the courts would adopt his interpretation of the Second Amendment, or was just plain stupid. Maybe it was because he was from Oklahoma (only kidding; I graduated from Oklahoma State University). In any event, as you might well expect, he was convicted of illegal possession of automatic weapons.

In upholding the conviction, the Tenth Circuit made clear that there had to be a relationship between not only the weapon, but also the person and the militia. In so doing, it issued a four-prong test that would guarantee that no Second Amendment challenge to any statute could ever survive in its courts:

> As a threshold matter, he must show that (1) he is part of a state militia; (2) the militia, and his participation therein, is "well regulated" by the state; (3) [the weapon in question is] used by that militia; and (4) his possession of the machinegun was reasonably connected to his militia service.[433]

The court then went on to explain that the militia of the Second Amendment is a governmental organization, and the unorganized militia cannot count, since it is not "well regulated".[434] Therefore, it could only be the National Guard. Now, presuming that an individual could show that he is part of a state governmental organization, which is well regulated, which under this court's ruling could only be the National Guard, and could show that the weapon at issue is used by the National Guard, the fourth part of the test can never be met. The National Guard does not let its members keep its weapons themselves. They are locked in an armory. Therefore, the Second Amendment becomes meaningless as to any "right of the people".

24. United States v. Emerson[435]

This is a huge case, both in size and in importance. In size, it runs 72 pages in length. In importance, it is the first time that I have been able to find, that a court of appeals expressly held that the Second Amendment protects an individual right, not a state power. And it is the only case that really examines the language and history of the Second Amendment.

In a more recent amendment to the federal statute prohibiting certain classes of people, such as felons, from possessing firearms, the Congress had added anyone who is subject to a court order that was issued after a hearing of which the person had been given actual notice and had an opportunity to participate in, and that prohibited the person from harassing, stalking, or threatening an intimate partner of the person, or the child of the intimate partner or person, and includes a finding that the person represents a credible threat to the physical safety of the intimate partner or child. While there are other provisions to this amendment to the statute, and it includes other situations, the general purpose, and the effect in this case, has to do with temporary injunctions while a divorce proceeding is ongoing. It is not unusual for one or both spouses in a divorce to ask the trial court for a temporary injunction to keep the other spouse from harassing them. Remember, they can't get along with each other. That is why they are getting a divorce. In order to reduce spousal violence and abuse during divorce, this amendment to the statute was passed to remove a tool of, and therefore arguably the opportunity for, such violence.

Mr. Emerson owned a Beretta pistol. He apparently acquired it in October 1997. In August 1998, Mrs. Emerson filed for divorce. In September 1998, a hearing was held on temporary orders (the request for a temporary injunction). There was some evidence produced that Mr. Emerson might be violent. There is a dispute about the extent of this evidence, with gun control advocates claiming more evidence of this than what gun rights advocates claim, and more than what is contained in the opinions in the case. While this is possible (I did not check the hearing transcripts at either the divorce court or the federal district court), I will stay with the facts listed in the opinions, because I can trust them to be correct. If there was more evidence of possible violence, it merely adds support to the final ruling of the court of appeals.

Mr. Emerson did not contest the entry of a temporary injunction against him. The divorce court entered a temporary injunction against him ten days after the hearing (though there was no express finding of the credible threat in the order). Automatically, Mr. Emerson lost any right to possess a firearm under federal law. Do you see the problem developing? How many of you knew about this law prohibiting the possession of a firearm by anyone under such an order? For that matter, how many attorneys knew about it? I did not, until I started to research this topic.

In December 1998, a grand jury indicted Mr. Emerson for violating the statute by possessing the Beretta pistol on November 16, 1998. The federal district court dismissed the case, holding that the Second Amendment does protect an individual right, and that without an express finding in the temporary injunction of a credible threat, that temporary injunction could not be used as a basis for a violation of the statute. There are other holdings in that case as well, but this will do for our purposes.

The federal government appealed the case. The Fifth Circuit held that the Second Amendment does protect an individual right, and rejected the collective right or states right/power theories.

> We hold, consistent with *Miller*, that it protects the right of individuals, including those not then actually a member of any militia or engaged in active military service or training, to privately possess and bear their own firearms, such as the pistol involved here, that are

suitable as personal individual weapons and are not of the general kind or type excluded by *Miller*.[436]

However, when applying the Second Amendment to Mr. Emerson, the court held that "that does not mean that those rights may never be made subject to any limited, narrowly tailored specific exceptions or restrictions for particular cases that are reasonable and not inconsistent with the right of Americans generally to keep and bear their private arms..."[437] The court went on to hold that since the statute requires a finding that a credible threat exists, based on an actual hearing at which the person involved has to have a chance to appear and contest it, that draws the statute narrowly enough to pass muster. Then the court finds that Texas law does not allow such an injunction to be issued without a finding of a likelihood that irreparable harm will occur. Therefore, there must have been such a required finding against Mr. Emerson, therefore, the Second Amendment does not protect him in this case.

While this is reasonable logic, having practiced law in Texas, and having done some divorce work there (though I no longer do divorce work), I can tell you that sometimes attorneys on the opposite sides of a divorce will get their clients to agree to mutual temporary orders (restraining each party from harassing, etc., the other). I never did that because I believe that it does more harm than good, especially if the parties are relatively friendly in the divorce (which may sound like an oxymoron; if they were friendly there would be no need for a divorce), and it needlessly increases the attorneys' fees the clients have to pay. My ex-wife even tried to get me to enter into such an agreement with her when we were going through our divorce, but I refused. Not because of this federal law, which did not exist at the time, but because in an otherwise stable environment, the parties are just asking for trouble. If one party gets a wild-hair, this gives them the opportunity to try to get the court to hold the other party in contempt of court. That is just too dangerous for me.

In any event, when this is done (mutual injunctions requested), there is merely a cursory hearing, at which there usually is no evidence of any danger from either party, only that both parties agree to the orders. The orders are then issued, without any possible finding of possible irreparable harm or credible threat, because no evidence thereon was given. As I read the majority opinion, just because the

Texas law requires such a finding in order to produce such a temporary injunction, that would be enough, even if the parties and the judge did not follow this law. This could cause vast unintended consequences for the parties, such as being charged with a federal crime. For my opinion, if this ever happens to someone, I would think that the attorney who represented him/her in the divorce would have been guilty of malpractice and could be sued, but that does not get the person out of the criminal charge.

For this reason, I do not like the end result of *Emerson*, but the problem can be avoided if people, especially divorce attorneys are educated in this matter. As for the rest of the reasoning in the case, it is way too long to quote here. It is the only opinion that goes into great depth on the analysis of the Second Amendment, especially the history of it. Besides it is very similar to what I have already said in Chapters 3 and 4 on the text and history of the Amendment. In fact, you may have noted that I have already used numerous quotes from it in those chapters.

There is a concurring opinion in *Emerson*, which complains about the court even addressing the constitutional issue, saying that the same result could have been reached without it. The point is that the court could have just said that whatever the Second Amendment does, Mr. Emerson's rights were not protected because of his special situation. However, this is hard to do without defining the scope of the constitutionally protected right, and, as the majority points out, all of the other cases holding that there is no individual right could have been decided without holding that, but merely holding that whatever the Amendment does, the individual involved is not protected. So, I see no problem with this. The bottom line is, in the Fifth Circuit, the Second Amendment does protect an individual right, but that right can be regulated by adequately drawn statutes. The Fifth Circuit includes Texas, Louisiana and Mississippi.

25. *Silveira v. Lockyear*[438]

While there have been a handful of cases decided since *Emerson*, most of them still have not provided any additional analysis of the issue, merely stating that they disagreed with the Fifth Circuit and/or were going to follow their own precedent and ignore the logic used in *Emerson*. However, in December 2002, the Ninth Circuit Court of Appeals gave its answer to *Emerson*. *Silveira* is a case involving restrictions placed by the State of California on the possession of semi-automatic weapons. The state law made it a felony to manufacture, possess, sell, transfer, or import into the state, certain semi-automatic weapons, with a grandfather clause that allowed people to keep those weapons they already had, if they would register them with the state, though the place the person could have it was strictly regulated. This law obviously implicates not only the Second Amendment, but also the issue of using the 14th Amendment to apply the Second Amendment to restrict the power of the states to regulate gun ownership.

While the Ninth Circuit comes to the opposite conclusion from the Fifth, there are some nuggets of gold in this opinion for gun rights advocates. First, even though the concurring opinion in this case chides the majority for doing so, the court writes an extensive analysis of the issue because it acknowledges that prior to *Emerson*, "there exists no thorough judicial examination of the amendment's meaning."[439] Finally someone other than gun rights advocates has admitted this fact! They go further to say that their prior holdings, like other courts, were reached "largely on the basis of the rather cursory discussion in *Miller*, and touched only briefly on the merits of the debate over the force of the amendment."[440]

The concurring opinion says that this analysis is not needed because all the court has to do is follow its own precedent, which has held that no individual right exists; only a collective right, which as we have seen, is no right at all. The three judge panel deciding this case could not reverse the earlier holdings if they wanted to, but would have to refer the case to a hearing of the whole court *en banc* if it was inclined to overrule the prior cases, so why bother with the analysis just to come up with the same result? While the concurring opinion might be technically correct, the majority is correct in doing what they did so as to try to clarify the reasoning behind their holdings, for only in this way can the people know the truthfulness of their court system.

The court also admitted that in actuality, "the *Miller* Court's opinion stands only for the proposition that the possession of certain weapons is not protected, and offers little guidance as to what rights the Second Amendment does protect", though it says that "*Miller* does strongly imply ... that the Supreme Court rejects the traditional individual rights view."[441] The first statement, again finally, is an admission of a correct analysis of *Miller*, though the second statement is open to strong debate.

While the question of the 14th Amendment's application is yet to be discussed in Chapter 9, I should note here that the Ninth Circuit admitted that the case law that holds that the 14th Amendment cannot be used to apply the Second Amendment to restrict the powers of the states to regulate gun ownership or possession is out dated. "One point about which we are in agreement with the Fifth Circuit is that *Cruikshank* and *Pressxer* rest on a principle that is now thoroughly discredited."[442] This could prove to be an important concession in later cases. However, the court also said that "[b]ecause we decide this case on the threshold issue of standing, ... we need not consider the question whether the Second Amendment presently enjoins any action on the part of the states."[443] As I have pointed out before, this statement is illogical. Merely stating that this presents a question acknowledges that the Second Amendment must provide for an individual right, for if it only provides for states' rights, the 14th Amendment cannot be used to cause the Second Amendment to restrict the states powers to regulate guns.

Finally, on the gun rights side, the court virtually says that if the Second Amendment did protect individual rights, then any statute restricting these rights would have to be subjected to the highest test of constitutionality and would be found constitutional only if "they are suitably tailored to serve a compelling state interest."[444] As you will see in Chapter 10, this is very important for deciding which regulations will be allowed and which will not.

Now let's look at the portions favoring the gun control advocates' position. As I stated at the first of this book, I will look at all arguments, whether I agree with them or not. Not surprisingly, the Ninth Circuit rejects the *Emerson*, and my, analysis of the language of the Second Amendment. They start off with the word "militia". "We believe the answer to the definitional question is the one that most persons would expect: 'militia' refers to a state military force."[445] While, as I pointed out in Chapter 3, this is a plausible reading, and probably the strongest argument of the gun control advocates, it ignores the prohibition contained in the Constitution against states maintaining troops without the consent of Congress.[446] Given that prohibition, it would seem to me that the "militia" would have to be something other than a state military force. In any event, the court said that since the Supreme Court had ruled that the word "people" should have the same meaning throughout the Constitution,[447] so too should the word "militia". And, the court says, "militia" consistently means a state military force. They refer to article II, section 2, clause 1, where the President is made the Commander in Chief of the army, navy and the militia, and in the Bill of Rights, in the Fifth Amendment where a defendant has a right to an indictment except in cases arising in the land or naval forces, " or in the Militia when in actual service in time of War or public danger…"[448] The continual relationship between the armed forces and the militia seems to indicate that the militia is a state owned military force. They also go to the Articles of Confederation, which required each state to maintain a well regulated and disciplined militia.[449] And with the inclusion of the adjective "well regulated", it makes it seem even more so that this must be a state military force.[450] Again, as I said in Chapter 3, there are good arguments on both sides of this. The court ignores the possibility that if "militia" referred to an organized armed citizenry it would fit in with the other uses in the Constitution, Articles of Confederation, and other uses just fine. Even so, this is a point, on definitional analysis, that could go either way.

After that, however, the court's analysis totally falls apart. They next look at the phrase "bear arms", and assert that it "is a phrase that customarily relates to a military function". While they cite some support for this usage, they totally ignore the examples given in Chapter 3 of this book that shows that it was also customarily used to refer to other reasons for bearing arms, including a prior proposed statute presented by the author of the Second Amendment himself, James Madison. Their argument simply does not hold water. To try to bolster their argument, the court says that "[n]o state at the time, nor any state before had ever compelled people to carry weapons in their private capacity."[451] Again, this simply is not true, as shown by the extensive history I gave in Chapter 4, where there were numerous laws that required men to carry their guns to church or when traveling. The court simply ignores this, although this information is very available.

The court then looks at the word "keep". Earlier in the opinion, the court said that it was significant that the Second Amendment does not protect the right to "possess" or "own" arms, but to "keep and bear arms".[452] This is despite the fact that the first definition of keep is to possess. In any event, the court then decides that the words "keep" and "bear" must be read together. This is a violation of grammatical structure. Finally, the court alludes to the right of the states to keep arms as being a catalyst for the Revolutionary War, saying that "it was the British troops' attempt to capture the Massachusetts militia's arsenal that prompted Paul Revere's warning and the battles at Lexington and Concord to defend that states' stores of munitions."[453] This is a tortured rewrite of history. The "state" government of Massachusetts at the time was under the control of the British military, with a military governor. Therefore, the arsenal spoken of could not have been the "state's". This is a case of the court taking an argument for individual rights, changing history, and using it against individual rights.

The court then puts the two clauses of the amendment together, and concludes that the first clause should control the second. Again, this violates grammatical structure. But even if we assume that all of the reasoning of the court listed so far is correct, it still does not answer the question as to whether the militia clause states the **only** reason to protect the right to keep and bear arms, or merely states **one** reason. As the court does admit, "given the history and vigor of the dispute over the meaning of the Second Amendment's language, we would be reluctant to say that the text and structure alone establish with certainty which of the various views is correct."[454] In this, they are probably correct.

So the court then turns to its historical analysis. Here they conclude that the only reason for passing the Second Amendment was to protect the states' militias. They then fall into the trap of looking only at the evidence that supports this reason, which I have acknowledged does exist. But that does not mean that evidence of other reasons does not exist. And even though this evidence has been published many times over, including in the *Emerson* opinion, which the court had to have read, they simply do not address 98% of it. They ignore it, as if it does not exist, which, to the uneducated, makes their opinion sound logical and correct. But it does exist. I will not repeat the history given in Chapter 4 here. Suffice it to say that what little the court does address, they mess up. They quote a portion of James Madison's Federalist No. 46, and then accuse the gun rights advocates of constantly taking it out of context. In fact, it is the court that has taken it out of context, leaving out much of what supports the gun rights advocates' case. I have quoted the whole applicable text in Chapter 4. You decide for yourself.

The court asserts that only in the New Hampshire ratification convention did a proposal for an individual right to possess arms pass. This is wrong. Again, see Chapter 4. The court says that there is *"not a single statement in the congressional debate about the proposed amendment that indicates that any congressman contemplated that it would establish an individual right to possess a weapon."*[455] Again, a twisting of history. I have explained why the record of congressional debate is slim to none. And there is plenty of other evidence that the congressmen did in fact consider the Second Amendment to protect, not establish, an individual's right to possess arms. Again, see Chapter 4.

Amazingly, the court does quote James Mason, from Virginia, yet ignores the obvious conclusion to be drawn from it:

> *I consider and fear the natural propensity of rulers to oppress the people. I wish only to prevent them from doing evil...* If the clause [U.S. Const. Art. I, section 8, clause 15] stands as it is now, it will take from the state legislatures what divine Providence has given **to every individual—the means of self defence.**[456]

While Mason may be talking to some extent about protecting the states' powers over the militias, he also clearly states that God has given every individual the right, and the means, of self-defense. Therefore, there is, preexisting the Constitution, an individual right to have weapons, for purposes other than serving in the militia. Therefore, the Second Amendment can be seen a protecting this individual right.

Any way, if you are interested in reading the rest of the opinion, you will see that it inexplicably leaves out most of the true history that I have set forth in Chapter 4. Of course, as I have said, that is the only way that they can come to the conclusion that no individual right exists, for to acknowledge the complete history forces one to recognize an individual right, for purposes in addition to militia service.

26. *Nordyke v. King*[457]

A little over two months after *Silveira* a different three judge panel from the Ninth Circuit had the occasion to again address the Second Amendment. This case involved a county in California making it illegal to have any firearm on county property, which effectively stopped the presentation of gun shows on the county owned property where they had been held for years. In addressing the Second Amendment issues, the panel, like the concurrence in *Silveira*, chided that panel for going into detail in its analysis of the issue (which, again, I disagree with this position). The *Nordyke* court chose to merely follow precedent. However, they then did something truly remarkable. They acknowledged the arguments made in *Emerson*, calling it "thoughtful and extensive", and stated that "if we were writing on a blank slate, we may be inclined to follow the approach of the Fifth Circuit…"[458] They add, "we feel that the *Silveira* panel exposition of the conflicting interpretations of the Second Amendment was both **unpersuasive** and, even more importantly, unnecessary."[459] How amazing is that? The court follows the precedent, but says, in essence, that it disagrees with it and with the reasoning just handed down less than three months before. Taking this one step further, one of the judges on this three judge panel, Justice Gould, wrote a concurring opinion in which he points out many of the problems with the *Silveira* reasoning, even though he still votes to follow the ruling, and then expressly asks the Ninth Circuit to take up this issue *en banc* (as a whole, instead of in three judge panels), to overturn the previous holdings of the court, and calls on the United States Supreme Court to take up the issue to reverse these holdings.[460] This is extremely unusual. While the law in the Ninth Circuit remains that there is no individual right, there is obviously a split of opinion among the judges on that court as to what the law should be. Will this result in a reconsideration of the issue *en banc*? Or will this all lead finally to a definitive ruling by the Supreme Court? Only time will tell. Stay tuned.

C. *Concluding Remarks on Case Law*

So what have we learned? First, the United States Supreme Court has not given any definitive ruling, one way or the other, as to what the Second Amendment really means or does, regardless of how much the advocates on each side want to claim that the law supports their position. Based on all of the cases available, including *Miller* because

A People Armed and Free

of its apparent adoption of the second argument from the government's brief, I believe that the better position is that it protects an individual right, but the case law is not clear-cut on this point from the Supreme Court.

From the lower courts, we have different positions. The Third, Fourth, Sixth, Seventh, Eighth, Ninth and Tenth Circuits clearly hold that there is no individual right. This covers the majority of states in the country. The Fifth Circuit clearly holds that there is an individual right. The First Circuit appears to support individual rights. All of the circuits uphold the restrictions that have been involved so far, with some of the state power courts even allowing blanket prohibitions of particular types of weapons from all citizens.

This situation, with the differing positions of the courts of appeals, is ripe for a case to go to the Supreme Court. If all courts of appeals were in unison, and ruling correctly, the Supreme Court would be inclined to not hear any of the cases. However, with diametrically opposed rulings, one or more of the courts have to be wrong. Even so, the Supreme Court decided not to hear the *Emerson* case. Maybe they thought that if it could be decided without reaching the constitutional issue, it would not be a good case to bring up on this point. There may have been other reasons. Maybe it will take a case with stronger facts, such as a squeaky-clean defendant being charged under a statute that clearly goes to far, or sweeps too broadly in prohibiting the possession of a firearm. We will discuss these possibilities in Chapter 10 when we discuss the extent of the Second Amendment's protection.

Anyway, you can see why the gun control advocates have generally been happy with the results in the lower courts, until *Emerson*, and even there the gun control statute was upheld. These results are why they claim that the law on the Second Amendment is well settled, when it is anything but, as finally admitted in *Silveira* and *Nordyke*.

Chapter 7
Public Policy

I believe that this is the least valid factor of all of the six that we will have looked at when we finish this journey. While looking at the public policy that existed at the time that a constitutional amendment was passed may help us understand the original intent of the Framers of that provision, in my humble opinion, current public policy is just not a good basis to hang constitutional interpretation on, whether it supports your position or is against it. There are several reasons for this.

First, we are talking about the constitution, not about some statute that can be changed by a mere majority of Congress and the concurrence of the President. While public policy certainly has a place in determining what is put into the constitution, once a provision is in there, its meaning should remain the same from then on. There is a reason that a super majority of both houses of Congress and then of the states is required to pass constitutional amendments. It is to protect the most basic principles of this government from every little change of wind in public opinion.

It is more than a little scary to me to see recent opinion polls that indicate that people would be willing to give up some of their rights, that many brave souls have suffered, fought and died to protect, in order to try to obtain some measure of additional security in today's terrorist threatened environment. I thank God that at least some of our rights are written in stone, as it were, in our Constitution so that they cannot be given away by mere majorities who may be fearing for their own safety and who do not have the fortitude to stand up and fight for them as our ancestors did. Freedoms of speech, assembly, religion, rights to have an attorney, to not testify against oneself, and all of the other rights protected in the Bill of Rights should remain regardless of the terrorist threat.

The same goes for the Second Amendment, regardless of whether public policy would indicate that it should protect individual rights to keep and bear arms, or be interpreted to protect state powers over the militia. Whether I believe that it is a good idea for many people to have guns, or that it would be a good idea for nobody to have guns simply should not enter into the process of what the Amendment actually means. If public policy calls for a change, then go through the method set forth in the Constitution to change it.

If a valid public policy reason ever exists to change any of these rights, then the appropriate method for that change is for the proponents of that change to get members of Congress to introduce a constitutional amendment, and obtain the support of sufficient members to pass it and then get enough states to ratify it. The use of the courts to try to change the interpretation of the right based on public policy grounds is not a valid method, in my opinion.

The second reason that I do not like this factor is that, unlike the factors of historical meaning, case law, or the grammatical structure of the provision itself, public policy, like beauty, is clearly in the eye of the beholder. Your view of public policy is every bit as good as mine. That does not mean that I will agree with you, but that you have as much right to your opinion as I do to mine. And this is fine; this is the way it should be, when we are talking about statutory enactments. However, when we are talking about constitutional protections, something more than opinions should be involved. We should trust to the collective wisdom of the ages, the genius of the Founding Fathers, the collective intellect of over 200 years of the best jurists this country has had to offer, to tell us what the constitution means, not new opinions that may influence today's judges to change that interpretation. Again, if we do not like the interpretation given, based on our opinions of public policy, it is incumbent on us to try to change what the Constitution says, not change how the courts interpret it.

Third, in an attempt to look as scientific as possible, and as impressive as historians, social scientists invariably turn to statistical analysis to support their opinions on what good public policy is or should be. Now I am not a trained statistician. However, I have studied statistics both from a mathematical viewpoint and from a political science/public-polling viewpoint, and I can tell you that there are many problems with basing anything on statistical studies. They say that statistics do not lie, but people who use statistics do.

How the study is set up can greatly affect its outcome. Time periods studied, population groups included or excluded, questions (if asked) can be worded to get the answers wanted, sources used for official statistics, all of these items and more can be manipulated to obtain the results desired. On some issues there are many variables that should be controlled for to get valid results, and it may not be possible to control for them, or if possible to control, the people conducting the study may not have done so. If not controlled, then the results may be due to these other variables, not the issue that is being studied. For example, in the area of the presence of guns, or the enactment of gun-control laws, and their relation to the level of crime, how do you control for changes in the economy, which may affect crime levels, or changes in the numbers of people put in prison, which may affect crime levels, or changes in security technology, which may affect crime levels, or improvements in hospital performance, which may reduce the number of deaths due to guns? More will be said on all of this later. Even if the study is basically valid, the public position on the results of the study may be spun out of control to make the impression that the users want, even if it is not a valid impression. A totally unrelated example here will show my point.

As I am writing this book, Ford Motor Company has an advertisement that appears on television and radio for their pickup trucks that says: "Five of America's ten best sellers; they're America's best." Now I assume that the statement is true, based on valid statistics, or otherwise Ford could be in trouble for false advertising. But what is really being said? The statement is clearly meant to impress people, that so many people like Ford pickups that they must be a good deal and you too should buy one. After all, they hold a lock on one-half of the top ten sales positions. But is that necessarily a good position? Let's look at some different scenarios that would make the above statement true, but would have vastly different meanings for the impact of how good Ford trucks are.

Ford could hold all five of the top five positions, with each of its five pickup models outselling all others, except for the other Ford products. This would certainly allow the advertisement statement to be true, and would certainly be impressive. But I doubt that this is the case, because if it were Ford would be saying that instead of five of the top ten. Which statement would you be more impressed by? On the other hand, all five of Fords models could be ranked six through ten, with each of the other manufacturers' models outselling all five of Ford's models put together. This would still allow Ford's advertised statement to be true, but would not be very impressive at all. Or the actual statistics could be somewhere in between these two extremes, but we do not know where. Are the true statistics really impressive or not? Do you see how statistics can be spun to make a silk purse out of a sow's ear? Now I must say that I am not accusing Ford of doing this, because I do not know what its statistics are. It just makes a convenient example. And if this spinning can be done for pickups, it can be done for guns, both for and against them.

So, the bottom line on my opinion of the use of statistics to try to determine what good public policy is or should be, is that I simply do not trust them. There is too much room for manipulation of the results for me to be very trusting. And I must add that this goes to the statistics used on both sides of the issue at hand. I do not trust the statistics of either the gun-control advocates or the gun-rights advocates, with one exception, which I will point out and explain shortly. Therefore, I do not believe that this is a valid method to try to influence the meaning of a constitutional provision.

With all of this said about my opinion of why current public policy is not a good or valid factor to use in determining what the Second Amendment means, the fact of the matter is that the courts are sometimes swayed by public policy, therefore we must look at it. The methodology that I will use to look at public policy is to look at the various reasons given to have a guarantee of an individual right, and the reasons given to not have that guarantee, or to just have the Amendment go to protect state powers over the militia, and compare them. In this chapter this will be done only at the constitutional level. There is another chapter dealing with the extent of the protection of the Second Amendment, and what gun control laws should be allowed, and that involves a separate, though obviously related and somewhat overlapping, question of public policy at the statutory level.

A. *Protection of State Militias*

According to gun-control advocates, this is the sole reason for the Second Amendment. Gun-rights advocates would generally accept the protection of the militias as **a** reason, though in a different vein and with a different result than the gun control advocates desire. The crux of the difference on this reason lies with the definition of militia. We have already discussed this in Chapter 3. Gun control advocates say that the militia in the Second Amendment is the National Guard, while the gun rights advocates say that it is the body of the people. There is a dispute over what, if any, affect the adjective phrase "well-regulated" has on the definitions used.

Jack Reynolds, J. D.

Beyond what I have already said about these arguments in previous chapters, the real problem that I have with the gun control advocates' position is that it basically argues the Second Amendment totally out of existence, to where it does not even provide the protection to the states that they say it does. Their logic goes like this. The Second Amendment protects only the state's right to have a militia. Therefore, there is no right for any individual to have a gun, even if he is in the militia, because it is only the state government that is protected. The only guns protected are those provided by the state, which are kept in the National Guard armories.

If you do not believe me, that this is the position that is being foisted on the American people, read the following exchange between one of the three judges on the Fifth Circuit panel that heard the *Emerson* case, and the U.S. Attorney (yes, the agent of the federal government) arguing the case on appeal (this was before Attorney General John Ashcroft changed the position of the government to one supporting individual rights):

> **Judge Garwood:** "You are saying that the Second Amendment is consistent with a position that you can take guns away from the public? You can restrict ownership of rifles, pistols and shotguns from all people? Is that the position of the United States?"
> **Meteja (attorney for the government):** "Yes"
> **Garwood:** "Is it the position of the United States that persons who are not in the National Guard are afforded no protections under the Second Amendment?"
> **Meteja:** "Exactly."
> Meteja then said that even membership in the National Guard isn't enough to protect the private ownership of a firearm. It wouldn't protect the guns owned at the home of someone in the National Guard.
> **Garwood:** "Membership in the National Guard isn't enough? What else is needed?"
> **Meteja:** "The weapon in question must be used IN the National Guard." [461]

Therefore, while the state may be protected in its "right" to have guns in the militia, the individual is not. Since the National Guard is the "militia", the unorganized militia does not count. The gun control advocates then stop, and do not carry this logic through to its inevitable result. But here comes the problem. The National Guard is not provided arms by the states, but by the Federal government, the very problem feared by the Founding Fathers; the very fear that the gun control advocates say caused the passage of the Second Amendment. So what would happen if the federal government stopped providing weapons to the National Guard, or took all of the weapons away, or nationalized the National Guard so that it no longer belongs to the states? The states would no longer have the ability to maintain a militia, as defined by the gun control advocates, and would therefore not have a right to have a militia or to provide their militias with arms. If the "right" exists only at the discretion of the federal government, then it is no right at all, and the Second Amendment might as well not exist, because it in effect does nothing. Do you really think that the Founding Fathers and Framers were so stupid that they put in all of the effort to enact this amendment that does nothing?

And let's look at this issue from another perspective. If the gun control advocates truly believe that the Second Amendment somehow protects the "right", or power, of the states to arm their militias, then they should be willing to stand up for this constitutional right every bit as strongly as they stand up and announce their position on the Second Amendment in their efforts to support gun control laws that they favor. So would they? What would they do if a state, exercising this protected "right" or power, were to decide to arm its unorganized militia as the states used to do at the time the Second Amendment was enacted?

Let us imagine that a state decides that it no longer trusts the federal government to provide for the militia (National Guard) and passes a statute requiring all adults, ages 18 through 60, to become a part of its militia, and to provide their own firearms and ammunition. Let us further assume that since today's American military uses weapons such as M-16's, the statute also requires that the weapon that each person has to provide for himself/herself is an M-16. Surely states could pass such a statute, since they had the power to do so after the Second Amendment was passed, and no other change has been made to the Constitution since then to affect either state powers over militias or individual ownership of guns. If they had the power to pass such laws then, they can do it now.

But, by the way, manufacturing of M-16's for sale to individuals is illegal under the federal gun control law that bans assault weapons. We now have a problem under the supremacy clause of the Constitution. Normally a federal law will preempt and override any state law in conflict with it. Here people would be required to do something by state law that is illegal under federal law. But, if the gun control advocates are right about what the Second Amendment does, then the Second Amendment steps in to say that the state governments can do this, therefore, the federal law prohibiting such ownership would be unconstitutional as applied in that state.

Would the gun control advocates stand up for the Constitution, for the Second Amendment, as protecting the "right", or power, of the states to arm its militia? I sincerely doubt it. And if they would not, then they are not making a legitimate argument as to what the Second Amendment does. For when you put forth a position on the Constitution, you must be willing to see it through to its logical conclusion, whether you like the end result or not. If you are not willing to do this, you had better rethink your position.

Since the Second Amendment must be interpreted so as to have some effect, and the gun control position would give it no effect, and since it is highly unlikely that anyone would stand up for any state trying to exercise its Second Amendment "rights" against federal laws which prohibit the manufacture of assault weapons, then it must actually be interpreted to guarantee a pre-existing individual right to keep and bear arms.

B. *Self-Defense vs. The Danger of Guns*

History clearly shows that self-defense was one reason that some of the Founding Fathers wanted to protect the individual's right to keep and bear arms. Additionally, it can be argued that while there is evidence that the Founding Fathers did have a concern for self-defense, there appears to be no evidence that they were concerned with any supposed dangers of individuals having guns. While there were some regulations of guns in colonial times and early on by the states, it came nowhere close to those proposed today. The assault weapons of the time, military muskets and rifles, were not only not banned, governments required people to possess them! While some governments did restrict the carrying of concealed weapons, some required the carrying of guns if a person was traveling away from his home, for the purpose of self-protection. All of this was addressed in more detail in Chapter 4 on history. Therefore, looking at the public policy of the time of the passage of the Second Amendment would indicate that the Framers were more concerned about the issue of self-defense than they were about the dangers posed by guns, therefore this would imply an individual right being protected by the Second Amendment.

And logically it must be conceded that even today a basic right to self-defense could rise to a constitutional level so as to form a basis under public policy for interpreting the Second Amendment to guarantee an individual right. If you have the right of self-defense, then you should have the right to have, and utilize, the tools, i.e. guns, that may be necessary to exercise that right of self-defense. The real question is whether under public policy the danger that the presence of guns may present should override this basic right of self-defense, or does public policy even strengthen this right by self-defense actually becoming societal defense?

Here we can get mired down into the statistics that I complained of at the beginning of this chapter. Gun control advocates assert that more than 180,000 Americans are injured by gunfire every year, and that over 30,000 are killed, mostly by handguns. They point out that suicides account for more than half of the annual gun deaths.[462] They claim that the increase of guns in America is the cause of all of this. They point to other countries, such as Canada and Japan, that have strict gun control laws and much lower rates of shootings, asserting that gun control therefore must work to reduce violence, injuries and deaths.[463] For example, they point out that in 1996, handguns were used to murder only 30 people in Great Britain, 106 in Canada, 15 in Japan, but 9,300 in the United States. They also point out, legitimately, that these shootings not only affect those who are shot, but also countless relatives and friends, causing much pain and grief to loved ones, financial hardship to those left behind, and a financial burden on society to deal with the medical treatment of the victims of gun violence, lost time from work, and countless other ways that this violence is a detriment to society. Therefore, the gun control advocates argue, public policy demands that the Constitution not provide a right to individuals to be able to have firearms, especially not handguns.

Gun rights advocates have their own statistics. They point to the supply of handguns going up in the Unites States recently, while the incidence of violence with guns has decreased. They point out that studies have indicated that the presence of guns may be a factor in the method chosen by a person to commit suicide, but it is not a factor in whether or not the person commits suicide. In other words, if a gun is readily available, it is likely to be used. But if a gun is not available, the person wanting to commit suicide will merely find another way to do so. They also point to other countries, most notably Switzerland, where gun ownership is pervasive, but where the incidence of gun violence is as low as the countries cited by the gun control advocates.

Let's look at other examples. The American Bar Association strays away from a legal analysis of the Second Amendment and involves itself with an apparent agenda, citing statistics clearly designed to inflame the emotions and encourage gun control. Some of the items cited on its web page include the following:

- "The United States has the highest rates of childhood homicide, suicide, and firearms-related death among all of the industrialized countries.
- The overall firearms-related death rate among U.S. children aged 15 years or less is nearly 12 times higher than among children in the other 25 countries combined.
- The homicide rate for U.S. children in the United States is five times higher than among children in the other 25 industrialized countries combined.
- Of the total homicides among children in the world, 73 percent occurred among U.S. children.
- The suicide rate for American children 14 and younger is twice that of the rest of the industrialized world.[464]

However, gun rights advocates have their own statistics responding to this. Guncite.com has two charts put together, which are reproduced here, which show that all is not as bad as the gun control advocates would have you believe:

International Homicide Rate Table (Death rates are per 100,000)[465]

Country	Year	Population	Total Homicide	Firearm Homicide	Non-Gun Homicide	% Households With Guns
South Africa	1995	41,465,000	75.30	26.60	48.70	n/a
Colombia	1996	37,500,000	64.60	50.60	14.00	n/a
Estonia	1994	1,499,257	28.21	8.07	20.14	n/a
Brazil	1993	160,737,000	19.04	10.58	8.46	n/a
Mexico	1994	90,011,259	17.58	9.88	7.70	n/a
Philippines	1996	72,000,000	16.20	3.50	12.70	n/a
Taiwan[1]	1996	21,979,444	8.12	0.97	7.15	n/a
N. Ireland	1994	1,641,711	6.09	5.24	0.85	8.4
United States[2]	1999	272,691,000	5.70	3.72	1.98	39.0
Argentina	1994	34,179,000	4.51	2.11	2.40	n/a
Hungary	1994	10,245,677	3.53	0.23	3.30	n/a
Finland[3]	1994	5,088,333	3.24	0.86	2.38	23.2
Portugal	1994	5,138,600	2.98	1.28	1.70	n/a
Mauritius	1993	1,062,810	2.35	0	2.35	n/a
Israel	1993	5,261,700	2.32	0.72	1.60	n/a
Italy	1992	56,764,854	2.25	1.66	0.59	16.0
Scotland	1994	5,132,400	2.24	0.19	2.05	4.7
Canada	1992	28,120,065	2.16	0.76	1.40	29.1
Slovenia	1994	1,989,477	2.01	0.35	1.66	n/a
Australia	1994	17,838,401	1.86	0.44	1.42	19.4
Singapore	1994	2,930,200	1.71	0.07	1.64	n/a
South Korea	1994	44,453,179	1.62	0.04	1.58	n/a
New Zealand	1993	3,458,850	1.47	0.17	1.30	22.3
Belgium	1990	9,967,387	1.41	0.60	0.81	16.6
England/Wales[4]	1997	51,429,000	1.41	0.11	1.30	4.7
Switzerland[5]	1994	7,021,000	1.32	0.58	0.74	27.2
Sweden	1993	8,718,571	1.30	0.18	1.12	15.1
Denmark	1993	5,189,378	1.21	0.23	0.98	n/a
Austria	1994	8,029,717	1.17	0.42	0.75	n/a
Germany[6]	1994	81,338,093	1.17	0.22	0.95	8.9
Greece	1994	10,426,289	1.14	0.59	0.55	n/a
France	1994	57,915,450	1.12	0.44	0.68	22.6

Country	Year	Population	Total Homicide	Firearm Homicide	Non-Gun Homicide	% Households With Guns
Netherlands	1994	15,382,830	1.11	0.36	0.75	1.9
Kuwait	1995	1,684,529	1.01	0.36	0.65	n/a
Norway	1993	4,324,815	0.97	0.30	0.67	32.0
Spain	1993	39,086,079	0.95	0.21	0.74	13.1
Japan	1994	124,069,000	0.62	0.02	0.60	n/a
Ireland	1991	3,525,719	0.62	0.03	0.59	n/a

Notes:

1. Number of homicides: Ministry of Interior, National Police Administration (link not always active), Taiwan.
   Population: As of April 1999, Government Information Office, Taiwan.
   Gun Homicides: Central News Agency, Taipei, November 23, 1997.
2. Total homicide rate and firearm homicide rates are from FBI Uniform Crime Report(1999).
3. The United Nations International Study on Firearm Regulation reports Finland's gun ownership rate at 50% of households.
4. Total homicides and gun homicides: Criminal Statistics, England and Wales, 1997.
   Population: 52.2 million in mid-1997, Office for National Statistics Monitor, press release.
5. Percent households with guns includes all army personnel.
6. Percent households with guns excludes East Germany.

Sources:

Homicide data for Colombia, Philippines, and South Africa are from the United Nations International Study on Firearm Regulation .
Population figures for Colombia, Philippines, and South Africa are estimates based on UN data.

Data for the remainder of the countries, except as noted above: *International Journal of Epidemiology* 1998:27:216.
Column "% Households With Firearms": *Can Med Assoc J*, Killias, M (1993), except United States (Gallup [2000] and Harris [2001] polls.)

Note: Argentina, Brazil, Estonia, Greece, Hungary, Mexico, Mauritius, Slovenia, Portugal, and South Korea are classified as upper-middle-income countries by the World Bank. GunCite does not know the classification for Colombia, South Africa and the Philippines. The remainder are considered high-income countries."

Points made by the Guncite.com link is that England already had a much lower homicide rate than the United States before it ever enacted any gun control laws. From the table, it can be seen that the Swiss, who have hundreds of thousands of fully automatic weapons in their homes, and the Israelis, who also allowed large numbers of gun owners at the time, both have low homicide rates. Also, if we look at **non-gun** murders, the U.S. has a higher rate than many European counties' **total** murder rates. But Taiwan, the Phillipines and Mexico have **non-gun** murder rates that exceed the United States' **total** murder rate. What all of this means is, as I said, statistics can say different things to different people, and there are many more variables at play here than just the availability of guns.

The other table from Guncite.com[466] shows similar statistical problems:

Jack Reynolds, J. D.

International Violent Death Rate Table (Death rates are per 100,000)

Country	Year	Population	Total Death	Total Homicide	Firearm Homicide	Total Suicide	Firearm Suicide	% Households With Guns
Estonia	1994	1,499,257	70.76	28.21	8.07	40.95	3.13	n/a
Hungary	1994	10,245,677	39.01	3.53	0.23	35.38	0.88	n/a
Slovenia	1994	1,989,477	33.37	2.01	0.35	31.16	2.51	n/a
Finland[1]	1994	5,088,333	30.72	3.24	0.86	27.26	5.78	23.2
Brazil	1993	160,737,000	25.34	19.04	10.58	3.46	0.73	n/a
Denmark	1993	5,189,378	23.46	1.21	0.23	22.13	2.25	n/a
Austria	1994	8,029,717	23.36	1.17	0.42	22.12	4.06	n/a
Switzerland[2]	1994	7,021,000	22.80	1.32	0.58	21.28	5.61	27.2
France	1994	57,915,450	22.67	1.12	0.44	20.79	5.14	22.6
Mexico	1994	90,011,259	21.74	17.58	9.88	2.89	0.91	n/a
Belgium	1990	9,967,387	20.77	1.41	0.60	19.04	2.56	16.6
Portugal	1994	5,138,600	18.95	2.98	1.28	14.83	1.28	n/a
United States[3]	1993	257,783,004	18.57	5.70	3.72	12.06	7.35	39.0
Japan	1994	124,069,000	17.34	0.62	0.02	16.72	0.04	n/a
Sweden	1993	8,718,571	17.12	1.30	0.18	15.75	2.09	15.1
Germany[4]	1994	81,338,093	17.00	1.17	0.22	15.64	1.17	8.9
Taiwan[5]	1996	21,979,444	15.00	8.12	0.97	6.88	0.12	n/a
Singapore	1994	2,930,200	15.77	1.71	0.07	14.06	0.17	n/a
Canada	1992	28,120,065	15.64	2.16	0.76	13.19	3.72	29.1
Mauritius	1993	1,062,810	15.42	2.35	0	12.98	0.09	n/a
Argentina	1994	34,179,000	15.25	4.51	2.11	6.71	3.05	n/a
Norway	1993	4,324,815	14.75	0.97	0.30	13.64	3.95	32.0
N. Ireland	1994	1,641,711	14.74	6.09	5.24	8.41	1.34	8.4
Australia	1994	17,838,401	14.65	1.86	0.44	12.65	2.35	19.4
New Zealand	1993	3,458,850	14.63	1.47	0.17	12.81	2.14	22.3
Scotland	1994	5,132,400	14.46	2.24	0.19	12.16	0.31	4.7
Hong Kong	1993	5,919,000	11.52	1.23	0.12	10.29	0.07	n/a
Netherlands	1994	15,382,830	11.25	1.11	0.36	10.10	0.31	1.9
South Korea	1994	44,453,179	11.17	1.62	0.04	9.48	0.02	n/a
Ireland	1991	3,525,719	10.68	0.62	0.03	9.81	0.94	n/a
Italy	1992	56,764,854	10.42	2.25	1.66	8.00	1.11	16.0
England/Wales[6]	1992	51,429,000	9.53	1.41	0.11	7.68	0.33	4.7
Israel	1993	5,261,700	9.80	2.32	0.72	7.05	1.84	n/a
Spain	1993	39,086,079	8.97	0.95	0.21	7.77	0.43	13.1
Greece	1994	10,426,289	4.61	1.14	0.59	3.40	0.84	n/a
Kuwait	1995	1,684,529	3.50	1.01	0.36	1.66	0.06	n/a
Country	Year	Population	Total Death	Total Homicide	Firearm Homicide	Total Suicide	Firearm Suicide	% Households With Guns

A People Armed and Free

Notes:
1. The United Nations International Study on Firearm Regulation reports Finland's gun ownership rate at 50% of households.
2. Percent households with guns includes all army personnel.
3. Total homicide rate and firearm homicide rates are for 1999, FBI Uniform Crime Report (1999).
4. Percent households with guns excludes East Germany.
5. Number of homicides: Ministry of Interior, National Police Administration (link not always active), Taiwan.
   Population: As of April 1999, Government Information Office, Taiwan.
   Gun Homicides: Central News Agency, Taipei, November 23, 1997.
6. Total homicides and gun homicides for 1997: Criminal Statistics, England and Wales, 1997.
   Population: 52.2 million in mid-1997, Office for National Statistics Monitor, press release.

Sources:
The first eight columns of data are from the *International Journal of Epidemiology* (1998). The "Total Death" column was calculated by including homicides, suicides, and unintentional and undetermined firearm (not shown here) rates.
Column "% Households With Firearms": *Can Med Assoc J*, Killias, M (1993), except United States (Gallup [2000] and Harris [2001] polls.)
Note: Argentina, Brazil, Estonia, Greece, Hungary, Mexico, Mauritius, Slovenia, Portugal, and South Korea are classified as upper-middle-income countries by the World Bank. The remainder are considered high-income countries.

What can be seen from this table is that while Northern Ireland has only 8.4% of its households with guns, its firearm homicide rate is 5.24, compared with the United States with 39% of its households with guns, and a firearm homicide rate of only 3.72. Then Norway, with a gun ownership rate comparable to the United States, at 32%, only has a firearm homicide rate of .3, less than 1/10th of the United States. Three countries, with unknown gun ownership rates, Estonia, Brazil and Mexico, have firearm homicide rates far in excess of anything even feared by the United States, at 8.07, 19.04, and 17.58 respectively. With Estonia having just recently come out from the Iron Curtain, I have a hard time believing that its gun ownership rate, in 1994 when these statistics were reported, would even closely approximate that of the United States. I also doubt that the gun ownership rates in Brazil and Mexico would greatly exceed ours.

Let's look at some other statistics compiled by the ABA:

- "According to the Centers for Disease Control and Prevention, every seven hours a child or teen was killed in a firearm-related accident or suicide in 1999.
- Gunfire killed 3,761 infants, children, and teens in 1998.
- http://www.cdfactioncouncil.org/children_and_guns_brief_stats.htm
- Of all the children killed by gunfire, 58 percent were victims of homicide and about 33 percent died from suicide. Guns remain the most common method of suicide for children. Accidental shootings accounted for most of the balance of the gun deaths of children.
- http://www.cdfactioncouncil.org/children_and_guns_brief_stats.htm
- In 1997, 85% of homicide victims 15 to 19 years old were killed with firearms. The firearm homicide rate increased by 67% between 1987 and 1997.
- http://www.cdc.gov/ncipc/pub-res/FactBook/fbkvio.pdf
- According to the Children's Defense fund, the latest numbers about children and gun violence in a single year show:
- 3,365 children and teens were killed by gunfire in 1999,
- 1,990 were murdered by gunfire
- 1,078 committed suicide with a firearm
- 214 died from an accidental shooting "[467]

However, again Guncite.com has a table[468] showing all accident types for all age groups, which shows that things are not as bad as they seem:

Deaths Due to Unintentional Injuries, 2000 (Estimates) (Chart compiled by GunCite. Source of data, except as noted, National Safety Council, *Injury Facts*, 2001 Edition, pp. 8-9, 84)

Accident Type	Age							
	0-4	5-14	15-24	25-44	45-64	65-74	75+	Total
All Automobile	900	1,500	10,500	13,300	9,200	2,700	4,900	43,000
Falls	70	70	210	950	1,900	1,700	11,300	16,200
Poisoning by solids, liquids	60	40	800	6,800	3,200	300	500	11,700
Pedestrian¹	250	300	750	1,300	1,400	450	850	5,300
Drowning	450	350	700	1,250	650	230	270	3,900
Fires, burns	400	260	240	700	800	500	700	3,600
Suffocation by ingested object	100	20	30	250	400	500	2,100	3,400
Firearms	20	60	150	190	110	30	40	600
Poisoning by gases, vapors	10	10	70	120	80	40	70	400
All other causes	700	400	1,100	3,000	3,200	1,600	4,500	14,500
TOTAL	2,700	2,700	13,800	26,600	19,500	7,600	24,400	97,300

1. Pedestrian fatalities are also included in motor vehicle fatalities. They are broken-out on a separate line to illustrate how often pedestrian fatalities occur.

As can be seen, despite the large number of firearms present in America, firearm related accidents rate relatively low on the list of causes of accidents. Nobody is arguing that we take away automobiles, or cleaning supplies or household poisons due to the high number of accidental deaths attributable to these causes.

More from the ABA:
- "Guns kept in the home for self-protection are more often used to kill somebody you know than to kill in self-

defense; 22 times more likely, according to a 1998 study by the *Journal of Trauma*. http://www.jtrauma.com/
- In 1999, according to the FBI's Uniform Crime Report, there were only 154 justifiable homicides committed by private citizens with a firearm compared with a total of 8,259 firearm murders in the United States.
- http://www.fbi.gov/ucr/ucr.htm
- Between 1988 and 1997, the suicide, homicide, and unintentional firearm death rates among women were disproportionately higher in states where guns were more prevalent. The elevated rates of violent death in states with more guns was not entirely explained by a state's poverty or urbanization and was driven primarily by lethal firearm violence, not by lethal nonfirearm violence.
- http://jurban.oupjournals.org/cgi/content/abstract/79/1/26"[469]

This will be responded to shortly. In the meantime, more ABA statistics:
- "According to the National Crime Victimization Survey (NCVS) in 2000, 533,470 victims of serious violent crimes (rape and sexual assault, robbery, and aggravated assault) stated that they faced an offender with a firearm. http://www.ojp.usdoj.gov/bjs/guns.htm
- In 1998, firearm-related injuries remained the second leading cause of injury death in the United States, accounting for approximately 31,000 deaths. http://www.cdc.gov/mmwr/preview/mmwrhtml/ss5002a1.htm
- The majority of these fatal and nonfatal firearm-related injuries result from interpersonal violence and intentionally self-inflicted gunshot wounds, but approximately 15,000 unintentional gunshot wounds are treated in U.S. hospital emergency departments (EDs) each year. http://www.cdc.gov/mmwr/preview/mmwrhtml/ss5002a1.htm

- Although firearm-related injuries represent <0.5% of injuries treated in hospital EDs, they have an increased potential of death and hospitalization compared with other causes of injury. http://www.cdc.gov/mmwr/preview/mmwrhtml/ss5002a1.htm
- In 1994, treatment of gunshot injuries in the United States was estimated at $2.3 billion in lifetime medical costs, of which $1.1 billion was paid by the federal government. These factors emphasize the importance of firearm-related injuries as a public health concern. http://www.cdc.gov/mmwr/preview/mmwrhtml/ss5002a1.htm"[470]
- "Over 3,500 students were expelled in 1998-99 for bringing guns to school. Of these, 43% were in elementary or junior high school. (U.S. Department of Education. *Report on State Implementation of the Gun-Free Schools Act: School Year 1998-99.* October 2000, p. 2.) http://www.ed.gov/offices/OESE/SDFS/GFSA/
- A 1999 survey conducted by the Center for Disease Control found that 4.9% of high school students reported having carried a gun at least once in the last 30 days. http://www.cdc.gov/ncipc/factsheets/schoolvi.htm "[471]

I cannot resist this one. This statement is made by the ABA to sound like almost 5% of our school children carry firearms to school at times. But that is not what it says. There were times when I was a teenager that if I had been asked if I had carried a gun within the last thirty days, my answer would have been yes. I occasionally went hunting with my cousin, or target shooting on my uncle's farm with my brother, my dad and my cousins. But I never carried a gun to school. This is a blatant attempt by the ABA to spin statistics to say something that they do not say, for propaganda purposes. I treat this as an attempt by the ABA to lie to the American people. In the meantime, more from the ABA:

- "The *New England Journal of Medicine* has determined that the presence of a gun in the home increases the risk of suicide fivefold.http://www.nejm.org

Jack Reynolds, J. D.

- Firearms are a highly lethal means of suicide. One study found that 92% of suicide attempts with firearms result in fatality. http://www.ajph.org/
- Suicide by firearms was the most common method for both men and women, accounting for 57% of all suicides, according to the National Institute of Mental Health. http://www.nimh.nih.gov/research/suifact.htm
- Firearms were the most common method of suicide by both males and females, 65 years and older, 1998, accounting for 78.0% of male and 34.8% of female suicides in that age group. http://www.cdc.gov/ncipc/factsheets/suifacts.htm
- Among persons aged 15-19 years, firearm-related suicides accounted for 62% of the increase in the overall rate of suicide from 1980-1997. http://www.cdc.gov/ncipc/factsheets/suifacts.htm
- In 1997, guns were used in 17,566 suicides, compared with 13,522 homicides, according to the National Vital Statistics Report. http://www.nytimes.com/library/national/101799suicide-hearings.html "[472]

I cannot improve on the response to these statistics from Dr. Gary Kleck, a Florida State University criminologist:

> The full body of relevant studies indicates that firearm availability measures are significantly and positively associated with rates of *firearm* suicide, but have no significant association with rates of *total* suicide.
> Of thirteen studies, nine found a significant association between gun levels and rates of *gun* suicide, but only one found a significant association between gun levels and rates of *total* suicides. The only study to find a measure of "gun availability" significantly associated with total suicide...used a measure of gun availability known to be invalid.
> This pattern of results supports the view that where guns are less common, there is complete substitution of

other methods of suicide, and that, while gun levels influence the choice of suicide method, they have no effect on the number of people who die in suicides.[473]

The problem with all of these statistics is multifold. First, what is the time period covered by these statistics? There may have been different trends in the 1970's than the 1980's, and the 1980's may have been different than the 1990's, and the 2000's may prove to be different yet. What were the sources of the statistics? Different government agencies collect data for different purposes, and the source used may be under inclusive or over inclusive of what really needs to be looked at. What jurisdictions were these statistics taken from? Different countries have different cultures, which provide different results. If from the United States, was it the country as a whole? If so, were there differences among the different areas of the country. Did gun violence go up in New York or California, while it went down in Texas, or was it exactly the opposite? This makes a difference because different states are treating gun ownership differently. So, if there is a connection between gun ownership or gun availability and gun violence, one would expect to find different statistics from the different states based on the way they regulate guns.

For example, gun control advocates assert that one reason for the recent reduction in violent crimes is the enactment of more gun control laws at both the state and federal level. They are especially found of saying that the Brady Law has had a great impact on the reduction of violent crime. On the other hand, gun rights advocates argue that the passage of concealed carry weapons laws has actually served to reduce violent crime, because criminals now do not know if their potential victims may be armed or not. There will be more on these points in Chapter 10 on the extent of the Second Amendment protection. In the meantime, both camps seem to totally ignore the possibility that a booming economy during the 1990's may have contributed to the reduction in violent crime. Also, how about the fact that most states have been on a prison-building spree, after many lawsuits in the 1980's complaining of overcrowding of the prisons forced the states to release a horde of criminals before their sentences were fully served. That resulted in more criminals on the street in the 1980's and fewer in the 1990's. That might have something to do with the statistics. I have even seen one report that claims that the increase in legal abortions has contributed to the reduction of violent crimes.[474]

Do you see the problem with the number of possible variables involved in this issue? But we are not finished yet. Gun control advocates claim that people who want to have guns in their homes are more likely to be shot by their own guns than they are by a criminal intruder. They claim that there are only about 108,000 defensive gun uses annually. A defensive gun use is any incident where a gun was used to protect yourself, or somebody else, or your property. This can include any incident where you shoot at someone, whether you kill him, wound him, or totally miss him, but it would also include any instance where a gun was merely brandished and the bad guy, upon seeing the gun, may have run away without any shot being fired. Defensive gun uses also include incidents where guns are used to protect people from animals, such as bears, wolves and the like. Gun control advocates assert that for every case of self-protection homicide involving a firearm kept in the home, there are 1.3 accidental deaths, 4.6 homicides, and 37 suicides involving firearms, meaning that if you have a gun in your home, you are 43 times more likely to be killed by it, than you are to use it to kill an intruder in self-defense.[475] But there are problems with the methodology of all of these statistics. For example, this only compares the times the gun was used to kill the bad guy. It does not look at all of the other defensive gun uses.

One author has pointed out that the methodology used to get the 43:1 ratio, if applied to non-gun related deaths versus non-gun related self-protection homicides results in a 99:1 ratio.[476] The author then uses the example of martial arts. If this 99:1 ratio holds true for non-gun use, perhaps martial arts experts are more likely to be killed by non-gun methods than they are to kill in self-defense. Does this mean that we should avoid martial arts training because it is too dangerous? And what about the other defensive gun uses that do not result in the bad guy getting killed? Even using the gun control advocates' lowest number, if a life is saved even half of the time a gun is used defensively, then 54,000 lives are being saved annually.

And there is reason to suspect that 108,000 number. One professor has pointed out that this number was derived from a governmental study of the National Crime Victimization Survey. It was not a total count, which in truth no one has been able to do, but is a statistical analysis and projection of the number of defensive gun uses that the statisticians think occur each year. This study was a non-anonymous survey of crime victims by a branch of the federal government, the U.S. Bureau of Census. The purpose was not to estimate the number of defensive gun uses, but to get an overall survey of crime victims. The survey interviewers acknowledged that they were federal officers, even showing an identification card with a badge. The interviewees were told that the interviews were being conducted on behalf of the Department of Justice. The interviewees had to give their names, addresses, telephone numbers, and the names of all members of their households over 12 years of age. Then, during the interview, they were asked if they did anything to defend themselves. Since most of the crimes these people were victims of were committed away from the home, if the victims had a gun it might have been in violation of some law for them to be carrying it. There might also be some concern that their use of the gun might have been a violation of the law, or at least there might be a fear that it was. So it would be very easy and understandable for numerous people to simply deny any defensive gun use, even if it had occurred.

Other studies have estimated the annual defensive gun use rate to range from 800,000 to 2.5 million. The study most often cited by gun rights advocates, by Dr. Gary Kleck, from 1993, estimated two million defensive gun uses per year. However, I have also read critical assessments of this study, to the effect that the numbers are impossible because some of the estimates would have our hospitals over flowing with gun shot victims.[477] To put it simply, I do not know what is true, but I generally believe that on such studies you can usually reject the lowest and highest numbers and find the truth somewhere in the middle. If that is done here, the number of defensive gun uses would number somewhere between 800,000 and 2 million annually. Does that justify society absorbing the numbers of non-defensive shootings, injuries and deaths, and the attendant financial and emotional costs? Well if the actual number is in the middle, say 1,250,000, and a life is saved even just 10% of the time, that would amount to 125,000 lives saved.

But we still are not finished. Gun rights advocates point out that in countries where guns have been basically banned recently, the violent crime rate has gone up! In a new book,[478] Joyce Malcolm, a Bentley College historian, points out that in the 1800's there was wide spread gun ownership in England. Even so, there were few gun fatalities. Over three years, there were only 59 fatalities from handguns, of which 19 were accidents, 35 were suicides, and 3 were homicides, out of almost 30 million people. Of course these records might not be complete, but they are still pretty impressive. Despite these low rates, certainly low compared to the United States, England began to regulate guns, ostensibly to reduce crime, but actually to disarm potential labor unionists and Bolsheviks. Since 1997, when guns were virtually outlawed, gun crime has risen dramatically in England, and according to some studies a person is six times more likely to be mugged in London than New York City now.[479] I have seen similar reports concerning statistics from Australia, which also recently banned guns. All of this lends credence to the slogan that "when guns are outlawed, only outlaws will have guns."

Another way of looking at these statistics deals with the way that some crimes are committed. Dr. Kleck asserts that in Britain and the Netherlands, where guns are not allowed, they have a "hot burglary" rate of 45%. A "hot burglary" is a burglary committed while someone is at home. In the United States, the "hot burglary" rate is under 13%. The concept here is that apparently criminals may feel safer themselves going into a home if they know that the owners do not have guns, therefore the higher "hot" rate. If they think the owner might have a gun, they are less likely to commit the burglary when someone is at home. Clearly, if a burglary is committed at your home, you are pretty safe, physically, if you are not there. If you are there, you stand at least some risk of being injured, raped or killed. So, how can we measure the reduction of deaths and injuries that result from the lower percentage of "hot" burglaries in the United States?

Do you see my problem with statistical studies? You can pick and choose which ones you want to believe, and most people do. They tend to cite or quote those that support their arguments, and ignore those that go against them. If I were to rely on the studies at all, I must confess that I would tend to believe the studies used by the gun rights advocates because they give the results that I would expect to see based on my common sense of what I would expect the results to be. In other words, they make more sense to me. But then, I could be biased in this. And these studies could be biased, just like the gun control advocates' favorite studies can be. So I choose to not rely on them at all, except for one coming up.

A People Armed and Free

Then there are the anecdotal studies. These are reports of many true incidents of what has happened, both in support of gun control and in support of gun rights. They include the news reports of violent and gruesome murders and massacres, many including schoolchildren such as the incident at Columbine. These types of incidents have been reported so often, and so many of them have involved the United States Post Offices, that our society has coined a new phrase for such events: "Going postal". For the life of me, I cannot see that much stress as a postal employee. These people should try working at my law office if they want to see stress. But, in any event, the gun rights advocates have their anecdotes too. They point to cases in England, for example, where a homeowner was arrested for stopping a burglary of his home with a toy pistol, while the burglar walked free. There are statements to the effect that the reason that the Palestinians now use bombs instead of guns to attack their intended victims in Israel is that when they tried to commit mass killings with guns against civilians there, with many Israelis carrying their own weapons legally, the Palestinians were being shot by the civilians before they could carry out their intended acts. If some teachers had had guns at Columbine, how many students' lives would have been saved? There is even a gun rights web site which posts, daily, links to news stories across the country pertaining to defensive gun uses: Operation Self Defense, found at http://www.keepandbeararms.com/opsd/default.asp. It seems to average about two defensive gun uses per day, which only comes to about 730 per year, but it must be realized that they probably do not have access to all of the news stories throughout the country, and even if they did, many defensive gun uses are never reported in the news media. Which brings us to the problem with the anecdotal reports. They are even less reliable than statistics. You can always find some number of incidents that will support your position on virtually any issue. They may be normal results, or they may be a few aberrations. We just do not know.

Reactions to emotionally charged incidents do not make good public policy. Just because Christopher Reeve was tragically paralyzed by falling off of a horse, should we try to restrict people from riding horses? Just because there is a rash of infants dying from heat stroke after being left in a locked car each summer, does that mean that we should deny people the right to take children in their cars? We must look at the policy as a whole, not based on a few incidents, which may be the norm, or may be totally aberrant.

One problem with the studies looking at foreign countries is that they are dealing with different cultures and a different mix of other laws. So Japan has a lower gun violence rate. I have been stationed in Okinawa in the Marine Corps, and while there are some admirable parts of the Japanese culture, I would not want to be subject to many of their laws that restrict freedom. These studies also do not look at all possible variables as noted above. So where does all of this leave us? As I said at the beginning of this chapter, I do not trust any of them, except one.

John Lott and David Mustard[480] examined crime statistics from 1977 to 1992 for each and every county in the United States. They looked at the results individually by county. They then compared the statistics before and after people in the county, due to changes in state laws as to the ability of people to carry concealed firearms, were allowed to carry concealed guns, if it ever happened. By doing the study in this manner, it covers all possible economic changes, it covers both times when more criminals were being let out, and more were being incarcerated. It looks at the statistics on a local basis, so that one area's statistics in one direction could not be offset by another area's statistics in the opposite direction. It basically eliminates the other variables, because they could all swing both ways. The only variable that can be related to any shifts, if there is a pattern, is the allowance of concealed weapons. And is there a pattern! In each and every county where concealed guns have been allowed, immediately after the allowance of concealed guns the crime rate went down. Murders by 8.5%, rapes by 5%, aggravated assaults by 7% and robbery by 3%, all on average. And the crime rate continues to go down for some years after the carrying of concealed guns is permitted. Lott and Mustard estimate that if those states that did not permit concealed handguns in 1992 had permitted them back then, we may have had 1,570 fewer murders, 4,177 fewer rapes, 60,000 fewer aggravated assaults, and 12,000 fewer robberies. In other words, they found that criminals act rationally. Where they have reason to fear that their victims might be armed, they reduce their criminal activity. And they found the largest affect in large cities, where gun control laws have usually been the strongest and where the crime rates have been the highest.

They also found that where crimes do occur, in regards to multiple victim shootings, the number of people killed or injured per attack is reduced if concealed carry is available, showing that the bad results from the crimes that are committed can be reduced.[481] Now there might be methodological problems with this study too, but I cannot see them. It appears clear to me that what common sense tells us would happen does in fact happen.

There are many other studies and reports, on both sides of this issue. Some of the papers go back and forth attacking each other's credibility. One could write a book just about this one perspective of the public policy issue, and indeed some people have. But it would be way beyond the scope of this book to try to look at all of these studies, as we did the legal issues and case law, or the historic aspect of the Second Amendment. And as I said earlier, it should not matter when dealing with a constitutional issue.

So what does all of this mean? I still stand fast on the concept that the right of self-defense is a natural right that we all have, and had before the Constitution was created. That right included the right to possess a firearm in order to exercise self-defense. The Second Amendment guarantees that the right to possess a firearm shall not be infringed, for self-defense among other reasons. Whatever your belief about the merits of having a firearm for self-defense as opposed to its inherent dangers should not affect this reading of the Constitution. But if the courts want to look at public policy to try to balance out these concerns and thereby determine what the Constitution should say about the right to possess guns, once they get through the problems of the studies, there is plenty of evidence to support the possession of guns for self-defense.

C. *Hunting*

You may recall that some of the Founding Fathers wanted to make sure that we could keep and bear arms for the purpose of hunting. Remember the discussion about bearing arms against rabbits? In any event, at the time of the Revolution, the establishment of the Constitution and passage of the Second Amendment, hunting was probably much more important to the livelihood of many Americans than it is today. Back then, many people used hunting to put food on their tables. Very few do so today. And of those who do, most do not have to, they merely do so because they enjoy hunting and do not want to kill for no reason at all, and do not want to waste the meat.

Jack Reynolds, J. D.

All of this shows that at the time the Second Amendment was passed, the policy of allowing people to have guns for hunting probably did rise to a constitutional level. But does it still do so today? I would say yes for two reasons. First, my position is once a constitutional right, always a constitutional right, at least until the constitution itself is changed. If hunting was a protected right at the beginning, or a reason for the constitutional guarantee of the right to keep and bear arms, then it should still be so now. This is similar to the point of the Third Amendment, which prohibits the federal government from quartering troops in private homes. Even though this was never tried, until one possible incident recently, and the government has made plenty of provision for other methods of quartering troops, does not mean that the right protected there has ceased to exist. It just means that it has never had to be invoked. So it is with the question of hunting as a public policy basis for the Second Amendment. It has not ceased to exist, but merely does not hold the spotlight that it once did.

The second reason may sound a little strange to some of you, but, without wanting to sound like I am a crazy survivalist, if there is some national or worldwide disaster that sets us all back a few years in our technology and living standards, we may find that hunting again becomes as important as it once was. It is much easier to protect a right than it is to get it back once it has been lost. It is not that I believe that any such disaster is about to happen, but if it does, the policy of allowing people to have guns for hunting should still be there for those who will need it.

D. *Sport*

What is sport? Some hunting could be considered sport. So could all forms of target practice, whether at a known distance range, skeet shooting, or like my brother, cousins and I used to do, taking some cans to my uncle's farm, putting them on the pond's levee to use it as an impact area, and then shooting at the cans from some distance away.

Now I can just hear the outcries of gun control advocates, that surely the mere enjoyment of firing guns cannot rise up to the level of constitutional protection. After all, would we protect football with the Constitution? Well, in a manner of speaking, we do protect football, because I am sure that football would be subject to the equal rights laws that other businesses are. In any event, there is even a better

A People Armed and Free

reason to look at sport as a reason to interpret the Second Amendment as protecting an individual's rights.

Remember that the gun control advocates say that the only reason for the Second Amendment is to protect the states' powers to maintain a "well-regulated" militia? And they say that "well-regulated" means trained. Well then, if people are allowed to use their own firearms, and their own ammunition, for sport shooting, such as target practice, then they become better marksmen at no cost to the government. Therefore, the militia becomes better trained, therefore, more of a "well-regulated" militia.

From my experience in the Marine Corps, I can tell you that generally those individuals who come to us from a background where they have been around guns, and have had some experience shooting guns, generally do better on the rifle and pistol ranges than those who do not. Of course, there are some exceptions, but overall, the civilian experience with guns does help an individual in the military to perform the required training with his issued weapon. Therefore, by the gun control advocates own arguments, there is a valid argument for sport to be a public policy basis for the Second Amendment guaranteeing an individual right to keep and bear arms.

E. The Insurrectionist Theory

I have saved this item for last because, if you could not tell from reading the chapter on the history pertaining to the Second Amendment, I believe that it is probably the most important reason for having the Second Amendment. This is not to say that I have changed my mind about the affect that we should give today's public policy in interpreting what the Second Amendment says or does. I have not. But, the insurrectionist theory was most certainly a big part of the public policy at the time it was passed and ratified, and therefore, like hunting and self-defense, remains a valid reason today for maintaining the original meaning of the Second Amendment, as protecting the rights of individuals.

At the same time, gun control advocates make probably their best-reasoned argument against the gun rights position in regards to this point. That does not mean that it is a correct argument, only that it is at least well reasoned and has a logic to it. I have presented plenty of well reasoned, logical arguments in court that have lost, so the mere fact that it is logical does not mean that the gun control advocates' argument will prevail. Even so, if a person is going to take a position on an issue, he must be willing to address the arguments of the opposing side, and if he cannot refute even the most logical of those opposing arguments, he should look at changing his position. Therefore, we will look at the gun control advocates' argument, and hopefully refute it. By that time you will see what I mean by it being their best-made position.

Their argument is founded on the notion that the insurrectionist theory is basically in conflict with the body of the Constitution.[482] Article I, Section 8, Clause 15 clearly provides that Congress is given the power "To provide for calling forth the Militia to **execute the Laws of the Union, suppress Insurrections** and repel Invasions". (Emphasis added). The Declaration of Independence does hold forth the principle that the people have the right to rebel against their government: "That whenever any Form of Government becomes destructive of these ends, **it is the Right of the People to alter or to abolish it**..." (Again, emphasis added). However, it is conceivable that the people, in making their social compact, called the Constitution, to form our government could have given away this right to the government, unless it is to be considered as one of the unalienable rights mentioned in the Declaration, in which case it could not be given away. The gun control advocates argue that clearly this has been done, since the federal government is given the power to suppress insurrections. Additionally, since this power is given in relation to the militias, it is inconceivable that the Second Amendment, which refers to the maintaining of a well-regulated militia, could be founded on the principle of insurrection, with that very same militia being planned for use in suppressing the insurrection. Do you see the conflict here?

They also question what would justify the people in exercising any supposed right to rebel. Could a group of people be protected from prosecution because they were supposedly exercising this right? For example, could the KKK execute liberal government officials, without facing prosecution, because they believe that forced integration violates their rights, therefore giving them a right to rebel and fight back against the federal government? If such a right exists surely it must be protectable by our court system.

Now arguments such as these have a certain logic. Usually courts try to read documents, be they statutes, contracts, or constitutions, to be internally consistent. And if there are two different interpretations

A People Armed and Free

of a provision, one of which would be in conflict with the rest of the document, and one of which would be in harmony with the rest of the document, the one in harmony with the rest will usually be adopted. Remember I pointed this out in Chapter 3 in relation to the text of the Second Amendment itself. This makes good sense, usually.

However, when you look at what went on in the Constitutional Convention, the different positions and interests fought over there, and the compromises made in the final result, you will see that our Founding Fathers wisely put many internal conflicts into the Constitution. First, think of the checks and balances that we all learned about in Freshman Civics classes, with the Congress having the power to pass laws, but the President having the power to veto them, but Congress then having the power, with a super majority, to override the veto, then the Supreme Court having the power to determine if the laws so passed are constitutional or not, and if not, they cannot be enforced. But the President has the power to appoint the members of the Supreme Court, but they have to be approved by the Senate. So who really has the ultimate power?

Then there is the conflict between the President and the Congress about who has the power to commit our armed forces to combat. The Constitution clearly gives only the Congress the power to declare war[483], but it also makes the President the Commander-in-Chief of the Armed Forces.[484] This power in the presidency has to include some power to direct the armed forces into combat. But where is the dividing line? This is an issue that has been argued since President Thomas Jefferson sent the navy and Marine Corps against the Barbary Pirates. It has come even more into play recently with the war on terrorism and the possibility of a war with Iraq. Certain incidents may clearly fall on one side or the other, but other incidents may also fall into a gray area where there is an internal conflict between these constitutional provisions.

Or how about the conflict between the representation of the people, and the rule of elites? While most of the Founding Fathers wanted a representative form of government, many of them did not trust the people and feared a tyranny of the people. Therefore, they instituted methods to allow the people to have a large say, through their popularly elected representatives, yet maintained a check on that by providing a protection to be provided by the elites of the country. The Senate was to be appointed by each state government, not elected by the people as they are today. The president was not to be directly elected, but to be elected by the Electoral College. That is why President Bush was able to win office in 2000, even though he received fewer votes nation wide that Al Gore.

When we get to the Bill of Rights, we find more internal conflicts. Look at the First Amendment. In it are two provisions, that when put together make up what most people call our freedom of religion. They are: "Congress shall make no law respecting an establishment of religion" and, "or prohibiting the free exercise thereof". Now let's take a look at how these provisions are applied in the context of public schools. If a principal was to come on the intercom first thing in the morning and announce that everybody in the school had to bow their heads for a prayer to be said by a school official, in the name of Jesus Christ (or Allah, or Jehovah, or any other specific religious entity) we would have a state requirement for people to participate in a religious act which they may or may not agree with, and this would therefore be a state sponsorship of religion, which tends to establish a religion, and would therefore be unconstitutional. At the other end of the spectrum, I have read of a six year old girl, in kindergarten in a public school, who was going to say grace over her lunch at school. She asked some of her friends to join hands with her and join her in the prayer, which they did of their own accord. All of this was done individually, without any encouragement from the school or its officials. In fact, the school officials stepped in and stopped the activity, asserting that there could be no prayers at the school. This was wrong and clearly violated the little girls' freedom to exercise their religion.

Now there are cases that fall in between these two extremes. Suppose a group of students get together and want to have a public prayer before some school event, say a football game or graduation. They appoint one of their own, a student, to give the prayer. While the school is not requiring participation in the prayer, school assets, such as microphones, are being used, and it is at a school event, and will be imposed on others, although they are not required to join in the prayer. However, a refusal to allow the prayer could be said to infringe on the students' free exercise of their religion. While people can disagree on which side of the fence such cases should fall, surely everyone can see the conflict built in here between the two provisions

A People Armed and Free

of the First Amendment, one prohibiting the state support of any given religion, the other guaranteeing the free exercise of religion.

So it is with the right of insurrection or rebellion. The right exists, as indicated in the Declaration of Independence. And I happen to believe that it is inalienable, since it is also called a duty, given the proper situation. However, the government is also given the power to put such rebellions down. To not grant that power to any government would amount to allowing total anarchy, because anyone who did not like any given law could disobey it and simply declare himself in rebellion and the government could do nothing about it. So how does this conflict of principles get resolved?

As a practical matter, by whoever wins the war of rebellion. Sad to say, logic, brilliant arguments, political persuasion and appeals to a higher moral authority will not determine whether the government is justified in putting down the rebellion, or the rebels are justified in their insurrection, except for the affect that such items may have to sway enough people from one side to the other to make a difference in the outcome. Think about it. Despite the beautiful prose in the Declaration of Independence, all of the glorious ideals contained therein, and what we consider today to surely be the truth found by our Founding Fathers, if we had lost the Revolutionary War it would have all been a side note in history. The signers of the Declaration of Independence would have all been hung as traitors. As Benjamin Franklin is reported to have said, "We must all hang together, or we shall surely all hang separately." This is not to say that "might makes right", only that the right side may lose.

We have some examples of failed rebellions, such as Shays' Rebellion, the Whiskey Rebellion, and the Civil War. Not that they were right or wrong, just that they existed. One wonders how many other rebellions throughout the history of mankind have had noble ideals, great potential for the human race, but have failed, and we simply do not know about it because the government that won repressed those ideals.

Therefore, my position is that there is a right of insurrection, that exists even today. It should be said that the Second Amendment does not guarantee that right directly, but it guarantees the right of the people to keep and bear arms so that they may have the tools necessary if they ever are forced to exercise that right. However, if they ever do, they had better make sure that they win. Forget about the courts letting them off because of the right of insurrection. The courts are a part of the same government they were rebelling against.

But there is more to the argument to be made against the gun control advocates position than just that. Their position is more internally inconsistent than they claim the insurrectionist theory to be. For, the gun control advocates' position on the historical reason why the Second Amendment was intended to protect the states' powers to maintain and arm their militias, is in effect the insurrectionist theory transposed from the people to the state governments. Remember, they argue that the only reason for passing the Second Amendment was that the states feared that the provisions of the Constitution pertaining to the militia would give the federal government total control over the arming and training of the militia. Therefore, the federal government could totally take over the militias, or totally disband them, or neglect them to where they would be useless. Why would the state governments fear this? Because then the state governments would be left defenseless. From whom or what? The federal government! The federal government, with a standing army (remember the discussion about the fears of a standing army), either with a militia co-opted from the states, or without any militia around to contest them, could then impose its will upon the states. If the Second Amendment was designed to alleviate these fears, then the purpose of the militia, under the gun control advocates argument, had to include the right of the states to resist the federal government and its standing army, in other words, an insurrection made not by the people, but by the states!

As I write this, it occurs to me that this is exactly what occurred in the Civil War, with the southern states attempting to secede and using their militias to resist the rule of the federal government, and the federal government using its standing army (and navy) and the militias of the states remaining in the Union, to impose its will on the southern states. And as I said before, the ultimate resolution depends on who wins. According to political scientists and historians, the Civil War determined that there is no right of secession. Was this because the logical arguments in favor of such a right were simply wrong? Maybe they were, maybe they were correct, but that is not the reason for this statement about no right of secession. The reason is that the federal government won the war.

So while the gun control advocates have a logical argument that must be taken seriously, it has holes in it, and when put together with the rest of their arguments as to why the Second Amendment should not be read to guarantee an individual right, it falls apart on its own weight. Their false logic, since their argument is so internally inconsistent, shows that they are not looking for what is the real meaning of the Second Amendment, but are looking for a specific result, in accordance with their agenda, and coming up with any argument that they think will get them to that result.

All of this begs the question: What would be a justifiable reason to conduct a rebellion or insurrection? The answer is that I do not know. One thing is for sure, though, and that is in order to win, which as we have seen is a requirement to be found to have had a justifiable reason to rebel, the cause of the rebellion has to be so bad that a large number of the people will support the rebellion. This is indicated as a truism in the Declaration of Independence: "Prudence, indeed, will dictate that Governments long established should not be changed for light and transient causes; and accordingly all experience hath shewn, that mankind are more disposed to suffer, while evils are sufferable, than to right themselves by abolishing the forms to which they are accustomed." Conditions have to be real bad to justify a rebellion. With that said, my personal opinion is that if the federal government had taken upon itself, at its beginning, in the 1790's, the powers that it exercises today, including the taxation we have now, the commercial regulation we have now, the restriction of property rights, the restriction of certain freedoms in some areas, yet the blatant allowance of activities that our Founding Fathers never dreamed of allowing, and the forcing of these activities on the states, our Founding Fathers would have rebelled against the government they had just instituted, throwing it out and starting over. The reason that we have not rebelled is that these changes have taken place over a long period of time, more than 200 years. Like drugs, what would have been a fatal dose if taken at the very first, becomes a mild high after years of increased use. So we have been numbed to the federal government's intrusion into our lives. However, in the words of the Declaration of Independence: "But when a long train of abuses and usurpations, pursuing invariably the same Object evinces a design to reduce them under absolute Despotism, it is their right, it is their duty, to throw off such Government, and to provide new Guards for their future security."

Jack Reynolds, J. D.

I have heard it said that as long as we have what most people call a democratic government (which is really a republican form of government, being representative in nature rather than direct action by the people; not to be confused with the political parties by the same names) that rebellion is totally inappropriate. Maybe this is true. As long as we only have ourselves to blame for the gradual erosion of our rights, by electing people to Congress and the presidency who are more interested in protecting their own power and keeping themselves in office than they are in doing what is right to protect the freedom of all Americans, then probably it will be impossible to obtain that large majority of people to support a rebellion that would be necessary to allow such a rebellion to succeed. If such a large majority could be obtained for a rebellion, elections, if still available, could throw the rascals out.

Do not get me wrong. I am not calling for a rebellion. I love my country, and with all of its faults I recognize that this is the freest place on Earth to live today. However, that does not mean that we have not strayed from the vision of our Founding Fathers. And that does not mean that we should not try, through our elected representatives, to regain a portion of that vision. And that does not mean that we should give up our individual right to keep and bear arms for the purpose of defending those freedoms and liberties that we have left, with the benefit that all politicians know that if they go too far, they may have to face an angry, armed public.

There are other, less convincing arguments presented against the insurrectionist theory. It is said that in today's world, with tanks, jet planes, rockets, large caliber and long-range artillery, any attempt to rebel against the government with the arms allowed under the Second Amendment would be futile. Of course, that presupposes that there is a restriction on the type of weapons allowed under the Second Amendment, which may not be true. But even if it is, this totally ignores the recent examples of Vietnam, where the enemy in the south had no planes, and was vastly inferior in other weapons. Or the Chinese in the Korean War, who had no artillery, only small caliber mortars, yet handed the U.S. Army an ignominious defeat when they first came into the war. Or how about the Palestinians against Israel? Israel surely has the strongest military in the Middle East, yet they cannot put an end to the Palestinian uprising. How about Afghanistan against the Soviet Union? The mujahadeen had no tanks, and no

A People Armed and Free

planes. Most of their weapons were small arms, with a few Stinger missiles provided from outside the country. Yet they were able to defeat the second most powerful military in the world. And that same military (now known as the Russians) was dealt a severe blow in Chechnya, again by a group of committed individuals with little more than small arms. Again, in Northern Ireland, the IRA continually caused the British army problems. One is left wondering what would have happened if the millions of Jews in Nazi Germany had had guns (remember how they held out in the Warsaw Ghetto when they finally did fight back?), or what would had happened if the students at Tianamen Square in China had had guns when they were crushed by the Communist government?

Some say that the concept is outdated. We now have a standing army far in excess of what the Founding Fathers ever feared in their worst nightmares. It has not been used against the people, so there is no longer any reason to worry. I have heard the Second Amendment called an anachronism. Anachronism is defined as "[t]he representation of something as existing or happening at other than its proper or historical time" or "[s]omething out of its proper time."[485] I refuse to find anything in the Bill of Rights to be an anachronism.

Another argument is that it cannot happen here. That is to say, while originally the Founding Fathers may have been justified in fearing the central government, with over two hundred years of history without any real oppression we do not have anything to worry about. After all, we are a civilized democracy in a modern world. So was Germany in the late 1920's. No one can say that the Chinese are not civilized; they probably had the world's first civilization. Yet their government has, in the 20th century, killed millions of its own people. In Kosovo, another modern civilization, the government practiced ethnic cleansing. Could it happen here? We hope not, but it certainly could. After all, power corrupts, and absolute power corrupts absolutely. Look at the abuses by the government at Ruby Ridge and Waco, and in seizing Elian Gonzales and sending him back to Cuba. Can anyone forget the picture of the federal agent holding the gun in the child's face? Yet at the same time, with the results of having many of the BATF agents shot in Waco, the public outcry over Ruby Ridge and the resulting lawsuits, and the outcry over Elian Gonzales, one would expect the government to be somewhat more circumspect about what it does in the future. Only by guaranteeing the people the right to keep and bear arms can we make sure that we continue to have a free state — a free federal government — and that was the main reason for the passage of the Second Amendment. It remains the main reason for such an interpretation today, if you want to apply today's public policy to the issue.

F. *Conclusion on Public Policy*

I still believe, despite all of the strong arguments in favor of the gun rights advocates position, that public policy has no place in this issue. However, if public policy is to be considered, in my opinion it favors the concept of an individual right. What is really important to me from this discussion is that, if I were not convinced before by the gun control advocates' lies about our history, I am completely convinced now that they are totally unscrupulous in their efforts to take away this natural right of the people. They are a lot like the attorney who was with a mathematician and a physicist, when the three of them were asked what 2 times 2 is. The mathematician responded that in order to multiply two numbers you have to take their logarithms and add them together, and when you do this the result is 3.99999...., which can be rounded off to 4. The physicist responded that it would be the square of two, which would be four. The attorney responded: **"What do you want it to be?"**

The gun control advocates' position on what the militia is (the National Guard according to them) defeats the very reason (according to them) for having the Second Amendment. They would never support a state, if one would ever try to assert the right that the gun control advocates claim the Second Amendment gives them, in trying to require everyone to have an assault weapon in the face of a federal statute prohibiting such weapons. They claim that the insurrectionist theory is inconsistent with the Constitution, ignoring other internal conflicts in the Constitution, but then claim the reason for the Second Amendment was so that the state governments could have a military capability in order to fight the standing army of the federal government if it was ever used in an attempt to oppress the states, which is nothing less than the insurrectionist theory for states! They are not arguing from principle as to what the Constitution, Bill of Rights, and specifically the Second Amendment is, but are making up multifarious arguments for a result they want. Their position would be more principled if they were to assert that the Second Amendment only grants a power to the states to arm their own militias, but then admitted that the insurrectionist theory was valid, at least to allowing the states to resist federal authority, and would support state actions that might conflict with the federal gun control laws that they helped to pass, but such is not their position. When we are talking about the Constitution, I can respect a principled argument based on a true philosophy of government, but not legal sophistry to try to bend the Constitution to your will.

Jack Reynolds, J. D.

Chapter 8
The Ethos of the Second Amendment

What in the world do we mean by this? What is "Ethos"? The same dictionary that I used in Chapter 3 defines "ethos" as "[t]he disposition, character, or fundamental values peculiar to a specific people, culture, or movement."[486] In other words, we are looking at the ideals and values of the American people that pertain to the Second Amendment. This is similar to what we looked at in Chapter 2 in regards to the Bill of Rights as a whole.

There are two portions to this, both of which we have already covered to some extent in previous chapters. The first is the notion of limited government. Being a libertarian, I love this part. Much of what can be said here was discussed in Chapter 2 in explaining where the Bill of Rights came from, and how our government was formed. The government was based on a social compact, and was only supposed to have those powers that the people gave to it, with the people retaining all other rights and powers to themselves as individuals.

How is this to be applied specifically to the Second Amendment? By definition, under the social compact theory, the people, prior to forming any government, had a natural right to keep and bear arms. Unless the people who joined in the forming of this government expressly gave the federal government the power to regulate the ownership, possession, and bearing of firearms, then that power and right remained with the people before the Second Amendment was even drafted.

Now people can argue that the interstate commerce clause gives the federal government the power to do just that, just as people argue that the same clause gives the federal government power to regulate drugs, cars, and thousands of other products in this nation. While I would have to agree that the courts have given the interstate commerce clause this broad, expansive interpretation, I believe that we have gone well beyond what the Founding Fathers had in mind when they put that clause into the Constitution. I believe that our Constitution and our government were founded as one of limited

A People Armed and Free

powers, with very little intended to go to the government, and a lot to be retained by the people.

This is especially true when we talk about the issue of the ownership of guns. The people who founded this country did not trust the government. As our review of the history shows, even if you accept the gun control advocates assertion that the reason for the Second Amendment was to ensure that the states could maintain and arm their militias, the underlining reason for the concern was the fear of a strong central government. It seems inconceivable to me that the same people who expressed such a fear of a strong central government, of the possibility of it using its standing army to oppress either the states or the people, of the concept of government usurping powers to the point of demanding a Bill of Rights despite the arguments against it, would have agreed to have given up their natural right to keep and bear arms.

Basically, what I am saying is that this country was founded on the notions of freedom and liberty. Therefore, the assumption that should be made in any dispute over any issue involving freedom is that the intention of the Founding Fathers was for the freedom to exist. Unless you can show me strong proof that the Founding Fathers intended for the people to forfeit their rights with the passage of the Constitution, I will come down on the side of the people keeping those rights. And in regards to the right to keep and bear arms, to the interpretation of the Second Amendment, I have not seen any good evidence that the Founding Fathers intended the people to give up the right to own, carry, and utilize their firearms either as a militia, in self-defense, for hunting, for sport, or to protect themselves from the government, to that same government, so as to allow that same government to restrict the ownership, the type of weapons, or to even confiscate the weapons! Yet this is what the gun control advocates claim!

So to me, this portion of the ethos, the disposition, character, or fundamental values peculiar to the American people, indicates that the Second Amendment should be interpreted to guarantee an individual right to keep and bear arms.

Now the second part of the ethos question is less political and more cultural. The American nation undeniably has a gun culture. Prior to 1965 the gun rate, per 1000 people, was about 100. Around that time the gun rate began to increase dramatically. As of 1997, it had reached around 320 per 1000 people. At a population of 300 million, that would translate to 96 million guns. There are estimates that go much higher. And despite the lies told by Bellesiles, guns have been a part our history from the very beginning. I cannot imagine the Pilgrims landing on these potentially hostile shores without guns, for defense and for hunting to provide food for their families. While this may smack of a public policy argument, if guns are inbred, are so much a part of our culture, then the Second Amendment should be read to protect the right of the people to keep them, because, with guns being a part of the culture when it was enacted, that is probably what the Framers meant to do anyway.

All of this combines, with the other five factors of the text, history, structure, case law, and public policy to indicate that, while a definitive answer to the question has not been given by the only authority that can give such an answer, the Supreme Court, the question as to what the Second Amendment does should be answered that it guarantees a right that the people had before the Constitution was created, as individuals to keep and bear arms.

Chapter 9

Is the Second Amendment Extended to Restrict State Regulation? The Effect of the 14th Amendment

The short answer to the above question is no. As shown in Chapter 6 on case law, the Supreme Court, a long time ago, ruled that the Bill of Rights, as originally enacted, were meant to restrict the powers of the federal government, and did not apply directly to the states. Later, but still a long time ago, the Supreme Court ruled that the 14th Amendment did not operate to extend the protection of the Second Amendment to restrict the state governments from regulating firearms. That ruling has never been reversed or overruled.

In a case that we looked at earlier, *Presser v. Illinois*,[487] in reference to the 14th Amendment, the Supreme Court said:

> It is only the privileges and immunities of citizens of the United States that the clause relied on was intended to protect. A State may pass laws to regulate the privileges and immunities of its own citizens, provided that in so doing it does not abridge their privileges and immunities as citizens of the United States.[488]

The Court went on to give an example of what it was talking about. In reference to the First Amendment right to peaceably assemble, if the attempt to assemble was for a national purpose, such as trying to petition the federal government for a redress of grievances, it would be protected against state encroachment under the 14th Amendment. However, if it was being exercised for some other purpose, such as associating together to protest state laws, or to associate together as a military company, it would not be an attribute of national citizenship, and would therefore not be protected against state restriction by the 14th Amendment.

More recently, several courts of appeal have refused to apply the Second Amendment against the state governments because, in a technically correct reading of the law, only the Supreme Court can overrule its prior holding on this point, and until it does so, the Second Amendment cannot be applied to restrict state regulation by the lower courts. So we have to wait on the Supreme Court if we ever hope to get a different result.

But perhaps this is not the question that needs to be asked. If it were, this chapter would be over. But in the effort to give you more material to read for the money you spent in buying this book, or perhaps because this issue is really more important than just the above answer, we will rephrase the question to ask: Should, or will, the Second Amendment be applied, through the 14th Amendment, to restrict state regulation of firearms?

The best exposition on this issue was given by Justice Black in his dissent, joined by Justice Douglas, in *Adamson v. California*.[489] We have already looked at this case, but just to refresh your memory, the issue was whether or not the Fifth Amendment's right against self-incrimination would be applied, through the 14th Amendment, against the states. The Supreme Court held, at the time, that it would not. Justices Black and Douglas dissented. In their dissent they gave a history of the question about applying the Bill of Rights to the states, and attached an appendix with an extensive history of the 14th Amendment. It is to this history that we now turn.

Prior to the Civil War, in 1833, the Supreme Court had ruled that the Fifth Amendment prohibition against taking private property for public use without just compensation could not be applied against the states.[490] The Court reasoned that the purpose of the Bill of Rights was to restrict the federal government, not the states, so none of the first eight amendments (note, for our purposes, this would include the Second Amendment) could be applied to the states. Realize that this was well before the passage of the 14th Amendment, which did not come about until after the Civil War. That rule was still in effect at the time the 14th Amendment was introduced in Congress.

The 14th Amendment had its beginnings with the formation, in 1865, of the Joint Committee on Reconstruction, a committee made up of members of both houses of Congress, with a mandate to determine whether or not the former Confederate States were entitled to be represented in either House of Congress. That committee began drafting proposed constitutional amendments that would outline the procedure for reconstruction.[491] On January 12, 1866, a subcommittee was appointed to consider suffrage proposals. That subcommittee also

A People Armed and Free

had a proposed constitutional amendment from Congressman Bingham referred to it. That proposal would have given Congress power to make laws to secure "to all persons in every State ... equal protection in their rights of life, liberty, and property."[492] This proposal underwent numerous revisions in committee, and finally was reported to the House of Representatives by Congressman Bingham on February 13, 1866, in the following format: "'The Congress shall have power to make all laws which shall be necessary and proper to secure to the citizens of each State all privileges and immunities of citizens in the several States (art. 4, sec. 2); and to all persons in the several States equal protection in the rights of life, liberty, and property (5th amendment)."[493]

On February 26, 1866, this proposed amendment came up for debate in the House of Representatives. Some opponents took the positions that it would destroy state's rights and grant Congress power to legislate on matters of purely local concern. Besides, they said, the amendment was unnecessary because the Bill of Rights would protect the people against state violation.[494] Of course, as we have seen, this was simply an incorrect statement of the law at the time. Congressman Bingham took them to task on this, citing the *Barron* case, and another case, *Lessee of Livingston v. Moore*,[495] which dealt with the Seventh Amendment (the right of trial by jury in common law cases), to show that the Bill of Rights do not extend to the states. Congressman Bingham, the original author of the amendment, a member of the committee that reported out the amendment, and the sponsor of the amendment in the House of Representatives, then proceeded to make an impassioned speech for the need of such an amendment, part of which is here now quoted:

> The question is simply whether you will give by this amendment to the people of the United States the power, by legislative enactment, to punish officials of States for violation of oaths enjoined upon them by their Constitution? ... **Is the Bill of Rights to stand in our Constitution hereafter, as in the past five years within eleven States, a mere dead letter? It is absolutely essential to the safety of the people that it should be enforced.**

269

Mr. Speaker, it appears to me that this very provision of the bill of rights brought in question this day, upon this trial before the House, more than any other provision of the Constitution, makes that unity of government which constitutes us one people, by which and through which American nationality came to be, and only by the enforcement of which can American nationality continue to be.

What more could have been added to that instrument to secure the enforcement of these provisions of the bill of rights in every State, other than the additional grant of power which we ask this day? ...

As slaves were not protected by the Constitution, there might be some color of excuse for the slave States in their disregard for the requirement of the bill of rights as to slaves in refusing them protection in life or property...

But, sir, there never was even colorable excuse, much less apology, for any man North or South claiming that any State Legislature or State court, or State Executive, has any right to deny protection to any free citizen of the United States within their limits in the rights of life, liberty, and property. **Gentlemen who oppose this amendment oppose the grant of power to enforce the bill of rights**. Gentlemen who oppose this amendment simply declare to these rebel States, 'Go on with your confiscation statutes, your statutes of banishment, your statutes of unjust imprisonment, your statutes of murder and death against men because of their loyalty to the Constitution and Government of the United States.[496]

Congressman Hotchkiss then suggested that the amendment should be put into language to prohibit the States from taking actions to deprive such privileges and immunities. Debate was then postponed until April 2, 1866.⁴⁹⁷ That tabling of the proposed amendment was a procedural device that effectively killed it.

During this time frame other events were transpiring that have an affect on how we look at the 14th Amendment. Congress had passed the Freedman's Bureau Bill, which made deprivation of certain civil rights of Negroes an offense punishable by military tribunal, but it applied only to the states in the south, not the entire country. President Johnson, on February 19, 1866 vetoed this bill because he considered it to be unconstitutional. The Congress then acted swiftly to enact the Civil Rights Bill, which empowered federal courts to punish those who deprived any person anywhere in the country of certain defined civil rights. The Senate sponsor of this bill, Senator Trumball, had stated in a speech that:

> [T]he late slaveholding States' had enacted laws ... depriving persons of African descent of privileges which are essential to freemen... (S)tatutes of Mississippi ... provide that if any person of African descent residing in that State travels from one county to another without having a pass or a certificate of his freedom, he is liable to be committed to jail and to be dealt with as a person who is in the State without authority. **Other provisions of the statute prohibit any negro or mulatto from having fire-arms**; and one provision of the statute declares that for 'exercising the functions of a minister of the Gospel free negroes ... on conviction, may be punished by ... lashes... [S]imilar provisions are to be found running through all the statutes of the late slaveholding States... **The purpose of the bill ... is to destroy all these discriminations.**⁴⁹⁸

In the House debate on this bill, an opponent, Congressman Raymond, admitted that it would guarantee to the Negro "the right of free passage... He has a defined status ... a right to defend himself ... **to bear arms** ... to testify in Federal courts..."⁴⁹⁹ Congressman Bingham himself, while in support of efforts to guarantee Blacks civil rights, was against the bill for two reasons. First, he thought that the bill would be unconstitutional. Due to the Supreme Court decisions,

Jack Reynolds, J. D.

he felt that the only way to guarantee the protections of the Bill of Rights against state infringement was by a constitutional amendment. Second, he was concerned that the bill went too far; stripping the states of power they needed to govern:

> I do not oppose any legislation which is authorized by the Constitution of my country to **enforce in its letter and its spirit the bill of rights** as embodied in that Constitution. I know that **the enforcement of the bill of rights is the want of the Republic.**
>
> … **I am with him in an earnest desire to have the bill of rights in your Constitution enforced everywhere**. But I ask that it be enforced in accordance with the Constitution of my country.
>
> … I submit that the term 'civil rights' includes every right that pertains to the citizen under the Constitution, laws, the Government of this country…
>
> … The law in every State should be just; it should be no respecter of persons. It is otherwise now, and it has been otherwise for many years in many of the States of the Union. I should remedy that not by an arbitrary assumption of power, but by amending the Constitution of the United States, expressly prohibiting the States from any such abuse of power in the future…
>
> If the bill of rights, as has been solemnly ruled by the Supreme Court of the United States, does not limit the powers of the States and prohibit such gross injustice by States, it does limit the power of Congress to prohibit any such legislation by Congress.
>
> … I have advocated here an amendment which would arm Congress with the power to compel obedience to the oath, **and punish all violations by State officers of the bill of rights**, but leaving those officers to

A People Armed and Free

discharge the duties enjoined upon them as citizens of the United States by that oath and by that Constitution.[500]

President Johnson also vetoed this bill, again because of constitutional concerns, but this time Congress overrode his veto.

We now return to the Reconstruction Committee. It had taken up another proposed amendment, this one put forth by Congressman Stevens, which provided that "No discrimination shall be made by any State, nor by the United States, as to the civil rights of persons because of race, color, or previous condition of servitude."[501] Congressman Bingham proposed an additional section providing: "No State shall make or enforce any law which shall abridge the privileges or immunities of citizens of the United States; nor shall any State deprive any person of life, liberty, or property without due process of law, nor deny to any person within its jurisdiction the equal protection of the laws."[502] On April 28, 1866, this change was made by the committee.

Congressman Stevens was the sponsor of this Amendment in the House of Representatives. In introducing it, and speaking for the committee, he said:

> The first section (of the proposed amendment) prohibits the States from abridging the privileges and immunities of citizens of the United States, or unlawfully depriving them of life, liberty, or property, or of denying to any person within their jurisdiction the 'equal' protection of the laws.
> I can hardly believe that any person can be found who will not admit that every one of these provisions is just. They are all asserted, in some form or other, in our Declaration or organic law. **But the Constitution limits only the action of Congress, and is not a limitation on the States. This amendment supplies that defect, and allows Congress to correct the unjust legislation of the States**, so far that the law which operates upon one man shall operate equally upon all.[503]

Congressman Bingham, in concluding the debate on the proposed amendment, further explained its effect:

> (M)any instances of State injustice and oppression have already occurred in the State legislation of this Union, of flagrant violations of the guaranteed privileges of citizens of the United States, for which the national Government furnished and could furnish by law no remedy whatever. Contrary to the express letter of your Constitution, 'cruel and unusual punishments' have been inflicted under State laws within this Union upon citizens…
>
> It was an opprobrium to the Republic that for fidelity to the United States they could not by national law be protected against the degrading punishment inflicted on slaves and felons by State law. That great want of the citizen and stranger, **protection by national law from unconstitutional State enactments, is supplied by the first section of this amendment**.[504]

In the Senate, Senator Howard introduced the amendment. In so doing, he made the following speech:

> I … present to the Senate … the views and the motives [of the Reconstruction Committee]…
>
> The first section of the amendment … submitted for the consideration of the two Houses, relates to the privileges and immunities of citizens of the several States, and to the rights and privileges of all persons, whether citizens or others, under the laws of the United States…
>
> It will be observed that this is a general prohibition upon all the States, as such, from abridging the privileges and immunities of the citizens of the United States…

It would be a curious question to solve what are the privileges and immunities of citizens of each of the States in the several States... I am not aware that the Supreme Court have ever undertaken to define either the nature or extent of the privileges and immunities thus guarantied... But we may gather some intimation of what probably will be the opinion of the judiciary by referring to ... Corfield v. Coryell (Fed.Cas. No. 3230) 4 Washington Circuit Court Reports, page 380. [Here Senator Howard quoted at length from that opinion.]

Such is the character of the privileges and immunities spoken of in the second section of the fourth article of the Constitution. To these privileges and immunities, whatever they may be-for they are not and cannot be fully defined in their entire extent and precise nature-to these **should be added the personal rights guarantied and secured by the first eight amendments of the Constitution;** such as the freedom of speech and of the press; the right of the people peaceably to assemble and petition the Government for a redress of grievances, a right appertaining to each and all the people; **the right to keep and to bear arms**; the right to be exempted from the quartering of soldiers in a house without the consent of the owner; ...

Now, sir, here is a mass of privileges, immunities, and rights, some of them secured by the second section of the fourth article of the Constitution, which I have recited, **some by the first eight amendments of the Constitution**; and it is a fact well worthy of attention that the course of decision of our courts and the present settled doctrine is, that all these immunities, privileges, rights, thus guarantied by the Constitution, or recognized by it, are secured to the citizens solely as a citizen of the United States and as a party in their courts. They do not operate in the slightest degree as a

> restraint or a prohibition upon state legislation. States are not affected by them, and it has been repeatedly held that the restriction contained in the Constitution against the taking of private property for public use without just compensation is not a restriction upon State legislation, but applies only to the legislation of Congress.
>
> Now, sir, there is no power given in the Constitution to enforce and to carry out any of these guarantees... **The great object of the first section of this amendment is, therefore, to restrain the power of the States and compel them at all times to respect these great fundamental guarantees.**[505]

Both those in favor of the amendment and those against it related the amendment to the Civil Rights Bill, especially as to the amendment guaranteeing the constitutionality of the bill.

With the addition of a first sentence regarding who the citizens of the United States are, the First Section of the 14th Amendment was passed with essentially the same language as was presented to the Congress:

> Section. 1. All persons born or naturalized in the United States and subject to the jurisdiction thereof, are citizens of the United States and of the State wherein they reside. No State shall make or enforce any law which shall abridge the privileges or immunities of citizens of the United States; nor shall any State deprive any person of life, liberty, or property, without due process of law; nor deny to any person within its jurisdiction the equal protection of the laws.

All of what we have seen so far indicates that the people who supported the passage of the 14th Amendment had in mind the purpose of making the whole of the Bill of Rights applicable to the states. Its opponents also thought that this would be the result of its passage. There are even some direct references to the language of the

A People Armed and Free

Second Amendment, along with the other portions of the Bill of Rights, to indicate that they specifically considered the need to apply it to the states. There are even indications that one of the problems that the 14th Amendment was designed to alleviate was the denial of the right to keep and bear arms to Blacks. This is all a pretty good indication that the Supreme Court should hold that the Second Amendment does apply to the states to restrict their ability to regulate the possession of firearms.

Similar to our treatment of the history of the Second Amendment, we must now turn to the subsequent history of the 14th Amendment. In 1871 a bill was presented to Congress to enforce a portion of the 14th Amendment. In the debate on this bill, Congressman Bingham, one of the authors of the 14th Amendment and still a member of Congress, addressed the reasons for the enactment of the 14th Amendment:

> The gentleman says that amendment differs from the amendment reported by me in February; differs from the provision introduced and written by me, now in the fourteenth article of amendments. It differs in this: that it is now, as it now stands in the Constitution, more comprehensive than as it was first proposed and reported in February, 1866. It embraces all and more than did the February proposition.
>
> ****
>
> I answer the gentleman, how I came to change the form of February to the words now in the first section of the fourteenth article of amendments, as they stand, and I trust will forever stand, in the Constitution of my country. I had read-**and that is what induced me to attempt to impose by constitutional amendments new limitations upon the power of the States**-the great decision of Marshall in Barron v. The Mayor and City Council of Baltimore, wherein the Chief Justice said, in obedience to his official oath and the Constitution as it then was: 'The amendments (to the Constitution) contained no expression indicating an

intention to apply them to the State governments. This court cannot so apply them.'-7 Pet. page 250.

In this case the city had taken private property for public use, without compensation as alleged, and there was no redress for the wrong in the Supreme Court of the United States; and only for this reason, the first eight amendments were not limitations on the power of the States.

And so afterward, in the case of the Lessee of Livingstone v. Moore ... the court ruled, 'It is now settled that the amendments (to the Constitution) do not extend to the States.' They were but limitations upon Congress. Jefferson well said of the first eight articles of amendments to the Constitution of the United States, they constitute the American Bill of Rights.

In reexamining that case of Barron, Mr. Speaker, after my struggle in the House in February 1866 to which the gentleman has alluded, I noted and apprehended as I never did before, certain words in that opinion of Marshall. Referring to the first eight articles of amendments to the Constitution of the United States, the Chief Justice said: 'Had the framers of these amendments intended them to be limitations on the power of the State governments they would have imitated the framers of the original Constitution, and have expressed that intention.' Barron v. The Mayor, &c., 7 Pet. 250.

Acting upon this suggestion I did imitate the framers of the original Constitution. As they had said 'No state shall emit bills of credit, pass any bill of attainder, ex post facto law, or law impairing the obligations of contracts;' imitating their example and imitating it to the letter, I prepared the provision of the first section of the Fourteenth Amendment as it stands in the

Constitution, as follows: 'No State shall make or enforce any law which shall abridge the privileges or immunities of the citizens of the United States, nor shall any State deprive any person, of life, liberty, or property without due process of law, nor deny to any person within its jurisdiction the equal protection of the laws.'

I hope the gentleman now knows why I changed the form of the amendment of February, 1866.

Mr. Speaker, that the scope and meaning of the limitations imposed by the first section, fourteenth amendment of the Constitution may be more fully understood, permit me to say that **the privileges and immunities of citizens of the United States**, as contradistinguished from citizens of a State, **are chiefly defined in the first eight amendments to the Constitution of the United States**. Those eight amendments are as follows: [Here Mr. Bingham recited verbatim the first eight articles, including the Second Amendment.]

These eight articles I have shown never were limitations upon the power of the States, until made so by the fourteenth amendment. The words of that amendment, 'no State shall make or enforce any law which shall abridge the privileges and immunities of citizens of the United States,' are an express prohibition upon every State of the Union, which may be enforced under existing laws of Congress, and such other laws for their better enforcement as Congress may make.

Jack Reynolds, J. D.

****

Is it not clear that other and different privileges and immunities than those to which a citizen of a State was entitled are secured by the provisions of the fourteenth article, that no State shall abridge the privileges and immunities of citizens of the United States, **which are defined in the eight articles of amendment, and which were not limitations on the power of the States before the fourteenth amendment made them limitations?**

****

Mr. Speaker, I respectfully submit to the House and country that, by virtue of these amendments, it is competent for Congress today to provide by law that no man shall be held to answer in the tribunals of any State in this Union for any act made criminal by the laws of that state without a fair and impartial trial by jury. Congress never before has had the power to do it. It is also competent for Congress to provide that no citizen in any State shall be deprived of its property by State law or the judgment of a State court without just compensation therefor. Congress never before had the power so to declare. It is competent for the Congress of the United States to-day to declare that no State shall make or enforce any law which shall abridge the freedom of speech, the freedom of the press, or the right of the people peaceably to assemble together and petition for redress of grievances. **For these are of the rights of citizens of the United States defined in the Constitution and guaranteed by the fourteenth amendment, and to enforce which Congress is thereby expressly empowered.**[506]

Additionally, in further debate on the same bill (in case you have forgotten, it was a bill to enforce the 14th Amendment) another

Congressman, Dawes, who had been involved in the passage of the 14th Amendment made the following speech:

> In addition to the original rights secured to him in the first article of amendments, he had secured the free exercise of his religious belief, and freedom of speech and the press. **Then he had secured to him the right to keep and bear arms in his defense.** Then, after that, his home was secured in time of peace from the presence of a soldier; and, still further, sir, his house, his papers, and his effects were protected against unreasonable seizure... [At this point he continued enumerating all of the other rights contained in the Bill of Rights.]
>
> And still later, sir, after the bloody sacrifice of our four years' war, **we gave the most grand of all these rights, privileges, and immunities, by one single amendment to the Constitution,** to four millions of American citizens who sprang into being, as it were, by the wave of a magic wand. Still further, every person born on the soil was made a citizen and clothed with them all.
>
> It is all these, Mr. Speaker, which are compresended in the words 'American citizen,' and **it is to protect and to secure him in these rights, privileges, and immunities this bill is before the House.**

Can it be made any more clear by anyone than what these two gentlemen have said, that the people who were involved in the passage of the 14th Amendment intended that by it all of the Bill of Rights, expressly including the Second Amendment, would be applied to the states to restrict their governments from infringing these rights of their citizens? It seems clear as a bell to me. In addition, a book that conducted a comprehensive analysis of the historical origins of the 14th Amendment, and which was published in 1908, found that the Congress had the following reasons for submitting the first section of the 14th Amendment to the states for ratification:

1. **To make the Bill of Rights (the first eight amendments) binding upon or applicable to, the States**.
2. To give validity to the Civil Rights Bill.
3. To declare who were citizens of the United States.[507]

The Supreme Court should have always been using the 14th Amendment to apply all of the Bill of Rights to the states. So what went wrong?

According to Justice Black,[508] the Supreme Court first considered the effect of the 14th Amendment in the Slaughter-House cases[509] in 1872. Apparently, because the issue did not involve any of the rights enumerated in the Bill of Rights, but a "natural right" of a person to do business and engage in his trade or vocation, the question of the application of the Bill of Rights through the 14th Amendment never came up, and was not briefed to the Court. The Court did reject this natural law argument, and held that the 14th Amendment protected only those rights held by an individual as a result of being a citizen of the United States.

Amazingly, Justice Black indicates that the Court in this case did not consider the congressional purpose or popular understanding of the 14th Amendment, quoting the following passage from a law review article written about seven years after the case:

> It must be admitted that the construction put upon the language of the first section of this amendment by the majority of the court is not its primary and most obvious signification. Ninety nine out of every hundred educated men, upon reading this section over, would at first say that it forbade a state to make or enforce a law which abridged any privilege or immunity whatever of one who was a citizen of the United States; and it is only by an effort of ingenuity that any other sense can be discovered that it can be forced to bear.
>
> It is a little remarkable that, so far as the reports disclose, no one of the distinguished counsel who argued this great case (the Slaughter-House Cases), nor any one of the judges who sat in it, appears to have thought it worth while to consult the proceedings of the

Congress which proposed this amendment to ascertain what it was that they were seeking to accomplish. Nothing is more common than this. There is hardly a question raised as to the true meaning of a provision of the old, original Constitution that resort is not had to Elliott's Debates, to ascertain what the framers of the instrument declared at the time that they intended to accomplish.[510]

From then through the case of *Twining v. New Jersey*[511], of all of the cases which considered the relation of the 14th Amendment and the Bill of Rights, in only one, *Maxwell v. Dow*[512], was the history concerning the 14th Amendment either presented to the Court in the parties' briefs, or mentioned in the opinions of the cases.[513] In *Maxwell*, the Court did acknowledge that the appellant had cited from a speech of Senator Howard, but then said that it was not advised of what other speeches were made in the Senate or House. The Court then made an outlandish statement:

> What individual Senators or Representatives may have urged in debate, in regard to the meaning to be given to a proposed constitutional amendment, or bill, or resolution, does not furnish a firm ground for its proper construction, nor is it important as explanatory of the grounds upon which the member voted in adopting it.[514]

This is a total violation of the principle of determining the original intent. It goes against all other cases that I have ever seen. While perhaps one odd statement from a Senator may not be conclusive evidence of what the original intent was, the history as shown by the congressional record most certainly is evidence to be considered and carries great weight. This statement is made even more incredible when one considers the rule announced by the Supreme Court in the earlier case of *Ex parte Bain*[515]: "It is never to be forgotten that in the construction of the language of the Constitution ..., as indeed in all other instances where construction becomes necessary, we are to place ourselves as nearly as possible in the condition of the men who framed that instrument."

Jack Reynolds, J. D.

What this shows is another example of the truism that I pointed out in reference to the *Miller* case, that is that bad cases, or in this instance, bad representation by the attorneys, make bad law. Had the attorneys adequately done their jobs and presented the evidence of the original intent of the Framers of the 14th Amendment to the Supreme Court, one could assume that they would have been forced to accept the logic that the Bill of Rights now applied to the states. But this did not happen, so we get incorrect results.

To make a long story short, and while this list may not be all-inclusive, from the time of the enactment of the 14th Amendment to the decision of *Adamson*, the Supreme Court published decisions that the following portions of the Bill of Rights were not "privileges or immunities" of national citizenship, therefore the states could not be prohibited by the federal government from infringing on them:

- 7th Amendment guarantee of a jury trial in civil cases.[516]
- 1st Amendment freedom of assembly.[517]
- 5th Amendment prohibition of taking of property for public purposes by regulation.[518]
- 5th Amendment prohibition of taking property without just compensation.[519]
- 5th Amendment requirement that accused be prosecuted under a grand jury indictment.[520]
- 2nd Amendment right to keep and bear arms.[521]
- 8th Amendment prohibition against cruel and unusual punishments.[522]
- 5th Amendment requirement for indictment by a grand jury, and 6th Amendment guarantee of trial by jury in criminal prosecutions.[523]
- 5th Amendment protection against self-incrimination.[524]
- 1st Amendment freedom of speech.[525]
- 5th Amendment protection against self-incrimination (again).[526]

What all of this indicates is that the Court did not just have it in for the Second Amendment, but universally refused to apply any of the Bill of Rights to the states, and declared that none of the rights protected in the Bill of Rights were "privileges and immunities" of citizens of the United States.

A People Armed and Free

The first chip in this rock of refusal to apply the Bill of Rights to the states occurred in 1897 in the case of *Chicago, B. & Q. R. Co. v. Chicago*[527], where the Supreme Court finally held that the states had to follow the Fifth Amendment requirement for the government to pay just compensation for private property taken for public use. This was done not under the privileges and immunities clause that we have been looking at, but through another portion of the 14th Amendment, called the due process clause. After the case of *Maxwell v. Dow*, in 1899, and before *Adamson* in 1947, the tide had begun to turn (though obviously not enough for poor Mr. Adamson). During that time frame, the following rights, protected under the Bill of Rights, were applied to the states through the 14th Amendment due process clause:

- 6th Amendment right to counsel in criminal cases.[528]
- 6th Amendment right of an accused in a criminal case to be informed of the charge against him.[529]
- 1st Amendment freedom of assembly.[530]
- 8th Amendment prohibition of cruel and unusual punishment and 5th Amendment protection from double jeopardy.[531]
- 1st Amendment, as to all of its provisions.[532]

Since *Adamson*, the Supreme Court has continued to apply portions of the Bill of Rights to the states, one-by-one, as they come before the Court:

- 4th Amendment right of privacy.[533]
- 6th Amendment requirement to provide counsel in criminal cases.[534]
- 5th Amendment right against self-incrimination, overruling *Twinning* and *Adamson*.[535]
- 6th Amendment right to a jury trial.[536]
- 4th Amendment freedom from unreasonable searches and seizures.[537]

Since the early 1960's, every Supreme Court case that I am aware of, which has addressed the issue of whether or not a specific right protected in the Bill of Rights would be applied to the states to restrict their infringement of those rights, has answered that question affirmatively, despite the early cases refusing to do so. As Justice

Jack Reynolds, J. D.

Brennan said: "The Court has not hesitated to re-examine past decisions according the Fourteenth Amendment a less central role in the preservation of basic liberties than that which was contemplated by its Framers when they added the Amendment to our constitutional scheme."[538] I do not know of any Supreme Court case since then that has refused to apply a portion of the Bill of Rights to the states.

Based on all of this, the history of the 14th Amendment, the fact that the early cases that refused to apply the Bill of Rights to the states did not have the history on the 14th Amendment presented to the Court, and the trend over the last 40 years or more to apply every right protected by the Bill of Rights to the states as they are presented to the Court, I have every reason to believe that whenever the Supreme Court again looks at the question of whether or not the Second Amendment applies to the states, the answer will be yes! True, no case has yet held that all of the Bill of Rights applies to the states — though individual judges have written that they should — therefore, there is some small sliver of a possibility that I could be wrong. But the reason for this lack of such a holding is probably that the Court is merely following its own rule of only deciding the issues actually presented before it. Since the Supreme Court has not addressed the question of applying the Second Amendment to the states for over 100 years, we are stuck with the early, erroneously decided cases.

But there is **no** doubt in my mind that the Second Amendment **should** be applied to the states. This was clearly the intent of the Framers of the 14th Amendment. It clearly should be applied if all of the other portions of the Bill of Rights are applied. It is the only result that makes sense.

Chapter 10

What is the Extent of the Second Amendment Protection? How Much Can the Government Infringe the Right to Keep and Bear Arms?

Not all rights are created equal. Most people do not realize this. They think that if it is written into the Constitution, then it must be fully protected, as are all other rights. As a libertarian, I might tend to agree that this **should** be the way things are done. But such is not the case. Whether through a bent sense of morals, that somehow personal rights are better than economic rights, or if you support the current results, through astute constitutional analysis, the Supreme Court has come out with basically three different tests to be used to determine the constitutionality of a law, depending on the right involved. While the words used differ at times between the cases, the three tests are basically, from most favored right to the least, the strict scrutiny test, the intermediate scrutiny test, and the reasonable basis test.

The most stringent test is usually reserved for those rights that the Supreme Court believes to be the most important, such as First Amendment freedom of speech. For example, in the case of *Boos v. Barry*[539] the issue was whether or not a law that provided that the posting of signs that diplomats might find offensive could be barred within 500 feet of a foreign embassy was constitutional. Also at issue was whether or not a law that allowed the police to disperse a gathering of three or more people within 500 feet of a foreign embassy was constitutional. The Supreme Court in analyzing these laws made the following observations:

> Our cases indicate that as a content-based restriction on political speech in a public forum, 22-1115 [the law involved] must be subjected to the most exacting scrutiny. Thus, we have required the State to show that the "regulation is **necessary** to serve a **compelling state interest** and that it is **narrowly drawn** to achieve that end."[540]

Jack Reynolds, J. D.

Notice the words in bold. These are the key words or phrases in this test. They are what form the really high hurdles, for laws to pass constitutional muster, which protect the individuals' rights. The Supreme Court ruled that the law restricting the signs in this case was unconstitutional, but allowed the constitutionality of the law allowing the dispersal of three or more people because the Court of Appeals had held that the statute allowed such dispersal only when the police reasonably believed that a threat to the security or peace of the embassy was present. Had the statute been interpreted to allow unfettered discretion for the police to disperse people, it too would have probably run afoul of the same constitutional test, pertaining to both the freedom of speech and the freedom of assembly, both under the First Amendment.

This same exacting scrutiny has also been applied to noncommunicative expressive conduct, such as burning the American Flag. In *Texas v. Johnson*[541] the state had passed a law making it a criminal act to burn the American Flag as an act of political expression. The Supreme Court treated this basically the same as the question of free speech and held the law unconstitutional.

However, not all expressive conduct can be absolutely protected. In 1968, the Supreme Court upheld a law making it illegal to burn your draft card. In *United States v. O'Brien*[542], the Supreme Court used basically the same test, somewhat modified for the situation, and acknowledged the use of some different words in different cases:

> This Court has held that when "speech" and "nonspeech" elements are combined in the same course of conduct, a sufficiently important governmental interest in regulating the nonspeech element can justify incidental limitations on First Amendment freedoms. To characterize the quality of the governmental interest which must appear, the Court has employed a variety of descriptive terms: compelling; substantial; subordinating; paramount; cogent; strong. Whatever imprecision inheres in these terms, we think it clear that a government regulation is sufficiently justified if it is within the constitutional power of the Government; if it furthers an important or substantial governmental interest; if the governmental interest is

A People Armed and Free

unrelated to the suppression of free expression; and if the incidental restriction on alleged First Amendment freedoms is no greater than is essential to the furtherance of that interest.[543]

As a result of applying this test, the Court found that the law prohibiting the destruction of the draft cards did further an important substantial governmental interest, unrelated to the suppression of free expression, and the incidental restriction on the First Amendment Freedoms was no greater than essential to the furtherance of that interest. Perhaps part of the problem, as we may see in the next few cases, has to do with the use of the terms: How strong must the governmental interest be to become compelling, or substantial, or important? How necessary does the law have to be? What does narrowly drawn mean? Does it mean that there are no other alternatives available, or that the legislature must use the best alternative, or that the one used was the only alternative that could be used without a lot of trouble for the government? Cases can sometimes be contradictory in their use of these terms.

Intermediate scrutiny is used in other situations where the problem supposedly addressed by the statute under constitutional review is more content neutral, or where other types of rights may be involved. For example, in *Craig v. Boren*[544], a case where a suit was brought in an attempt to invalidate the statutory distinction between males and females as to the legal age to buy beer in Oklahoma (females could buy beer at age 18, while males had to be 21), the Court held that the intermediate scrutiny test applied to statutes that distinguish based on gender: "[S]tatutory classifications that distinguish between males and females are 'subject to scrutiny under the Equal Protection Clause.' To withstand constitutional challenge, previous cases establish that classifications by gender must serve **important governmental objectives** and must be **substantially related** to achievement of those objectives."[545]

Notice the subtle difference in the words used in this test. The Government interest is no longer compelling or substantial, but important. The law no longer has to be necessary and narrowly drawn, but must be substantially related to the achievement of the objective. Incidentally, the difference in ages was declared to be unconstitutional.

A couple of free speech cases also have had the intermediate scrutiny test applied to them, because the laws were supposedly content neutral. For example, in *Ward v. Rock Against Racism*[546], the city had passed an ordinance that required that the city's employee control the volume of the bands at public outdoor concerts. This was contested as being government control of the freedom of expression. Even though the Supreme Court recognized that there is a freedom of expression in music that is constitutionally protected, because this statute did not involve the content of the music, but the volume, which the city did have an important interest in controlling, the lesser test of intermediate scrutiny would be used:

> [W]e reaffirm today that a regulation of the time, place, or manner of protected speech must be **narrowly tailored** to serve the government's **legitimate, content-neutral interests** but that it need not be the least restrictive or least intrusive means of doing so. Rather, the requirement of narrow tailoring is satisfied "so long as the ... regulation promotes a substantial government interest that would be achieved less effectively absent the regulation." To be sure, this standard does not mean that a time place, or manner regulation may burden substantially more speech than is necessary to further the government's legitimate interests. Government may not regulate expression in such a manner that a substantial portion of the burden on speech does not serve to advance its goals. So long as the means chosen are not substantially broader than necessary to achieve the government's interest, however, the regulation will not be invalid simply because a court concludes that the government's interest could be adequately served by some less-speech-restrictive alternative. "The validity of [time, place, or manner] regulations does not turn on a judge's agreement with the responsible decisionmaker concerning the most appropriate method for promoting significant government interests" or the degree to which those interests should be promoted.[547]

Here we have returned to the narrowly tailored concept, but now the government interest must only be legitimate, not compelling or important. Incidentally, the statute was upheld.

In a more recent case that involved the freedom of religion as well as the freedom of speech, *Watchtower Bible and Tract Society of New York, Inc. v. Village of Stratton*[548], where the village passed an ordinance requiring that all door-to-door solicitors, including salesmen, political advocates and religious proselytizers, had to apply for and be issued licenses before they could go door-to-door, the Court used a similar test, but this time found that while the stated governmental interests of the prevention of fraud, the prevention of crime, and the protection of residents' privacy were indeed important, it had to balance these interests with the amount of speech affected by the ordinance. The Court found that the ordinance was overbroad, and therefore not drawn narrowly enough to pass constitutional muster.

At the lower end of the spectrum are the economic rights. As an example, the Fifth Amendment prohibits the taking of property for public purposes without just compensation. Now if you own property, such as land, you may have numerous rights pertaining to this ownership. For example, you may own the minerals beneath the land, with the attendant right to mine the land to remove those minerals. You have the right to exclude whomever you want to from the land. You have the right to let whomever you choose to come onto the land. You have the right to the use of the airspace above the land, either to build into, or to keep others out of, up to some reasonable height. Property law professors liken ownership of land to having a bundle of sticks, with each stick representing some right that you own. If any of these "sticks" or rights are taken away from you, then you have lost some of the value of your ownership of the property.

Now there is no doubt that many laws restrict the use of certain property. Zoning laws, environmental laws, historical preservation laws, and many others. Arguably, since these laws take away some of the sticks, or rights, of an owner, they amount, to some degree, to a taking of property for a public purpose, and should therefore, under the Fifth Amendment, result in just compensation to the owner. Yet these laws, whether federal, state or local, are almost always upheld without requiring compensation. Why?

Usually the courts approach these cases not from the initial concept of a fundamental constitutional right being potentially violated, but from the point of the exercise of the police power of the state, which carries a presumption of constitutionality validity with it. Then, the court applies the lesser test, of a reasonable relationship to a legitimate state interest, to the law. Notice the difference in the words used: legitimate v. compelling or important, and reasonable relationship v. necessary or substantially related. And narrowly drawn does not even have a counterpart.

Some examples are in order. In *Penn Central Transportation Co. v. New York City*[549], the city had prohibited the owners of Grand Central Station from building a modern office complex above the station, due to the desire to maintain the historic nature of the artistic beauty of the original building. Now while this may be a laudable goal (although I am reminded that beauty is in the eye of the beholder), it was clear that the government was taking away a financially valuable use of the property from the owners, for an avowed public purpose. If the government wants to preserve historic buildings for the public, it should pay for them and pay for their upkeep. If it is not willing to do that, it should let the owners do what they will with the buildings. That is my opinion. But, my opinion lost. The U.S. Supreme Court upheld the restriction, despite the takings clause of the Fifth Amendment.

In *Goldblatt v. Hempstead*[550], the landowner had been mining gravel from the land for decades. As a result, a lake had been formed, around which a large development had been made. Then, the city passed an ordinance that prohibited any more excavations below the water table. The Supreme Court's comments are interesting:

> Although this concededly prohibited the beneficial use to which the property had previously been devoted, a state court granted the Town an injunction to enforce this prohibition. Held: On the record in this case, appellants have not sustained the burden of showing that the depth limitation is so onerous and unreasonable as to result in a taking of their property without due process of law in violation of the Fourteenth Amendment…
> Indulging in the usual presumption of constitutionality, … we find no indication that the prohibitory effect of Ordinance No. 16 is sufficient to render it an

unconstitutional taking if it is otherwise a valid police regulation.

> To justify the State in ... interposing its authority in behalf of the public, it must appear, first, that the interests of the public ... require such interference; and, second, that the means are reasonably necessary for the accomplishment of the purpose, and not unduly oppressive upon individuals."
>
> Even this rule is not applied with strict precision, for this Court has often said that "debatable questions as to reasonableness are not for the courts but for the legislature."[551]

So, the courts will presume constitutionality, and will defer to the legislative bodies on the questions of reasonableness. This amounts to almost no right at all, if the courts really want to follow this test and want to uphold a statute.

However, recently some laws and regulations have tried to go too far, even in the area of economic rights. In the case of *Nollan v. California Coastal Commission*[552], a California state regulatory agency tried to force an owner of a home on the beach to grant a public easement across his property in order to obtain a building permit to modify his house. The Supreme Court ruled that this was a regulatory taking of the owner's property without just compensation. In so doing, the Court said the following:

> Given, then, that requiring uncompensated conveyance of the easement outright would violate the Fourteenth Amendment, the question becomes whether requiring it to be conveyed as a condition for issuing a land-use permit alters the outcome. We have long recognized that land-use regulation does not effect a taking if it **"substantially advance[s] legitimate state interests"** and does not "den[y] an owner economically viable use of his land," ... Our cases have not elaborated on the standards for determining what constitutes a **"legitimate state interest"** or what type of connection between the regulation and the state interest satisfies the requirement that the former **"substantially**

advance" the latter. They have made clear, however, that a broad range of governmental purposes and regulations satisfies these requirements. See Agins v. Tiburon, supra, at 260-262 (scenic zoning); Penn Central Transportation Co. v. New York City, supra (landmark preservation); Euclid v. Ambler Realty Co., 272 U.S. 365 (1926) (residential zoning).[553]

Notice that the words used have now been changed slightly. While it is still only a legitimate state interest (not important or compelling) that is involved, there now has to be a substantial advancement of this interest, not merely a reasonable relationship.

So what does all of this have to do with the Second Amendment? Well, assuming that I am right, that the Second Amendment does guarantee a right to individuals to keep and bear arms, then the next question that must be asked is: Which test is to be applied to any law or regulation that tends to infringe on that right?

Very few people have ever contended that the Second Amendment is absolute. Even the First Amendment, the holy grail of all individual rights, has exceptions to it. On its face, the First Amendment, ("Congress shall make **no law** ... abridging the freedom of speech ...") is absolute. Yet it has always been recognized that libel or slander is not allowed and can be punished. The proverbial rule that freedom of speech does not allow one to yell, "FIRE!" in a crowded theater when there is no fire, is also applied. Even the cases cited above recognize a possibility of governmental regulation of free speech, if the regulation can pass the most strenuous test. Therefore, one should expect that some regulation, or infringement, of the right to keep and bear arms would be allowed, despite the absolute language of the Amendment. So, if some infringement is to be allowed, how much will be allowed, or how much infringement will be too much? To answer this question, we must know which test the courts will use in determining the constitutionality of any attempt to infringe on this right.

This is not any easy question to answer, because most cases that have addressed the issue of the Second Amendment have ruled that there is no individual right, so the question of what test to apply simply did not come up. Remember that only one case at the Supreme Court level has addressed the Second Amendment, and it did not reach this question at all. Gun control advocates argue that if an individual right is ever declared, the least stringent test of a reasonable basis should be applied. In support of this they cite *Lewis v. United States*[554]. To refresh your memory, the issue in this case was whether or not a prior felony conviction, though probably unconstitutional because the defendant was not given counsel at the time, could be used against the defendant as the predicate offense to cause his possession of a firearm to be illegal. The Second Amendment was not in issue. In that case the Court did say that "[t]he firearm regulatory scheme at issue here is consonant with the concept of equal protection embodied in the Due Process Clause of the Fifth Amendment if there is 'some **rational basis** for the statutory distinctions made ... or ... they have **some relevance** to the purpose for which the classification is made.'"[555] This sounds like the rational basis test, but again, it was not in consideration of applying the regulatory statute to the Second Amendment, although it must be said that the Court did append its footnote 8 to the quoted statement, which did mention the Second Amendment by quoting *Miller* as requiring a reasonable relationship to the preservation or efficiency of a well regulated militia. So, it is arguable whether or not this case would support the application of the reasonable basis test to the Second Amendment right.

Gun control advocates also point to several court of appeals cases, such as *United States v. Nelsen*[556], *United States v. Day*[557], and *United States v. Synnes*[558], as holding that the reasonable basis test is to be applied. But remember that each of these cases denied that an individual right exists. The reasonable basis applied in these cases was not applied to the Second Amendment, but to the basic power of the government to regulate interstate commerce. It is almost universally recognized (despite my opinions) that this is the test to be applied to the application of the interstate commerce clause, to determine if the government has the power to regulate or restrict something. However, that has never been the question in this book. The question has been whether, despite that power, the Second Amendment steps in to prohibit the government from exercising that power so as to infringe the rights of individuals to keep and bear arms. And now, in this chapter, the question becomes, if it does, what test is to be used to determine whether any given attempt by the government to restrict firearms has gone too far. These court of appeals cases simply do not reach this issue.

The one case that has held that there is an individual right, *United States v. Emerson*[559], does not fully answer the mail on this question. The closest that the court gets to enunciating a test is the following:

> Although, as we have held, the Second Amendment *does* protect individual rights, that does not mean that those rights may never be made subject to any **limited, narrowly tailored specific** exceptions or restrictions **for particular cases** that are **reasonable** and **not inconsistent** with the right of Americans generally to individually keep and bear their private arms as historically understood in this country.[560]

The government interest, compelling, important or legitimate, is not even addressed. The relationship of the law to that interest, necessary, substantially related or reasonably related, is not clear; though the word reasonable is used I am not sure that it applies to the relationship, or just to being reasonable in general. It does appear that the law in question has to be limited and narrowly drawn for specific or particular cases, which sounds like a portion of a higher test. Overall, this language from the Fifth Circuit simply does not enable me to pigeonhole where the court thinks the Second Amendment should go as to the three traditional tests used to protect people's rights.

It should be noted that the United States Attorney General, Mr. John Ashcroft, in a letter stated that "the individual rights view of the Second Amendment does not prohibit Congress from enacting laws restricting firearms ownership for **compelling state interests**, such as prohibiting firearms ownership by convicted felons..."[561] While not of the same authority as a court decision, the Attorney General's opinion is entitled to be given some persuasive authority. And his statement would indicate the strict scrutiny test should be used. The problem with this argument is that his predecessor said there was no individual right at all, and who knows what his successor will say. It will probably depend who the next President is.

Once again, the only court that can answer this question is the United State Supreme Court. What test should it use? Well, in my

A People Armed and Free

opinion, it should use the strict scrutiny test, just like I think it should use the strict scrutiny test for all rights; but I am obviously wrong, as a legal matter, at least as to economic or property rights. What test will it use? This is a big wild card. I do not believe that anyone, attorney or not, can sit here and with confidence tell you what the Court will do on such an issue. I certainly would not bet the farm on one result or another.

So, as we go through this chapter, I will attempt to distinguish between the different results that I think should apply if each of the different tests are used. So, now on to the specific issues as to what the government can, or should, regulate, and what they cannot.

A. *Nobody Wants to Take Away Your Guns*

As a first issue, we need to address this comment that is made virtually every time the debate comes up over specific gun regulation issues. Remember that I am careful about using absolutes. Even so, I must say that every time that I have listened to a debate on these topics, on television or radio, or read a debate in the newspaper, at some point the gun control advocate says something to the effect that we should not be so paranoid, "Nobody wants to take away your guns." This statement is a lie and the people making it know that it is a lie. I doubt that even the people making the statement do not want to take away people's guns, but even giving them the benefit of the doubt, by saying that the person making the statement may not want to take away people's guns, the statement is still a lie, because plenty of people do want to take away guns, and the people making these statements know it!

Some polls show that approximately 40% of the American people want to do away with the civilian ownership of handguns, and almost 20% want to get rid of all guns.[562] While opinion polls fluctuate somewhat from time to time, this is still a significant percentage. And this is not just limited to people on the street. Many of these are powerful people. Some quotes are in order:

> The need for a ban on handguns cannot be overstated. Unlike rifles and shotguns, handguns are easily concealable. Consequently, they are the weapons of choice in most murders, accounting for the deaths of 25,000 Americans in 1991.

> A 6-month grace period would be established during which time handguns could be turned in to any law enforcement agency with impunity and for reimbursement at the greater of $25 or the fair market value of the handgun. After the grace period's expiration, handguns could be turned in voluntarily with impunity from criminal prosecution, but a civil fine of $500 would be imposed.[563]

"As you know, my position is we should ban all handguns, get rid of them, no manufacture, no sale, no importation, no transportation, no possession of a handgun."[564]

> I am introducing the Handgun Control Act of 1992. This legislation would outlaw the possession, importation, transfer or manufacture of a handgun except for use by public agencies, individuals who can demonstrate to their local police chief that they need a gun because of threat to their life or the life of a family member, licensed guard services, licensed pistol clubs which keep the weapons securely on premises, licensed manufacturers and licensed gun dealers.[565]

"The only way to discourage the gun culture is to remove the guns from the hands and shoulders of people who are not in the law enforcement business."[566] "There is no reason for anyone in this country, for anyone except a police officer or a military person, to buy, to own, to have, to use, a handgun. The only way to control handgun use in this country is to prohibit the guns."[567] "The goal is an ultimate ban on all guns, but we also have to take one step at a time and go for limited access first."[568] "Gun violence won't be cured by one set of laws. It will require years of partial measures that will gradually tighten the requirements for gun ownership, and incrementally change expectations about the firepower that should be available to ordinary citizens."[569] "We are inclined to think that every firearm in the hands of anyone who is not a law enforcement officer constitutes an incitement to violence."[570]

> We are beyond the stage of restrictive licensing and uniform laws. We are at the point in time and terror when nothing short of a strong uniform policy of domestic disarmament will alleviate the danger which is crystal clear and perilously present. Let us take the guns away from the people. Exemptions should be limited to the military, the police and those licensed for good and sufficient reasons.[571]

"My own view on gun control is simple. I hate guns and I cannot imagine why anyone would want to own one. If I had my way, guns for sport would be registered, and all other guns, would be banned."[572] Gary Wills, a historian and writer, often cited, quoted and relied on by the Brady Center and Handgun Control, Inc., in their efforts to promote gun control has said: "Mutual protection should be the aim of citizens, not individual self-protection. Until we are willing to outlaw, the very existence or manufacture of civilian handguns we have no right to call ourselves citizens or consider our behavior even minimally civil."[573] He also said: "Every civilized society must disarm its citizens against each other. Those who do not trust their own people become predators upon their own people. The sick thing is that haters of fellow Americans often think of themselves as patriots."[574] Even the venerable Sarah Brady has made a similar statement: "The only reason for guns in civilian hands is for sporting purposes."[575]

Now I am not a conspiracy theorist (though I must admit that I do not believe that Lee Harvey Oswald killed President Kennedy by himself), but this sounds like a lot of people, politicians, news media moguls, and gun control activists who market themselves as being moderate on the issue of gun control, want to take away guns. While Handgun Control Inc. claims that it does not want to ban guns, it did file a friend of the court brief in the case of *Quilici v. Village of Morton Grove*[576], supporting the village's ordinance banning the private ownership of handguns. Clearly, when a gun control advocate comes on television and piously announces that **no one** wants to take away your guns, he is lying.

And given the gun control advocates position on the Second Amendment, as show by the U.S. Attorney's argument in *Emerson* quoted earlier in Chapter 7, there could be no way to stop the government from taking all guns from people if it decided to do so, unless they are wrong about the Second Amendment. Given all of these statements and actions, and the logical conclusion of the gun control argument, I do not count this as paranoia, but as logical skepticism. Or perhaps another way to put it would be: Even if you are paranoid, it doesn't mean that the bastards aren't out to get you!

B. *Current Federal Gun Control Laws*

I do not intend to go into depth as to every federal law touching on the issue of firearms. But I will address the statutes restricting the right of certain classes of individuals to possess firearms, the regulations concerning the transfer of ownership of firearms, and the Brady Act.

In my opinion, it is probably good for good people to have guns, and bad for bad people to have guns. A gun by itself is neutral. I once gave a class in church to a group of young men, ages 12 and 13, about the church's position on sexual behavior. My intention was to show that under the right circumstances, i.e. being married, that sexual relations are good, but under the wrong circumstances, i.e. outside of marriage, they are bad. To do this I led off with the question: What kind of tools can you think of that can be used both for good and bad purposes? I expected them to answer something like hammers (when used to build a house it is good; when used to bash somebody's head in it is bad) or automobiles (when used to go to school or work, good; when used to drag race, resulting in a wreck that kills somebody, bad). The first response I received was "guns". Now, I had never thought of guns as being tools, but darned if the kids aren't right! If I am at a restaurant with a gun placed on my table, as long as it stays there, it is neither good nor bad, it simply is. If I pick it up and use it as a tool to rob the cashier, it is bad. If, on the other hand, I pick it up and use it to shoot someone else who is trying to rob the cashier, as a tool to prevent a robbery and possibly a murder of the cashier, it is good.

With all of that said, let us first look at the Gun Control Act of 1968, as amended. 18 U.S.C. section 922(g) makes it illegal for certain classes of people "to ship or transport in interstate or foreign commerce, or possess in or affecting commerce, any firearm or ammunition; or to receive any firearm or ammunition which has been shipped or transported in interstate or foreign commerce." These classes include the following:

1. People who have been convicted in any court of a crime punishable by imprisonment for a term exceeding one year (in other words, a felony).

This falls into the category of not allowing bad people to have guns. This seems like a good idea to me. And it is not just me thinking my opinions are superior to other people. A look at history, as we did some chapters ago, shows that the original colonies and states often restricted criminals from being able to have guns. So this restriction seems to have been recognized at the time the Second Amendment was enacted, and therefore would probably be valid under any of the three potential tests of constitutionality.

It should be noted that the individual does not have to be sentenced to more than a year of imprisonment, only that the crime convicted of had a potential punishment of more than a year. I have one friend who asked about potential rehabilitation. Suppose someone is convicted of a minor felony (is that an oxymoron?) and then lives for ten or twenty years without any further problems. Is he to be denied this constitutional right for all of his life? Perhaps, since arguably more important rights, such as the right to vote can be denied him. But perhaps not, because the statute does grant a process to have this restriction removed, and maybe such a situation would merit the removal of the restriction. If there is any constitutional problem with this restriction being applied for life, then this procedure for removal may save the statute constitutionally.

2. People who are fugitives from justice.

Like these people care. They are running away from the law anyway. Actually, 18 U.S.C. section 921(a)(15) defines a "fugitive from justice" as "any person who has fled from any State to avoid prosecution for a crime or to avoid giving testimony in any criminal proceeding." The Seventh Circuit has held that this means that the person has to know that charges are pending against him, but he does not have to know that he is classified as a "fugitive from justice".[577] It is also clear that this means that the person has to leave the state that he is wanted in. In *United States v. Duncan*[578], the court held that "an indispensable requisite of the prosecution's proof was that Duncan had left Florida with the intent to avoid arrest or prosecution."[579] In that case, the defendant was arrested on August 22, 1975, coming into the country from Canada for smuggling stolen goods. The arresting officers did a records check and discovered the outstanding warrant from Florida. They also found a gun in his possession. The defendant claimed that he had just found out about the warrant and was in the process of returning to Florida to deal with it. The only evidence at trial as to why the defendant left Florida was that he had left on June 16, 1975, on a vacation. The warrant was not issued until July 21, 1975, therefore, it would have been impossible for the defendant to have left Florida with the intent to avoid the warrant. Therefore, he was acquitted.

If caught with a gun, that is probably just one more crime to add to the list on these people. But if enforced, it may be a tool to remove some criminals from the streets for a longer period of time. As to the constitutionality, I would classify it like the first class of people, as keeping guns out of the hands of bad people. And it probably has the same chance of standing constitutional muster as the first.

3. *People who are unlawful users or addicted to any controlled substance.*

This one may be more of a problem. This does not just reach drug dealers, smugglers and the like, who would also fall under numbers one and two, but also the user. The problem is, how is user defined? The statute does not define it. So the courts are left to determine their own definition. For example, does the accused person have to have been using the drug at the instance that he is found with a weapon, or would something like daily use, weekly use, or monthly use during the time frame that he possessed a gun suffice? In *United States v. Ocegueda,*[580] the defendant admitted to using heroin at least ten times from March to August, 1976, which would average about 2 times a month. On June 24 and July 5, 1976, he purchased firearms from a licensed gun dealer. The court found that a common sense meaning of the term "user" would clearly include the conduct of the defendant, but that if his use of heroin had been infrequent and in the distant past, they might have to rule differently. In *United States v. Corona,*[581] the court ruled that there is no requirement that the defendant be shown to have been using drugs at the moment he purchased the firearms, and that in that particular case there was plenty of evidence to show that the defendant used and was addicted to cocaine during the three years that he made six separate purchases of a total of nine firearms.

The best analysis of this problem is by a district court in the case of *United States v. Reed.*[582] There the defendant was charged with six counts of possession of a firearm by a user. However, there was no direct evidence of his use of any drugs. On one occasion, there was the odor of marijuana coming from his car, which might indicate contemporaneous drug use. The court said that the United States Attorney admitted that the statute applies only to a person who **is** a drug user, not someone who **was** a drug user, although the use does not have to be at the exact some moment as the possession of the firearms. The problem is that there is no standard for when a person transfers from one who **is** using drugs to one who **was** using drugs.

While this again may be used to reduce crime, it seems a little broad if the higher level tests are applied, for what, really, does the possession of a gun have to do with someone occasionally smoking a joint, regardless of what you may think of the action of using marijuana? For many people, the two are totally unrelated. And to deny a constitutional right based on such occasional use would be like denying the same constitutional right for being found drunk in public. With that said, it would probably pass constitutional muster under the lowest level test, because we can make the argument that there is a legitimate governmental interest in stopping the drug trade and keeping guns out of the hands of those who would break the law by using drugs (legitimate, though not compelling) and there is a reasonable relationship of the law to this interest (though not a substantial relation, and it certainly is not narrowly drawn). I have problems with it under the two higher tests.

4. People who have been adjudicated as mental defectives or who have been committed to a mental institution.

This falls into the category of people who have been determined to be a danger to themselves or others. As long as this category is kept narrowly drawn or interpreted to this purpose, it should pass muster under all of the tests. However, we have definition problems in this category too. What does it take to be "adjudicated"? What is a mental defective? What is a commitment to a mental hospital?

There are two different approaches to this provision among the courts. One approach is to read the statute, as a criminal statute, narrowly; the other is to read it broadly to accomplish its intended results. In the narrow category, in the case of *United States v. Hansel*,[583] a state board had found the defendant to be mentally ill and in need of hospitalization. However, the court determined that he was not committed to a mental institution because the state law for such commitments was not complied, and, in reading the statute strictly and narrowly, the determination of mental illness is not the same as mental defective, which the court said means mentally retarded. A similar case from the Fifth Circuit, *United States v. Giardina*,[584] held that the hospitalization of a person for two weeks on certificates from two doctors, without a judicial hearing, could not amount to being committed to a mental hospital. The court said "criminal statutes are to be strictly construed and give to '[committed]' its narrow meaning ... An essential element of that federal offense is either a formal adjudication that a person suffers a mental defect, or a formal commitment, which latter, in the instance of Louisiana, requires formal action by the state district court."[585]

On the other track, in *United States v. Waters*[586] the court held that an involuntary commitment without a judicial hearing qualified under the statute because the state law in that case did not require a judicial hearing. Then in *United States v. Midgett*,[587] the court determined to read the statute broadly, to define commitment as "to place officially in confinement or custody."

What about people who commit themselves? In *United States v. Vertz*[588] the court quotes a portion of the federal firearms regulations:

> Committed to a mental institution. A formal commitment of a person to a mental institution by a court, board, commission, or other lawful authority. The term includes a commitment to a mental institution involuntarily. The term includes commitment for mental defectiveness or mental illness. It also includes commitments for other reasons, such as for drug use. The term does not include a person in a mental institution for observation or a voluntary admission to a mental institution.[589]

If the statute is restricted to applying only during the time that the person is a danger to himself or others, it is OK. But if it goes beyond that to include all of a person's life, even after he recovers from his mental problems, then, in my opinion, there is a problem, at least under the strict scrutiny test. This differs from the criminal and drug provisions, since those are voluntary actions of the people involved, while mental illness is not. Under the reasonable basis test, since the statute does not have to be narrowly drawn, but only have a reasonable relationship to a legitimate government interest, it may be OK.

5. *Illegal aliens and aliens here under nonimmigrant visas.*

Constitutional rights do not necessarily apply to non-citizens, and I have no problem with denying the Second Amendment protection to all aliens, especially since I consider the most important reason for the Second Amendment to be the insurrectionist theory. Aliens have no business starting insurrections here, whether they are here legally or not. It would make sense to allow legal aliens, here on immigrant visas, to have guns for self-defense, but I could also argue that they should have to wait until they become naturalized citizens. In any event, if the Second Amendment is extended to aliens, certainly the illegal aliens should not fall under its protection. As to the aliens here under nonimmigrant visas, I would need help from an immigration attorney to form an opinion. I punt on this one.

6. *People who have been discharged from the armed forces under dishonorable conditions.*

This can only happen through a general court martial, for an offense that would be a felony in the civilian world. Therefore, everything said about the first class of people applies here.

7. *People who have been citizens of the United States, but who have renounced their citizenship.*

Since they are no longer citizens, I have no problem not giving them constitutional protections. This is especially true since they have voluntarily renounced their citizenship. This is just a consequence of their conscious action that they should be aware of. Again, we do not want them involved in any insurrection. Maybe they should be allowed to defend themselves, but then if they desire to have a gun to do so, maybe they should think about that before taking such drastic action. However, if the Second Amendment is to be applied to noncitizens, this one probably has a problem under all three tests. While there may be a legitimate government interest in keeping subversive people, who used to be citizens, from being able to use guns against our government and people, and this statute could be said to be reasonably related to that interest, it just seems way too broad to me. Again, this only applies if we are going to apply the Second Amendment to noncitizens.

Jack Reynolds, J. D.

8. People under a restraining order that restrains such person from harassing, stalking, or threatening an intimate partner of such person or child of such intimate partner or person.

Actually there is a lot more to this provision than just that. The court order must be issued after a hearing that the person had notice of, and an opportunity to participate in. The court order must include a finding that such person represents a credible threat to the physical safety of such intimate partner or child; or by its terms explicitly prohibits the use, attempted use, or threatened use of physical force against such intimate partner or child that would reasonably be expected to cause bodily injury. That is a mouthful. This is the portion of the statute that Mr. Emerson was charged with violating. That means that it was found to be constitutional by the Fifth Circuit in *Emerson*, even applying the Second Amendment to protect an individual right. However, there is an indication in *Emerson* that if the restraining order was issued without the required findings (in *Emerson*, due to Texas state law and rules of procedure, these findings were implied in the order) the statute would not be applied.

As noted before, a problem with this is that it can be applied to boilerplate language in temporary orders and divorce decrees. This problem is not restricted to Texas. A Superior Court Judge in Porter County, Indiana, Judge Thomas Webber, has pointed out the unintended consequence of people making themselves into federal criminals by agreeing to divorce decrees that invoke the prohibition of this law, even though there is no evidence of any violent intent of either party.[590]

While the ruling is probably correct if either of the reasonable basis or intermediate scrutiny tests are used, if strict scrutiny is used an argument can be made that the statute is not narrow enough. Since it already requires a court hearing, why not require the judge to address the issue of whether or not the individual gets to keep his gun and make an express ruling on the subject, instead of having a statute that automatically makes the person a federal criminal? While there is a compelling government interest in keeping divorcing spouses from killing each other, the statute would still need to be narrowly drawn, which it is not. It includes many boilerplate orders entered in divorces by agreement. Too broad!

9. People convicted of misdemeanor crimes of domestic violence.

The government interest here seems to rest on the assumption that those who commit minor spousal abuse may later try to kill their spouse, so we have to keep them from having guns. Perhaps this would reach the category of a legitimate interest, but hardly compelling. And while the law might be somewhat related to this interest, it certainly is not substantially related to it, and I would argue that it is not even reasonably related to it. And it is certainly too broad. Most people who have minor problems do not try to kill each other.

And this provision has a retroactive effect. Those who were convicted years ago, even prior to the passage of the provision, became federal criminals if they possessed a firearm on the effective date of the provision. Even if there is no evidence of any further threat. There are cases being reported now where a person, during an argument with her spouse, threw her car keys, not at her spouse, but they landed close to him. Due to her spouse calling the police, she was charged with, and convicted of, a misdemeanor assault, even though her spouse decided he did not want to press charges. Now she cannot own a gun for any reason for the rest of her life? Give me a break. We might as well say if you are ever convicted of speeding, even one time, even if only one mile per hour over the speed limit, you can never drive again. This section should not pass muster even under the least stringent test. There has to be a better way to keep spouses from killing each other.

With that said, at least one court disagrees with me and thinks it will pass even the strict scrutiny test. See, *Gillespie v. City of Indianapolis*, 185 F.3d 693, 699 (7th Cir. 1999), *cert. denied*, 528 U.S. 1116 (2000).

All of this brings us to the Brady Act, probably the most well known, by name at least, of all of the gun control measures. Initially, it applied only to handguns (pistols) but it now applies to all firearms. The major provision of the bill requires a background check for all purchases of firearms. Although the provisions listed above made it illegal for certain people to possess firearms, prior to the Brady Act people in each of those categories, if residing in a state that did not have its own background check system, could just walk into a gun store and buy a gun. Federal law did require the purchaser to sign an affidavit that he did not fall into any of these categories, but it was easy for them to lie on the form and buy a gun anyway. Therefore, the basic concept of the Brady Act is good, to the extent that the categories of restricted persons are themselves constitutionally valid. However, there were some problems with parts of the bill.

First, there was initially a requirement for a mandatory five-day waiting period to purchase a handgun. The concept here is that if someone wanted to buy a gun because they were mad at someone else, or wanted to commit suicide, then this would provide a cooling down period and possibly avoid a death. The problem with this is that it could also cut the other way. What if a person knew that someone else was mad at him, and had threatened his life? He now wants to buy a gun for self-defense. But, faced with a five-day waiting period, he might not be able to obtain a gun to defend himself with, and might be killed by the other person. This seems to me to be a tragic denial of a constitutionally protected right.

Then there was a problem with the background check system. In today's world of the Internet and high-speed computers everywhere, you would think that this would be easy. But when the law was passed, there was no national system to check all criminal records in all fifty states. So, the law required that the local officials had to run the background checks. This was ruled unconstitutional.[591] Even so, most local authorities probably continued to perform the background checks, just because it was a good idea for somebody to do it.

The law has now evolved. The federal government now has the responsibility to provide background checks under the National Instant Criminal Background Check System (NICS). This is a computerized national system. The seller of the gun is required to take information from the purchaser and run it through the computer. He normally gets a response within a few minutes. If the person is cleared, the dealer can go ahead and sell the gun to him, and provide immediate delivery of the gun to the purchaser. Two other results are possible. The purchaser may be quickly denied the ability to buy a gun through the background check, in which case the seller cannot sell him the gun. Or the system may come back with a notice that there may be some question as to this person's background, in which case up to three days are given to complete the background check. At the end of the three days, either the person will be denied permission to buy the gun, or, even if the system is still pending, he is allowed to go forward with the purchase.

A People Armed and Free

All of this is quite a bit better than the original system. And with improvements in technology and getting more local court and legal systems on board, one would hope that the system continues to improve. Even the NRA seems to support the basic concept of NICS, although they still have a problem with the potential of a law abiding citizen having to wait three days to exercise a constitutionally protected right, for the same reasons that they opposed the five-day waiting period.

It should be noted that there is an appeal process that a person can go through if he is wrongly denied permission to buy a gun. The results of these appeals so far show that most of the rejections are justified, but a substantial number of rejections were wrongful, and the people involved were eventually allowed to buy the guns. This also gives gun rights activists some problems, much as wrongfully incarcerating an innocent person should give people pause.

Various claims are made about the effectiveness of the Brady Act. Most gun rights activists say that its impact on crime has been negligible. Gun control advocates claim that over 600,000 people have been denied the purchase of guns, and that this has contributed significantly to drop in violent crimes involving firearms. I suspect that the answer probably lies somewhere in the middle. I am very suspicious of the 600,000 number. First, how many of those are repeat attempts, that is to say, how many of those represent people who were denied at one location, so they went to another location and tried again? Then, how many of those who were denied simply obtained a firearm somewhere else, through some other means? I also believe that other laws may have had some impact on the violent crime rate, such as the right to carry concealed weapons and the practice during the 1990's of putting more criminals behind bars. And we cannot discount the better economy during the 1990's. Even so, as I said earlier, it is probably a good idea to prevent bad people from having guns, and as long as this can be done without infringing the rights of law-abiding citizens to have guns, then I am OK with it. And, it probably has reduced the violent crime rate some amount, though with all of the other variables involved, I do not believe that we can ever know how much.

This leads us into another area of contention between the two camps – whether or not the current laws, if enforced, are adequate, or do we need more gun control laws? This goes back into a dispute over statistics. But first let us set the stage: The law that makes it a federal crime for certain people to possess a firearm prescribes a ten-year sentence for each violation. The Brady Act makes it a crime to lie on the application form, and this federal crime carries with it a one-year sentence. So, if 600,000 people were denied the purchase of a gun because of the Brady Act, why aren't 600,000 people behind bars for that federal crime? Of course, some of the people may have innocently made mistakes on the forms, others have been shown to have been wrongfully denied the purchase, still others may have disappeared while waiting for their background results to come in. Even so, a large number of these people should be known, and should have been accessible. All it should take is a phone call to the local law enforcement agency, have them picked up and delivered to the federal authorities, and a very simple trial, with the signed application form and the background check result entered into evidence, and presto, the person would be convicted. And another potentially violent criminal would be off the street for a period of time. But, as of this writing, I do not know of more than seven prosecutions under the Brady Act!

The following table shows what I am talking about:

Prosecutions of Federal Firearms Laws
CASES REPORTED, EXECUTIVE OFFICE, U.S. ATTORNEY REQUESTED FIREARMS SECTIONS COUNTS CHARGED, CALENDAR YEARS 1996-1998

Title 18 U.S.C.	
Penalty	
1996	
1997	
1998	
Providing a firearm to a prohibited person unspecified category	
10 years	
17	
25	
10	
Providing a firearm to a felon	
10 years	
20	
13	
24	
Possession of a firearm by a prohibited person, unspecified category	
10 years	
683	
752	
603	
Possession of a firearm by a felon	
10 years	
1213	
1366	
1550	

311

Possession or discharge of a firearm in a school zone
5 years
4
5
8

*All violations under the Brady act, Instant Check phase
1 year
0
0
0

**Transfer of a handgun or handgun ammunition ta a juvenile
1 year
9
5
6

Possession of a handgun or handgun ammunition by a juvenile
1 year
27
3
8

***"Enhanced penalty: Use of a firearm during crime of violence or drug-related crime prosecutable in federal court
5 years
1987
1885
1763

---

*For knowingly making any false statement or representation on Federal Form 4473, the penalty is 10 years.
***But if he knew or had reasonable cause to believe that juvenile would commit crime of violence the penalty is 10 years.
***10 years if short-barrelled rifle or shotgun or "assault weapon." 30 years if machine gun, destructive device, or firearm with silencer. On subsequent conviction: 20 years; life if machine gun, destructive device. or firearm with silencer.

A People Armed and Free

You can see that these laws could be a very strong deterrent to violent crime by getting violent criminals off of the street for long periods of time. For example, take an average criminal. He has been convicted for at least one prior felony. He has committed others, and is wanted by the law, so he is a fugitive. He probably uses some kind of drugs. So, under three provisions of the Gun Control Act, he is prohibited from possessing a gun or ammunition. Now he goes into a gun store to buy a gun. He is shopping for a gun, so he picks up a couple and handles them. Bingo, violation numbers one and two, each carrying a ten-year possible sentence. He then tries to buy one, filling out information on the Brady form and lying about his background. Three additional violations of one-year each. He probably presents a false ID. Another violation, more jail time. Do see where we are going? After all is said and done, he could probably be put away for 30 years or more, easily. But, the government officials seem to be satisfied with the feel good statistics of over 600,000 people being turned away from the doors. To make a real impact on violent crime, we should not just turn criminals away from one door, so that they may go to others, only to commit crimes again, but should lock them up whenever we can. And this criminal should be easy to catch.

This recommended approach has been tried in Richmond, Virginia, since 1997. Called Project Exile, the local and federal authorities have gotten together to cooperate in this area. When a local law enforcement agency arrests a person with a gun, who falls into one of the prohibited categories, he is turned over to the federal authorities, who prosecute. The following results were obtained, as of April 1, 2000 (approximately three years of applying this action):

- 607 individuals have been indicted for federal firearm violations
- 460 individuals have been arrested on the federal charges
- 311 (approx. 69%) have been held without bond
- 383 have been sentenced to an average 56 months (4.7 years) in a federal prison

Federal prosecutors report that in 1999, homicides in Richmond were 46% below the number in 1997, and gun crimes overall had declined over 65%. The point is to get bad guys off of the streets. Letting good guys have guns does not hurt people.

With all of that said, the Brady Act has some good points, and if kept within reason is probably constitutional, to the extent that the prohibited classes are constitutional.

What about the laws pertaining to who can sell guns? Without going into more painful detail than you would ever want to endure, suffice it to say that if a person is going to have a business of selling firearms, he has to have a federal license. He has to keep voluminous records for a long period of time, which federal agents can inspect. He is subject to criminal penalties if he sells a firearm to someone in a prohibited category, just like a prohibited purchaser is. In other words, it is a very regulated industry. Certainly, under the interstate commerce clause, as currently interpreted, the federal government has the power to do this. But, does the Second Amendment step in to stop such regulation? Probably not. Even under the gun rights advocates' position of individual rights, it would only protect the right to have firearms, not a right to run a business of selling firearms. Therefore, as long as the government regulations of the businesses do not attempt to bar individuals from having firearms, the business itself can probably be regulated without violating the constitution.

All of this extensive regulation, both of the business and of certain individuals, calls to mind the accusation by the gun control advocates that guns are not as regulated as teddy bears are. Their point on this seems to be that the Consumer Product Safety Commission has the authority to regulate certain aspects of the manufacture of teddy bears for the safety of children. Things such as the material used in making the teddy bears, so that they are flame retardant and are not poisonous; how the eyes are attached, so that they do not come off where a small child might put one in his mouth, swallow it and choke on it. But they do not have similar regulations pertaining to the type of metal that goes into guns. While that may be true, I think you can see that there are loads of regulations pertaining to the selling, distribution and possession of firearms that do not pertain to teddy bears. As far as I know of, no federal license is required to sell teddy bears. No one is in a restricted category to where they cannot buy a teddy bear. This is really a red herring of an argument that tries to compare apples to oranges, or more appropriately, apples to rocks, since oranges are at least related to apples in that both are fruits, while

A People Armed and Free

there is no relationship between teddy bears and guns, except that both are bought and sold.

Another point should be made here. Nothing in the law protects gun manufacturers from tort responsibility for negligence or products liability. Torts are the kind of suits brought for personal injury, such as in car accidents or medical malpractice. If a gun manufacture uses a faulty design for a gun, which causes it to explode and kill its user, then they can be found responsible. If they are negligent in the manufacturing process and that causes injury, they can be held responsible. So again, guns are subject to the applicable laws, just like teddy bears.

Let us now turn our attention to one last current federal law. In 1994 a law was passed that bans the manufacture or importation of "assault weapons". These were defined as certain semiautomatic weapons, usually of military type. Other semiautomatic weapons, such as hunting rifles, are not banned. Pre-existing "assault weapons" are not banned, and can still be owned and sold. The ban goes through 2004 when, unless extended by Congress and the president, it will expire of its own accord.

Why do this? What is the reason behind the ban on "assault weapons"? The reasons given by the gun control advocates include that such weapons have become the weapon of choice for drug dealers and gangs.[592] Gun rights advocates dispute this, pointing out:

> Assault weapons are not the weapons of choice among drug dealers, gang members or criminals in general. Assault weapons are used in about one-fifth of one percent (.20%) of all violent crimes and about one percent in gun crimes. It is estimated that from one to seven percent of all homicides are committed with assault weapons (rifles of any type are involved in three to four percent of all homicides). However a higher percentage are used in police homicides, roughly ten percent. (There has been no consistent trend in this rate from 1978 through 1996.) Between 1992 and 1996 less than 4% of mass murders, committed with guns, involved assault weapons. (Our deadliest mass murders have either involved arson or bombs.)[593]

They further accuse the gun control advocates of supporting this ban only because the use of assault weapons make sensational news, and therefore it may be easier to gain public support for a ban, and this ban can be used as a step toward more extensive gun control or bans in the future. They quote the Washington Post: "No one should have any illusions about what was accomplished (by the ban). Assault weapons play a part in only a small percentage of crime. **The provision is mainly symbolic; its virtue will be if it turns out to be, as hoped, a stepping stone to broader gun control**."[594]

Gun control advocates point to mass killings. However, as pointed out above, they are but a small percentage of these killings. Gun control advocates say that assault weapons are too powerful, being able to penetrate police vests. So will most other rifles, because the vests are not designed to protect against rifle rounds. In fact, the assault weapons are less powerful than most hunting rifles. While good for what they were designed for, their smaller caliber and overall power actually make them less deadly in some circumstances. I have been pulling butts on a rifle range (running the target up and down, marking the shot holes and pasting them up), when I have actually seen M-16 rounds bounce off the paper targets when fired from 500 yards. Not often, but I have seen it happen. That would never happen with a good hunting rifle.

Gun control advocates say that all policemen support the ban. While certainly some do, some do not. Guncite.com has a large inventory of opposing police views, including the following statement:

> What limited polling of law enforcement has been done does not support the claims of Handgun Control, Inc., that all the police want "assault weapon" prohibition. The Florida chapter of the Fraternal Order of Police polled its membership, and found 75% opposed to an "assault weapon" ban. The most recent poll of police opinion was carried out by *Law Enforcement Technology* magazine in March 1991. The results were reported in the July/August 1991 issue: "75% do not favor gun control legislation ... with street officers opposing it by as much as 85 %." In

particular, 78.7% opposed a ban on "assault weapons." (About 37 % of top management supported a ban, and about 11% of street officers.)[595]

So what is the real constitutional issue here? Regardless of whether or not you support the gun control position as to the statistics or the gun rights position, should this ban be allowed under the Second Amendment? This law, unlike the regulations of sellers, does affect the right of individuals to own certain types of guns, because they cannot be made. Therefore, it does bring to bear the Second Amendment. While it can always be said that the government has a legitimate interest in reducing crime, and it can be said that a ban of certain types of weapons is reasonably related to that interest, because people can always come up with statistics to support such a ban and the courts will generally defer to the wisdom of the legislature under the reasonable basis test, the same could be said for a total ban on all guns, which would thereby reason the Second Amendment out of existence. That is why I do not believe that the least restrictive test should be used in relation to the Second Amendment. Under either the intermediate scrutiny test or the strict scrutiny test, it seems to me that the total ban of any type of firearm is too broad. It will automatically impact many law-abiding citizens, probably more so than it will impact criminals. Therefore, I do not believe that the ban should be upheld (although it has been by lower courts) and it should not be renewed by Congress and the President in 2004.

As an additional matter, this ban makes the least sense of all of the gun control laws if the real reason for the Second Amendment was to preserve the militia. If the people, who make up the militia, have the ability to obtain their own military type weapons and train with them, at their own expense, the militia gets a better-trained individual at no expense to the government. It is clear that the gun control advocates are not interested in supporting the constitution, but are only interested in whatever argument they can come up with to allow them to get the government to take away the people's guns.

C. Handguns

There is no federal ban on handguns at this time, despite the constant plea for such a ban by gun control advocates and many politicians. There are some such bans by some localities. Not all criminals are smart, but some are. If I were a smart criminal, which I am not (a criminal that is; whether or not I am smart may still be open to debate), I would certainly prefer to pick my victims from a group that I could be reasonably sure of could not defend themselves. In my mind, any town that outlaws handguns has just placed an open invitation to criminals to pay them a visit.

Handguns are the weapons most often used in homicides. Therefore, it seems logical to try to get rid of them, right? Except that they are used even more often in self-defense. Even without a shot being fired. If handguns were banned, who would lose them? Law-abiding citizens, of course. Criminals would keep theirs. And even if all handguns could be magically disintegrated, criminals would simply choose other weapons, be they other firearms, such as shotguns or rifles, or knifes, boxcutters (like the terrorists on 9/11) or something else. Banning handguns will not stop crime. Nor will it stop homicides, as the almost 3,000 people killed on 9/11 can attest.

But since handguns are easily concealable, wouldn't a ban make it harder for criminals to conceal their weapons, such as shotguns or rifles? No. Shotguns and rifles can be sawed off. Isn't that illegal? Yes, but do you think that matters to someone who is going to try to rob you and who is prepared to kill you to begin with? I doubt it.

What about the so-called "Saturday-Night Specials"? These are relatively cheap, small handguns. They are constantly the brunt of gun control advocates attempts to ban certain firearms. However, a law review article has pointed out that this term, Saturday-Night Special, has its origins in racial conflict shortly after the Civil War.[596] These were the only weapons that blacks could afford for self-defense, so the states tried to outlaw them. Due to these racial overtones, the gun control advocates have changed their terminology in some writings to "junk guns". They are supposed to be of inferior quality and therefore more dangerous. However, the gun control advocates do not cite any statistics about how many people have been killed or injured due to this alleged inferior quality. No, they still argue about their concealability and use in crime. And when asked about whether or not a ban on them would deprive poor people of the ability to defend themselves, they equivocate:

> Price is NOT the overriding factor in determining whether a handgun is a Saturday Night Special - the weapons are defined by inferior quality and

A People Armed and Free

> concealability. These weapons are not suited for self-defense or target shooting because they are inaccurate at a distance, lack essential safety features, and are made of unreliable and unsafe materials.
> Furthermore, firearms are not necessarily the best method of self-defense, and may actually place the user at greater risk of harm.[597]

Price is a factor. Self-defense is usually done within ten yards, so accuracy at a distance is not a factor for suitability for self-defense. I know of no extensive statistics that show more of a danger to the user than the person he is trying to defend himself from. Even high quality revolvers do not have a safety on them, as semi-automatic pistols do. And we have already seen the arguments over the use of guns for self-defense. Again, it appears that the gun control advocates are simply trying to do away with guns, one category at a time.

Which gets us back to the constitutional issue. As I said about the assault weapons ban, bans of handguns should not be constitutional. While assault weapons have their primary purpose in supporting the militia (or under the insurrectionist theory, if you prefer), handguns have their best justification under the purpose of self-defense (though they too can be related to the militia). Outside of the home, handguns are the best method of self-defense, because of their ability to be easily carried, their concealibility, their ease of use, and their relatively good accuracy at short distances. Of course, all of these attributes also make them attractive to criminals, but again, banning them will not change that; it would only take away a right of self-defense from law-abiding citizens. Under either the intermediate scrutiny or the strict scrutiny tests, such bans should be declared unconstitutional, because they are not substantially related to the government interest, and they are not narrowly drawn.

D. Cop Killer Bullets

Like most of you, I have read the news reports, and seen the television exposes concerning Cop Killer Bullets. I have seen the results of using Cop Killer Bullets in numerous movies (**NEVER** trust Hollywood). Yet I found out in my research that all that I thought I knew on this subject was wrong. Surprised? So was I. Apparently, the news media, only going for sensational stories that fit its agenda simply do not want to let the people know the truth. Do you want to know what the truth is? Read the following from Mike Casey (a pseudonym). He is currently a Patrol Officer, Firearms Instructor and Field Training Officer in a municipal police department in Maine. He previously served as a Deputy Sheriff in the Detroit area and as a U.S. Army Armored Cavalry officer. Mike has served in a variety of law enforcement positions including horse-mounted patrol, bicycle patrol and as a Special Response Team member. He holds a BA in Criminology. Why would a police officer use a pseudonym? Perhaps because the following statement, while true, is not politically correct, and could endanger his job:

> In the mid 1960's, Dr. Paul Kopsch (an Ohio coroner), Daniel Turcos (a police sergeant) and Donald Ward (Dr. Kopsch's special investigator) began experimenting with special purpose handgun ammunition. Their objective was to develop a law enforcement round capable of improved penetration against hard targets like windshield glass and automobile doors. Conventional bullets, made primarily from lead, are often ineffective against hard targets especially when fired at handgun velocities. In the 1970's, Kopsch, Turcos and Ward produced their "KTW" handgun ammunition using steel cored bullets capable of great penetration. Following further experimentation, in 1981 they began producing bullets constructed primarily of brass. The hard brass bullets caused exceptional wear on handgun barrels, a problem combated by coating the bullets with Teflon. The Teflon coating did nothing to improve penetration, it simply reduced damage to the gun barrel.
> Despite the facts that "KTW" ammunition had never been available to the general public and that no police officer has ever been killed by a handgun bullet penetrating their body armor, the media incorrectly reported that the Teflon coated bullets were designed to defeat the body armor that law enforcement officers were beginning to use. The myth of "Cop-killer" bullets was born.

A People Armed and Free

In January of 1982, NBC Television broadcast a sensationalist prime time special titled "Cop Killer Bullets." Law enforcement officials had asked NBC not to air the program as the use of body armor by police officers was still not common knowledge and the "KTW" ammunition was virtually unheard of outside law enforcement circles. The safety of law enforcement officers took a back seat to ratings at NBC however and they not only broadcast the show, but re-broadcast it again six months later.

Following significant media hype and widespread misconceptions, Congress got into the act and proposed legislation that would have outlawed any bullet based on it's ability to penetrate certain bullet resistant material. The FBI, Bureau of Alcohol Tobacco and Firearms, and other forensic experts cautioned that the proposed ban was too vague to be enforceable. The NRA opposed the proposed law since it would have banned not only the controversial armor piercing handgun rounds, but nearly all conventional rifle ammunition as well. (Most rifle ammunition will easily penetrate the most commonly worn protective vests.)

The NRA proposed alternative legislation based upon the actual design and construction of the bullets. The final, approved version of the bill (H.R. 3121 passed in 1986) prohibited the sale of armor piercing ammunition [which may be used in a handgun] other than to law enforcement and the military. Representative Mario Biaggi (D-N.Y.) the original bill's sponsor, stated that the final legislation "... was not some watered down version of what we set out to do. In the end there was no compromise on the part of police safety..."

Gun control advocates and the news media jumped on the NRA's opposition to the original, vague and ineffective proposal. They ignored the NRA's contribution to the final legislation insisting to this day

> that the NRA wants "Cop Killer" bullets to be available to the public.

Here are the facts:

> - "Armor piercing" ammunition is only legally available to law enforcement agencies and to the armed forces.
> - Rather than opposing the ban on "armor piercing" ammunition, the NRA was in fact instrumental in crafting the law that Congress ultimately passed.
> - When properly wearing the appropriate body armor, not one law enforcement officer has ever been killed by a handgun bullet penetrating their vest. The National Institute of Justice (NIJ) certifies three levels of body armor. The most commonly worn, Level IIA, offers realistic protection against all .22, .25, .32, .380, and .38, caliber handgun ammunition, against most 9mm, .357 Magnum, .40 S&W, .45 ACP and .44 Magnum handgun ammunition and against 000 buck shotgun pellets. Level II and Level IIIA armor protects from even greater threats including 12 gauge shotgun slugs and the "hottest" .44 Magnum rounds.
>
> "Cop-killer" bullets are a myth born from media hype and nurtured by unrealistic Hollywood portrayals and the deliberately misleading claims of the anti-gun lobby. An objective, rational look at the facts quickly separates the myth from the reality. Knowledge is power.[598]

With this being from an author using a false name on the Internet, how do I know this is true? I checked it out. I talked with other police officers and military MP officers I know, including my brother, who I trust completely, and they confirmed it. My brother, in addition to being a sergeant on a large city police force, has trained their police recruits at their academy. He told me that it has been common knowledge for some time among law enforcement trainers that the "cop killer" bullets were a myth.

A People Armed and Free

Now I have no problem, constitutionally, with the restriction of this type of ammunition to the military and police. There is no need, or constitutionally recognized purpose, for individuals to have it. But what I do have a problem with is the continued lack of integrity of the gun control advocates, in the way they presented the issue, in their attempts to pass a ban that would have included virtually all rifle ammunition, and in their false accusations against the NRA, when in fact the NRA helped write a good piece of legislation that was passed. This makes me distrust their other arguments, and more importantly, their actual intentions, even more.

E. *Trigger Locks and Safe Storage Laws*

Gun control advocates are calling for laws that require people to safely store their guns and ammunition. The proposals take various forms. Some would require trigger locks. Some would require some type of locked container. Some require that the gun and its ammunition be stored separately, both locked up. All of this is designed to keep guns from being obtained by small children and accidentally discharge, or by irresponsible older children who might then use the guns in a wrong manner resulting in the death or injury of someone. Sounds like a laudable goal. So what is wrong with the suggestion?

Gun locks reduce the time available for self-defense. Gun control advocates say that the gun can be quickly unlocked, but I can still see a governor (I do not remember which one, but I can see him) who on television was going to prove this point. It took him an awfully long time to get the lock off of the gun. And he was not scared out of his wits because he had a criminal coming at him. And the proposal that the ammunition and gun be stored separately, both locked, is ludicrous. You might as well not have them for self-defense. Let's see, first I have to unlock my gun, then I have to unlock my ammunition, then I have to load my gun. I'm dead!

Gun control advocates point to the statistics of young children being killed by guns improperly stored. Of course, any loss of a young child is tragic. But do the storage laws work? Gun control advocates say they do: "In Florida, which was the first state to pass a CAP law, the results were dramatic — unintentional shooting deaths dropped by more than 50% the first year. California has shown similar results."[599] However, gun rights advocates cart out their own statistics:

The researchers found that accidental deaths among children younger than 15 were '23 percent lower than expected.

Using the 23 percent figure, the researchers estimated that the lives of 39 children were spared in the CAP law states [over a period of up to 4 years]. In states without the laws, it was estimated that 216 children who died could have been saved [again over a 4 year period].

[A] Free Press analysis of child mortality statistics from the Centers for Disease Control and Prevention in Atlanta indicated that although there was some impact from safe storage laws, it was barely measurable and dwarfed by a sharp decline nationally in accidental shooting deaths.

That decline includes all manner of unintentional shootings, such as when a child finds a loaded gun in the house, plays with it and accidentally kills someone. Between the mid-1980s and the mid-90s, unintentional firearm fatalities in U.S. children younger than 15 dropped nearly 44 percent, the analysis found.

In states that enacted CAP laws during that period, the decline was marginally greater — 45.1 percent vs. 42.6 percent for non-CAP states.

If the slight differences between CAP and non-CAP states could be **entirely** attributed to trigger locks, the laws were responsible for saving the lives of 1.75 children a year, the Free Press found." [emphasis added]

Don Kates, a civil rights lawyer in California who has written several books about gun-related issues, said many of the public health researchers studying gun violence are open advocates of gun control whose work is twisted in public debate.

Children younger than 5 are twice as likely to die from ingesting household poisons than by gunfire, said Kates, a gun-rights advocate.

'So the question for the Legislature should be: Is a parent criminally responsible for leaving an unlocked container of bleach below the sink?' Kates said.[600]

So, maybe the accidental death rates in Florida and California were going down anyway, even if the CAP laws had not been passed. An additional concern is whether or not these laws have resulted in more homicides because people have not been able to defend themselves:

> During the first five full years after the passage of the safe storage laws, the group of fifteen states that adopted these laws faced an annual average increase of over 300 more murders, 3,860 more rapes, 24,650 more robberies, and over 25,000 more aggravated assaults. On average, the annual costs borne by victims averaged over $2.6 billion as a result of lost productivity, out-of-pocket expenses, medical bills, and property losses.[601]

Now I have said before, and I will say again, I do not trust any of these statistics. It is easy to see how these can be manipulated based on the time frame looked at, the location, and other variables involved. It is impossible to determine a cause-and-effect basis on this issue from these statistics. It does make sense to me that such laws would prevent some accidents, but at what costs to people who cannot defend themselves?

On the constitutional issue, I question whether the federal government even has the power, even under the broadest interpretation of the interstate commerce clause, to require trigger locks or other safe storage laws. If they do, then the law should be narrowly drawn, allowing for a full ability of the gun owner to use it in self-defense, or it should be declared unconstitutional.

State governments probably do have the power to enact such laws, but again, they should meet the same constitutional requirements as any federal law, because the Second Amendment should be applied to the states through the 14th Amendment. Any law that requires a gun to be unloaded and stored separately from the ammunition, with both locked, is totally unreasonable.

Jack Reynolds, J. D.

F. Smart Guns

New technology might resolve all of the above problems. Some proposed solutions are guns that recognize the owner by fingerprint, therefore a lock is not necessary, but children would still be protected. An added benefit would also be that if a criminal stole your gun, he could not use it, unless there is some way around the technology. So is there anything wrong with this?

Not with having the new technology available. But if the gun control advocates want to require that it be used on all weapons, we may have a problem. Like any new technology, when it is initially made available, the cost is prohibitive for most people. Additionally, for now we do not have enough actual use data to know how reliable the technology is. Will people actually be able to use the guns when needed, or will sweat, dirt on the hands, or nervousness affect the recognition mechanism so that it may not be useable when needed? Will the technology actually prevent unwanted use, or will it be easy to get around? It is too early to tell. Again, I have a problem with the government requiring us to do anything, and this is just one more intrusion that would best be left to the individual to decide on.

With all of this, we should remember that the vast majority of parents do have the interests of their children at heart. Nobody wants to see their children get killed needlessly by stupid accidents involving guns. Admittedly, some parents will always be careless, but gun owners are generally more knowledgeable about the dangers of guns than the average person is about other dangers, such as cleaning compounds, automobiles, etc. Let's let the people involved decide how best to protect their families.

G. Limits on the Numbers of Guns or the Frequency of Purchase

Gun control advocates have convinced a number of states, including South Carolina, Virginia, Maryland and California, to enact what they call "One-Handgun-A-Month Laws". They are attempting to get such a law enacted at the federal level. What is the reason for such laws, and how do they work?

Gun control advocates point out that while the Brady Act effectively stops certain people from directly buying guns from licensed dealers, it does not stop straw purchases. In other words, a person who is qualified to buy a gun, and can pass the background check, can go into a gun store and buy a gun for someone else who is not qualified, who cannot pass the background check. "Gun traffickers often employ straw purchasers to buy firearms in bulk — the guns, in turn, are sold on the illegal market, often to juveniles, and eventually wind up on our nation's streets."[602] Of course, such mass selling of guns by an unlicensed person is already illegal. But, these new laws would endeavor to prevent any such sales to unqualified persons, by limiting the number of handguns that any individual could buy to just one a month. Of course, even this would not completely stop this practice. If a previously convicted person wanted a gun, he could still go to a friend or relative who has no convictions, and get him to go to a gun store and buy one for him, as long as he has not bought a gun within the last month. It should be relatively easy to find someone who could do this. Still, gun control advocates claim that such laws do work.

> Virginia's law has greatly disrupted the gun trafficking pattern from Virginia to states in the northeastern United States. For guns purchased after implementation of the new law that were recovered in the Northeast, Virginia's share fell by 54% — to 16% of all guns traced back to the Southeast. Even more dramatically, the percentage of guns traced back to Virginia gun dealers fell by 61% for guns recovered in New York, 67% for guns recovered in Massachusetts, and 38% for guns recovered in New Jersey. Further, according to law enforcement officials in Virginia, straw purchases of handguns that had made that state the "firearms supermarket" dropped sharply after the law was passed.
> Reports from public officials in Virginia have been very encouraging. The Virginia State Crime Commission concluded that, "Virginia's [One-Handgun-Per-Month] statute has had its intended effect of reducing Virginia's status as a source state for gun trafficking. The imposition of the law does not appear to create an onerous burden for law-abiding gun purchasers." According to Helen Fahey, U.S. Attorney for the Eastern District of Virginia, "Since passage of the [One-Handgun-Per-Month] legislation, instances of gunrunning have decreased dramatically."

> In Maryland, handgun sales dropped more than 25 percent during the first year of that state's "One-Handgun-Per-Month" law. Maryland officials attributed much of the drop to an 80 percent decrease in the number of multiple sales. Furthermore, the number of Maryland multiple-sale guns turning up at crime scenes in Washington, D.C. dropped from 23 to zero, and from 26 to four in Baltimore.[603]

Gun rights advocates contest the effectiveness of such laws. Moreover, they claim that such laws infringe on a constitutionally protected right. They equate this restriction to limiting the number of times a person could go to church each month, or the number of times he could assemble in a protest march, or the number of times he could write letters to the editor of a newspaper each month. I prefer to analyze this law, along with some other gun control laws, to another dearly held right of the people, that if charged with a crime, we are presumed innocent until proven guilty beyond a reasonable doubt. This law seems to turn this presumption on its head. It presumes that everybody who may want to buy more than one gun during a thirty-day period is going to do something illegal with it. Therefore, everybody, including law-abiding citizens, is prohibited from doing so. This would be bad enough if it was merely restricting a privilege, but when restricting a constitutionally protected right, I find this reversal of the right of the presumption of innocence very offensive and insulting.

While there is a logic to the laws, and there is at least an argument as to their effectiveness, I have my doubts that they would pass constitutional muster under either the intermediate scrutiny test or the strict scrutiny test. They probably would pass the reasonable basis test.

H. *Waiting Periods*

While the federal waiting period is no longer in effect (as long as you quickly pass the background check), 18 states still have their own required waiting periods, ranging from two days to over thirty. The logic, as said earlier, is to reduce the availability of guns to those who might be emotionally disturbed, whether suicidal or angry with someone else. By forcing them to have a cooling-off period, we might prevent some murders/suicides. Of course, this ignores the

A People Armed and Free

substitution theory, that if they really want to kill themselves or someone else, they will simply find another way to do it. Beyond that, as I pointed out earlier, this infringes on a constitutionally protected right and affects one of the very purposes for which the Second Amendment was passed, self-protection. By again assuming that all gun buyers are guilty of some intended wrongdoing, instead of presuming innocence, we may be causing some people to be killed because we are denying them timely access to the tool they need to defend themselves.

In my opinion, the waiting periods would probably pass the reasonable basis test, but not the other two.

I. Gun Shows and Secondary Sales

One of the big cries that we hear from the gun control advocates is to close the gun show loophole. The implication here is that guns are sold by dealers at gun shows without having to go through the Brady Act background check. This is not true. Licensed dealers have to conduct the background check on **all** sales, whether from their storefronts, cars, or gun shows. Most of the people who set up booths at gun shows and are not licensed dealers are not selling guns. They are selling books, clothing, camping or hunting gear, and other accessories. A few collectors sell and trade guns from their collections, but this is not done as a business, but as a hobby, and therefore is not subject to the federal law that applies to dealers. The number of such transactions is very small.

What the gun control advocates really want to do is to control private sales. For the same reasons that they want to impose a one-gun-per-month limit, they want to require every individual, before he conveys a gun to someone else, to have to run a background check on that individual. Imagine this: Before I could give, or sell, a gun to my brother, who I know better than any federal or state agency does, I would be required to run a background check on him. Then add the cost of such checks to the individuals. While dealers can afford the equipment, software and connections to be able to make numerous checks due to the volume of their business, an individual doing this on a one-time basis could not afford such an extravagance. And to assume they could go to a gun dealer to do a check for them, when obviously he is losing out on a sale of a gun, without him also charging a large amount of money for the service, is living in a fairytale world.

Jack Reynolds, J. D.

One might think that the gun control advocates would be satisfied with one approach or the other, but no! They want both. Once again, the gun control advocates are presuming law-abiding citizens to be guilty of bad intentions, and therefore severely restricting their rights needlessly, just because of a few bad people. It would make as much sense to require everybody who wants to sell their car to someone else to have to do a background check on that possible buyer to make sure he had never had any accidents, tickets, drunk driving charges, and the like, before he could convey the car. The laws impose too much of a burden on innocent people, and on their constitutionally protected rights.

J. *Lawsuits Against Gun Manufacturers*

For many years gun control advocates have been attempting to destroy the ability of the people to exercise their right to keep and bear arms by doing away with the source of the arms: The gun manufacturers. Much like law suits against breast implant manufacturers and the makers of Fen-Phen caused the FDA to remove these items from the market. Even if the government had not acted, the economic impact of the suits, judgments and settlements would have forced their removal. Anyway, gun control advocates have brought many suits against gun manufacturers alleging that the mere manufacturing of guns is a dastardly practice and that anyone who has been shot by a gun should be able to recover damages from the manufacturers. All of these suits have failed.

More recently, taking a cue from successful governmental suits and settlements against the tobacco industry, gun control advocates have convinced some cities to bring such suits against the gun manufacturers for damages caused to the cities: More crime, more money spent on law enforcement, more money spent on hospital emergency room services to treat gun shot victims, etc. But there are some large differences. Tobacco has no good use. However it is used, it is still addictive; it is still a carcinogen. Guns, on the other hand, are like the other tools I mentioned at the beginning of this chapter. They can be used for bad purposes, by criminals robbing someone, or for good purposes, by someone in self-defense, or for hunting. The gun itself is neutral, with the manufacturer not being able to control what the user does with it. Tobacco, however, is bad; its purveyors know it's bad, and regardless of who uses it or how, it will cost society. A big difference.

A People Armed and Free

Handgun Control Inc., and the Brady Center, on their web sites, support these frivolous lawsuits. They encourage them, and report positively on their progress. While some states have passed laws prohibiting such lawsuits, and Congress is considering such a law at the federal level, these websites decry such laws. Recently California, which had passed such a law, repealed its law protecting gun manufacturers. Gun control advocates rejoiced!

Now I should make it clear that the types of lawsuits that we are talking about are not the usual negligence or products liability suits. If a gun manufacturer uses a faulty design, or is negligent in the making of the gun, and this fact causes someone an injury (such as it blows up in the hand of the user, or is so inaccurate that it shoots someone when it was aimed to shoot someone or something else), then such suits should be, and are, allowed. The gun manufacturers should be held responsible for their mistakes just like the manufacturer of any other useful product. But they should not be put out of business just because some people do not like the product.

These suits would basically be the same as cities suing all automobile manufacturers for the costs they incur for traffic control, accident investigation, and ambulance and emergency room service incurred because of all of the injuries by people from the use or operation of automobiles. Sure automobiles have good uses, and any attempt to put Ford, GM and Chrysler out of business would be devastating to our economy and our lifestyle. But guns have good uses too, and the removal of the ability of law-abiding citizens to have access to guns for self-defense purposes, would also have devastating effects.

This has two constitutional implications. As to the Second Amendment, one would have to question whether such suits violate it, because it is not the legislative bodies that are making laws to infringe the right of the people. But then again, the Second Amendment does not say "Congress shall make no law . . ." as the First Amendment, only that the right of the people shall not be infringed. Then there is an issue on the other side of the question. Can the government restrict the ability of individuals or entities, including cities, to access the courts to redress wrongs that they feel have been done them, no matter how ridiculous I may think their claims are? My position is that legislatively enacted laws that completely ban such suits should not be allowed, but laws should be put in place that allow the defendants in such suits to recover all costs they have incurred when the suits are summarily dismissed as being frivolous. That would include forcing these cities to pay the gun manufacturers the damages the cities caused by this attempted extortion.

One final thought on this issue. It seems to me that the gun control advocates' support of these lawsuits, including the so-called moderate organizations such as Handgun Control, Inc. and the Brady Center, show that they are anything but moderate. Their agenda is clearly to do away with the ability of all people, including honest law-abiding citizens, to have access to guns, be it for hunting, self-defense, sport, or to protect our liberties. They do not care. They just hate guns and want to see them disappear. Except for the government's guns.

K. *Registration/Licensing of Guns and Owners*

This has been one of the laws most sought after by gun control advocates for years. I can remember in the 1960's, as a child, watching the news after the assassination of President Kennedy, with people calling for gun registration back then.

Gun control advocates claim that gun registration would make it harder for criminals to obtain guns, and make it easier for law enforcement agencies to solve crimes.

> Registration in its strictest form places the burden on the owners of firearms to register their weapons, usually by serial number and description, with a governmental authority, either local or state police... Registration allows for speedier and more reliable tracing of guns used in crime... An untold number of criminals escape conviction because there is no paper trail or evidence linking them to the crime guns they used... Registration is designed to reduce illegal gun trafficking by providing for more efficient tracing of guns used in crimes and tougher prosecution of those who sell guns to illegal purchasers. State-based registration of handgun transfers can achieve that objective.[604]

They also want to require all gun owners to have a license to just have a gun: "Handgun licenses are necessary to stem the flow of guns into the wrong hands. No one who is prohibited by law from

A People Armed and Free

purchasing or owning a firearm should have one. By the same token, licensing would not affect the ability of law-abiding citizens to own or buy guns."[605] So, just what do they want to see done in this area?

"The proposed system for an applicant to receive a license would include:

1. **Minimum age of 21.** Currently, federal law prohibits federally licensed firearms dealers from selling handguns to persons under 21. However, a loophole in federal law allows the private sale of handguns to persons between the ages of 18 and 20. Only 12 states prohibit such sales to juveniles. Most states do not even require a background check for private sales to people under 21.
2. **Background check with fingerprint identification.** A name-based criminal history background check must be complemented with a fingerprint check. An FBI fingerprint background check provides the most reliable proof of identity and will ensure that felons and other prohibited persons are denied licenses.
3. **Proof of residency.** It is illegal to purchase a handgun outside the purchaser's state of residence. In addition to providing a driver's license, the applicant should be required to provide concrete proof of current residence such as a utility bill.
4. **Successful completion of a firearms safety test or course.** Currently only six states require any type of training or safety test before the purchase of a handgun. An untrained handgun owner is a danger to themselves, their family and the community, and should be required to demonstrate that he can load, fire and store a weapon safely. Training would also include education on federal, state and local laws related to gun ownership and use. Just as drivers must show they know the rules of the road, so should gun owners must show that they are familiar with basic gun laws."[606]

What are the problems with all of this? First, the analogy to requiring licenses to drive a car, and requiring automobiles to be registered, is inappropriate. As a matter of fact, registration of automobiles and drivers' licenses are required in most states only if

333

the automobile is being operated on a public roadway. An unlicensed person can legally drive an unregistered car on private property, such as a farm or ranch. In fact, that is how I legally learned how to drive at age 14, well before I was eligible for a driver's license. So why shouldn't a person be able to keep a gun at home without a license or registering it? Especially since driving a car is universally considered a **privilege**, not a **right**. However, having a gun does involve the **right** to keep and bear arms.

Second, did you know that the government cannot force criminals to register their guns? Forget for a moment the fact that criminals probably would not do it anyway. If they are going to break laws against stealing and murdering, why would they feel they had to obey a law requiring them to register their guns? But even so, once caught with an unregistered gun they could not be prosecuted for the failure to register it precisely because they are criminals. You say this doesn't make sense? Read the case of *Haynes v. United States*.[607] There a person was charged with the possession of an unregistered firearm and failure to register it. Because of the nature of the firearm, the Supreme Court held that the requirement for the possessor to register it was tantamount to requiring him to commit self-incrimination, which is prohibited by the Fifth Amendment. Therefore, he was set free on both charges. This problem has been modified somewhat on these types of weapons by a change in the law requiring the transferor to register the weapon, instead of the possessor. In *United States v. Freed*,[608] the Supreme Court held that this change relieved the possessor of the duty to register the weapon, and therefore of the requirement to incriminate himself. But this type of change would not affect the law that we are presently considering, and that the gun control advocates are proposing.

Think about it. Anyone who has been convicted of a felony, who uses drugs, or who is a fugitive from justice, commits a federal crime just by possessing a firearm. Therefore, forcing him to register that firearm would require him to admit that he was committing a crime, and would therefore be requiring him to incriminate himself. Therefore, he cannot be required to register the gun, and any charges against him for failure to register, and apparently for the possession of the gun itself at that point, would have to be dismissed under the Fifth Amendment. The only people that such a law could be enforced against would be otherwise law-abiding citizens who had failed to register their firearms! Talk about a misguided policy! Let's punish the good people in the name of going after the bad people. Of course it is easier to go after good people than bad, and arrest and conviction statistics would probably go up under such a law, but real violent crime would not be affected at all.

Third, what other constitutionally protected rights have licensing and registration requirements placed on them? Does anyone have to get a license to express his political views, or write a book like this one? I hope not, or I may be in trouble. Or, does anyone have to get a license to preach the gospel? Do you have to register your computer in order to petition your Congressman? Then neither should the exercise of your Second Amendment rights be put under such a burden.

Fourth, it is doubtful that registration would have much affect on the ability of law enforcement agencies to solve crimes. Many times the trace of the gun is irrelevant to solving the crime. The district attorney only has to prove that the defendant committed the crime using the gun, which may have his fingerprints on it, not what the history was as to how he got the gun. And where it might be relevant, odds are that the gun will have been stolen and the trace lost anyway. Of course, this is not true in all cases, but it is in enough of them to dilute the gun control advocates' argument.

Finally, the real reason that gun right advocates do not want such laws passed, apart from the mere principle of the thing, is that they suspect that this is merely a ruse of the gun control advocates to obtain a complete list of all gun owners (except for the criminals, who will not register), so that they can later be forced to give the guns up. Call them paranoid if you will, but read the earlier section about nobody wanting to take away your guns first. Of course, such confiscation would not all occur at once. First it would be the firearms that the gun control advocates label as the most dangerous, such as, at this point in time, "assault weapons" and "Saturday-night Specials". Then once all of those weapons are taken up (except for the criminals' guns), and crime does not decrease, they will look to confiscate the next group of firearms that they will then label as being the most dangerous, probably handguns. Then, once those have been taken up, the next most dangerous weapons, maybe rifles and shotguns. Then everything.

Don't think they would do that? Take a look at what has happened in various places around the world. Since 1921 New Zealand has required firearms to be registered. In 1974, they confiscated all revolvers that had previously been legally held for self-protection and registered. In 1965, Canada outlawed previously legal and registered small-caliber handguns, with the provision that the current owners could keep them until their death, at which time they had to be turned over to the government. In Australia, its states and territories provided for registration of firearms. In 1996, the national government outlawed most semi-automatic rifles and semi-automatic and pump shotguns. "Since 1921, all lawfully-owned handguns in Great Britain are registered with the government, so handgun owners have little choice but to surrender their guns in exchange for payment according to government schedule... The handgun ban by no means has satiated the anti-gun appetite in Great Britain."[609] Do you think that this is just a problem in other countries? How about New York City, where in 1967 they required all long guns to be registered, then in the 1990's used the registration roles to confiscate legally owned and registered semi-automatic rifles, despite testimony from the chief of police that no registered rifle had ever been used in a crime?[610] Then, in California, they initially required certain rifles, SKS Sporters, to be registered, giving a grace period to do so. Then they revoked that grace period, declared such rifles illegal, and confiscated all of the previously registered rifles.

This does not sound like paranoia to me. It sounds like a reasonable skepticism on the part of gun owners. Remember: Those who fail to learn from history are condemned to repeat it.

L. *Concealed Carry Laws*

The interesting flip side of the coin to registration and licensing are the concealed carry laws. At one point in time in our history the philosophy was that only bad people, with something to hide and some bad purpose in mind, would want to carry a gun concealed on their person. If you had a concealed gun, it must be concealed for a bad reason, so such actions were outlawed. Early cases indicate that despite the Second Amendment and similar state constitutional protections, the state governments could regulate the carrying of concealed weapons, so, since this was being done by some states at the time the Second Amendment was enacted, such laws were probably a valid exercise of governmental power. But at that time, it

A People Armed and Free

was generally legal to carry a gun in the open. The theory was that if a criminal saw that you had a gun, he would probably leave you alone.

But then, things began to change. People became uncomfortable with seeing other people with guns strapped on. Guns were scary to them. So people were not allowed to carry guns in the open either. Then philosophy began to change again. If some people carried guns in the open, and concealed carry was not allowed, the criminals would know when it was safe to attack someone, because they would see that no one had a gun. So, maybe it would be better for society as a whole if people were allowed to carry concealed weapons. That way, criminals would not know if some one had a gun, so they might be wary of attacking anybody. With weapons concealed, other people would not be so uncomfortable, since they would not see the guns. It could be a win-win situation.

In the last twenty years, many states have passed laws allowing people to carry concealed weapons. Of course, these laws differ from state to state. However, there are basically two categories: Shall issue and permissive. Shall issue laws require the state officials to issue a license to carry a concealed weapon once the applicant has met the statutory requirements, which, again, differ from state to state. Permissive laws allow state officials to issue such permits, but grant them some discretion to deny the permits even if the statutory requirements are met.

Only a few states had any concealed carry laws until about 15-20 years ago. Since then, many states have enacted them in one form or another. The map shown below lists the states and what type of law they have:

Jack Reynolds, J. D.

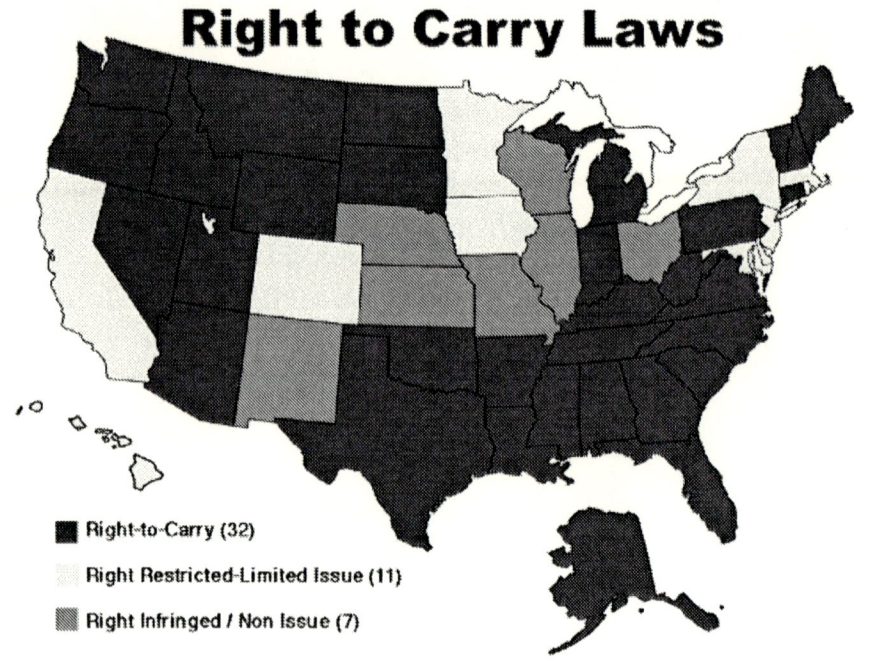

Gun rights advocates point to studies that show that in every county that has issued concealed carry permits in this country, the violent crime rate has gone down immediately when they started issuing permits. No matter when, or where.

These laws do bring up some additional issues, such as are the permits valid in other states? One part of the Constitution requires states to recognize and accept acts of other states. For example, if you are married in one state, that marriage is recognized in all states. If you have a driver's license in one state, you are authorized to drive in all states. Would this extend to a license to carry a concealed gun? While gun control advocates like to analogize to driver's licenses when talking about gun ownership, registration of guns and wanting to require licenses to just own a gun, I bet they don't when talking about concealed carry licenses. In any event, the answer appears to be that the recognition of your right to carry a concealed gun is not automatic. It appears that different states accept different other states licenses. For example, as of this writing, a Texas license is recognized in Arizona, Arkansas, Florida, Idaho, Indiana, Kentucky, Louisiana,

Michigan, Montana, Oklahoma, Tennessee, Utah, Virginia and Vermont. However, Texas only recognizes the licenses from Arizona, Arkansas, Florida, Kentucky, Louisiana, Oklahoma and Tennessee. So if you have a concealed carry license and want to go out of state, you had better check with the states you are planning on going into before trying to carry concealed there. And while some lists exist on this, laws change so frequently that they may be out of date. By the time you read this, the list above pertaining to Texas may be out of date. The best rule is to always check. Incidentally, one state does accept all licenses, because in that state you do not even have to have a license to carry concealed; all people who can legally possess a gun can carry one concealed. The state? Vermont.

Not surprisingly, the gun control advocates oppose concealed carry laws. They start off with a scare tactic: "Do you feel safer sitting next to someone carrying a gun?"[611] My answer is, it depends on who that someone is. If he is a criminal, no. If he is a good, law-abiding citizen, yes. Then they allege that crime rates either have not gone down as much in concealed carry states as they have in other states, or they have actually gone up. For example:

> More guns = more crime — or at least a much smaller reduction in the crime rate. A 1999 study by the Brady Center to Prevent Gun Violence (formerly the Center to Prevent Handgun Violence), using FBI crime statistics, demonstrated that liberalizing CCW laws may have an adverse effect on a state's crime rate. Between 1992 and 1998, the violent crime rate in states which kept strict CCW laws fell by an average of 30%. The violent crime rate for the states that had weak CCW laws during this same time saw their violent crime rates drop by only 15%. Nationally, violent crime declined by 25% during that same period.[612]

Gun rights advocates have responded to this statement in this way:

> In Jan. 1999, HCI claimed that between 1992-1997 violent crime rates declined less in RTC states than in other states. It was the first time HCI admitted RTC

does not cause crime to rise. But HCI's comparison of the crime trends of RTC and non-RTC states had flaws. HCI categorized states according to whether they had RTC in 1997, but calculated their crime trends from 1992-1997. The error: Of the 31 states that had RTC in 1997, only 17 had it in 1992. Also, HCI misclassified Alabama and Connecticut as "restrictive" states; both states had decreases in crime, so HCI presumably wanted to keep them out of the RTC group. HCI's 1992 starting point under-represented the impact of RTC laws on crime. By 1992, many states had had RTC for many years and had already experienced decreases in crime. HCI also credited restrictive laws for the decrease in crime in some states. But states that have restrictive carry laws have had them for many years and crime did not begin to decline in those states until the 1990s, due to a variety of factors unrelated to firearms.[613]

Then there was a study by the Center for Disease Control, released in 1995, which claimed that gun homicide rates in Miami, Jacksonville, and Tampa, Florida had increased after Florida passed its concealed carry (or right-to-carry (RTC) law). Florida passed this law in 1987. Read some of the problems with this study:

Deceptively, McDowell, et al., calculated Jacksonville and Tampa homicide from the early 1970s, when rates were lower than in 1993. They calculated Miami's trend from 1983, since rates before 1983 were higher and their inclusion in the comparison would have shown that the city's homicide rate decreased. None of the homicides was committed by a license holder, and no distinction was made between homicides that occurred in situations where a license would be required to carry a firearm and other homicides. (McDowell previously claimed D.C.'s homicide rate decreased after its 1977 handgun ban. In fact, the rate tripled after the ban.)[614]

Gun rights advocates claim that the gun homicide rates actually "fell 10%, 18% and 20%, respectively, in those metropolitan areas, from 1987 until 1993."[615] Do you see what I mean about statistical studies being so easy to manipulate for your own purposes, and why I do not trust them from either side.

Gun control advocates also argue that concealed carry laws cannot have been a factor in reducing violent crime, because "[t]he number of crime victims who successfully use firearms to defend themselves is quite small. According to the FBI Uniform Crime Reports and the Centers for Disease Control, out of 30,708 Americans who died by gunfire in 1998, only *316 were shot in justifiable homicides* by private citizens with firearms."[616] Of course, we have already seen that this totally discounts the bad guys who were shot and not killed, and those who just ran away when they saw that their victim had a gun, and it also ignores the crimes that were never attempted because the criminal was afraid that someone might have a gun.

Gun control advocates claim that many criminals get concealed carry permits, and therefore the laws actually make society more dangerous by allowing criminals to carry guns:

> The gun lobby claims that only law-abiding citizens get CCW permits. But an August 2000 study by the Violence Policy Center revealed that, from January 1996 through April 2000, the arrest rate for weapon-related offenses among Texas concealed handgun license holders was 66% higher than that of the general adult population of Texas. CCW license holders are committing crimes - including murder, rape, assault and burglary — but because the gun lobby makes it difficult if not impossible for the public to determine if a shooter has a CCW license in most states, the full story has not yet been told.[617]

Let's look at the gun advocates' response:

> [T]hey ignore the fact that more than 55 percent of licensees arrested for violent crimes are cleared of the crimes for which they are arrested. Most tellingly, when the arrest rates of Texas' concealed carry holders

are compared with those of the general population, licensees are found to be more law-abiding than the average person.

In an unpublished report, engineering statistician William Sturdevant found that concealed carry licensees had arrest rates far lower than the general population for every category of crime. For instance:

** Licensees were 5.7 times less likely to be arrested for violent offenses than the general public—127 per 100,000 population versus 730 per 100,000.
** Licensees were 13.5 times less likely to be arrested for nonviolent offenses than the general public—386 per 100,000 population versus 5,212 per 100,000.

** Further, the general public is 1.4 times more likely to be arrested for murder than licensees, and no licensee had been arrested for negligent manslaughter.[618]

As a further example of this distortion by the gun control advocates, look at the case of Gordan Hale III. Shortly after Texas passed its concealed carry law, Mr. Hale was involved in a minor traffic accident. An altercation with the other driver ensued, with the end result that Mr. Hale, who had a concealed carry permit, shot and killed the other driver. Gun control advocates point to this case as the very reason that concealed carry should not be allowed:

The incident started when an employee being trained for a messenger service had his side mirror clipped by the CCW licensee, who was driving another vehicle. There was no damage to the messenger's car, and he intended to drive on, but the CCW licensee slowed down and pulled over. The unarmed messenger then approached the stopped car and the two men began to argue. When the messenger reached in and punched the CCW licensee, he was shot in the chest by the licensee's .40 caliber handgun. Witnesses said the

> messenger did not appear to have any hostile intent when he approached the car, but matters escalated and he was killed. Others called the messenger who was killed "a teddy bear kind of guy and very easygoing." Dallas police initially charged the CCW licensee with murder, claiming he clearly exceeded the legal use of deadly force. A grand jury, however, later failed to indict him.[619]

This sure makes it sound like the messenger was an innocent victim and the CCW licensee, Mr. Hale, was a gun-crazed killer. Now, as Paul Harvey would say, let me tell you the rest of the story. While I was not there, and therefore do not know what happened first hand, I was aware of the incident through newspaper accounts at my home in Texas. First, the messenger was reported to be about twice the size of Mr. Hale. Contrary to the quoted passage, the newspapers reported that the messenger was very angry and agitated when he approached Mr. Hale's car. He immediately began punching Mr. Hale through the driver's side window, not once, but repeatedly. At this point I have read two versions of what happened next. In one, Mr. Hale tried to retreat to the other side of the car, but the messenger tried to come in after him. In the other version, the messenger tried to pull Mr. Hale through the window. In any event, Mr. Hale, fearing for his life, shot the messenger in self-defense; the exact reason that the concealed carry law was passed. Incidentally, the messenger was not a "teddy bear". He had a history of physical assault and battery, with a prior criminal record of such.

One thing I can talk about with certainty. Grand juries are notorious for being tools of the district attorney's office. The district attorney in Dallas wanted an indictment on this case because he was against the concealed carry law. Usually grand juries rubber-stamp the district attorney's request for an indictment. In fact, defendants are not even given the right to tell their side of the story to the grand jury, and if called to testify before a grand jury, they do not have a right to be represented by an attorney. Also to be considered is the low hurdle that has to be cleared to obtain an indictment. Unlike a criminal trial, where guilt has to be shown by evidence beyond a reasonable doubt, or even a civil trial, where the plaintiff has to prove his case by a preponderance of the evidence, a grand jury only has to find probable

Jack Reynolds, J. D.

cause to indict. If you want to put numbers to this, to convict on a criminal charge the jury has to be, maybe 95-98% sure of the defendant's guilt. To find for a plaintiff in a civil trial, the jury only has to be 51% sure. To indict, the grand jury only has to be 10-25% sure. With all of the cards in the deck stacked against him, as it is for all defendants before grand juries, the grand jury still could not find enough evidence to merely indict. In fact they said what I just said. This was the classic case of why the concealed carry of guns should be allowed.

Are you ready for more statistics concerning concealed carry licenses?

Fla: (10/1/87-2/29/02) 798,732 issued, 146 (0.02%) revoked due to firearm crimes by licensees. (Dept. of State)

Ky.: As of 10/31/01, 71,770 valid permits. From 10/1/96-12/31/01, 585 (0.8%) revoked for any reason. (State Police)
La.: (11/1/96-2/28/02) 15,319 issued, 67 (0.4%) revoked for any reason. (State Police)
Okla.: Through Feb. 2, 2002, 35,329 issued, 108 (0.30%) revoked for any reason. (SBI)
N.C.: (12/1/95-9/29/01) 47,046 issued, 242 (0.5%) revoked for any reason. (SBI)
S.C.: (8/96-5/26/02) 33,492 issued, 164 (0.5%) revoked for any reason. (SLED)
Tex.: (1/1/96-5/1/02) 223,584 issued, 1,772 (0.8%) revoked for any reason. (DPS)
Tenn.: (12/96-5/4/02) 130,187 issued, 1,126 (0.9%) revoked for any reason. (DPS)
Ut.: As of Dec. 31, 2001, 44,173 issued, 565 (1.3%) revoked for any reason.
Va.: (7/95-4/02) 172,347 issued, 372 (0.2%) revoked for any reason. (State Police)
Wyo.: (10/1/94-2/02) 7,480 issued, 20 (0.3%) revoked for any reason. (Dept. of Criminal Investigation)[620]

So the rate of problems with the people who have been granted concealed carry permits seems to be rather low, contrary to what the gun control advocates would have you believe. Of course, these statistics are subject to the same manipulation that the gun control advocates are accused of. If I could ignore all of these statistics, on both sides, I would, because I do not trust any of them. But, since they are an integral part of the arguments on both sides, and we are now talking about statutory enactments, not constitutional interpretation, they are unavoidable. You can choose who to believe, but for me, the gun control advocates have shown a complete lack of integrity.

Just a couple of more items before leaving this section. First, the Violence Policy Center published a report in 1995 claiming that Florida's concealed carry law puts guns into the hands of criminals.[621] Now this does not make sense to me for two reasons. First, it would be in violation of federal law, which prohibits convicted felons from even possessing guns. The state law could not override that, and with the Brady Act's required background check, and the Florida required check before issuing a license, it should not happen. Second, I doubt that very many criminals even care to try to obtain a permit. Notice I said "very many", not "any". If they are going to use a gun to commit a crime, I would doubt that they would be very concerned about not having a license to carry that gun. As a counter to this second point, the Violence Policy Center states that criminals do apply for permits, but they fail to point out that when they do, they are denied:

> To set the record straight, as of November 30, 1995, the Department had denied 723 applications due to criminal history. The fact that these 723 individuals did not receive a license clearly indicates that the process is working... [T]he majority of concealed weapon or firearm licensees are honest, law-abiding citizens exercising their right to be armed for the purpose of lawful self-defense."[622]

723 applications from criminals in eight years is not a very high rate, considering the number of criminals on the street.

Gun control advocates always have contested concealed carry laws on the grounds that they will lead to more gun violence, such as road rage incidents, drunks losing control (I agree that alcohol and guns do not mix), people resisting police officers, and the like. However, this simply has not proven to be the case.

> Concerns that permit holders would lose their tempers in traffic accidents have been unfounded. Worries about risks to police officers have also proved unfounded... National surveys of police show they support concealed handgun laws by a 3-1 margin....There is also not a single academic study that claims Right to Carry laws have increased state crime rates. The debate among academics has been over how large the benefits have been.[623]

"Whenever a state legislature first considers a concealed-carry bill, opponents typically warn of horrible consequences... But within a year of passage, the issue usually drops off the news media's radar screen, while gun-control advocates in the legislature conclude that the law wasn't so bad after all."[624]

> Both John B. Holmes, Harris County district attorney, and Glenn White, president of the Dallas Police Ass'n, initially opposed concealed carry in Texas but have subsequently embraced it. Holmes said, "I ... (felt) that such legislation ... present(ed) a clear and present danger to lawabiding citizens by placing more handguns on our streets. Boy was I wrong. Our experience in Harris County, and indeed statewide, has proven my initial fears absolutely groundless." And White said, "All the horror stories I thought would come to pass didn't happen. ... I think it's worked out well, and that says good things about the citizens who have permits. I'm a convert." The evidence indicates that concealed carry is a vital tool in the fight against violent crime.[625]

Finally, I have read a rather long paper put out by some gun control advocates that encourages businesses to deny people the right to carry guns on their premises.[626] The point here is that most of these concealed carry laws allow certain establishments, such as churches and businesses to put up signs, if they so desire, that expressly state that no one is allowed to carry a gun on the premises. I agree that business owners have the right to make up their own mind about this activity. However, I disagree with the scare tactics the gun control advocates use. Without going into each and every argument put forth by the gun control advocates (I simply do not have the space in this book) I do want to address one that hits home on my practice as a personal injury attorney.

The gun control advocates assert that if a business does not put up a sign telling people that they cannot carry a weapon on their premises, when the law allows them to do so, if they so desire, and someone carries a gun into the business, and then shoots an innocent person on the premises, whether in the course of committing a crime or in the course of attempting to defend against a crime (and just accidentally shoots the wrong person), the business could be sued under a premises liability theory for not maintaining a safe place for its customers. While this theory is plausible, I have some problems with it. First as to a criminal carrying a gun on the premises, a sign telling them not to do it will not stop them. They are about to commit a real crime. Do you really think they care about the sign, or the additional crime of carrying a concealed gun where it is not allowed? "Oh, I am about to rob this store, but because they have a sign up telling me I can't carry a concealed gun on the premises I better not." Get serious. Or to look at it another way, if there are two convenience stores across the street from each other, one with a sign up prohibiting the carrying of weapons on the premises and declaring it a gun free zone, and the other with a sign up warning people that employees and customers may be armed, and I want to rob a convenience store, which store do you think I will choose to rob? Additionally, the premises owner is not responsible for the intentional tort of a third party (the act of the criminal in shooting someone). Simple personal injury law.

As to the potential negligent tort of third parties – the accidental shooting of the wrong person by someone trying to stop the crime—while the cause of action might be plausible, so could the opposite scenario result in a similar claim.

In October 1991, in Killeen, Texas, a man came into a Luby's cafeteria with a gun and just started shooting people at random. 22 innocent people were killed. This was before Texas had a concealed carry law, but the state did allow people to carry guns in their cars if they were "traveling". One woman in the cafeteria claimed that she had a gun in the car, but because it was illegal to carry it inside the cafeteria, she had left it there. She felt confident that she could have stopped the killer if she had had her gun with her. She didn't, and as a result, many people were killed.

Now what happens today if the same thing were to happen, and Luby's just happened to have a sign up telling people that they cannot bring guns on the premises. This same lady, being obedient to the law, leaves her gun in the car, as do all other people who may have concealed carry licenses. The bad guy, not caring about the law – after all, he is about to murder a bunch of people; do you think he cares about the sign?—comes into the cafeteria with his gun and carries out his plan. Now, does this woman, and all of the others who may be killed or wounded in the shooting, have a cause of action against Luby's for not allowing them their right to self-defense, for not allowing them to have weapons with which they could have defended themselves and saved many lives? For thereby maintaining an unsafe premises where criminals can come in and kill people with impunity? Such a cause of action is certainly as plausible as the one proposed by the gun control advocates. And as the saying goes: "I would rather be judged by twelve than be carried by six."

While this may sound like a recent quote from a NRA advocate, it is really from Thomas Jefferson in 1774-1776:

> Laws that forbid the carrying of arms ... disarm only those who are neither inclined nor determined to commit crimes ... Such laws make things worse for the assaulted and better for the assailants; they serve rather to encourage than to prevent homicides, for an unarmed man may be attacked with greater confidence than an armed man.[627]

M. Gun Control Compromise?

Gun control advocates accuse gun rights advocates of being radical, of being paranoid, of being hardheaded, of refusing to compromise to enact reasonable gun control legislation. They claim that the NRA is opposed to any and all gun control. When I started this research, I did not know if that allegation was true or not. I found out that it is false. The NRA supports background checks, if they can be done instantly, such as the way the NCIS is supposed to work, and not infringe on law-abiding citizens by making them wait needlessly to exercise their constitutionally protected right. The NRA supports

A People Armed and Free

restrictions on criminals being allowed to possess guns, and vigorously supports the Project Exile program, such as has been applied in Richmond, Virginia. The NRA helped draft the legislation regulating handgun bullets designed for more penetration.

However, gun rights advocates do draw a rather strong line in the sand to protect their right to keep and bear arms. Actually, it is more like a deep trench from a World War I battlefield. They have gone as far as they are willing to go, and they will go no farther.

The real problem is that they do not trust the gun control advocates or the politicians they support. They look at them as having the same insatiable appetite for gun control that Hitler had for more land. When he was given the Rhineland, he wanted the Sudetenland. When he got that, he wanted the rest of Czechoslovakia. We he got that, he wanted Austria. When he got that, he wanted Poland. They see the gun control advocates as always wanting more gun control, no matter what has already been passed. They fear, as has already been pointed out, that this will eventually lead to total confiscation. And with the gun control advocates arguments on the Second Amendment, if accepted, it could literally come to that, because, according to them, there is nothing to stop the government from taking away all of the people's guns.

Also, there is no such thing as compromise in this matter. When I compromise a personal injury case for my client, we reach a final settlement with the other side. I have never heard the gun control advocates say that they would be satisfied if they just got certain measures passed. I have never heard them say that if the NRA would allow a certain bill to pass, they would drop their attempts to obtain more gun control. In any event, even if they were to say that, that can never take place here, because the political system is always in flux. Some other problem will always raise its head, with some advocate and politician coming up with a new gun control measure to try to solve it. No, whatever portion of the right to keep and bear arms that may be given up by the gun rights advocates will simply be lost, with nothing given in return, which is what usually happens in a compromise.

If the gun control advocates really wanted to obtain support from the other side for a compromise, to obtain reasonable gun control, they would try to alleviate the fears of the gun rights camp. How can this be done? By admitting that the Second Amendment protects the

Jack Reynolds, J. D.

rights of individuals to keep and bear arms, and obtaining a clear, unequivocal holding from the United States Supreme Court saying so, employing a higher test of constitutionality of any restrictions on that right. Only by constitutional protection of the basic right to keep and bear arms will the gun rights advocates be willing to allow more regulation of guns.

For example, if the gun control advocates want registration of guns and licensing of gun owners, if there was a constitutionally protected right, recognized by all, for individuals to keep and bear arms, then such registrations and licenses could not be used by the government to later confiscate such weapons. This might alleviate the fears of the gun rights advocates, and remove the main reason for their opposition, allowing such a measure to pass. But until the gun control advocates support the basic right, and we have such a strong ruling from the United States Supreme Court, this compromise will never happen.

Nor will any others.

Chapter 11
Some Concluding Thoughts, and Where Do We Go From Here?

We have made a long journey. Perhaps now you can see why the people on Hannity & Colmes could do little more than yell at each other over this issue. It is way too involved to address in a short five-minute segment. Maybe you can see why I was surprised when I found as much information as I did, and wound up deciding, after putting in a mountain of work in just researching the Second Amendment, to put that work to use in writing this book. I hope that it has helped you understand the issues involved, and come to some resolution as to what you think the Second Amendment means, and how to back that opinion up, whether you agree with my conclusions or not.

So what is my final take on the Second Amendment? By its words alone, it says that the right belongs to the people, not the states. It says that we want to have a free nation (State). In order to do that, it is necessary that we have a well-regulated militia, which at the time of the enactment of the Second Amendment was the body of the people being armed, not the National Guard, which is the very type of militia feared by the Founding Fathers, and this fear was one factor that led to the enactment of the Second Amendment. In order to make sure that the body of the people could always be armed, thereby providing a well-regulated militia, the federal government guaranteed that the right of the people to keep and bear arms could not be infringed. The history of the Constitution and the Second Amendment bears this interpretation out. The structure of the government and the overall ethos of our governmental system support the notion that this would be an individual right. While public policy is in the eye of the beholder, and therefore can be argued both ways, in my opinion the better argument supports the right of the individual. Case law, at the court of appeals level, admittedly supports the gun control position for the most part, though some, including the only federal case to fully look at the history and analyze the text of the Amendment, supports the individual right position. The Supreme Court, despite arguments to the contrary from both camps, has failed to rule on the issue, though most of its opinions that mention the Second Amendment seem to treat it as an individual right, and the opinions that do so are much better reasoned than those few that go the other way. We will not know for sure what the Second Amendment does until the Supreme Court expressly rules on the subject.

Beyond all of the above, which is certainly sufficient for me to come down in favor of the gun rights position (remember, I was approaching this matter as if I was a judge, looking at the arguments from both sides and trying to decide based on the best arguments), what has really convinced me to support the individual right interpretation of the Second Amendment, and the strongest test in order to protect that right, is the gun control advocates' lack of integrity. As noted many times in this book, I have caught them in many deceptions, unjustified spins, and outright lies. Now, as with any group of people, I am sure that the gun rights advocates are not pure as the driven snow. For example, I found out that the references to Hitler insisting on gun control are probably inaccurate.[628] Hitler did not take away the Germans' guns, the Weimer Republic, a democratically elected government, did, in 1928, before Hitler came to power. This is not to say that Hitler was not in favor of gun control, only that he was not the one who implemented it, as claimed by some gun rights advocates. But this is a minor point when compared to the problems with the gun control arguments. They just don't wash.

As I mentioned in Chapter 1, I was not a member of the NRA when I started this book, nor have I ever been. After the research I have done, I have become convinced, not by being duped by propaganda, but by a detailed analysis of the best arguments put forth by the most notable proponents of both sides, and by my own reading of historical and legal documents, that I should join the NRA. And I will as soon as my wife lets me have the money to do so. So please get your friends to buy this book so I can do this.

What will happen in the future? I am cautiously optimistic. While some gun control legislation has passed in the last ten years, some of which I would agree with, such as background checks, some of which I would not, such as broad prohibitions on people subject to restraining orders and those who have been convicted of misdemeanor domestic violence offenses, other protections have been added. Many states have passed concealed carry laws. Forty-four states have some sort of guarantee on the right to keep and bear arms in their own constitutions, and since 1970, 15 either enacted such provisions for the first time, or strengthened them.[629] Congress has refused the more egregious proposed legislation. The Fifth Circuit has ruled in favor of individual rights. Supreme Court Justice Clarence Thomas has virtually invited the right Second Amendment case to be brought before the Supreme Court so that it could rule in favor of an individual right. If I were a betting man, and if such a case was to come before the Court within the next few years, I would bet on the gun rights position being vindicated; the Supreme Court would rule in favor of an individual right. That is what the great weight of authority indicates it should do. Of course, I have been known to be wrong before in trying to predict what courts were going to do.

And all of this does not mean that we can relax or let our guard down. That is why gun rights advocates refuse to "compromise" on these issues. We can never relax in the defense of any of our freedoms. I have one more quote for you that, while it expressly applies to the whole Bill of Rights, I feel has a special application to the Second Amendment, especially in light of the arguments that it is outdated, that it is an anachronism, that we do not have to worry about government oppression, or it could never happen here. It is from Justice Black in his dissent in *Adamson v. California*,[630] in his explanation of why the Bill of Rights should be applied, in their entirety, to the states through the 14th Amendment:

> I cannot consider the Bill of Rights to be an outworn 18th Century 'strait jacket' as the Twining opinion did. Its provisions may be thought outdated abstractions by some. And it is true that they were designed to meet ancient evils. But they are the same kind of human evils that have emerged from century to century wherever excessive power is sought by the few at the expense of the many. In my judgment the people of no nation can lose their liberty so long as a Bill of Rights like ours survives and its basic purposes are conscientiously interpreted, enforced and respected so as to afford continuous protection against old, as well as new, devices and practices which might thwart those purposes. I fear to see the consequences of the Court's

practice of substituting its own concepts of decency and fundamental justice for the language of the Bill of Rights as its point of departure in interpreting and enforcing that Bill of Rights.

Remember that I have said that the most important reason for the enactment of the Second Amendment was what is called the insurrectionist theory. It was to make sure that the people would be armed in order to resist any attempt by the government to take away the other freedoms that we enjoy. Blackstone himself, as noted in Chapter 4, had indicated that ultimately all of the people's liberties rested on their ability to resist oppression by force. And the danger of the federal government taking away our liberties is still there, and will always be there as long as we have humans running the government. Do not forget that the constitution of the Soviet Union guaranteed the freedom of speech. That did not stop that government from interpreting it out of existence. But as pointed out by Justice Black, as long as the Bill of Rights survives, and is correctly interpreted, our freedoms can remain safe.

I would go one more step to say that as long as the Second Amendment remains, and is correctly interpreted, to guarantee the right of the **people** to keep and bear **arms,** in order to maintain a **free** state, we will remain A **People, Armed** and **Free!**

And the debate rages on.

About the Author:

Jack Reynolds has been a practicing attorney in Houston, Texas since November 1983. He is licensed in both Texas and Utah, and practices before both state and federal courts. He is also licensed before the Fifth Circuit Court of Appeals. He is Board Certified in Personal Injury Trial Law by the Texas Board of Legal Specialization. He graduated *cum laude* from the University of Houston School of Law in 1983, where he served as a research editor on the Law Review. He retired as a lieutenant colonel infantry officer in the Marine Corps Reserve.

Active in his church and community, he has a wife and three children at home, whose freedoms and physically security he is determined to protect.

Chapter 1
[1] U.S. CONST. amend. II.
[2] Brief filed for the government in *Emerson v. United States* before the United States Supreme Court.
[3] *United States v. Miller,* 307 U.S. 174 (1939).
[4] Neal Boortz, *Home Page.* 22 July 2002. http://www.boortz.com/index.htm.

Chapter 2
[5] I Samuel 10:1-25 KJV
[6] Jack N. Rakove, *Original Meanings,* pp. 8-20 (Alfred A. Knopf, Inc. 1997)
[7] The term state at the time did not mean a subdivision of the country, as most of us think of it today, but instead meant a body politic constituting a nation.
[8] Rakove, pp. 103-07
[9] In my humble opinion, history has proven portions of both arguments to be correct. The federal government has certainly expanded its powers beyond what the Founding Fathers could have even imagined, yet at the same time, the listing of rights has, it seems, implied to the courts that other rights that people should have, are not there.
[10] Rakove, p. 115. The ratification dates for the first five states were: Delaware, December 7, 1787; Pennsylvania, December 12, 1787; New Jersey, December 18, 1787; Georgia, January 2, 1788; and Connecticut, January 9, 1788. See http://www.house.gov/Constitution/Constitution.html, fn. 1.
[11] These states and their dates of ratification are: Massachusetts, February 6, 1788; Maryland, April 28, 1788; South Carolina, May 23, 1788. *Id.*
[12] New Hampshire, June 21, 1788; Virginia, June 25, 1788; New York, July 26, 1788. The remaining states ratification dates are: North Carolina, November 21, 1789; Rhode Island, May 29, 1790; and Vermont, January 10, 1791. . See http://www.house.gov/Constitution/Constitution.html, fn. 1.
[13] Actually, twelve amendments were sent by Congress to the States. The first two were not ratified at the time, though one of those not ratified then, was later ratified and became the 27th Amendment. *Id.*

Chapter 3
[14] I must say, however, at times I have seen both federal courts and state courts, through legal sophistry, construe a statute or clause in a contract, or some other writing, to mean exactly opposite what it says.
[15] *The American Heritage Dictionary, Second College Edition* (Houghton Mifflin Co. Boston, 1982) 1062.
[16] *Id.*
[17] *Id.* 971.
[18] The term "states' rights" was always a misnomer. What is really meant by that phrase is the desire to have the "power" under discussion exercised by the state government rather than the national government since the state government, being

closer to the people, should be more responsive to the wants and needs of the people. You can agree or disagree with this concept, but either way it is not correct to call the concept "states' rights".

[19] *"The powers not delegated to the United States by the Constitution, nor prohibited by it to the States, are reserved to the States respectively, or to the people."*

[20] *The American Heritage Dictionary, Second College Edition* (Houghton Mifflin Co. Boston, 1982) 1063.

[21] *Id.*

[22] *Id.* 919.

[23] *Id.* (emphasis in original).

[24] See http://www.house.gov/Constitution/Constitution.html (emphasis added).

[25] U.S. CONST. amend. I.

[26] U.S. CONST. amend. IV.

[27] U.S. CONST. amend. V.

[28] U.S. CONST. amend. IX.

[29] U.S. CONST. amend. X.

[30] 494 U.S. 259 (1990).

[31] *Id.* at 265.

[32] Hennigan, *Our Second Amendment Rights Have Not Been Eroded, Our Understanding of Them, However, Is,* Church & Society Magazine, Vol. 90, No. 5 (May/June 2000).

[33] *Id.*

[34] *Id.*

[35] *The American Heritage Dictionary, Second College Edition* (Houghton Mifflin Co. Boston, 1982) 127. The definition used is for the second listing of "arm".

[36] *Id.*

[37] *Id.*

[38] *The American Heritage Dictionary, Second College Edition* (Houghton Mifflin Co. Boston, 1982) 698.

[39] *Id.* 164.

[40] *United States v. Emerson,* 270 F.3d 203, 230-31 (5th Cir. 2001), *cert. denied,* 122 S. Ct. 2362, 153 L.Ed. 2d 184 (U.S. 2002).

[41] *Id.* 230 and n. 29.

[42] *Id.* 231.

[43] *Id.*

[44] *Muscarello v. United States,* 524 U.S. 125 (1998).

[45] *Id.*

[46] *Id.* 661.

[47] U.S. Const. art I, section 8, clauses 15 and 16

[48] *Id.*

[49] U.S. Const. art I, section 8, clause 12.

[50] U.S. Const. art I, section 10, clause 3. There is some dispute over whether this prohibition is complete, or only applies during times of peace. The complete clause states: "No State shall, without the Consent of Congress, lay any Duty of Tonnage,

keep Troops, or Ships of War in time of Peace, enter into any Agreement or Compact with another State, or with a foreign Power, or engage in War, unless actually invaded, or in such imminent Danger as will not admit of delay." It is not clear whether the "in time of Peace" language applies only to "Ships of War", or to keeping troops as well. This distinction does not make any difference for our discussion.

[51] 381 U.S. 41 (1965).

[52] 28 U.S.C. 1346 (1958 ed.). The concept here is that of sovereign immunity, stemming from the English rule that a person could not sue the king. No one can sue the government unless the government gives its consent. The cited Federal Tort Claims Act gives that consent for certain specified situations.

[53] 381 U.S. at 46.

[54] 496 U.S. 334 (1990).

[55] 3 J. Elliott, *Debates in the General State Conventions* 425 (3d e. 1937)(statement of George Mason, June 14, 1788).

[56] *Letters from the Federal Farmer to the Republican* 123 (W. Bennett e. 1978)(ascribed to Richard Henry Lee).

[57] *An American Citizen* (Oct. 21, 1787).

[58] *The Pennsylvania Gazette* (Feb. 20, 1788).

[59] *The American Heritage Dictionary, Second College Edition* (Houghton Mifflin Co. Boston, 1982) 796..

[60] 10 U.S.C. section 311(a).

[61] Nelson Lund, *The Second Amendment, Political Liberty, and the Right to Self-Preservation*, 39 Ala. L. Rev. 103 (1987)(emphasis in original).

[62] "Exploding the NRA's Second Amendment Mythology", 23 July 2002, http://www.gunlawsuits.org/defend/second/articles/nramyths.asp

[63] *Id.*

[64] Lund, 107 (emphasis in original).

[65] *The American Heritage Dictionary, Second College Edition* (Houghton Mifflin Co. Boston, 1982) 1041.

[66] Dennis A. Henigan, *Arms, Anarchy and the Second Amendment*, Valparaiso Univ. L. Rev. Vol. 16, No. 1 (Fall 1991).

[67] *The American Heritage Dictionary, Second College Edition* (Houghton Mifflin Co. Boston, 1982) 1190.

[68] *Id.*

[69] *"The powers not delegated to the United States by the Constitution, nor prohibited by it to the States, are reserved to the States respectively, or to the people."*

[70] 4 Documentary History of the First Federal Congress 9-10 (Charlene B. Bickford & Helen E. Veit eds., 1986); quoted in Stephen P. Halbrook, *The Right of the People or the Power of the State: Bearing Arms, Arming Militias, and the Second Amendment*, 26 Val. U.L. Rev 131, 170 (1991).

[71] *Id.*

[72] *The American Heritage Dictionary, Second College Edition* (Houghton Mifflin Co. Boston, 1982) 834.

[73] *The American Heritage Dictionary, Second College Edition* (Houghton Mifflin Co. Boston, 1982) 1109.
[74] Dennis Henigan, *The Right to be Armed: A Constitutional Illusion,* San Fransico Barrister, Vol. 8, No. 12 (December 1989)(emphasis added).
[75] John E. Warriner and Francis Griffith, *English Grammar and Composition*, Revised ed. With Supplement (New York: Harcourt, Brace & World, Inc., 1969) 53.
[76] *Ibid.*
[77] Robert J. Cottrol & Raymond T. Diamond, *The Fifth Auxiliary Right*, 104 Yale L.J. 995, 1002 (1995); quoted in Glenn Harlan Reynolds, *A Critical Guide to the Second Amendment*, 62 Tenn. L. Rev. 461, n.22 (1995).
[78] Don't be too hard on him for this. Most attorneys do not know what rights are contained in any specific amendment unless they happen to use them all of the time, such as criminal defense attorneys using the Fourth, Fifth, and Sixth Amendments.
[79] Warriner and Griffith, 53-63.
[80] *Ibid.* 4.
[81] *Ibid.* 62.(italics in original, bold added).
[82] Testimony of Eugene Volokh on the Second Amendment, Senate Subcommittee on the Constitution, Sept. 23, 1998, reprinted as *A Right of the People*, California Political Review (Nov/Dec. 1998).
[83] "Exploding the NRA's Second Amendment Mythology", 23 July 2002, http://www.gunlawsuits.org/defend/second/articles/nramyths.asp
[84] Sanford Levinson, *The Embarrassing Second Amendment*, 99 Yale L.J. 637-659.
[85] *Emerson*, 270 F.3d 249 and n. 57.
[86] Journal of the First Session of the Senate 75 (Washington, D.C. 1820); quoted in *Emerson*, n. 57.

Chapter 4
[87] In case you do not recognize this date, it is the birthday of the United States Marine Corps!
[88] Carl vonClauswitz, *On War*, ed. Michael Howard and Peter Paret (Princeton, N.J.: Princeton Univ. Press, 1987), p. 87.
[89] Dennis Henigan, *The Right to be Armed: A Constitutional Illusion*, San Francisco Barrister, Vol. 8, No. 12 (Dec. 1989)(emphasis added).
[90] Keith A. Ehrman & Dennis A. Henigan, *The Second Amendment in the Twentieth Century: Have You Seen Your Militia Lately?*, Dayton L. Rev. Vol. 15, No. 1 (Fall 1989).
[91] *Id.*
[92] *Id.*
[93] Clayton E. Cramer, *For the Defense of Themselves and the State: The Original Intent and Judicial Interpretation of the Right to Keep and Bear Arms* 24-25 (1994) and Joyce Lee Malcolm, *To Keep and Bear Arms: The Origins of an Anglo-American Right* 2 (1994), both cited in *United States v. Emerson*, 46 F.Supp. 2d 598 (N.D. Tex. 1999), *reversed on other grounds*, 270 F.3d 203 (5th Cir. 2001), *cert. denied*, 122 S. Ct. 2362, 153 L. Ed. 2d 184 (U.S. 2002).

[94] Ehrman & Henigan
[95] *Emerson*, 46 F. Supp. 2d at 602.
[96] Ehrman & Henigan
[97] *Id.*
[98] *Emerson*, 46 F. Supp. 2d at 602.
[99] *Id.*
[100] 1 B. Schwartz, *The Bill of Rights: A Documentary History* 42-43 (1971); quoted in Ehrman & Henigan, supra n. 89.
[101] Ehrman & Henigan
[102] Ehrman & Henigan. "[T]he law at the time greatly circumscribed who could possess arms. In addition . . . there is little historical support for the idea that the English Bill of Rights was attempting to ensure some absolute right of individuals to have arms. Instead, the focus of this section of the Bill of Rights was a conflict between Protestants and Catholics over respective roles in the militia and the army." *Id.*
[103] William Blackstone, *Commentaries on the Laws of England.*
[104] 22 Cor. 2 ch. 25, A section 3, cited in Nelson Lund, *The Second Amendment, Political Liberty, and the Right to Self-Preservation*, 39 Ala. L. Rev. 103-130, at n. 22 (1987).
[105] Cited in Nelson Lund, *The Second Amendment, Political Liberty, and the Right to Self-Preservation*, 39 Ala. L. Rev. 103-130, at n. 22 (1987).
[106] 2 William Blackstone, *Commentaries*, 412; quoted in Nelson Lund, *The Second Amendment, Political Liberty, and the Right to Self-Preservation*, 39 Ala. L. Rev. 103-130, at n. 23 (1987).
[107] Joyce Lee Malcolm, *To Keep and Bear Arms: The Origins of an American Right* 138 (1994); quoted in *Emerson* 46 F. Supp 2d at 602.
[108] Ehrman & Henigan
[109] *Emerson*, 46 F. Supp. 2d at 602.
[110] *Id.*
[111] J. Hammond Trumbull et al., eds., *The Public Records of the Colony of Connecticut*, 15 vols. (Hartford, CT 1850-1890), 8:380; quoted in *More Bellesiles: "Cite Correction"*, http://www.guncite.com/gun-control-more-bellesiles.html.
[112] Alexander S. Salley, Jr., ed., *Journal of the Grand Council of South Carolina*, 2 vols. (Columbia, S.C., 1907) 1:10-12; http://www.guncite.com/gun-control-more-bellesiles.html.
[113] John Russell Bartlett, ed., *Records of the Colony of Rhode Island and Providence Plantations, in New England,* 10 vols. (Providence, R.I. 1856-65), 1:79-80, 94, 223-34; http://www.guncite.com/gun-control-more-bellesiles.html.
[114] Browne et al., eds., *Archives of Maryland*, 3:103, 46:398-99, 58:122-24, 340-42, 390, 395, 58:146-47; http://www.guncite.com/gun-control-more-bellesiles.html.
[115] Shurtleff, ed., *Records of Massachusetts Bay* 1: 84, 190; http://www.guncite.com/gun-control-more-bellesiles.html.
[116] *Id. 1:134-35.*
[117] *Emerson*, 46 F. Supp. 2d at 602.
[118] Ehrman & Henigan n. 66.

[119] Michael A. Bellesiles, *Arming America: The Origins of a National Gun Culture* (New York: Alfred A. Knopf, 2000).
[120] Clayton E. Cramer; *Arming America: A Novel Rewrite of American History* (May 14, 2001); http://www.nraila.org/articles.asp?FormMode=Detail&ID=52&1=View
[121] *Id.*
[122] *Id.*
[123] *Id.*
[124] John G. Fought, *"Magic History": Constructing a Past in Arming America;* http://www.guncite.com/gun_control_bellesiles.html
[125] *More Bellesile: "Cite Correction",* January 5, 2002, http://www.guncite.com/gun-control-more-bellesiles.html
[126] *Boston Gazette and County Journal,* Sept. 26, 1768, at 3 cols. 1-2; quoted in Stephen P. Halbrook, *The Arms of the People Should Be Taken Away;* http://www.nraila.org/articles.asp?FormMode=Detail&ID=9&1=View
[127] *New York Jornal,* Feb2, 1769, at 2, col. 2; quoted in Stephen P. Halbrook, *The Arms of the People Should Be Taken Away;* http://www.nraila.org/articles.asp?FormMode=Detail&ID=9&1=View
[128] *Boston Gazette and Country Journal,* October 17, 1768, at 2, col. 3; quoted in Stephen P. Halbrook, *The Arms of the People Should Be Taken Away;* http://www.nraila.org/articles.asp?FormMode=Detail&ID=9&1=View
[129] *Massachusetts Spy,* Sept. 8, 1774, at 3, col. 3; quoted in Stephen P. Halbrook, *The Arms of the People Should Be Taken Away;* http://www.nraila.org/articles.asp?FormMode=Detail&ID=9&1=View
[130] Stephen P. Halbrook, *The Arms of the People Should Be Taken Away;* http://www.nraila.org/articles.asp?FormMode=Detail&ID=9&1=View
[131] *Id.*
[132] *Id.*
[133] *Sources of American Independence* 176 (H. Peckman ed. 1978); quoted in Stephen P. Halbrook, *The Arms of the People Should Be Taken Away;* http://www.nraila.org/articles.asp?FormMode=Detail&ID=9&1=View
[134] John W. Jackson, With The British Army In Philadelphia, 1777-1778, At 20 (1979); cited in Stephen P. Halbrook and David B. Kopel, Tench Coxe and the Right to Keep and Bear Arms, 1787-1823, William and Mary Bill of Rights Journal (Feb. 1999).
[135] Ehrman & Henigan
[136] http://www.usconstitution.net/articles.html
[137] Jack N. Rakove, *Original Meanings* 316 (New York, Alfred A. Knopf 1997).
[138] *Ibid.*
[139] Rakove, 318.
[140] *Id.* 288.
[141] *Id.* It should be noted that the votes at the convention were taken by state, so that while some individuals may have been in favor of the motion, none of the state delegations had a majority in favor of it.
[142] Ehrman & Henigan

[143] U.S. Const. art I, section 8, cl. 12.
[144] *United States v. Emerson*, 270 F.3d 203, 270 (5th Cir. 2001), *cert. denied*, 122 S. Ct. 2362, 153 L. Ed. 2d 184 (U.S. 2002).
[145] Even gun control advocates have admitted this. See Ehrman & Henigan text at n. 142.
[146] Jonathan Elliot, *Debates on the Adoption of the Federal Constitution* 464-65 (1845); quoted in Stephen P. Halbrook, *The Right of the People or the Power of the State: Bearing Arms, Arming Militias, and the Second Amendment*, 26 Val. U.L. Rev 131, 137-38 (1991).
[147] Letter to William S. Smith (1787), in Thomas Jefferson, *On Democracy* 31-32 (S. Padover ed., 1939); quoted in Stephen P. Halbrook, *The Right of the People or the Power of the State: Bearing Arms, Arming Militias, and the Second Amendment*, 26 Val. U.L. Rev 131, 137-38 (1991).
[148] Letter of 1788, 1 Jonathan Elliot, *Debates in the Several State Conventions* 382 (1836); quoted in Stephen P. Halbrook, *The Right of the People or the Power of the State: Bearing Arms, Arming Militias, and the Second Amendment*, 26 Val. U.L. Rev 131, 137-38 (1991).
[149] quoted in Stephen P. Halbrook, *The Right of the People or the Power of the State: Bearing Arms, Arming Militias, and the Second Amendment*, 26 Val. U.L. Rev 131, 137-38 (1991).
[150] James Madison, *Federalist No. 46*; http://memory.loc.gov/const/fed/fed_46.html. (emphasis added).
[151] Richard Henry Lee, *Letters of a Federal Farmer*, in 14 Documentary History of the Ratification of the Constitution 38-39 (1983); quoted in Stephen P. Halbrook, *The Right of the People or the Power of the State: Bearing Arms, Arming Militias, and the Second Amendment*, 26 Val. U.L. Rev 131, 140-41 (1991)(emphasis added).
[152] 2 *Documentary History of the Ratification of the Constitution* 509 (Merrill Jensen ed., 1976); quoted in Stephen P. Halbrook, *The Right of the People or the Power of the State: Bearing Arms, Arming Militias, and the Second Amendment*, 26 Val. U.L. Rev 131, 142 (1991)
[153] 2 Documentary History at 336; quoted in Stephen P. Halbrook, *The Right of the People or the Power of the State: Bearing Arms, Arming Militias, and the Second Amendment*, 26 Val. U.L. Rev 131, 142 (1991)
[154] Please realize that firearms and the militia questions were only two of many issues that were involved in the ratification process. While we concentrate on those because they are the subject of this book, many other issues were involved.
[155] 2 Documentary History at 623-24; quoted in *Emerson*, 270 F.3d at 241.
[156] 2 Jonathan Elliot, *2 Debates in the Several State Conventions* 545 (1836): quoted in Stephen P. Halbrook, *The Right of the People or the Power of the State: Bearing Arms, Arming Militias, and the Second Amendment*, 26 Val. U.L. Rev 131, 144 (1991)
[157] 2 Elliot at 545-46; quoted in Stephen P. Halbrook, *The Right of the People or the Power of the State: Bearing Arms, Arming Militias, and the Second Amendment*, 26 Val. U.L. Rev 131, 145 (1991)
[158] http://memory.loc.gov/const/fed/fed_29.html

¹⁵⁹ *Pennsylvania Gazette*, Feb. 20, 1788; quoted in Stephen P. Halbrook, *The Right of the People or the Power of the State: Bearing Arms, Arming Militias, and the Second Amendment*, 26 Val. U.L. Rev 131, 146 (1991).(All Caps in original; bold added).

¹⁶⁰ *2 Debates in the Several States* at 74; quoted in Stephen P. Halbrook, *The Right of the People or the Power of the State: Bearing Arms, Arming Militias, and the Second Amendment*, 26 Val. U.L. Rev 131, 147 (1991)

¹⁶¹ *Id.* at 97. quoted in Stephen P. Halbrook, *The Right of the People or the Power of the State: Bearing Arms, Arming Militias, and the Second Amendment*, 26 Val. U.L. Rev 131, 147 (1991).

¹⁶² *Debates of the Massachusetts Convention of 1788*, at 86-87, 266 (Boston, 1856); quoted in Stephen P. Halbrook, *The Right of the People or the Power of the State: Bearing Arms, Arming Militias, and the Second Amendment*, 26 Val. U.L. Rev 131, 147 (1991).

¹⁶³ 1 Johnathan Elliot, *The Debates in the Several State Conventions on the Adoption of the Federal Constitution* 326 (2d. ed. 1836); quoted in *Emerson*, 270 F.3d at 242.

¹⁶⁴ *Winchester Gazette* (Virginia), February 22, 1788; quoted in Stephen P. Halbrook, *The Right of the People or the Power of the State: Bearing Arms, Arming Militias, and the Second Amendment*, 26 Val. U.L. Rev 131, 150-51 (1991).(emphasis added).

¹⁶⁵ All of this may also bring to your mind, if such rights pre-existed the Constitution and the federal government had no power over them, how do we get the federal laws restricting hunting, fishing, etc, to protect endangered species? That is a whole additional matter outside the scope of this book. In fact, that question could inspire a whole book of its own. Suffice it to say, it is good that the Second Amendment is there to form a barrier to such encroachments on the right to keep and bear arms as have occurred on other rights.

¹⁶⁶ Richard H. Lee, *Additional Letters From the Federal Farmer* 169-70; quoted in Stephen P. Halbrook, *The Right of the People or the Power of the State: Bearing Arms, Arming Militias, and the Second Amendment*, 26 Val. U.L. Rev 131, 150-51 (1991).(emphasis added).

¹⁶⁷ Most of the articles cited in this book during this time frame were written under pseudonyms. For example, James Madison used "Publius". It has taking a lot of work by many historians to discover who the actual authors were. Some of the actual authors remain unknown.

¹⁶⁸ *The Government of Nature Delineated* (1788), in 2 Documentary History of the Ratification of the Constitution (Microfilm Supp. At 2524-26) (Merrill Jensen ed., 1976): quoted in Stephen P. Halbrook, *The Right of the People or the Power of the State: Bearing Arms, Arming Militias, and the Second Amendment*, 26 Val. U.L. Rev 131, 153 (1991).

¹⁶⁹ *State Gazette* (Charleston), Sept. 8, 1788; quoted in Stephen P. Halbrook, *The Right of the People or the Power of the State: Bearing Arms, Arming Militias, and the Second Amendment*, 26 Val. U.L. Rev 131, 153 (1991).

¹⁷⁰ 3 Jonathan Elliot, *Debates in the Several State Conventions* 45 and 51 (1836); quoted in Stephen P. Halbrook, *The Right of the People or the Power of the State:*

Bearing Arms, Arming Militias, and the Second Amendment, 26 Val. U.L. Rev 131, 154-55 (1991).

[171] 3 Elliot at 112; quoted in Stephen P. Halbrook, *The Right of the People or the Power of the State: Bearing Arms, Arming Militias, and the Second Amendment,* 26 Val. U.L. Rev 131, 153 (1991).

[172] 3 Elliot at 380; quoted in Stephen P. Halbrook, *The Right of the People or the Power of the State: Bearing Arms, Arming Militias, and the Second Amendment,* 26 Val. U.L. Rev 131, 153 (1991).

[173] 3 Elliot at 386; quoted in Stephen P. Halbrook, *The Right of the People or the Power of the State: Bearing Arms, Arming Militias, and the Second Amendment,* 26 Val. U.L. Rev 131, 158-59 (1991).(emphasis added).

[174] 9 *Documentary History of the Ratification of the Constitution* 659 (John Kaminski & Gaspare Saladine eds., 1990); quoted in Stephen P. Halbrook, *The Right of the People or the Power of the State: Bearing Arms, Arming Militias, and the Second Amendment,* 26 Val. U.L. Rev 131, 161 (1991).

[175] 9 *Documentary* at 657; quoted in Stephen P. Halbrook, *The Right of the People or the Power of the State: Bearing Arms, Arming Militias, and the Second Amendment,* 26 Val. U.L. Rev 131, 161 (1991).

[176] 3 Elliot at 660; quoted in Stephen P. Halbrook, *The Right of the People or the Power of the State: Bearing Arms, Arming Militias, and the Second Amendment,* 26 Val. U.L. Rev 131, 162 (1991).

[177] *New York Journal and Daily Advertiser,* April 21, 1788, at 2, col. 2; quoted in Stephen P. Halbrook, *The Right of the People or the Power of the State: Bearing Arms, Arming Militias, and the Second Amendment,* 26 Val. U.L. Rev 131, 162 (1991).

[178] 1 *Debates in the Several States* at 327-28; quoted in Stephen P. Halbrook, *The Right of the People or the Power of the State: Bearing Arms, Arming Militias, and the Second Amendment,* 26 Val. U.L. Rev 131, 163 (1991).

[179] 1 *Debates in the Several States* at 331; quoted in Stephen P. Halbrook, *The Right of the People or the Power of the State: Bearing Arms, Arming Militias, and the Second Amendment,* 26 Val. U.L. Rev 131, 163 (1991).

[180] 1 *Debates in the Several States* at 327-28; quoted in *Emerson,* 270 F.3d at 243.

[181] It was not until after the Bill of Rights had been passed by Congress and sent to the states for ratification that North Carolina ratified the Constitution.

[182] 4 Jonathan Elliott, *Debates in the Several State Convention* 245 (1836); quoted in Stephen P. Halbrook, *The Right of the People or the Power of the State: Bearing Arms, Arming Militias, and the Second Amendment,* 26 Val. U.L. Rev 131, 164 (1991).

[183] *Emerson,* 270 F.3d at 244.

[184] Ehrman & Henigan

[185] It should be remembered that at that time senators were appointed by the state legislatures.

[186] James Madison, *Extract of a letter from the Hon. James Madison, jun. To his friend in the county,* Fredericksburg Virginia Herald, January 29, 1788; quoted in *Emerson,* 270 F.3d at 245.

[187] 4 Madison Papers 60 (Robert Rutland ed., 1979); quoted in Stephen P. Halbrook, *The Right of the People or the Power of the State: Bearing Arms, Arming Militias, and the Second Amendment,* 26 Val. U.L. Rev 131, n. 183 (1991).

[188] Robert Rutland, *The Birth of the Bill of Rights 196 (1962);* quoted in Stephen P. Halbrook, *The Right of the People or the Power of the State: Bearing Arms, Arming Militias, and the Second Amendment,* 26 Val. U.L. Rev 131, 169 (1991)(emphasis added).

[189] James Madison, House of Representatives, June 8, 1989; quoted in *Emerson,* 270 F.3d at 246.

[190] 4 Documentary History of the First Federal Congress 9-10 (Charlene B. Bickford & Helen E. Veit eds., 1986); quoted in Stephen P. Halbrook, *The Right of the People or the Power of the State: Bearing Arms, Arming Militias, and the Second Amendment,* 26 Val. U.L. Rev 131, 170 (1991).

[191] *Id.*

[192] *Id.*

[193] *Id.*

[194] Letter from Fisher Ames to Thomas Dwight (June 11, 1789), in 1 Works of Fisher Ames 52-53 (1854); quoted in Stephen P. Halbrook, *The Right of the People or the Power of the State: Bearing Arms, Arming Militias, and the Second Amendment,* 26 Val. U.L. Rev 131, 174 (1991).

[195] Ames to F.R. Minoe, June 12, 1789; id.(emphasis added)

[196] Letter from Senator William Grayson to Patrick Henry, June 12, 1789, in 3 Patrick Henry 391 (1951); quoted in Stephen P. Halbrook, *The Right of the People or the Power of the State: Bearing Arms, Arming Militias, and the Second Amendment,* 26 Val. U.L. Rev 131, 174 (1991)(emphasis added).

[197] Letter from Joseph Jones to James Madison, June 24, 1789, in 12 Madison Papers 258 (Robert Rutland ed., 1978); quoted in Stephen P. Halbrook, *The Right of the People or the Power of the State: Bearing Arms, Arming Militias, and the Second Amendment,* 26 Val. U.L. Rev 131, 174 and n. 202 (1991)(emphasis added).

[198] Letter from William L. Smith to Edward Rutledge, Aug. 9, 1789, in 79 S.C. Hist. Mag 14 (1968); quoted in Stephen P. Halbrook, *The Right of the People or the Power of the State: Bearing Arms, Arming Militias, and the Second Amendment,* 26 Val. U.L. Rev 131, n. 202 (1991)(emphasis added).

[199] Federal Gazette, June 18, 1789, at 2, col. 1; quoted in Stephen P. Halbrook, *The Right of the People or the Power of the State: Bearing Arms, Arming Militias, and the Second Amendment,* 26 Val. U.L. Rev 131, n. 202 (1991)(emphasis added).

[200] Letter from James Madison to Tench Coxe, June 24, 1789; quoted in *Emerson,* 270 F.3d at 252.

[201] Letter from Samuel Nasson to George Thatcher, in Creating the Bill of Rights: The Documentary Record from the First Federal Congress 260 (Helen E. Veit et al. ed., 1991); quoted in Stephen P. Halbrook, *The Right of the People or the Power of the State: Bearing Arms, Arming Militias, and the Second Amendment,* 26 Val. U.L. Rev 131, 176 (1991)(emphasis added).

[202] *Emerson,* 270 F.3d at 245 (emphasis added).

[203] James Hutson, *The Bill of Rights: The Roger Sherman Draft*, This Constitution, No. 18 at 36 (Spring/Summer 1988); quoted in Stephen P. Halbrook, *The Right of the People or the Power of the State: Bearing Arms, Arming Militias, and the Second Amendment*, 26 Val. U.L. Rev 131, 178 (1991).
[204] 4 Documentary of the First Federal Congress at 28; quoted in Stephen P. Halbrook, *The Right of the People or the Power of the State: Bearing Arms, Arming Militias, and the Second Amendment*, 26 Val. U.L. Rev 131, 179 (1991).
[205] quoted in Stephen P. Halbrook, *The Right of the People or the Power of the State: Bearing Arms, Arming Militias, and the Second Amendment*, 26 Val. U.L. Rev 131, 180 (1991).
[206] Creating the Bill of Rights: The Documentary Record from the First Federal Congress 272-73 (Helen E. Veit et al. ed., 1991); quoted in Stephen P. Halbrook, *The Right of the People or the Power of the State: Bearing Arms, Arming Militias, and the Second Amendment*, 26 Val. U.L. Rev 131, 181 (1991)(emphasis added).
[207] Quoted in *Emerson*, 270 F.3d at 254.
[208] James Hutson, *The Bill of Rights: The Roger Sherman Draft*, This Constitution, No. 18, at 36 (Spring/Summer 1988); quoted in Stephen P. Halbrook, *The Right of the People or the Power of the State: Bearing Arms, Arming Militias, and the Second Amendment*, 26 Val. U.L. Rev 131, 181-82 (1991).
[209] 1 Annals of Congress 767 (Joseph Gales & William Seaton eds., 1834); cited in Stephen P. Halbrook, *The Right of the People or the Power of the State: Bearing Arms, Arming Militias, and the Second Amendment*, 26 Val. U.L. Rev 131, 184 (1991).
[210] Centinel Revived, no. xxix, Independent Gazetteer, Sept. 9, 1789, at 2, col. 2; quoted in Stephen P. Halbrook, *The Right of the People or the Power of the State: Bearing Arms, Arming Militias, and the Second Amendment*, 26 Val. U.L. Rev 131, 185 (1991).
[211] Journal of the First Session of the Senate 71 (Washington D.C. 1820); quoted in Stephen P. Halbrook, *The Right of the People or the Power of the State: Bearing Arms, Arming Militias, and the Second Amendment*, 26 Val. U.L. Rev 131, 186 (1991).
[212] *Id.* 75.
[213] *Id.*
[214] *Id.* 77.
[215] *Id.*
[216] 4 Documentary of the First Federal Congress, 45; quoted in Stephen P. Halbrook, *The Right of the People or the Power of the State: Bearing Arms, Arming Militias, and the Second Amendment*, 26 Val. U.L. Rev 131, 190-91 (1991).
[217] One dealt with postponing any pay raise that Congress might vote itself until after the next Congress is elected. While not ratified at the time, it was ratified in the 1990's, and became the 27th Amendment to the Constitution.
[218] Gazette of the United States, Oct. 14, 1789, at 211, col. 2; quoted in Stephen P. Halbrook, *The Right of the People or the Power of the State: Bearing Arms, Arming Militias, and the Second Amendment*, 26 Val. U.L. Rev 131, 193 (1991).

[219] Letter from Albert Gallatin to Alexander Addison, Oct. 7, 1789; quoted in Stephen P. Halbrook, *The Right of the People or the Power of the State: Bearing Arms, Arming Militias, and the Second Amendment,* 26 Val. U.L. Rev 131, n. 265 (1991).
[220] Speech from President Washington to the House of Representatives, Jan. 7, 1790, in Independent Chronicle (Boston), Jan 14, 1790, at 3; quoted in Stephen P. Halbrook, *The Right of the People or the Power of the State: Bearing Arms, Arming Militias, and the Second Amendment,* 26 Val. U.L. Rev 131, 193-94 (1991).
[221] Letter from Edmund Randolph to James Madison, Aug 18, 1789, in 12 Madison Papers 345 (1978); quoted in Stephen P. Halbrook, *The Right of the People or the Power of the State: Bearing Arms, Arming Militias, and the Second Amendment,* 26 Val. U.L. Rev 131, n. 266 (1991).
[222] Letter from Richard Henry Lee to Charles Lee, Aug. 28, 1789, in 2 Letters of Richard Henry Lee 499 (1914); quoted in Stephen P. Halbrook, *The Right of the People or the Power of the State: Bearing Arms, Arming Militias, and the Second Amendment,* 26 Val. U.L. Rev 131, n. 266 (1991).
[223] March 19, 1790, in 3 Patrick Henry 417-18 (1951); quoted in Stephen P. Halbrook, *The Right of the People or the Power of the State: Bearing Arms, Arming Militias, and the Second Amendment,* 26 Val. U.L. Rev 131, 194 (1991).
[224] Letter from Thomas to James Madison, 12 Madison Papers 363-64; quoted in Stephen P. Halbrook, *The Right of the People or the Power of the State: Bearing Arms, Arming Militias, and the Second Amendment,* 26 Val. U.L. Rev 131, n. 266 (1991).
[225] Massachusetts and the First Ten Amendments 28 (D. Meyers ed., 1936); quoted in Stephen P. Halbrook, *The Right of the People or the Power of the State: Bearing Arms, Arming Militias, and the Second Amendment,* 26 Val. U.L. Rev 131, n. 266 (1991).
[226] 5 Documentary History of the First Federal Congress 1458-59 (1986); quoted in Stephen P. Halbrook, *The Right of the People or the Power of the State: Bearing Arms, Arming Militias, and the Second Amendment,* 26 Val. U.L. Rev 131, 195 (1991).
[227] 2 Annals of Congress 1804-09(Dec. 16, 1790); quoted in Stephen P. Halbrook, *The Right of the People or the Power of the State: Bearing Arms, Arming Militias, and the Second Amendment,* 26 Val. U.L. Rev 131, 195-97 (1991).
[228] *Id.*
[229] "Mentor," AURORA (Phila.), May 21, 1799, at 2; quoted in Stephen P. Halbrook and David B. Kopel, Tench Coxe and the Right to Keep and Bear Arms, 1787-1823, William and Mary Bill of Rights Journal (Feb. 1999)(emphasis added).
[230] St George Tucker, Blackstone's Commentaries: with Notes of Reference, to the Constitution and Laws, of the Federal Government of the United States; and of the Commonwealth of Virginia (1803)(emphasis added).
[231] Tench Coxe, Digest of Manufactures, reprinted in 2 AMERICAN STATE PAPERS (FINANCE) 666, 687 (Wash., Gales & Seaton 1832; cited in Stephen P. Halbrook and David B. Kopel, Tench Coxe and the Right to Keep and Bear Arms, 1787-1823, William and Mary Bill of Rights Journal (Feb. 1999).

²³² 12 Ky. (2 Litt.) 90, 13 Am. Dec. 251 (1822).
²³³ *Id.* 93.
²³⁴ William Rawle, A View of the Constitution of the United States of America 125-26 (Da Capo Press 1970)(2d ed. 1829)(emphasis added); quoted in *Emerson,* 270 F.3d at 256-57.
²³⁵ Joseph Story, Commentaries on the Constitution of the United States 708-709 (Carolina Academic Press 1987) (1833) (emphasis added); quoted in *Emerson,* 270 F.3d at 257-58.
²³⁶ The Handbook of Texas On Line; at http://www.tsha.utexas.edu/handbook/online/articles/view/GG/qvg1.html
²³⁷ The Handbook of Texas On Line; at http://www.tsha.utexas.edu/handbook/online/articles/view/TT/mjtce.html
²³⁸ Republic of Texas Constitution, 1836.
²³⁹ 4 Ark. (4 Pike) 18 (1842).
²⁴⁰ 1Ga. (1 Kelly) 243 (1846).
²⁴¹ *Id.* 249-251 italics in original; bold added).
²⁴² Southerners also sometimes call it the War of Yankee Imperialist Aggression, but this is of rather recent use, not applied at the time of the war, so I will abstain from its use here.
²⁴³Constitution of the Confederate States of America, at http://web.archive.org/web/20010419023233/www.civilwar.com/csa.htm
²⁴⁴ James M. McPherson, *For Cause & Comrades, Why Men Fought in the Civil War* (Oxford University Press, New York 1977).
²⁴⁵ Report of the Subcommittee on the Constitution of the Committee on the Judiciary, United States Senate, 97th Cong., 2d Sess., The Right to Keep and Bear Arms, 68-82 (1982).
²⁴⁶ 14 Stat. 27 (1866).
²⁴⁷ From the earliest times of our government through the time of these early cases, if state governments wanted to restrict rights of the people, the federal Constitution was no obstacle. While there may be Bills of Rights in the state constitutions, it was left as a matter for internal state resolution. And in fact some states early on had state supported religion. If they had wanted to restrict freedom of religion, freedom of speech, or freedom of the press, while their own state constitutions might have prohibited this, the federal Constitution and its Bill of Rights did not.
²⁴⁸ 332 U.S. 46 (1947).
²⁴⁹ http://homepages.rootsweb.com/~mwellis/book/chapter12.html
²⁵⁰ *Id.*
²⁵¹ *State v. Kerner,* 181 N.C. 574, 577 (1921)
²⁵² Thomas M. Cooley, The General Principles of Constitutional Law in the United States of America 270-72 (Rothman & Co. 1981)(original ed. 1898)(footnotes omitted)(emphasis added); quoted in *Emerson,* 270 F.3d at 258-59.
²⁵³ First Annual Message to Congress, Dec. 3, 1901, 14 Messages and Papers of the Presidents 6672; quoted in *Perpich v. Department of Defense,* 496 U.S. 334, 341 and n. 10 (1990).

²⁵⁴ 31 Stat. 748, 758.
²⁵⁵ H. R. Rep. No. 1094, 57th Cong., 1st Sess., 22 (1902).
²⁵⁶ Section 4, 35 Stat. 400.
²⁵⁷ 29 Op. Atty. Gen. 322, 323-324 (1912).
²⁵⁸ 39 Stat. 166.
²⁵⁹ *Id.*
²⁶⁰ 48 Stat. 160-161.
²⁶¹ *Perpich* at 346.
²⁶² 100 Stat. 3871.
²⁶³ App. 12 (testimony of James H. Webb, Assistant Secretary of Defense for Reserve Affairs, before a subcommittee of the Senate Armed Services Committee on July 15, 1986).
²⁶⁴ P.L. 274, 77th Cong., 1st Sess., Ch. 445, 55 Stat., pt. 1, 742 (1941).
²⁶⁵ Rept. No. 1120 (to accompany S. 1579), House Committee on Military Affairs, 77th Cong., 1st Sess., at 2 (Aug. 4, 1941).
²⁶⁶ Pub. L. No. 99-308, sec. 1 (b) (1986)
²⁶⁷ *The Right to Keep and Bear Arms*: Report of the Subcommittee on the Constitution, Senate Judiciary Committee, 97th Cong., 2d Sess., 12 (1982).
²⁶⁸ Former Chief Justice Warren Burger, The MacNeil/Lehrer NewsHour, December 16, 1991

Chapter 5
²⁶⁹ Sanford Levison, *The Embarrassing Second Amendment,* 99 Yale L.J. 637, 651 (1989).

Chapter 6
²⁷⁰ *United States v. Emerson,* 270 F.3d 203 (5th Cir. 2001), *cert. denied,* 122 S. Ct. 2362, 153 L. Ed. 2d 184 (U.S. 2002).
²⁷¹ There have been times when this number was increased. It is up to Congress to set the number of judges on the Supreme Court. But for most of the history of the United States, that number has been nine.
²⁷² 18 U.S. (5 Wheat) 1 (1820).
²⁷³ At this point I should point out that I am deeply indebted to the work done by David B. Kopel, the Research Director of the Independence Institute of Golden, Colorado, as published in his paper, *The Supreme Court's Thirty-Five Other Gun Cases: What the Supreme Court Has Said About the Second Amendment,* Saint Louis University Public Law Review, Symposium on Gun Control 99 (1999). I would not have found the *Houston* case without his paper. While I would have found most of the other cases he discusses, his paper saved me much time in doing the research that would have been necessary to find them.
²⁷⁴ In early cases, the briefs of the parties were published along with the opinions of the Supreme Court. That is no longer done.
²⁷⁵ *Houston,* 18 U.S. at 51.
²⁷⁶ *Id.* 52-53.
²⁷⁷ *Id.* 53.

[278] 60 U.S. (19 Hou.) 393 (1856).
[279] *Id.* 417.(emphasis added)
[280] 71 U.S. (4 Wall.) 2 (1866).
[281] *Id.* 32.
[282] 92 U.S. 542 (1875).
[283] *Id.* 551-53.
[284] 116 U.S. 252 (1886).
[285] *Id.* 264-65.
[286] 144 U.S. 263 (1892).
[287] 153 U.S. 535 (1894).
[288] *Id.* 538.
[289] *Id.*
[290] *Id.* 539.
[291] David B. Kopel, , *The Supreme Court's Thirty-Five Other Gun Cases: What the Supreme Court Has Said About the Second Amendment*, Saint Louis University Public Law Review, Symposium on Gun Control 169 (1999).
[292] 161 U.S. 591 (1896).
[293] *Id.* 635 (J. Field, dissenting) (emphasis added).
[294] 165 U.S. 275 (1897).
[295] *Id.* 281-82 (emphasis added).
[296] 176 U.S. 581 (1899).
[297] *Id.* 597.
[298] 199 U.S. 521 (1905).
[299] *Id.* 528.
[300] 211 U.S. 78 (1908).
[301] 378 U.S. 1 (1964).
[302] 236 U.S. 75 (1915).
[303] 279 U.S. 644 (1929).
[304] *Id.* 650.
[305] 293 U.S. 245 (1934).
[306] *Id.* 260-61.
[307] *Dunne v. People*, 94 Ill. 120, 132-33 (1879).
[308] 307 U.S. 174 (1939).
[309] 26 U.S.C.A. section 1132d (passed June 26, 1934).
[310] I once had a child custody case where the mother had custody, I represented the father, who wanted custody, and the mother did not show up. The court would not formally change custody, but I got the judge to order such extensive visitation for my client that he essentially had custody, although it was still called visitation.
[311] *Miller*, 307 U.S. at 178.
[312] *Id.* 178-79.
[313] 21 Tenn. 152, 2 Hum. 158 (1840).
[314] *Id.* 156-57, 2 Hum. At 158-59.
[315] *United States v. Emerson*, 270 F.3d at 222.
[316] 332 U.S. 46 (1947).
[317] 339 U.S. 763 (1950).

318 *Id.* 784 (emphasis added).
319 357 U.S. 371 (1958).
320 367 U.S. 497 (1961).
321 *Id.* 515 (J. Douglas dissenting).
322 *Id.* 542-43 (J. Harlan, dissenting)(emphasis added).
323 366 U.S. 36 (1961).
324 *Id.* 49-50 n. 10.
325 Hugo L. Black, The Bill of Rights, 35 N.Y.U.L. Rev. 865 (1960).
326 *Id.* 873.
327 378 U.S. 1 (1964).
328 *Id.* 4-6 and n. 2.
329 391 U.S. 145 (1968).
330 *Id.* 164 (J. Black concurring).
331 *Id.* 166-67 (J. Black concurring)(emphasis added).
332 394 U.S. 812 (1969).
333 *Mandel v. Bradley*, 432 U.S. 173, 176 (1977).
334 408 U.S. 1 (1972).
335 *Id.* 16.
336 *Id.* 22-23.
337 407 U.S. 143 (1972).
338 392 U.S. 1 (1968).
339 *Adams,* 407 U.S. at 150-51 (J. Douglas dissenting).
340 410 U.S. 113 (1973).
341 See text at footnotes 320-322.
342 431 U.S. 494 (1976).
343 American Bar Association Speech, Toronto, Canada, Aug. 7, 1988; quoted in David B. Kopel, , *The Supreme Court's Thirty-Five Other Gun Cases: What the Supreme Court Has Said About the Second Amendment*, Saint Louis University Public Law Review, Symposium on Gun Control n. 135 (1999).
344 The McNeil Lehrer NewsHour, Mar 16, 1989, trans. No. 3389, Lexis Transcripts library; quoted in David B. Kopel, , *The Supreme Court's Thirty-Five Other Gun Cases: What the Supreme Court Has Said About the Second Amendment*, Saint Louis University Public Law Review, Symposium on Gun Control n. 136 (1999).
345 *Id.*
346 445 U.S. 55 (1980).
347 372 U.S. 335 (1963).
348 *Lewis,* 445 U.S. at 62-63.
349 *Id.* 65.
350 *Id.* 66-67.
351 *Id.* 65-66, n. 8.
352 *Cody v. United States,* 460 F.2d 34, 36-37 (8th Cir. 1972).
353 494 U.S. 259 (1990).
354 *Id.* 264-65(emphasis added).
355 Those are the . . .'s that you see in some of the quotes. They mean that some words, hopefully irrelevant, have been left out.

[356] David B. Kopel, , *The Supreme Court's Thirty-Five Other Gun Cases: What the Supreme Court Has Said About the Second Amendment*, Saint Louis University Public Law Review, Symposium on Gun Control 131 (1999).
[357] 505 U.S. 833 (1992).
[358] See text at footnotes 320-322.
[359] 510 U.S. 266 (1994).
[360] 521 U.S. 898(1997).
[361] "In my "revisionist" view, . . . the Federal Government's authority under the Commerce Clause, which merely allocates to Congress the power "to regulate Commerce . . . among the several states," does not extend to the regulation of wholly intrastate, point of sale transactions. See United States v. Lopez, 514 U.S. 549, 584 (1995) (concurring opinion). Absent the underlying authority to regulate the intrastate transfer of firearms, Congress surely lacks the corollary power to impress state law enforcement officers into administering and enforcing such regulations. Although this Court has long interpreted the Constitution as ceding Congress extensive authority to regulate commerce (interstate or otherwise), I continue to believe that we must "temper our Commerce Clause jurisprudence" and return to an interpretation better rooted in the Clause's original understanding. Id., at 601; (concurring opinion); see also Camps Newfound/Owatonna, Inc. v. Town of Harrison, 520 U. S. ___, (1997)" (Thomas, J., dissenting). *Prinitz,* 521 U.S. at 937-38 (J. Thomas concurring). While I agree with Justice Thomas's position, I must note that it is against the vast majority of case law which has basically held that anything and everything can be regulated under the interstate commerce clause.
[362] *Id.* 938-39.
[363] *Id.* n. 1 and 2.
[364] 524 U.S. 125 (1998).
[365] *Id.* 139-50 (J. Ginsburg dissenting).
[366] 523 U.S. 1 (1998).
[367] *Id.* 36 (J. Stevens dissenting)(emphasis added).
[368] 131 F.2d 261 (3d Cir. 1942), <u>reversed on other grounds,</u> 319 U.S. 463 (1943)
[369] *Id.* 266
[370] *Id.*
[371] 131 F.2d 916 (1st Cir. 1942), cert. denied sub nom, *Velazquez v. United States*, 319 U.S. 770 (1943).
[372] *Id.* 922-23 and n. 3.
[373] *Id.* 921(emphasis added).
[374] *Id.* 922 (emphasis added).
[375] 313 F. Supp. 1330 (S.D. Ind. 1970), aff'd on other grounds, 451 F.2d 1355 (7th Cir. 1971).
[376] *Id.* 1334.
[377] 438 F.2d 764 (8th Cir., 1971), vacated on other grounds, 404 U.S. 1009 (1972).
[378] See text at footnote 361 and footnote 361 itself.
[379] *Synnes,* 438 F.2d at 767-68.
[380] *Id.* 770.
[381] *Id.* 771 and n. 9 (emphasis added).

382 *Id.* 772.
383 *Id.*
384 440 F.2d 144 (6th Cir., 1971).
385 *Id.* 149 (emphasis added).
386 441 F.2d 1134 (5th Cir. 1971).
387 446 F.2d 164 (8th Cir. 1971).
388 *Id.* 167.
389 340 F. Supp 147 (E.D. Wis., 1972).
390 *Id.* 148.
391 460 F.2d 34 (8th Cir., 1972).
392 *Id.* 36.
393 *Id.* 36-37.
394 476 F.2d 562 (Sixth Cir., 1973).
395 *Id.* 566.
396 *Id.* 568.
397 *Id.*
398 *Id.*
399 497 F.2d 548 (4th Cir. 1974).
400 *Id.* 550 (emphasis added).
401 521 F.2d 1255 (10th Cir., 1975).
402 *Id.* 1259.
403 530 F.2d 103 (10th Cir., 1976), cert. Denied 426 U.S. 948 (1976).
404 *Id.* 105 (emphasis added).
405 *Id.* 105-06 (emphasis added).
406 564 F.2d 384 (10th Cir. 1977), cert. Denied 435 U.S. 926 (1978).
407 *Id.* 387.
408 518 F. Supp 1082 (D.N.H. 1981), <u>cert. denied</u>, *469 U.S. 842 (1984)*.
409 *Id.* 1090 (emphasis added).
410 See text at footnotes 371-374.
411 549 F. Supp. 297 (D. Utah, 1982).
412 *Id.* 299.
413 695 F.2d 261 (7th Cir., 1982).
414 See text at footnotes 284-285.
415 *Id.* 270 (emphasis added).
416 *Id.* (emphasis added).
417 *Id.* n. 8 (emphasis added).
418 *Id.* 272 (J. Coffey, dissenting).
419 *Id.* 278-80.
420 859 F.2d 1318 (8th Cir., 1988).
421 *Id.* 1320.
422 *Id.*
423 965 F.2d 723 (9th Cir., 1992).
424 978 F.2d 1016 (8th Cir., 1992).
425 *Id.* 1019-20 (emphasis added).
426 *Id.* 1021 (J. Beam, concurring).

[427] 1 F.3d 1231 (1st Cir., 1993).
[428] *Id.*
[429] *Id.*
[430] 81 F.3d 98 (9th Cir. 1996).
[431] *Id.* 101
[432] 264 F.3d 1161 (10th Cir. 2001), *cert. denied* 122 S. Ct. 2362, 153 L. Ed. 2d 183 (U.S. 2002).
[433] *Id.* 1165.
[434] *Id.* 1165-66.
[435] 270 F.3d 203F.3d (5th Cir. 2001), *cert. denied*, 122 S. Ct. 2362, 153 L. Ed. 2d 184 (U.S. 2002).
[436] *Id.* 260.
[437] *Id.* 261.
[438] 312 F.3d 1052 (9th Cir. 2002).
[439] *Id.* 1061.
[440] *Id.* 1063 and n. 11.
[441] *Id.* 1061.
[442] *Id.* 1067 n. 17.
[443] *Id.*
[444] *Id.* 1087-88.
[445] *Id.* 1069.
[446] U.S. Const. Art. I, section 10, clause 3.
[447] *United States v. Verdugo-Urquidez*, 494 U.S. 259 (1990).
[448] *Silveira*, 312 F.3d at 1070-71.
[449] *Id.* 1071.
[450] *Id.* 1072.
[451] *Id.* 1074.
[452] *Id.* 1072.
[453] *Id.* 1074.
[454] *Id.* 1075.
[455] *Id.* 1085.
[456] *Id.* 1083 (italics in original, bold added).
[457] No. 99-17551, page 2215 (9th Cir. February 18, 2003).
[458] *Id.* page 2226.
[459] *Id.* page 2227 n. 4 (bold added).
[460] *Id.* page 2231 (J. Gould, concurring).

Chapter 7
[461] Excerpt of oral arguments in U.S. v. Emerson, 5th Circuit Court of Appeals, June 13, 2000; quoted on GunCite.com at http://www.guncite.com/gun_control_gcnobody.html
[462] http://www.jointogether.org/gv/issues/problem/impact/crisis/; http://www.jointogether.org/gv/issues/problem/impact/victims/
[463] *Id.*; http://www.jointogether.org/gv/issues/problem/global/

[464] Special Committee on Gun Violence, *The U.S. Compared to Other Nations*; http://www.abanet.org/gunviol/uscompar.html
[465] *International Homicide Comparisons*; http://www.guncite.com/gun_control_gcgvinco.html
[466] *International Violent Death Rates*; http://www.guncite.com/gun_control_gcgvintl.html
[467] Special Committee on Gun Violence, *Kids and Guns*; http://www.abanet.org/gunviol/youth.html
[468] *Gun Accidents (and Kids & Gun Accidents)*; http://www.guncite.com/gun_control_gcgvacci.html
[469] Special Committee on Gun Violence, *Guns and Family Violence*; http://www.abanet.org/gunviol/family.html
[470] Special Committee on Gun Violence, *Firearms and Public Health*; http://www.abanet.org/gunviol/pubhealth.html
[471] Special Committee on Gun Violence, *Guns in Schools*; http://www.abanet.org/gunviol/schools.html
[472] Special Committee on Gun Violence, *Guns and Suicides*; http://www.abanet.org/gunviol/suicide.html
[473] Gary Kleck, *Targeting Guns: Firearms and Their Control* p 285 (Walter de Gruyter, Inc., New York 1997).
[474] *Los Angeles Daily News*, August 8, 1999, pp. 1, 18; quoted in *The Gun Supply Myth*, http://www.guncite.com/gun_control_gcgvsupp.html
[475] Arthur Kellermann and Don Reay, *Protection or Peril? An Analysis of Firearms Related Deaths in the Home*, 314 New England J. Medicine 1557-60 (1986).
[476] http://www.guncite.com/gun_control_gcdgaga.html
[477] David Hemenway, Survey Research And Self-Defense Gun Use: An Explanation Of Extreme Overestimates, Journal of Criminal Law and Criminology (Northwestern) 87 (1997): 1430.
[478] Joyce Malcolm, Guns and Violence: The English Experience (Harvard University Press 2002).
[479] *Guns Banned in Britain: Crime Soars*, NewsMax.com
[480] *Crime, Deterrence and Right to Carry Concealed Handguns*, Journal of Legal Studies vol. XXVI (Jan. 1997).
[481] John R. Lott and William Landes, Multiple Victim Public Shootings, Bombings, and Right-to Carry Concealed Handgun Laws: Contrasting Private and Public Law Enforcement; http://papers.ssrn.com/sol3/papers.cfm?abstract_id=161637
[482] Dennis A Henigan, *Arms, Anarchy and the Second Amendment*, 16 Valparaiso Univ. L. Rev. No. 1 (Fall 1991)
[483] U.S. CONST. Art. I, Section 8, clause 11
[484] U.S. CONST. Art. II, Section 2, clause 1.
[485] *The American Heritage Dictionary, Second College Edition* (Houghton Mifflin Co. Boston, 1982) 105.

Chapter 8

[486] *The American Heritage Dictionary, Second College Edition* (Houghton Mifflin Co. Boston, 1982) 467.

Chapter 9
[487] 116 U.S. 252 (1885).
[488] *Id.* 266.
[489] 332 U.S. 46 (1947).
[490] *Barron v. Baltimore*, 32 U.S. (7 Pet.) 240 (1833).
[491] *Adamson*, 332 U.S. at 92.
[492] *Id.* 92-93.
[493] Cong. Globe, 39th Cong., 1st Sess. (1866) 813; quoted in *Adamson* 332 U.S. at 93-94.
[494] Cong. Globe, *supra*, 1054, 1057, 1059, 1063-66, 1083, and 1085-88; cited in *Adamson* at 95.
[495] 32 U.S. (7 Pet.) 469, 551 (1833).
[496] Cong. Globe, *supra*, 1089-91 (emphasis added); quoted in *Adamson* at 96-97.
[497] Cong. Globe, *supra*, 1095; cited in *Adamson* at 98-99.
[498] Cong. Globe, *supra*, 474; cited in *Adamson* at 99-100.
[499] Cong. Globe, *supra*, 1266-67; cited in *Adamson* at 100.
[500] Cong. Globe, *supra*, 1291-92; quoted in *Adamson* at 101-02.
[501] *Adamson* at 103.
[502] *Id.*
[503] Cong. Globe, *supra*, 2459 (emphasis added); quoted in *Adamson* at 104.
[504] Cong. Globe, *supra*, 2542-43 (emphasis added); quoted in *Adamson* at 107.
[505] Cong. Globe, *supra*, 2764 (emphasis added); quoted in *Adamson* at 104-07.
[506] Cong. Globe, App. 1st Sess., 42d Cong., 81, 83-85 (emphasis added); quoted in *Adamson* at 111-18.
[507] Flack, The Adoption of the Fourteenth Amendment, p. 94 (1908) (emphasis added); quoted in *Adamson* at 73, n. 5.
[508] *Adamson* at 75-76.
[509] 16 Wall. 36 (1872).
[510] Royall, *The Fourteenth Amendment: The Slaughter-House Cases*, 4 So. L. Rev. 558, 563 (1879); quoted in *Adamson*, 332 U.S. at 75-76, n. 6.
[511] 211 U.S. 78 (1908).
[512] 176 U.S. 581 (1899).
[513] *Adamson* at 72-73.
[514] 176 U.S. at 601-02.
[515] 121 U.S. 1, 12 (1887).
[516] *Walker v. Sauvinet*, 92 U.S. 90 (1875).
[517] *United States v. Cruikshank*, 92 U.S. 542 (1875).
[518] *Munn v. Illinois*, 94 U.S. 113 (1877).
[519] *Davidson v. New Orleans*, 96 U.S. 97 (1878).
[520] *Hurtado v. People of California*, 110 U.S. 516 (1884).
[521] *Presser v. Illinois*, 116 U.S. 252 (1886).
[522] *In re Kemmler*, 136 U.S. 436 (1890).

[523] *Maxwell v. Dow*, 176 U.S. 581 (1899).
[524] *Twining v. New Jersey*, 211 U.S. 78 (1908).
[525] *Gitlow v. New York*, 268 U.S. 652 (1925).
[526] *Adamson v. California*, 332 U.S. 46 (1947).
[527] 166 U.S. 226.
[528] *Powell v. Alabama*, 287 U.S. 45 (1932).
[529] *Snyder v. Massachusetts*, 291 U.S. 97 (1934).
[530] *De Jonge v. Oregon*, 299 U.S. 353 (1937).
[531] *Louisiana ex rel Francis v. Resweber*, 329 U.S. 459 (1947).
[532] *Everson v. Board of Education*, 330 U.S. 1 (1947); *West Virginia State Board of Education v. Barnette*, 319 U.S. 624 (1943); *Bridges v. California*, 314 U.S. 252 (1941).
[533] *Mapp v. Ohio*, 367 U.S. 643 (1961).
[534] *Gideon v. Wainwright*, 372 U.S. 335 (1963).
[535] *Malloy v. Hogan*, 378 U.S. 1 (1964).
[536] *Duncan v. Louisiana*, 391 U.S. 145 (1968).
[537] *Terry v. Ohio*, 392 U.S. 1 (1968).
[538] *Malloy v. Hogan*, 378 U.S. 1, 5 (1964).

Chapter 10
[539] 485 U.S. 312 (1988).
[540] *Id.* 321 (emphasis added).
[541] 491 U.S. 397 (1989).
[542] 391 U.S. 367 (1968).
[543] *Id.* 376-77 (footnotes oitted).
[544] 429 U.S. 190 (1976).
[545] *Id.* 197 (emphasis added).
[546] 491 U.S. 781 (1989).
[547] *Id.* 798-800 (emphasis added, footnotes and citations omitted).
[548] 122 S. Ct. 2080 (U.S. 2002).
[549] 438 U.S. 104 (1978).
[550] 369 U.S. 590 (1962).
[551] *Id.* 594-95.
[552] 483 U.S. 825 (1987).
[553] *Id.* 834-35 (emphasis added).
[554] 445 U.S. 55 (1980).
[555] *Id.* 65 (emphasis added).
[556] 859 F.2d 1318 (8th Cir., 1988).
[557] 476 F.2d 562 (6th Cir., 1973).
[558] 438 F.2d 764 (8th Cir. 1971).
[559] 270 F.3d 203 (5th Cir., 2001), *cert. denied,* 122 S. Ct. 2362, 153 L. Ed. 2d 184 (U.S. 2002).
[560] *Id.* (italics in original; bold added).

[561] Letter from John Ashcroft to James Jay Baker, dated May 17, 2001 (emphasis added); http://www.gunlawsuits.org/downloads/070301complaint/ashcroft_letter.pdf

[562] Kleck, Gary, *Targeting Guns: Firearms and Their Control*, p 105, 345-46. (Walter de Gruyter, Inc., New York 1997); cited in Guncite.com at http://www.guncite.com/gun_control_gcnobody.html

[563] Hon. Major R. Owens (Rep. NY, Extension of Remarks - September 23, 1993. Source: The Congressional Record, 103rd Congress, 1993-1994); quoted in Guncite.com at http://www.guncite.com/gun_control_gcnobody.html

[564] Senator John H. Chafee, Rhode Island (June 11, 1992, The Congressional Record, 102nd Congress, 1991-1992); quoted in Guncite.com at http://www.guncite.com/gun_control_gcnobody.html

[565] Rep. Stephen J. Solarz, New York (August 12, 1992, The Congressional Record, 102nd Congress, 1991-1992, Daily Edition E2492-2493.); quoted in Guncite.com at http://www.guncite.com/gun_control_gcnobody.html

[566] New York Times, September 24, 1975; quoted in Guncite.com at http://www.guncite.com/gun_control_gcnobody.html

[567] Michael Gartner, former NBC News President, USA Today, January 16, 1992; quoted in Guncite.com at http://www.guncite.com/gun_control_gcnobody.html

[568] Joyner Sims, Florida State Health Dept., Deputy Commissioner, Chicago Tribune, November 7, 1993; quoted in Guncite.com at http://www.guncite.com/gun_control_gcnobody.html

[569] New York Times, December 21, 1993; quoted in Guncite.com at http://www.guncite.com/gun_control_gcnobody.html

[570] Washington Post, August 19, 1965; quoted in Guncite.com at http://www.guncite.com/gun_control_gcnobody.html

[571] Patrick V. Murphy, New York City Police Commissioner, December 7, 1970; quoted in Guncite.com at http://www.guncite.com/gun_control_gcnobody.html

[572] Deborah Prothrow-Stith, Dean of the Harvard School of Public Health; quoted in Guncite.com at http://www.guncite.com/gun_control_gcnobody.html

[573] Garry Wills, John Lennon's war, Chi. Sun-times, Dec. 12, 1980.; quoted in Guncite.com at http://www.guncite.com/gun_control_gcnobody.html

[574] Gary Wills, *Or Worldwide Gun Control?*,Phila. Inquirer, May 17, 1981.; quoted in Guncite.com at http://www.guncite.com/gun_control_gcnobody.html

[575] Sarah Brady, Jackson, Keeping the Battle Alive, Tampa Trib., Oct. 21, 1993 (interview with Sarah Brady); quoted in Guncite.com at http://www.guncite.com/gun_control_gcnobody.html

[576] 695 F.2d 261 (7th Cir., 1982).

[577] *United States v. Ballentine*, 4 F.3d 504, 506 (7th Cir. 1993), *cert. denied,* 510 U.S. 1179.

[578] 539 F.2d 29 (9th Cir. 1976).

[579] *Id.* 31.

[580] 564 F.2d 1363 (9th Cir. 1977).

[581] 849 F.2d 562 (11th Cir. 1988), *cert. denied,* 489 U.S. 1084 (U.S. 1989).

[582] 924 F. Supp. 1052 (D. Kan. 1996), reversed on other grounds, 114 F3d 1067 (10th Cir. 1997).
[583] 474 F.2d 1120 (8th Cir. 1973).
[584] 861 F.2d 1334 (5th Cir. 1988).
[585] *Id.* 1337.
[586] 23 F.3d 29 (2d Cir. 1994).
[587] 198 F.3d 143 (4th Cir. 1999).
[588] 102 F. Supp 2d 787 (W.D. Mich. 2000).
[589] *Id.* 789
[590] Bob Kasarda, *Surprise Discovered in Local Divorce Cases*, Northwest Indiana News The Times Online, July 31, 2002, www.Northwest Indiana News TheTimesOnline_com - Surprise discovered in local divorce cases.htm
[591] *Printz v. United States*, 521 U.S. 898 (1997).
[592] The Assault Weapons Ban: Questions and Answers; C:\Documents and Settings\reynoldsrj\My Documents\2d Amendment\Brady Campaign - Facts & Information - Gun Laws - The Assault Weapons Ban.htm
[593] Assault Weapons; http://www.guncite.com/gun_control_gcassaul.html. They also point to the following statistics: The following summary of police statistical surveys is excerpted from Kopel, David B, *Rational Basis Analysis of "Assault Weapon" Prohibition*. (Kopel's paper contains the citations for these surveys and lists a few more studies as well.)

- *California*. In 1990, "assault weapons" comprised thirty-six of the 963 firearms involved in homicide or aggravated assault and analyzed by police crime laboratories, according to a report prepared by the California Department of Justice, and based on data from police firearms laboratories throughout the state. The report concluded that "assault weapons play a very small role in assault and homicide firearm cases." Of the 1,979 guns seized from California narcotics dealers in 1990, fifty-eight were "assault weapons."

- *Chicago*. From 1985 through 1989, only one homicide was perpetrated with a military caliber rifle. Of the 17,144 guns seized by the Chicago police in 1989, 175 were "military style weapons."

- *Florida*. Florida Department of Law Enforcement Uniform Crime Reports for 1989 indicate that rifles of all types accounted for 2.6% of the weapons used in Florida homicides. The Florida Assault Weapons Commission found that "assault weapons" were used in 17 of 7,500 gun crimes for the years 1986-1989.

- *Los Angeles*. Of the more than 4,000 guns seized by police during one year, only about 3% were "assault weapons."

- *Maryland*. In 1989-90, there was only one death involving a "semiautomatic assault rifle" in all twenty-four counties of the State of Maryland.

- *Massachusetts*. Of 161 fatal shootings in Massachusetts in 1988, three involved "semiautomatic assault rifles." From 1985 to 1991, the guns were involved in 0.7% of all shootings.

- *Miami*. The Miami police seized 18,702 firearms from January 1, 1989 to December 31, 1993. Of these, 3.13% were "assault weapons."

- *New Jersey*. According to the Deputy Chief Joseph Constance of the Trenton New Jersey Police Department, in 1989, there was not a single murder involving any rifle, much less a "semiautomatic assault rifle," in the State of New Jersey. No person in New Jersey was killed with an "assault weapon" in 1988. Nevertheless, in 1990 the New Jersey legislature enacted an "assault weapon" ban that included low-power .22 rifles, and even BB guns. Based on the legislature's broad definition of "assault weapons," in 1991, such guns were used in five of 410 murders in New Jersey; in forty-seven of 22,728 armed robberies; and in twenty-three of 23,720 aggravated assaults committed in New Jersey.

- *New York City*. Of 12,138 crime guns seized by New York City police in 1988, eighty were "assault-type" firearms.

- *New York State*. Semiautomatic "assault rifles" were used in twenty of the 2,394 murders in New York State in 1992.

- *San Diego*. Of the 3,000 firearms seized by the San Diego police in 1988-90, nine were "assault weapons" under the California definition.

- *San Francisco*. Only 2.2% of the firearms confiscated in 1988 were military-style semiautomatics.

- *Virginia.* Of the 1,171 weapons analyzed in state forensics laboratories in 1992, 3.3% were "assault weapons."

- *National statistics.* Less than four percent of all homicides in the United States involve any type of rifle. No more than .8% of homicides are perpetrated with rifles using military calibers. (And not all rifles using such calibers are usually considered "assault weapons.") Overall, the number of persons killed with rifles of any type in 1990 was lower than the number in any year in the 1980s.

Gary Kleck, in *Targeting Guns: Firearms and Their Control* (Walter de Gruyter, Inc., New York 1997), summarizes the findings of forty-seven such studies, indicating that less than 2% of crime guns were assault weapons (the median was about 1.8%). According to Bureau of Justice Statistics, (*Criminal Victimization in the United States, 1993*, May 1996) offenders were armed with a firearm in 10% of all violent crimes. *That would mean less than .20%* (one-fifth of one percent or 1 in 500) *of violent crime offenders used an assault weapon* (1.8% X .10% = .018%).

http://www.guncite.com/gun_control_gcassaul.html

[594] Washington Post editorial, September 15, 1994, quoted in Assault Weapons; http://www.guncite.com/gun_control_gcassaul.html (emphasis in original).
[595] *The Assault Weapon Panic* (247K). Morgan and Kopel, Independence Institute, 1991; quoted in Assault Weapons and the Police Viewpoint, http://www.guncite.com/aswpolice.html
[596] Stefan B. Tahmassebi, *Gun Control and Racism,* George Mason University Civil Rights Law Journal
Vol. 2 (1991): 67.
[597] Saturday Night Specials: Questions & Answers, http://www.bradycampaign.org/facts/gunlaws/saturday.asp
[598] Mike Casey, "*Cop-killer Bullets*", http://www.guncite.com/gun_control_gcgvcopk.html
[599] Child Access Prevention (Cap) Laws And Gun Owner Responsibility Questions & Answers, http://www.bradycampaign.org/facts/issuebriefs/cap.asp
[600] Bell, Dawson, "Trigger locks may not be solution to gun problems," *Detroit Free Press,* March 29, 2000, quoted at http://www.guncite.com/gun_control_rrtrigger.html

[601] Lott, John Jr., and Whitely, John E., "Safe Storage Gun Laws: Accidental Deaths, Suicides, and Crime," March 29, 2000, quoted at http://www.guncite.com/gun_control_rrtrigger.html
[602] *"One-Gun-Per-Month" Laws: Questions & Answers*, http://www.bradycampaign.org/facts/gunlaws/onegun.asp
[603] *Id.*
[604] *Licensing And Registration: Questions & Answers*, http://www.bradycampaign.org/facts/gunlaws/licensing.asp
[605] *Id.*
[606] *Id.*
[607] 390 U.S. 85 (1968).
[608] 401 U.S. 601 (1971).
[609] Joseph E. Olson and David B. Kopel, *All The Way Down The Slippery Slope: Gun Prohibition In England And Some Lessons For Civil Liberties In America*, 22 Hamline L. Rev. 399, 433 (1999
[610] *Id.*
[611] Concealed Weapons, Concealed Risk, http://www.bradycampaign.org/facts/issuebriefs/ccw.asp
[612] *Id.*
[613] Right To Carry 2002, http://www.nraila.org/factsheets.asp?FormMode=Detail&ID=18
[614] *Id.*
[615] *Id.*
[616] Concealed Weapons, Concealed Risk, http://www.bradycampaign.org/facts/issuebriefs/ccw.asp (emphasis in original).
[617] *Id.*
[618] H. Sterling Burnett, Texas Concealed Handgun Carriers Are Law-Abiding..., http://www.nraila.org/articles.asp?FormMode=Detail&ID=6
[619] The Center to Prevent Handgun Violence, Legal Action Project, *Guns & Business Don't Mix, A Guide to Keeping Your Business Gun-Free*, p. 9, n. 38 (1997), http://www.gunlawsuits.org/pdf/articles/gunsnbusiness.pdf
[620] Right To Carry 2002, http://www.nraila.org/factsheets.asp?FormMode=Detail&ID=18
[621] Concealed Carry: The Criminal's Companion
[622] Interview with Sandra B. Mortham, Florida Secretary of State, St. Petersburg Times, January 11, 1996; quoted in Right To Carry 2002, http://www.nraila.org/factsheets.asp?FormMode=Detail&ID=18
[623] Should Michigan keep new concealed weapon law? Don't believe gun foe scare tactics, *Detroit News*, 1/14/01, quoted in Right To Carry 2002, http://www.nraila.org/factsheets.asp?FormMode=Detail&ID=18
[624] David Kopel, "The Untold Triumph of Concealed-Carry Permits," *Policy Review*, July-Aug. 1996, p. 9, quoted in Right To Carry 2002, http://www.nraila.org/factsheets.asp?FormMode=Detail&ID=18
[625] H. Sterling Burnett, Texas Concealed Handgun Carriers Are Law-Abiding..., http://www.nraila.org/articles.asp?FormMode=Detail&ID=6

[626] The Center to Prevent Handgun Violence, Legal Action Project, *Guns & Business Don't Mix, A Guide to Keeping Your Business Gun-Free*, (1997), http://www.gunlawsuits.org/pdf/articles/gunsnbusiness.pdf

[626]Thomas Jefferson, Commonplace Book (1774-1776); quoted at http://www.guncite.com/gc2ndfqu.html

Chapter 11

[628] N.A. Browne, *The Myth of Nazi Gun Control*, http://www.guncite.com/gun_control_gcnazimyth.html

[629] http://www.guncite.com/gc2ndstc.html

[630] 332 U.S. 46, 89 (1947).

Printed in the United States
16236LVS00002B/97-198